Investing with Young Guns

FINANCIAL TIMES

Prentice Hall

In an increasingly competitive world, it is quality
of thinking that gives an edge. An idea that opens new
doors, a technique that solves a problem, or an insight
that simply helps make sense of it all.

We work with leading authors in the fields of
management and finance to bring cutting-edge thinking
and best learning practice to a global market.

Under a range of leading imprints, including
Financial Times Prentice Hall, we create world-class
print publications and electronic products giving readers
knowledge and understanding which can then be
applied, whether studying or at work.

To find out more about our business and professional
products, you can visit us at www.financialminds.com

For other Pearson Education publications, visit
www.pearsoned-ema.com

Pearson
Education

Investing with Young Guns

The next generation of investment superstars

James Morton

FINANCIAL TIMES

Prentice Hall

PEARSON EDUCATION LIMITED

Head Office:
Edinburgh Gate, Harlow CM20 2JE
Tel: +44 (0)1279 623623 Fax: +44 (0)1279 431059

London Office:
128 Long Acre, London WC2E 9AN
Tel: +44 (0)20 7447 2000 Fax: +44 (0)20 7240 5771
Website: www.financialminds.com

First published in Great Britain in 2001

© Pearson Education Limited 2001

The right of James Morton to be identified as author of this work has been asserted by him in accordance with the Copyright, Designs and Patents Act 1988.

ISBN: 0 273 65264 8

British Library Cataloguing in Publication Data
A CIP catalogue record for this book can be obtained from the British Library.

10 9 8 7 6 5 4 3 2 1

Typeset by Pantek Arts Ltd, Maidstone, Kent
Printed and bound in Great Britain by Bell & Bain Ltd, Glasgow

The Publishers' policy is to use paper manufactured from sustainable forests.

The author

James Morton is director of Investments at European American Securities (EAS) and manager of the Chelverton Fund. Chelverton is a global microcap equity fund. Since inception in April 1994, the Chelverton Fund has increased its net asset value by 294 per cent, outperforming all relevant indices by a wide margin for the period to December 2000. He also manages the Chelverton Dividend Income Fund which emphasizes high yield equities. James Morton is investment adviser to Tailwind Inc., which manages the Tail Wind Fund Ltd. Tailwind invests in private placements of publicly traded equities at a discount and has grown its NAV by more than 550 per cent over five years. He is also international investment adviser on the European portfolio of funds managed by Cundill Investment Research, a Canadian firm with C$2.5 billion under management.

His 25 years in the financial services sector span commercial banking, corporate finance and investment management, and embrace 16 separate countries. Before EAS, James was a director of Samuel Montagu Inc. and worked at Arthur Young, Bain and Citibank. He has a BA in law from Cambridge, an MBA from Stanford Business School and an MA in Third World Economics from the Stanford Food Research Institute. He was the editor of the *Financial Times Global Guide to Investing*, published in October 1995, author of *Investing with the Grand Masters*, initially published by FT Pitman in October 1996, and then updated and re-released in paperback in September 1998, and is a columnist for *The IRS Report*, a financial newsletter. His latest book, *Prince Charles: Breaking the Cycle*, published in November 1998 on the Prince's fiftieth birthday, contains the only comprehensive assessment of the work of the Prince of Wales.

Contents

Note from the publishers

Investing with Young Guns contains information, opinions and views on a range of investment topics. All information contained has been obtained from sources considered to be reliable and every effort has been made to present a balanced and fair assessment of the topics covered in this publication. Nonetheless, neither the accuracy nor the completeness of the information contained herein, nor any of the conclusions or recommendations, can be guaranteed. There is no guarantee that future performance will in any way relate to the past, nor that any specific investment outlined in *Investing with Young Guns*, nor any of the strategies described herein, will be profitable.

Views expressed by the author and by all individuals whose comments are contained in *Investing with Young Guns* are subject to change, based on market and other conditions, including events that may have already occurred by the time you read this book. Opinions are intended solely for information purposes and should not be viewed as any kind of recommendation by either the publishers, the author, or the individuals profiled, or their respective organizations, and should not be relied upon in any respect by investors in making investment decisions. Investors should consult with their own professional advisers regarding investment decisions.

All financial markets are volatile and subject to fluctuations that cannot be reasonably foreseen. Any investment may result in losses as well as in gains. No responsibility for loss occasioned to any person acting, or refraining from acting, as a result of the material contained in this publication will be accepted by the publishers, the author, the individuals featured, or their respective organizations. The information presented in *Investing with Young Guns* is not, and should not, be construed as an offer to sell or a solicitation to promote any of the securities referred to anywhere in the publication.

Acknowledgements

Many experts were canvassed for ideas in selecting the people profiled in *Investing with Young Guns* – far too many to name every one – but I would, in particular, like to thank the following. To the extent the ultimate selection shines, they share the credit.

Simon Lee	Shanghai International Asset Management
Lindsay Cooper	Arisaig Partners (Singapore)
Mario Gabelli	Gabelli Asset Management
Shayne Norman	RCP & Partners GmbH

I also want to acknowledge my colleagues at European American Securities who have been most tolerant of the way writing books disrupts office life. Claire Powell, as always, made my job easier with her usual efficiency in turning my scribbling into presentable material. Dr Jonathan Agbenyega at Financial Times Prentice Hall is a model editor, knowing just when to make a helpful suggestion. Lastly, but most important, I want to thank my wife, Ellen, who is so understanding of this time-consuming activity and consistently encourages me in my writing. Without her unstinting support, this book would not have seen the light of day.

Introduction

For decades investors have looked backwards to look forwards, learning the lessons of yesterday in order to improve the returns of tomorrow. Those who made the effort and invested time in understanding why a small, select group consistently managed to outperform the market were usually rewarded with improvement in their own investment returns.

Less than five years on and the question has to be asked: 'does this approach still work?' If nothing else, confidence in the system that survived for so long has been severely shaken. Extrapolation was considered bad form for company financials; but analytical tools and investment insight appeared evergreen, more suitable to be carried forward, and capable of providing a level of stability in a constantly changing market mosaic. Now even that bedrock for decisions seems in doubt.

How else to explain recent poor performance from so many of the world's leading lights? Over the past five years, stars like George Soros lost the plot; Julian Robertson wound up Tiger, licking his wounds; Long-Term Capital Management, chock full of Nobel-prize winners, imploded. When even the greatest of the great, Warren Buffet, turns in a poor year, and *Barrons* ended 1999 by asking, 'has he lost his touch?' then what hope is there for the individual investor, or even the middle-of-the-road manager?

A few, like Colin McClean of Scottish Value Management, have succeeded in reinventing themselves and gone from strength to strength, but markets have moved on, and former heroes seem to have missed the move. It is astonishing how so many extremely astute and successful investors could, all of a sudden, turn in such mediocre numbers after heading their peer group for so long. Most of the top-rated names of the 1980s, and the early 1990s, have seen standards slip, been relegated to the second division, or simply faded away. What went wrong?

Four factors may have contributed to their decline.

1. One style over all

Most investors develop a particular approach that serves them well. Historically, the market tended to accommodate and reward superior stock picking, whatever the methodology employed. Rotation meant above average results could be achieved over five year periods while remaining wedded to a particular discipline. The market, of late, has been less tolerant of single-style investors who stick to their knitting.

2. Time warp

When you have done well for a long time, it is natural, and perhaps even reasonable, to assume that if the old magic stops working the interruption is only temporary. Normal service will be resumed sooner or later. Which may still turn out to be the case but, so far, for all too many managers this has yet to happen; and the longer the delay, the greater the damage to compound annual rates of return.

Barry Riley, a distinguished *Financial Times* journalist, made a telling observation in October 2000: 'Investment methodology refined during previous decades has failed to work; indeed, it has become dangerously misleading. History has become useless as a guide. Perhaps this is only temporary, and eternal investment truths will be re-asserted one day. But an awkward reality is that today's troubled companies do not simply bounce back, they often keep on fading away.'

As with companies, so, too, with investment professionals.

3. It is different this time

And, even if difference does not endure, it certainly has been different for at least the last three to four years. Valuations went off the charts, as expressed in traditional measures and compared against historical yardsticks. Top quartile returns mainly came from companies that barely existed five years ago. Billion-dollar businesses emerged from nowhere with few sales, negative cash flow and no profits. Long-term investors were not well equipped to deal with the explosion of new economy stocks which infected every major market, even inserting themselves into longstanding indices such as the S&P 500 and FTSE 100. To do well recently has involved not just a suspension of past beliefs but adoption of a completely new culture. It may all change again as we enter 2001, with the technology sector suffering more than the market as a whole and P2P replacing B2B as the mantra that matters, but that does not mean that happy days for the old ways are here again.

4. Revolution has replaced evolution

Markets in the past have tended to favour reflective thinking and consistency. Buy and hold has usually been the best strategy, always assuming the initial purchase was not fundamentally flawed. Developments at a company and change in its environment occurred at a pace which, for the most part, enabled investors to take stock of the situation, evaluate new information and make a considered decision.

Combine chaos on the investment pitch with an information-overload of unprecedented proportions and more choice in markets than ever before, and investors are faced with an environment that operates on a different set of rules, or possibly does without rules altogether. It is a scary investment climate out there, arguably more complicated and challenging than ever before.

Enter the young guns

Help is at hand. This sea change has thrown up a new group of professionals who understand what is happening and have figured out how to prosper even in unpredictable and unstable markets. When seismic shifts of this magnitude rock an industry, the old guard usually finds itself overtaken, outflanked and unable to adapt. The investment industry is no exception. To stay in touch with what works now, investors need to study a different group for ideas and insights.

The majority of today's performance leaders are relatively new to the profession, by and large in their early thirties. They began their careers just as technology started to destabilize eighties-style investing, ushering in whole new categories of companies which, in their turn, destabilized traditional industrial relationships. Perhaps it takes one to know one. Many of the stock market successes of the last five years have been started by entrepreneurs who are tuned into technology and are often not a lot older, maybe even younger in some instances, than the managers who have to assess the investment merit of these new economy companies.

While seasoned professionals stumbled and their results wilted, the next generation has embraced the opportunity to capture impressive gains. Look around the world and, over the past five years, the reality is that returns have not been terrific for investors outside the US and selected continental markets. To inject just one statistic, the average UK investment trust rose 86 per cent over that period, a compound annual rate of return of just over 13 per cent – not too shabby but somewhat below what most investors think they made, and a lot less than some of the headline indices. Global funds have delivered something similar, while, for emerging markets and large parts of Asia, including Japan, breakeven was not bad. The bonanza has been uneven to an unprecedented degree. Much of the world marked time, yet a few sectors created wealth at an unprecedented pace.

Investors need to reassess their tools and techniques to regain the initiative. Their focus has to become more forward looking. Again, younger professionals tend to find thinking about the future more relevant to their own lives and, as a group, tend to defer less to the past. Possibly they are also more optimistic; certainly they are less cynical. A mindset blending those attributes would have been helpful over the last few years.

The market has been asking a whole new set of questions. Where better to find answers than among those who have mastered the turbulence of recent times, specifically younger professionals more attuned to volatility? This conclusion led me to conceive *Investing with Young Guns*. Out with the old: in with the new. It is time to search for the next generation of global gurus, those who have grown up with current market conditions and have no baggage. I am not alone in seeking salvation among 30-something managers. Alan Stokes at the Investors Partners, a research firm that advises professional managers, had this to say to the *Wall Street Journal* in May 1999: 'The better fund managers are young, yet mature. They don't just think in straight lines, but are aware of what's happening around the world.'

Tapping the thought processes of the most talented 30-something professionals is the single most valuable source of continuing investment education – eye-opening to experienced investors and novices alike. My research into individuals who have come out on top after arguably the most demanding period of investing history in the last 25 years reveals new ways to make money – and also provides confirmation of a legacy of evergreen investment truths that have weathered the storm. The closing chapter delves into some of these techniques and explains how today's most successful young professionals have used them to increase their returns.

Of at least equal importance, the emphasis in *Investing with Young Guns* is on that most valuable currency of all, the future direction of financial markets. Portfolio composition has to keep abreast of change, with key holdings under constant examination. Only by looking ahead to anticipate those trends that will have the greatest impact on industries can investors hope to realign to take advantage of favourable market movements. Forward thinking is a key theme throughout the book.

Today's investors are searching for the right recipe to blend the best of what has worked in the past with those aspects of new economy thinking that have lasting validity. *Investing with Young Guns* intro-

duces just such insights and provides a preview into successful investing for the twenty-first century. No-one who reads this book should
fail to come away with fresh ideas and relevant methodologies to
improve their own investment performance.

Jamesm@easi.co.uk
April 2001

New names for a new century

The first decade of the new century follows a period of extraordinary turbulence in financial markets worldwide. The pace of change has also accelerated. Moore's Law may not have been intended to apply to investing, but what is happening to investors seems to mirror the development of the microchip with the amount of information to be processed doubling every 18 months.

The investment community is in a state of constant change: change in style, change in hot country or sector, and change in people who capture media attention. Managers rise to the top and no sooner have they established a reputation than markets move on and new names percolate up.

A few, very few, investment managers have stood the test of time, consistently delivering superior returns. I profiled the cream of the 1990s crop in *The Financial Times Global Guide to Investing* and *Investing with the Grand Masters*. Much of their wisdom, derived from many years of often painful and humbling experience, continues to have relevance to investors the world over. Some guidelines for making good investments are timeless.

I believe that the extent of change, not only in the structure of financial markets and the mechanics of investing, but also the composition of investment opportunities, demands at least different emphasis and, perhaps, an entirely new approach, if investors are to prosper in the 2000s. Consider just one statistic. Of the 81 companies in the FT information technology group, as of October 2000, only a quarter were listed ten years ago.

Technology is both creator and destroyer. Schumpeter's process of creative destruction descended on financial markets with a vengeance in the 1990s. Summarizing selected recent developments is essential to understanding today's markets. Among the most dramatic are:

● Availability of timely information: almost everyone can access real-time prices and, for those who care to click, there is a surfeit of data at their fingertips.

● Level playing fields: the same data is available to individuals and professionals alike, though cost constrains what most private investors utilize. Financial screening alone no longer provides any advantage. Data mining has largely replaced data gathering as the primary analytical task. In theory, the information edge the industry once had over clients has largely evaporated. In practice, the importance of direct communications with companies or issuers, including lunches (although 'lite' these days and a lot less liquid), still preserves a gap.

- Proliferation of ECNs: alternatives to established trading systems have begun to chip away at the power of established exchanges and the profits of market makers. Additional transparency, including bids and offers that reflect real buying and selling interest rather than market-maker positions or picture painting, is of genuine benefit to all investors. Direct participation, however, means trading skills become increasingly important at the margin, alongside analysis.

- Analytical tools everywhere and not a single insight: go back a decade, and clever clogs who could romp through regression creating complex time-series analyses were one up in the pursuit of mispriced securities. Now every investment software package bundles basic analytics. It helps to understand how charts that can be conjured up with one keystroke were created, but the competitive investment advantage has shifted from construction to interpretation in technical analysis, just as it has in data gathering.

The 1990s was the decade in which technology descended on financial markets with a vengeance. Technology has altered the playing field in so many ways, and placed greater demands than ever before, particularly on investment professionals. The daily life of investors has to reflect these new realities:

- Instant information is part of the daily diet. Not just dynamic pricing, which is a prerequisite to trading effectively, but press releases, too, go global at the press of a button. If you do not have your eye on the screen, you could miss that vital piece of information that can change a company's value for better or worse. Equally, if you are glued to the screen, how do you ever find the time to complete any analysis?

- The speed of market reaction to information has accelerated to a degree that is almost scary. Profit forecasts and trading statements can add or subtract 10, 20, even 30 per cent from a company's market value in minutes. When a blue chip with the stature of Procter & Gamble can plummet nearly 50 per cent in three trading days, the market has entered a new era.

- Information overload: no team, let alone a single individual, however talented, can cope with the onslaught of data that daily deluges investors. Filtering has become an essential element of the skill set: more so now then ever before.

- Proliferation of information sources: net chatter matters. Your broker may be the last to know. A recommendation from the likes of Goldman Sachs can still stimulate a share price; but, in specialized areas, lesser known names carry surprising clout. Cowen calls the shots in certain technology sectors. Kauffman Brothers stands alongside early stage companies they follow as their expertise, especially in telecommunications, raises the firm's profile. It is more difficult to know who to follow. Durlacher, the UK dot-com broker, enjoyed a purple patch for a couple of years before sinking along with the sector.

Influential publications such as *Barrons* move markets. Commentators, like Edmund Jackson in *The Sunday Telegraph*, Paul Kavanagh of Killik in *The Sunday Times*, or the Midas Column in *The Mail on Sunday*, have huge readership. Some newsletter writers can make a material difference to a company's share price. It is not always the well-known names who deliver. *The Bowser Report* and *The Cheap Investor* are two US sources that deservedly retain a loyal following. *Sharewatch* is a UK sleeper.

The ordinary investor somehow needs to keep tabs on as many sources as possible, while constantly pruning a shortlist that delivers superior, useable information. New venues for sharing, such as clubs or online communities, can have as much impact as top-tier broker buys or sells.

● The attention span of the average investor has declined. The MTV culture has captured pension fund advisers and punters alike. Liquidity lubricates markets, but you can have too much of a good thing. Traders acting on signals totally divorced from underlying operations undermine sound analysis and cause a disconnect between business performance and stock-price performance.

Investors for the next decade

So does the current environment call for different skills? Will the money managers of tomorrow need to jettison the tried and true precepts of sound investing to succeed? Yes and no. There is still a place, or rather a requirement, for fundamental analysis. Balance-sheet reconstruction should become easier as accounting standards around the world converge and the insistence of institutions on greater disclosure leads to more consistent and complete presentation. Understanding cash flow will be every bit as critical in 2010 as it was in 1990, even if the jargon changes and burn rate, rather than the change in the net cash position, is the buzz word *du jour*.

Yet to stay on top in an increasingly competitive profession, the stars of tomorrow will need to master a more holistic skill set. Superior analysis, though essential, will not, on its own, be sufficient. Snapshot numerical indicators, such as price to earnings, will satisfy a decreasing percentage of the total picture that investors must decipher to arrive at productive investment decisions.

I shall revisit this question in the closing chapter, but let me lay out up front my starting hypothesis. The most successful investors of the next decade will differ from the legends of the 1980s and stars of the 1990s:

- They will be more complete and more varied in their personal portfolio of ability and knowledge.
- They will be constantly fine-tuning their investment approach and regularly reinventing their analytical tool kit.
- They will be technologically astute and aware and, even where lacking personal expertise, at least attuned to what is leading edge, able to access and interrogate experts and assess the impact technology can have on any business.
- To come out on top will require an unusual tolerance for change – not just being comfortable with, but embracing, or even initiating, change.
- They will have to be both incisive analysts, and instinctive traders. This is tough, since few people are temperamentally suited to both roles. Big firms often segregate functions, but division of labour can impair effectiveness of execution.

For the individual, searching for someone to trust with their savings, the task has become immensely more difficult. Any attempt to trivialize the process with one-dimensional ratings or government-approved labels is an insult to investors and the profession alike. The plethora of options is overwhelming. In the UK and US, there are now more funds than listed companies. Megabucks go on advertising, but selecting a product simply because it is part of a well-known stable is rarely

> **You have to follow people who make money, not firms who collect fees.**

the right choice. Some long-established firms have been resting on past laurels, hoping to gloss over recent poor performance. Backing a manager who did well in a different climate is no guarantee of good future performance. The argument of company versus manager is over.

Individual managers won. You have to follow people who make money, not firms who collect fees.

Most of those few superstars who maintained a record of outper-formance over many years are now close to retirement or have ceased active involvement in the industry. Sir John Templeton is still the inspi-ration of the organization that bears his name, but no longer actively participates. Recent returns have been nothing to write home about. Michael Price sold Mutual Shares to the same conglomerate that also owns Templeton. Leonard Licht, formerly centre-stage at Mercury in its heyday, retired from Jupiter and does his own thing. Howard Flight became a Conservative MP, sold his firm to Investec and, while still involved, has to juggle dual responsibilities. A small handful, like Mario Gabelli in New York, Robert Lloyd George in Hong Kong and Colin McClean of Scottish Value Management in Edinburgh, all of whom had a strong 1999 and kept ahead of the crowd in 2000, should continue to top industry performance tables for many years to come. They have proven their ability to flourish, regardless of the market environment.

But readers whose concern is how to make money over the next 10 or 20 years have to start searching for the next generation of wealth builders now. Where will the best performing managers emerge in the first half of this decade? This is a question with immense ramifica-tions. Allocate investment to Manager A rather than Manager Z and, if the past decade is a reliable guide, results could vary from a highly satisfactory return of 600 per cent with someone who achieves in the top decile, to less than your original stake, if you stuck with a man-ager in the bottom decile. Take a more extreme set of statistics cited by Ben Yearsly of independent financial adviser Hargreaves Lansdown. The sum of £5,000 invested – and reinvested – into each year's top performing fund for the decade up to 1 November 2000 turned into £7.3 million! While the same sum invested in the *previous* year's top fund over the same period ended up at only £11,587. Never has the parable of the talents seemed more relevant. *Investing with Young Guns* intends to make the search for Group A easier by profiling indi-viduals whose record suggests they have every chance of joining that select band of superstars.

Identifying the new superstars

Every investment product carries a wealth warning stating that past performance is no guide to future returns, or some such bromide. You have to start somewhere. Only historic data is available, yet prediction is the only advice that has real value. Increasing the probability of future success is, therefore, desirable and to a degree, I believe it is also a realistic goal. *Investing with Young Guns* highlights a truly talented team 12 strong. These professionals combine both a demonstrated record of investment excellence with clear strategies for investing and an understanding of market dynamics that give them a head start for the next decade.

A pertinent question is how were these individuals chosen from the potential pool? I used four filters to find 12 exceptional young professionals who, to me, match the demographic profile and investment qualities of someone capable of joining the next generation of global gurus:

1. Age

The manager had to be 37 or younger on 1 January 2000. No-one profiled in *Investing with Young Guns* will be older than 46 by the end of this decade – in investment terms, still in their prime. However well they have done so far, hopefully, future performance should be even better as they mature.

Managers in this age bracket and below tend to be technology literate to a much greater degree than their older peers. Those in their thirties or younger will have been weaned on computers in school and accept the revolution of the 1990s as the natural order, rather than as an extraordinary upheaval, which is, of course, what it was. A comfort threshold with technological change is crucial as we look ahead. Like a *négociant* of fine wines, I have been searching for a balance of qualities: in this case of sufficient experience combined with enormous enthusiasm and a pinch of vision.

2. Experience

The individual had to have been working in the industry for at least seven years prior to publication. The seven-year itch is one of those sayings that seems to have remarkable resilience in professional, as well as private life. Seven years in one line of work for people in their early thirties confirms a degree of commitment, especially in a culture where changing profession is now commonplace. A seven-year period is sufficient to weed out the weaker brethren or simply those whose abilities are better deployed elsewhere. Seven years is long enough for a propensity to make mistakes to surface. To do well over that period suggests more than a statistical fluke.

In reality, almost every person selected has a decade or more under their belt, but seven seems a suitable cut-off point, though tenure need not necessarily have happened all at the same firm, nor in the same position.

3. Performance

Their track record has to be exceptional – not merely good, but exceptional. Markets have evolved and the next ten years are more likely to mirror the climate of 1995–2000 rather than 1990–5, let alone any earlier period. So what interests me most is how have they done recently? Let me be clear. No 'one-minute wonders' made it into these pages. I am not advocating a hot-hands strategy. Chopping and changing is more likely to rack up fees than profits. To be selected for *Investing with Young Guns* the individual had to be close to top of the class in the most recent relevant period leading up to publication. That is top out of *all* professionals. This is not a novice handicap. Look on this list as the Olympiads of the industry, all demonstrably capable of getting gold in their specific sector.

Each stands on his or her own merit. Readers will learn about a group of people who have all done remarkably well for clients during their careers, winning awards and delivering superior returns. Take a look at the results. If you are not impressed, you should be. Outperformance is the norm. Inclusion in *Investing with Young Guns* requires investment achievement that any objective observer would accept as *summa cum laude*.

Just because they are young does not mean they are not already among the very best. The flagship fund run by Chip Morris for T. Rowe Price was ranked number one out of 691 US equity mutual funds by Lipper through 1999. No surprise then, that *Money Magazine* included him on their list of the top ten managers in the US during the 1990s. Roger Guy also ranked top out of the entire UK in a survey by Greig Middleton of 1,500 unit trusts. So youth and performance, far from being mutually exclusive, seem remarkably compatible. Mark Slater came in fifth over five years out of all UK funds tracked by *The Investors Chronicle*. Catherine Tan runs the top performing Islamic fund in the world.

Most of those chosen have already racked up a long list of awards and prizes in recognition of their superior performance. Katherine Garrett-Cox has been voted into the Ultimate Investment Club 2000 by *Money Magazine*, along with such luminaries as John Bogle, Abby Cohen, Peter Lynch and Roger McNamee. Dave Nadig was nominated for Finance Oscar for the web in 2000. Sam Lau won the *South China*

Morning Post award for 1999 as top in his category over five years, the same year in which Francis Tjia won as Fund Manager of the Year. *Morningstar* has bestowed its top classification on Barbel Lenz, and Chip Morris also received this accolade.

I do not claim that the names that survived the screening process are indisputably the best 12 investment professionals in their age bracket; but I do claim that they are, without doubt, already among the best in the world at what they do, even at this relatively early stage in their careers. Others can devise their own lists containing different names, but I challenge anyone to produce a more qualified group.

4. Diversity

Investing with Young Guns set out to find the best up-and-coming professionals anywhere, but also had the goal of including representatives from all regions with active and accessible financial markets. A secondary objective was to capture a variety of investment styles.

Naturally numbers matter. At the end of the day, net return is the single most important criterion, qualified by the degree of risk incurred. Investing is about wealth creation, pure and simple. For a financial product, total after tax return tells you whether you made a good or bad decision. This ranking is clean, unambiguous, and leaves no room for argument.

> **Net return is the single most important criterion, qualified by the degree of risk incurred.**

Since, however, only a handful of those in the industry under 37 have undiluted management responsibility for any length of time, the sample would be too small and too narrow to justify using quantitative measures alone. A study based on Morningstar data at the back-end of 2000 illustrates why I rejected a quantitative screen as the sole selection mechanism. Their universe was 1,909 diversified domestic funds. The hurdle was top quartile performance that beat the S&P in both the most recent 6 and 12 months, and also over three years. A mere 27 names emerged, and only one was in the right age bracket.

If I had simply chosen those 12 managers aged 37 or younger whose funds had racked up the highest percentage gains over a fixed period – inevitably short, and also recent – that iteration would have yielded a very narrow group of committed technology buffs: almost all US-centric and 100 per cent long, or – better yet – geared to the gills via futures and options and willing consistently to roll the dice.

Some of those focused in this technology field whose progress has been spectacular are included – and rightly so. They even constitute the largest single category, which is as it should be. Especially when you consider the way technology stocks blossomed during the 1990s. In the US alone, the sector rose from a market capitalization of around $300 billion to $4.5 billion at the turn of the millennium. Its importance is underscored when you consider that, at one point in 1999, the value of Microsoft exceeded the GDP of Canada, qualifying the company for membership of the G7!

While acknowledging the importance of technology, *Investing with Young Guns* deliberately takes a broader-based and comprehensive look at the investment scene. Many commentators believe technology will continue to drive superior returns, but diversity reduces risk, and there is more than one way to make money. Trends, however powerful, peter out. No-one knows when technology stocks will pause for breath, reverse, or even go into free-fall. Those who bought dot coms last year only to watch as they collapsed by 90 per cent or more will know just how rapidly sentiment can flip over.

What matters most in identifying investment prowess is relative performance. Breakeven in Asia in 1998 could be a better indicator of an exceptional investor than up 50 per cent in a NASDAQ-linked fund. The crucial question is, has their approach produced results consistently superior to a defined peer group and relevant benchmarks? Investors should insist on a degree of diversification, even at the expense of absolute return.

Hedging bets is a good strategy for writers as well as investors. Hence a diverse group with varying records, but one common denominator: exceptional relative performance. One additional dimension: it seemed appropriate to weight professionals who not only were able to demonstrate top decile sector returns, but also are actively changing the face of their industry. Innovation in product structure and delivery reinforces the case for believing that someone has the ability to sustain a superior record.

The final selection

To find the right individuals was no easy task, once a database-driven solution had been jettisoned in favour of a more holistic approach. Fortunately, exchange of information is the common currency of fund managers. My questions were, 'Who would you pick as one of the superstars of the next decade?' and maybe more telling, 'Who would you entrust with your own money?' A cross-section of over 100 people actively involved in investing, and spanning all main financial centres, were polled and asked for suggestions of suitable professionals. Those responding included a number of fund managers whose livelihood depends on their ability to spot talent ahead of the herd, as well as financial journalists who are always on the lookout for new names. A quantitative filter served as an overlay to the recommendations that came back, and numerical performance acted as the ultimate arbiter between competing claimants. While not structured as a scientific survey, the result can withstand the most severe critic.

The final 12 represent the rich mosaic of twenty-first-century investing. There is balance and a cross-section of investment approach, as is only appropriate in such a diverse environment where change is the only constant. So, alongside the next generation of technology-rich gurus like Dan Chung and Dave Nadig, you will find Wayne Cooperman, who is that rarity among younger managers in the year 2001, a value investor; Japanese expert, Bill Kennedy; and Francis Tjia, who specializes in Asian debt.

A similar argument demands regional diversity. The US has been the main powerhouse driving growth in wealth during the last decade. No surprise then, that *Investing with Young Guns* includes more professionals of US origin than from any other country, reflecting US investment pre-eminence. London still ranks second as a global financial centre, so it is logical that Brits form the second largest group; while rapid recovery in Asia, with its important high-growth economies, confirms the rationale behind including four managers who are active in that region.

Even allowing for a deliberate intention to search out managers from around the world, the degree of diversity in the 12 who were finally chosen derives from a bottoms-up approach, not a desire to tick boxes. Encouragingly, 25 per cent are women and, again, this was not an objective, merely an outcome. Our young guns encompass six separate nationalities, which qualitatively confirms the globalization of financial markets. The profiles include a German covering Europe from San Francisco; an American looking after South-East Asia based in Tokyo; a Malaysian running Japanese equities out of Hong Kong; a Brit topping US performance tables while living in London; and one manager who is half Dutch and half Indonesian, but educated in Canada.

The stars of tomorrow will be a diverse group. I had no knowledge of the

The stars of tomorrow will be a diverse group.

backgrounds of individuals approached before talking to them. The only certainty was that their professional achievements caused them to stand out. Demographics of top performers in the investment world look set to change along with the markets.

Another interesting outcome, again by accident rather than design, is the spread of firms that emerged. Alongside Bill Kennedy from Fidelity and Chip Morris from T. Rowe Price, whose inclusion confirms that even the largest investment houses still know how to bring managers through their ranks who are capable of generating market-beating performance, you find Cobalt, a small hedge fund run by Wayne Cooperman, which deserves to be better known, and Dave Nadig's MetaMarkets.com, a pioneer changing the face of the mutual fund investment market in the US. Just as Francis Tjia, another entrepreneur, is changing the way investors approach Asian debt at his firm, Income Partners Asset Management. Yet also out of Hong Kong is Sam Lau of ING Baring, an established powerhouse on the Asian investment scene. In London, Roger Guy, arguably the top European fund manager in the industry, works at Gartmore, a household name, while Mark Slater operates out of a boutique that bears his name. The range of firms featured runs the gamut.

All-round investment skills

One final aspect of the make-up of the group deserves comment. All ended up in fund management but, interestingly, several started in research, and Slater wrote for *The Investors Chronicle* before managing money, while Nadig began life as a marketing manager. The line between analysis, portfolio management and trading is no longer so clear-cut. It is important for investors to hear views of people who can succeed in all aspects of the investment process.

Equity managers are over-represented, which does not require an apology; rather the reverse. Other asset classes have their place, but long-term evidence is overwhelming. I defer to the Barclays Equity-Gilt study that calculated that, over the last century, equities trounced all other categories. This may not seem the most sensible statement to make after the poor performance of stock markets in 2000, but if history repeats itself, then most investors should put most of their money in equities most of the time. Equities deserve to dominate, as they do in *Investing with Young Guns*, capturing 11 out of 12 core chapters. To put meat on the bones, £100 invested in bonds in 1899 without reinvesting income would have shrunk to less than £1 in real terms by the end of 1999. At the same time, the same £100 invested in equities, income reinvested, would have grown to £1.28 million! Not a fair comparison, perhaps, but this result does not require a re-count.

The key to accumulating wealth lies in choosing assets – overwhelmingly, equities – where value is created consistently: consistent value creation can only take place where profit growth is possible. Warburg Dillon Read has played St Paul to this strand of investment religion, which defines the ability of a company to achieve returns in excess of its WACC (Weighted Average Cost of Capital) as the primary distinguishing analytical tool between good and bad investments. The need for companies to create value in excess of WACC may have been the most important investment insight of the mid-1990s. Tacked on to low EV/EBITDA (Enterprise Value/Earnings Before Interest, Taxes, Depreciation and Amortization) multiples, a late 1980's cash-flow tool of the LBO/MBO crowd, and allied to low PEG (Price to Earnings Growth) ratios, a Jim Slater device of the early 1990s, those three measures combined to identify attractive opportunities for investors during the past decade.

But what if there are no earnings – and unlikely to be any for some time? All those approaches, each excellent in its own way, depend on operating earnings as a necessary ingredient. Many newly listed companies fall into the category of 'jam tomorrow'. Investors have to learn to assess potential. New valuation metrics are required: clicks, duration, pops, visits. Dynamic measures assume greater importance. Higher multiples for growth place pressure on accuracy in forecasting achievable margins and steady-state earnings. Predicting burn rate enters the essential category. Evaluating a realistic P2P (Path to Profitability) is as relevant as analyzing historic profitability.

Tricky stuff, and not easy to come to terms with if, for the last 10 or 20 – or even 30 – years, you have been able to get by with tools that tie into the balance sheet, cash flow and income statement. Most successful investors outperformed by learning how to interpret company accounts. This skill is far from obsolete but, apart from the need to assess the issue of when will a business run out of money (which was always more of a bond investor's bag), fundamental analysis took a bit of a back seat since 1996. The highest returns recently flowed to those who embraced the *Star Trek* method of investing: going boldly where investors had not gone before. Generation X embraced that revolution and understood the investment implications better than those who had been around the game for a long time.

Younger managers are more receptive to new ideas, less set in their ways, and quicker to change. Gross generalities, of course, and lacking in the scientific underpinning that runs through the rest of this book, but directionally accurate nonetheless. Soft stuff is more prominent. Such characteristics are useful when the mix of available investment opportunities, especially in equities, is changing more rapidly than ever before; when some of the largest listed companies in the world did not exist ten years ago; when important indices, and even whole markets, such as Techmark, EASDAQ and JASDAQ did not exist ten years ago; when, more than ever before, the world is an oyster of opportunity and almost every country is opening up in a way that was unimaginable at the start of the 1990s.

The change in the investment landscape requires agility and independence of thought like never before. Who would have predicted, at the start of 1999, that the top performing stock market would be Cyprus? And how many of the world's greatest investors got in on the ground floor of a little known Pokémon toy distributor which was the top performing US share that year? Traditional thinking can be a handicap when the menu of investments expands beyond historic confines.

> **The change in the investment landscape requires agility and independence of thought like never before.**

My contention is that with a few exceptions, investment managers best able to cope with complex conditions are those in their mid-thirties who have the right mix of just enough experience, but still are flexible in approach and have not found a one-size-fits-all solution, whether as torch or crutch. Entering the twenty-first century, it seems that the pendulum is swinging away from concept and story stocks that held centre stage in 1999 and early 2000. Old-economy companies are regaining some cachet. Yet excessive pessimism over technology prospects will be as misplaced as excessive enthusiasm for companies that never had a viable business plan. Finding companies capable of blending the best of the old and the new will be the key, and no group is better placed than those who have a good grounding in traditional investment skills but also see how to take advantage of the positive aspects of technology in an investment context.

Learning from the professionals

Successful investing has never been more of a challenge, but the rewards for getting it right have never been greater, either; nor the penalties for getting it wrong more severe. All of which underlines the importance for individuals who want to be active in managing their own money of understanding how the best professionals operate. Particularly those who have prospered throughout this period of turbulence and who understand how to adapt to change.

Perhaps even more relevant for those who have neither the aptitude, nor inclination, nor the time to look after their own assets (and that applies to the vast majority, even in mature economies) – how does one identify managers to do that job in an ever more confusing, fragmented and volatile investment industry?

Investing with Young Guns is the place to start. Here we present 12 individuals chosen with great care after an exhaustive search, each of whom is undeniably extremely talented and who has already demonstrated superior investment expertise that marks them out from the crowd.

Anyone can argue about one or more of those names, and readers are entitled to their own opinion of suitable candidates who did not make the list. Let me encourage you to put forward the credentials of others whom we should consider for future editions. It is our intention at the *Financial Times* to update *Investing with Young Guns* on a regular basis, so supportable suggestions are welcome. In the meantime, even if you do not agree with this exact group, there is a lot to learn and a great deal to enjoy in the balance of the book.

To succeed, today's investor has to keep up with developments in every arena from market psychology to analytical techniques. Our next generation of investment gurus reveal a range of knowledge and skill in application that should ensure anyone who reads even one chapter of *Investing with Young Guns* will come away better informed and better equipped to face the challenging markets of the first decade of the twenty-first century.

2

Dan Chung

Out-analyzing the competition

Became a technology bull and embraced the
internet at exactly the right time

Backstopped Spectra, the top performing US diversified fund in
the 1990s, which gained 1,200 per cent during the decade

Caught America Online at the inflexion point in October 1995,
which became a core holding and made a close to 1,500 per cent
return

Selected Yahoo as pre-eminent in sector, up 20 times since purchase rather than rival Lycos, which rose a lot less

There are many ways to get ahead in business, but one time-tested method is to marry the boss's daughter. So when you realize that Daniel Chung is Fred Alger's son-in-law, you start to wonder. But then you learn he was a successful attorney at the prestigious firm of Simpson, Thacher and Bartlett, with no intention of entering the investment industry until he met his prospective father-in-law. Alger sized up the man about to join his family and decided he wanted him at the family firm as well. Several dinners later, Chung succumbed, left the legal profession and embarked on a new career in money management.

'Fred is one of the more driven, dynamic and persuasive, and also stubborn, people you'll ever hear or meet. He asked me whether I really wanted to be a lawyer. After convincing me that life as a lawyer was not that exciting, he then persuaded me that investment management was very exciting.'

Once on the inside, Chung found no special favours. Entry point was the lowest rung of research assistant. He was required to qualify as a certified financial analyst as a prerequisite for promotion to analyst. Chung credits this programme, in part, for easing his transition. In-house training, however, under the tutelage of the firm's seasoned analysts and portfolio managers, had the greatest influence on him. Fred Alger's investment approach requires analysts to make their own assessment of a company's financials and prospects. Independence of thought and robust analytical underpinning is central to the firm's superior investment record.

'Analysis is key. Financials "as presented" by a company will always attempt to cast as favourable a light on performance as possible within Generally Accepted Accounting Practices (GAAP) rules. The analyst's job is to make an independent assessment of revenue growth, margin trends, operating income, cash flow from operations and, of course, earnings growth.'

The word to emphasize is 'independent': independent of the company; independent of accounting conventions, which can often mask what is actually going on, especially at an acquisitive company; and independent of consensus research from the broker community.

Alger already had a reputation as a growth house when Chung arrived in the mid-1990s. His early experience reflected the firm's orientation. He was pointed in the direction of two themes that looked as if they might yield suitable prospective investments.

One was in industries undergoing consolidation. Well-run consolidators can rack up the sort of sustainable earnings growth that appeals to Alger, both by growing revenues and through the extra margin leverage that can come from savvy cost cutting. Chung made himself an expert in funeral homes, modelling the rapid expansion of Service Corp International, the leader in a sector that was consolidating and that, at the time, was announcing excellent results. Another early home run was Tyco International, a conglomerate that was rolling up companies in security services and electronics.

'From an analytical perspective, these companies were great training. Because of the rapid pace of acquisitions, careful financial modelling of the acquired companies and of expected returns to the acquirers was critical.'

Make mine technology

Chung's search for new growth areas was to prove a watershed. The year 1995 may not seem long ago, but six years in the new economy era can constitute half a career. In June of that year, Chung was promoted and given a new analytical brief for information technology services, with a small group of stocks under the heading 'internet' thrown in for good measure. He was one of the first professionals to suspect that the handful of internet-related companies, back then no more than a minor appendage, could turn into something much more important. Chung had been aware of the existence of the net since 1990 or so, which is one reason he saw its commercial possibilities early.

'I might have some advantage. I grew up in the heart of Silicon Valley. My father was a mathematics professor at Stanford University, which I attended. Stanford *alumnae* have founded many technology companies, including Cisco, Hewlett-Packard, and, more recently, Yahoo, Akamai and others. In that setting, academics created the internet and were doing, ten years ago, what everyone does now – sending e-mails, collaborating and exchanging files.'

Chung began to investigate how the internet might be useful, and, more to the point, how an understanding of those uses could make money for investors – specifically Fred Alger's clients.

'The most basic step is how do you get on to the internet? Most people that I was talking to came from science and education. They had access at work – as did many professionals – but, at home, they often had nothing. At the time, America Online was the only consumer-friendly version of internet access.'

Once Chung began to explore what the internet had to offer, it was almost inevitable that he would gravitate to America Online (AOL).

'America Online was one of the easier companies to research. To evaluate the product, you just had to sign up. I spent a heck of a lot of time on the services. The key was clearly subscriber growth, which was terrific and accelerating. We looked at what it was charging per month and the economic returns from its subscription business model. Once people get online, they don't get off. They may switch providers, but they go online and stay.'

Possibly the single insight that tipped the scales came with the realization that the services America Online could offer would become *the* reason to buy a PC.

'Late one night, I realized I had spent more time on the computer in a single session than ever before, yet couldn't wait to get back online. Most PC software for consumers (accounting software like Quicken, tax preparation and home-office software) is essentially boring. I thought America Online would attract regular people.'

Great company, then. Pity about the financials or, perhaps more accurately, lack of financials. In 1995 a dearth of earnings and uncertain prospects offered little to go on in terms of traditional value metrics. Most professionals logged off and ignored the stock, but Chung was able to pursue his analysis because numbers are only one part of the process at Alger.

'The first thing to say is that our investment philosophy here has never been driven just by valuation. We don't buy or sell stocks based on a predetermined P/E multiple. We are not driven in our selection process by formulae or screens. Our process is driven by bottoms-up research. So the first impulse is to spend a lot of time on the service, or in a company, learning its products.'

The first impulse is to spend a lot of time on the service, or in a company, learning its products.

Which suited Chung fine. The numbers left a lot to be desired, the cost structure and cash flow were horrendous, but everything else about the company put America Online in a class of its own. If you could get comfortable with the revenue projections, you just had to buy the stock – and buy big.

'We saw great subscriber growth, we saw a service that was revolutionizing PC usage – that could really make you go, "Yes! I want to go on the computer".'

Chung recommended that Alger portfolios own America Online, based upon what some saw as wildly optimistic forecasts of likely internet traffic and the subscriber base. In retrospect, he realizes now that what he got wrong was that his projections have proved too pessimistic, even though they were way ahead of what anyone on Wall Street was willing to contemplate.

'The internet is becoming an essential service like the telephone or a utility more rapidly than anyone predicted. I looked at our old model recently, and at subscriber projections. The most interesting thing is that America Online, by itself, has surpassed our entire market forecast for 1999. And, of course, the market has turned out to be all of us. Right? It's not 35 per cent of people who have PCs will go online, it's 75 per cent of us will have PCs and 100 per cent of the 75 per cent will have internet access.'

This was one of the earlier projects in which Chung became involved, and he emerged from hours online to champion purchase, a proposal which might not have found favour at every firm. Fortunately, the investment case suited the Alger philosophy, because America Online promised to deliver in spades on the thing that mattered most to the firm's founder: sustainable growth. The audience was also receptive, since many managers at the firm have a technology background; one reason why, since the mid-1990s, Fred Alger Management has normally had at least 25 per cent invested in technology stocks. Chung's timing could hardly have been better. He caught the new wave of investing just as it was beginning to build.

Growth, growth and more growth

Much of the success at Fred Alger Management has come from buying growth – and not just any old growth, but the fastest growth it can find. Companies that are leaders also attract the team at Alger. And leadership inside a fast-growing sector combines the best of both worlds, because leadership usually links to the fastest growth, especially in sectors that themselves are high growth. Chung concedes that his firm has an ingrained bias on the topic of growth, but, hey, why knock what works so well? One trade-off between two potential positions captures the firm's investment hierarchy rather neatly.

'We like to buy the fastest growing companies, the leading companies: often those are the most expensive companies by P/E ratio measures. A couple of years ago we looked very hard at both Lycos and Yahoo. Lycos was cheaper, based on the numbers, and Yahoo expensive, but Yahoo was the leader.'

Which led Chung to focus his analysis on Yahoo, though he was careful to make sure his research placed the company in the context of its competitors.

'A lot of people (especially die-hard techies) thought Yahoo's manual directory classification was a poor approach to organizing the web, and would be killed by futuristic "spiders" combing the web [more automated search paradigms like AltaVista]. But using the site convinced me that Yahoo had superior ease of use. Its directory structure mapped closer to the way people actually think about searching for information, rather than a "key word" mapped against the entire web – the approach of the massive search "engines". Also, by avoiding fancy graphics on its main pages, we noted that Yahoo was, and remains, one of the fastest sites for flipping through pages. Finally, Yahoo's decision to focus on aggregation of content and not on creation of its own editorial made it more attractive as a partner to established content creators, and so a better business model.'

So not merely leadership, but in-built advantages likely to lead to greater growth, especially as Chung had a couple of questions over the numbers Lycos was showing.

'Analysis of their acquisitions and traffic metrics convinced me that there was recirculation of traffic within Lycos, a lot of it from acquisitions, that did not represent true-user loyalty or "depth" of use for their site.'

Chung came away, convinced that Yahoo would leave its competition trailing, and strongly recommended purchase. Alger made it one of the firm's largest holdings.

The company is the epitome of a growth stock. In modern markets, investors pay up for growth, so 30 per cent annual, if sustainable, is worth more than twice 15 per cent. Leadership also merits a premium. How much? Further comparison of Yahoo and Lycos from an interview given to *Smart Money* towards the end of 1999 is instructive:

'Yahoo in early 1998, at approximately $15 (split adjusted), looked tremendously expensive to many investors, sporting a $3.5 billion market cap. Its market cap to sales was 60 times, and it had a P/E that was "not meaningful". Yahoo's market cap today is roughly $90 billion, and the stock is a "20 bagger". Thinking Yahoo "overvalued", one might have invested in its "cheaper" competitor, Lycos, and the return, while outstanding, would have fallen short by a factor of four.'

No surprise, then, that a succinct definition of how Chung operates, and why the Fred Alger formula has been so successful, contains the 'G' word. Many times over – and at least once per sentence. 'We buy companies that have the potential to grow the fastest and dominate in the biggest markets.' With the 'L' word usually not

DAN CHUNG | 23

far behind. 'We look for the next generation of leading companies.'

There is still the matter of value. In case this point is not clear it should be stressed that Chung never loses sight of earnings, which are the most important valuation driver. Indeed, the whole culture at Fred Alger Management revolves around the search for superior earnings growth. What separates Chung from others is his willingness to look through today's reported profit, or lack thereof, and to see the earnings power of tomorrow. Leadership in a rapidly expanding sector is a positioning that can infer superior earnings growth.

'Often companies with the highest market cap/sales and market cap/operating income are those that are moving the fastest to claim new markets. The main controversy following Amazon's IPO was its "sky high" valuation relative to bricks-and-mortar book retailers like Barnes & Noble. Initial appraisals focused mostly on the book and music categories that Amazon was in or "clearly going to be in" and attempted to estimate the share of online sales to offline, and then Amazon's share online.'

Such a narrow analytical structure could not do justice to the intrinsic value created, the platform and all the other elements that make Amazon a best of breed. But what about positive cash flow and post-tax profits? Exceptional growth and instant profitability do not often go hand in hand. Establishing leadership is akin to staking out prime property in a Kansas land rush and gobbling up all the adjacent plots, for good measure, to stifle potential competition before anyone can pose a serious threat. Chung comments on the impact the drive for market position can have but, at the same time, makes no apology. Costs have to be incurred. Coming second is nowhere near as interesting.

'Sometimes, to achieve long-term goals, heavy investment is required, and operating losses are incurred: America Online's "carpet bombing" marketing in 1994–6; Amazon's investment in owning its distribution and fulfilment capability in 1999; Ebay's ongoing investment in its highly trafficked site, while simultaneously adding over 50 new regional sites, automotive auctions, and suite of new services to improve its customers' experience; Yahoo's investment in its

> **The best investments are companies that continually expand their business's long-term vision and opportunity.**

international properties, for which 2000 looks like a breakout year. The best investments are companies that continually expand their business's long-term vision and opportunity.'

There is an interesting convergence in Chung's approach with the way top managers talk about strategy. The bad news for investors is that, with new economy companies, out go simplistic rules and ratios, to be replaced by time-intensive business analysis. Shortcuts like historic Price/Earnings ratios have no place here. A holistic approach is essential.

Fundamentals come first

Fund managers are paid to show judgement and make decisions. Chung is firmly in the camp of those who believe that investing by numbers is not likely to produce above-average returns. You need something more than quantitative analysis. Which is why he repeats, several times in our conversations, that, as a firm, 'We're not driven by a financial metric like a P/E, or P/E to growth. We're more driven by the fundamentals.'

His first instinct is to find the rationale for the company and a business model that makes sense: one like America Online, which grabs you saying 'buy me'. Once the business passes this test, Chung turns to management as an equally important dimension. All of which calls for primary research at the company and in its market.

'The most important thing I do is spend time talking to management, competitors, customers, industry gurus, IT consultants and just about anybody else who might be able to educate me about a company or its industry.'

Only then is he going to prepare a full analytical package, creating a detailed financial model of prospects based on primary research.

A reasonable question, at this point, is whether all this effort – and an enormous amount of effort goes into building these financial models – is worth it. On one level, the answer is easy. The need to understand whether growth is sustainable leaves no alternative but to learn the business backwards. And that knowledge is then encapsulated in the model. As for the numbers, some level of error is inevitable, but results can come in surprisingly close to projections. Chung built his first set of pro formas for Yahoo when it went public in 1996. The model almost matched reported numbers in 1999. In the fourth quarter, Yahoo's revenues were $201 million. Chung's model had predicted $200 million. The model's profit-and-loss estimate proved to be within a few hundred thousand dollars of the actual results. The first half of 2000 saw similar tracking. The devil can sometimes be uncovered if you dig in sufficient detail. Still, Chung is cautious in interpreting such accuracy.

'Is this total blind luck? I have no idea, but I like to think that I didn't waste my time separately modelling Broadcast.com, Geocity and Yahoo. I track their individual costs including sales and marketing, general and admin. and R&D lines.'

His diligence and drive to get underneath headline numbers go way beyond where regular investment coverage ends. Only through digging one layer down do discrepancies in earnings-growth forecasts emerge. Which is what gives Fred Alger an edge over competitors who stop short of this degree of detail. Through identifying variation from *Wall Street* consensus, Chung and his cohorts earn their keep and spotlight stocks likely to outperform. Amazon was a large position for several years, as he explained in a 1999 interview:

'Amazon widely exceeded analysts' original revenue estimates for the company, and continues to raise the bar today. Why? Because it has rapidly moved beyond its successful book and music core, adding video, consumer electronics, auctions, z-shops, toys and home improvement to its online business. As its operations have expanded, so have our near-term and long-term revenue and profit estimates.'

Here the net, there the net, everywhere the internet

The early investment in America Online led to a series of investments in internet and technology companies. Chung saw the net as a catalyst for change in behaviour across a whole range of products and services. No surprise then to find that portfolios at Alger contain many net-related stocks such as infrastructure software, communications equipment and business-software applications companies. The top holdings vary by account and are a moving target but, as of October 2000, the ten largest in the fund run by Chung included pedigree names such as Ciena, Ebay, I2 Technologies, PMC Sierra, and Software.com. Also high up were EMC and Sun Microsystems, both of which benefited from the boom in new-economy investment. It is hard to pin down the precise percentage of Alger's portfolios that could be classified as net driven. Suffice it to say that the weighting is significant. As Chung points out, demarcation is difficult, and getting more difficult.

'Lines are beginning to blur. Sun Microsystems clearly wouldn't have the multiple that it has now if it hadn't been for the internet phenomenon. Sun had great performance on top and bottom line, but it is also trading at multiples we didn't see in 1996. And part of that is because the company is viewed as key hardware plumbing for the building out of the internet.'

Having picked up early on pioneers who went public first, Chung also examined, with the same sort of rigour, businesses that are the most likely beneficiaries of this explosion of activity: technology companies finding a new lease on growth by bringing established businesses into the networked economy and on to the net. Enterprise computer companies stood to be frontline beneficiaries from this expansion.

'Internet computing has greatly increased the performance and reliability requirements for servers. At the high end of processing power in the server market are mainframes; in the middle, Unix-based servers; and, at the bottom, NT/Intel servers. The standard view, four years ago, was a pyramid: mainframe at the top, losing market share to Unix servers. However, Unix was losing share to Wintel servers, Microsoft NT and Intel-powered servers from Compaq and Dell, because NT servers were also increasing in computing power and therefore gaining at the lower end, where price was more sensitive. This pyramid of markets and market growth assumed static relationships among tiers and implied processing power advancements. The model failed to take into account the demand for processing power, reliability, scalability, and all other important aspects of a server system.'

And here is where Chung's original research reaped huge dividends for Alger's clients.

'Internet businesses operating 24 by 7 had no tolerance for downtime or reboots. Consumer and business applications, like e-mail, chat and interactivity, were far more demanding than "file and print", the biggest use of NT servers in the enterprise. Interviews with webmasters reinforced the volatility of traffic patterns, the tremendous growth of traffic, and the reliability required.'

The next connection was crucial.

'The internet increased, by a quantum step, market demand for processing power. This increased requirement shifted the minimum level of performance upwards, right into the sweet spot of Unix servers. NT servers could not deliver, in particular, the reliability needed, so would not gain market share as quickly as pre-internet. Looking into which Unix vendor best met this new demand for performance, we surveyed benchmarking engineers who test servers and databases, and interviewed ISPs [Internet Service Providers], telecommunications and internet-hosting companies like Exodus and UUNET. It was clear from their responses that Sun was the internet leader.'

So Chung recommended Sun as a core holding while most of the market's attention was elsewhere. Those first purchases returned over 400 per cent profit in under two years.

The Grand Central Station of information

Once a company showed strongly on the radar screen as sectoral leader, and market validation of the business case justified a full analysis, Chung returned, as he does for each prospect, to the preparation of a multi-layer financial model. Time to go direct to the company – another prerequisite of a thorough financial forecast.

'Sun's never actually broken out revenues by product line, but, by talking to people who are engineers, it quickly became apparent that in their core, mid-range and upper-end workgroup servers, they were probably growing at over 50 per cent, while workstations had been holding them back. The P/E then was around 30 times, but they had this business growing much faster, and customer pressure on performance requirements meant less pressure on price. The question everyone was asking was, "Can the server handle traffic and not go down?" While most analysts were focusing on Y2K, we saw demand accelerating and the potential for over 30 per cent growth (which duly arrived).'

Of course, identifying likely losers is every bit as important as picking win-

> # Identifying likely losers is every bit as important as picking winners.

ners. The internet is not an unmixed blessing, even for new economy companies. One well-known name where Chung still has to make up his mind is Oracle.

'For Oracle the internet is a plus, but also a minus. It's a challenge to their business model. Can they capitalize on their position in databases, and sell applications to the faster growth markets in customer relationship management, B2B [Business-to-Business] exchanges and supply chain management? They have to re-architect a lot of their software and they face a host of new competitors who all want to dethrone Microsoft and Oracle.'

Not just businesses but entire sectors can come under attack, with established companies outflanked overnight.

'ERP [Enterprise Resource Planning] companies like Baan and Peoplesoft have been dethroned pretty rapidly. It's interesting to see how some companies were caught off-guard by the internet.'

Alger was not caught off-guard, courtesy of in-depth field research by Chung and his colleagues.

'Customers were buying ERP software to fix Y2K, but were not happy. Many complained about high price, long, difficult implementation, and, ultimately, non-delivery of promised benefits and features.'

Which was one red flag raised over forecasts, even for the market's favourite SAP. Chung dug deeper.

'Analysis based on new contracts, average size of contract, and how SAP recognized revenue over the period of implementation showed deceleration in new business and an end to the flow from the backlog of big deals sold in 1997 and 1998.'

Alger, as a firm, largely stayed away from the ERP sector in the late 1990s, sensing instability to come, and so avoiding significant stumbles suffered by SAP, Peoplesoft, JD Edwards, Oracle, and others in the ERP software space starting in 1998 and continuing through 1999 and on into 2000.

New economy, new values

All the number crunching in the world is, on its own, insufficient in this environment. All the research conceivable is still not enough. Every investor still has to grapple with the elusive issue of valuation and, as Chung admits, this element of the process is less than ideal, especially when evaluating internet or hypergrowth companies with little or no near-term earnings.

'There are a variety of yardsticks that analysts frequently refer to. We use the terms "yardstick" and "evaluate" as opposed to ratios and rules in a deliberate fashion: ultimately, valuing and investing in many, if not all, technology companies is an art, not a science. Most of these yardsticks are useful only in comparing one internet company to another internet company.'

Yardsticks suffice only because of the depth of research that enables Chung to use them in the context of a thorough understanding of the company and its markets. Factors that affect the interpretation of the yardstick include: 'The size, structure and growth of the market addressed by the company, the number and relative position of competitors, the potential for new competitors to enter, the advantages and disadvantages of the new technology, new service or new way of "doing business" *vis-à-vis* the old, and how rapidly the company will change a marketplace and an industry.'

Which begs the question, what are some of these yardsticks? Ideally there will be earnings visibility.

'We love companies with lots of earnings, operating margin expansion, revenue growth and selling at reasonable P/Es.'

But that combination of characteristics is not always on offer, so an investor has to become more creative. In those circumstances, Chung proffers several options as worthy of consideration.

'Market capitalization [MCAP] to sales, MCAP to gross margin dollars, MCAP to operating earnings or cash flow, and MCAP per subscriber/customer. We might use forward projections of operating earnings. I run discounted cash flows. But usually more as a methodology to look at very conservative-based value for checking my sanity and market sentiment. Then sensitivity analysis gives a feel for the range of stock prices in a bull or bear case.'

Anyone looking for a definitive set of quantitative benchmarks will, however, be disappointed. We are in the realm of relativity and dealing with degrees of difference, not absolutes. Chung is even cautious about ranking his yardsticks in order of importance.

'We do not view any one as most useful. And, though looking at such yardsticks across different internet companies can, on occasion, provide some sense of valuation, our investment philosophy is not driven by an arithmetic calculation of the "under" or "over" valuation on any given stock. In our experience, many of the best investments have never been "cheap stocks".'

So where does that leave a technology investor? Unfortunately, with more work still to do; at least under Chung's approach, where fundamentals overpower formulae.

'I get annoyed by over-focus on P/E or PEG ratios or other metric nonsense. We try to find the best growth, companies where fundamentals are improving and where markets are expanding. I try to understand all that, and then keep up with the news and noise in the real world. Valuation usually takes care of itself if I get that right.'

A researcher's work is never done

The amount of analytical ground covered by Chung and his team in researching potential investments is impressive. This has been alluded to earlier in the context of specific recommendations; but it is important to revisit the process to appreciate why his results are superior. Experimentation with the product was a factor in the decision on Yahoo, though the key insight that Chung took away from this exercise was not that one portal was better than another, but that leadership was likely to be validated by user behaviour.

'You get accustomed to a particular service. Whether it's the best or not doesn't really enter into most people's calculations. I don't know many consumers who would spend an equal amount of time every day using three different services just for the fun of it. As long as your service doesn't let you down, you stick with it. So the question is, which do you go to first? Initial use becomes very important. And it's usually the brand or market-share leader that you get led to.'

No easy let-off for Chung, who forced himself to undergo first-hand experience of all the majors.

'I formulated ten different things to find or do on the internet. Then I tried each on Yahoo, Lycos, American Online, MSN [Microsoft's online service] and Excite and appraised the experience. I also talked to companies that were doing early e-commerce deals with them.'

A company that survives a rigorous examination of its business case, both in terms of users and customers, also has to pass a test of its earnings growth potential. After all, profit is what Alger ultimately cares about: growth at the top, but also, in due course, at the bottom line. For every recommendation, Chung's team will have prepared a detailed forecast and run sensitivity scenarios, both to test projected profit and to prepare for the grilling from portfolio managers.

'We're committed to earnings models for all our companies. We have multi-year cash-flow models, and we test the models. The models reflect not just a series of numbers, but things like how many people do they need to grow, how much investment in marketing are they making, are they getting a good number of customers from this marketing? What is the effect of rising or falling telecommunications costs? We model to make sure that we really understand the company and its business.

> ## We don't believe anyone can really understand a company unless they have put together and analyzed its financials.

'A lot of people ask us, "Why don't you just use the Street model?" Well, we don't. We don't believe anyone can really understand a company unless they have put together and analyzed its financials. Looking at someone else's model leaves questions – what assumptions, what sensitivity to changes, etc. Some analysts have terrific models – it is not that their models are bad, or even worse than ours. It is just that I can't understand all that complexity by looking at someone else's work. I need, and Alger requires, that we work it through ourselves.'

The degree of detail Chung requires of himself is almost scary, and goes way beyond what individual investors could realistically hope to accomplish. Still, it is useful to understand what is involved, if only to marvel at the information shortfall. And, for Chung and his colleagues, here is the explanation for their outperformance.

Another point worth making is that this intensity of analysis is not forced. What might seem a drudge to some makes Chung's eyes light up. He loves what he does. You can sense enthusiasm for the challenge inherent in deconstructing a complex new-economy company like Amazon. He revels in the task of learning more about the business than his competitors, and emerging at the end of the exercise with a better understanding of every facet of its operations.

'I've got every detail you can imagine on what Amazon did in books in the US, in Germany and in the UK separately, and for music, and what their gross margin might be in books or music, with new accounts, and then distribution costs and shipping costs. Toys, electronics, home improvement items – each has a separate model. For z-shops I'm modelling the number of shops, the average items per shop, items added per day, how much they sell per quarter, the average price of those items, how much they get in listing fees. All of this is based on my estimates of how many Amazon customers might visit that site and what they buy: their look to book.

'Why do I do all this? Someone will say, "Yes, but it comes out with a gigantic loss, so how could he possibly buy? What's the metric that tells him to buy this?" Well, it isn't a single metric. What it is is trying to understand – and modelling intensely – the real business.'

Readers can see where all the work goes. Figure 2.1 encapsulates less than one in ten line items in the base-case model that Chung created as the primary input to Fred Alger's investment evaluation of America Online. Each e-commence relationship, for example from GTE Yellowpages to Cybermeals, has its own forecast. There were seemingly endless iterations; and, of course, since a model is a living reflection of the business, it is instantly updated the moment new information is gleaned either as a result of an event, such as company news, or indirectly through research at another situation that impinges on AOL's activity.

The level of detail is almost overwhelming, but the process to piece together the data and understand all the relationships means that, when complete, Chung can present to his colleagues with a high degree of confidence. Almost inevitably, original in-house analysis generates insights that drive the ultimate investment decision and allows Chung to extract one or two pivotal recommendations for the portfolios. Amazon was added in February 1998 at a split adjusted $5 and sold when close to $100 under two years later.

'What we look for in an internet stock, where valuation questions are the most philosophical, is where we think consensus opinion about a company is wrong. They either over or undervalue the company.

Figure 2.1 Extract from Fred Alger Management model of America Online, compiled by Dan Chung

AMERICA ONLINE										
Segment	Q1/99	Q2/99	Q3/99	Q4/99	1999E	Q1/00	Q2/00	Q3/00	Q4/00E	2000e
All Brands	13,242,000	14,461,000	15,983,000	16,618,000		17,776,000	18,262,000	19,843,000	20,747,000	
Avg All Brands Subs	12,839,000	13,851,500	15,222,000	16,300,500		17,197,000	18,019,000	19,052,500	20,295,000	
Avg Aol Subs						15,858,000	16,846,000	18,046,000	19,027,000	
AOL NA	12,042,000	13,261,000	14,783,000	15,468,000		16,248,000	17,444,000	18,648,000	19,406,000	
% + pr yr	38.32%	35.73%	37.98%	37.66%		34.93%	31.54%	26.14%	25.46%	
% + pr quarter	7.2%	10.1%	11.5%	4.6%		5.0%	7.4%	6.9%	4.1%	
Avg Min/member	47	48	55	52		55	57	64	58	
Avg rev/mo	$20.5	$20.5	$20.7	$20.8	$20.6	$20.8	$20.7	$20.6	$19.9	$20.5
% + pr yr	17.9	17.7	10.3	2.5	11.7	1.5	0.8	-0.1	-6.0	-0.5
Aver subs	11,639,000	12,651,500	14,022,000	15,125,500	13,359,500	15,858,000	16,846,000	18,046,000	19,027,000	17,444,250
Churn						change to net aolWW adds				
net Mkt cost/sub	$110.6	$82.3	$71.4	$298.4	$139.1	$217.7	$135.2	$156.7	$297.4	
% + pr yr	-15.7	-9.6	-20.0	63.8	21.8	96.8	64.2	119.4	-0.3	
Incr Mkt cost/sub	8.5	28.9	28.1	189.7	AOL only	115.2	107.9	115.4	92.3	
Avg Oth Rev/Sub	12.32	14.31	15.69	20.23		22.07	25.94	30.87	32.01	
% chg yty	17.32%	21.44%	36.24%	77.91%		79.18%	81.32%	96.73%	58.21%	
vs % chg in Subs	-21.00%	-14.29%	-1.74%	40.25%		44.25%	49.78%	70.58%	32.75%	
Ads/Ec Rev	156.10	209.00	252.00	276.00		319.00	399.00	521.00	562.00	
Avg EC rev/Sub	12.16	15.09	16.55	16.93	60.73	18.55	22.14	27.35	27.69	95.73
Chy % yty	48.35%	63.99%	71.79%	84.35%	AOL only	52.57%	46.75%	65.18%	63.55%	57.62%

AMERICA ONLINE

Gross Margin Analysis

Segment	Q1/99	Q2/99	Q3/99	Q4/99	1999E	Q1/00	Q2/00	Q3/00	Q4/00E	2000e
AOL Revs Historical	858.10	960.00	1089.00	1192.00	4156.10	1298.00	1457.00	1663.00	1746.27	6164.27
Netscape SW	100	140	109	128	437	122	117	126	135	500
Netcenter	32.3	48	55	47	184.3	47	47	47	47	188
Other acquisitions (spin)	4									
Total AOL Revs	994.40	1148.00	1253.00	1367.00	4777.40	1467.00	1621.00	1836.00	1928.27	6852.27
Restated Revs	999	1148	1253	1377	4777					
AOL Gm reported	312.65	370.00	448.00	477.57		540.35	652.70	752.83	820.65	
AOL Cogs reported	545.45	590.00	641.00	714.43		757.65	804.30	910.17	925.62	
AOL Cogs Est	547.73772	589.45	641.63			757.65	804.30	910.17	925.62	
AOL GM %	36.43%	38.54%	41.14%	38.54%		40.17%	43.40%	44.03%	45.76%	
Netscape SW cogs	10.00	14.00	10.90	12.80		12.20	11.70	12.60	13.50	
Netcenter Cogs	7	9.6	11	0		0	0	0	0	
Other Acq Cogs	18.26	25.95	25.47	13.77		14.00	14.00	14.00	14.00	
Restated Cogs	583.00	640.00	689.00	741.00	GM EST	783.85	830.00	936.77	953.12	
Restated GM										

And not in the sense of a metric, but in the sense that they're not appreciating what customer loyalty means in Amazon, or they're not appreciating where growth may or may not come from. That they're not appreciating the potential for gross margin expansion in a company.

'A great example is sales and fulfilment at Amazon, which cost about 16 per cent of revenues in the fourth quarter. People said, 'That's tremendously high. A lot of the industry is much lower.' They had been about 10 per cent the year before.

'The glass is either half full or half empty. Half empty says those are terribly high costs, higher than competitors, and bad; or you could look at it as half full, and as a tremendous opportunity for Amazon to leverage their infrastructure. If they could reduce their cost to, say, 6 per cent, that's 1,000 basis points of extra operating margin. So that's where I spend a lot of time to determine whether they can reduce fulfilment costs. If I see them progressing along those lines faster than I think people realize, we would probably call that a catalyst for buying the stock again.'

A big bonus is when Chung determines that not only has the mainstream investment community misconstrued an earnings forecast, but also it has failed to understand the financial end-game. The mismatch between his estimate and the public-market value can be most marked when they come to differing conclusions about the underlying business model. This valuation gap is best exemplified by Ariba and CommerceOne, two competitors in B2B e-commerce.

'In August 1999, Ariba's market capitalization was roughly twice that of CommerceOne, the market's rationale perhaps being that Ariba's larger revenues reflected larger market share. CommerceOne and Ariba traded at similar MCAP/sales multiples (roughly 25 times). Both address a gigantic market, but from subtly different starting points. CommerceOne's model is based on the development and growth of business-to-business internet exchanges built on its software and operated by CommerceOne or its partners, which include General Motors and British Telecom. If successful, the business will have a recurring, long-tailed revenue stream of subscriber and transaction-based fees from those internet exchanges.

'CommerceOne's model, however, also has the characteristic of less up-front revenue from software licences, in exchange for recurring revenue in the future, than the traditional enterprise software model. We concluded that the market undervalued the business model that CommerceOne had established, and consequently the stock. However, our research also concluded that Ariba was an early leader in the business-to-business internet category.'

Over the following year both stocks roughly tripled, though they suffered along with the whole technology sector at the back end of 2000.

Average up, not down

All the high-quality analysis and insights into valuation can be undone unless individual holdings are managed with vigilance once in the portfolio. The prevailing attitude at Alger is illustrated by America Online:

'The style here is to add to winning positions, to stocks doing well. America Online was bought first in October 1995. It did well, and more was bought. The position was added to through early 1996.'

A long-term love affair is not on, or even online. Take America Online, which is as close as Alger comes to a keeper. Chung, who was pushing the share to start with, was alert to the need to sell when things showed signs of coming off-track.

'By April 1996 we were already concerned regarding its ability to keep up with demand, which resulted in a disconnect problem and customer churn.'

The initial purchase was sold for a double, just before news about difficulties caused the price to halve. While still loving the story, Alger re-entered in July 1997 only after becoming convinced that the company had sorted out its problems and was ready to resume its advance. Top slicing followed later by buying back has occurred at regular intervals since.

Amazon, another long-time favourite, and once upon a time a top-ten position all across the firm, went when Chung concluded the price was too rich at the end of 1999.

'We sold because we know the difference between what's going to make a good stock and what drives the stock, and what is a great company. I think it's a great company, but we knew that the stock had probably got ahead of itself.'

An excellent call, as events showed by late 2000, because the price has since plunged from around $100, when sold, to below $20. Chung acknowledges that it is all too easy to become enamoured of a business when dealing with technology stocks. Great ideas can be so seductive you never want to let go.

> **Great ideas can be so seductive you never want to let go.**

'I get tied to my stocks, for sure. Everybody gets tied to stocks that they love.'

For which reason, regular internal investment reviews can be a rough ride. These are known as Monday morning yell *fests*. A poor argument is soon picked apart. The danger of hanging on too long is one to which everyone is sensitive. The need to remain immune to the siren call of a sexy story led Fred Alger to put in place a structured process, with defined sell limits to force a full-fledged review of the case for disposal once a stock hit its original target. Chung believes that challenges from seasoned and successful professionals at the firm, notably David Alger the CEO and chief investment officer, and Ron Tartaro and Seilai Khoo, both senior portfolio managers, provide the extra element that can expose a flaw or confirm a conclusion.

'Analysts are required to set formal targets: price, or a P/E, or a revenue multiple. When any stock hits that target, or the upside is single-digit percentage, it is time for re-evaluation. The analyst has to justify a higher price. That's where you see the difference between someone defending a stock because they love it, or whether there really are reasons to continue to own it.'

Of course, not every investment does what it is supposed to do. Even with the most thorough analysis, some fail to live up to their promise. The selling discipline for those that underperform is equally hard-nosed. Fall short and its the fast track to an exit from Alger portfolios. Chung explains the mechanism, a sort of internal stop loss that triggers a reality check:

'The other reason, clearly, to sell is if a stock falls short of the model that we've built. Following Service Corporation, we saw them pay increasing prices to acquire companies, and that, along with a slowing death rate, suggested they would have trouble making our earnings estimates. Sometimes reasons to sell scream out. Sometimes they whisper that something isn't quite as good as the story that's being told.'

Service Corporation screamed. Fred Alger managers all sold for a triple, netting over $80 in July 1998, and were long gone before the story unravelled. As of October 2000, Service trades at around $3.

The next wave

Chung is confident that we ain't seen nothing yet. He expects technology to continue to drive change in a way that will be positive both for business and consumers. In a 1999 interview he identified three separate spaces of opportunity that are here to stay, and which he expects, even with the odd hiccup along the way, will grow fast for the foreseeable future.

1. Consumer e-commerce

'Business to consumer is still interesting, but in a different way. That market seems to be consolidating around clear leaders very rapidly. There are great companies among those leaders. I think you will do very well financially by investing in some of those.'

His favourites, at the time of writing, are Yahoo, Ebay and America Online, but he has Amazon on his watch list and sees the possibility for that company to be a big holding again at some point in the future, when its fundamentals improve.

'In the consumer sector there is a core group that has already established broad customer bases, operating scale and strong brands with which they will continue to lead and outdistance their competitors. Yahoo and Ebay, in particular, we believe are internet franchises. Are these stocks cheap? No. Are they likely to be on the high end of some of the yardsticks that we have discussed? Yes. Are they likely to have growth, new business opportunities and profitability that continue to redefine their markets? We think so.'

2. Business to Business

'We're seeing a variety of marketplaces form. Some are adjuncts to traditional ones, but others are more revolutionary.

'The key is to determine the strategic technology providers of infrastructure software, hardware and services to the Global 2000 corporations that enhance the efficiency of their business processes – everything from sales and support services to manufacturing and supply chain management – by use of the internet and related technologies.'

The two big competitors are both picking up blue chip clients, as Chung observes. 'Ariba has major customers like Cargill, Cisco and IBM implementing its software: CommerceOne has the auto exchange Covisint with GM, Ford and other auto manufacturers participating, as well as international customers like British Telecom; Oracle has announced major wins at Citigroup. In the initial formation, most activity is just to try to automate the purchasing process.'

Chung sees B2B going way beyond creating a marketplace for electronic transactions – evolving into a fully fledged information exchange, linking purchasers and suppliers through the length of the value-added chain.

'Part of that is to allow searching for new suppliers, or for auctions, or to determine prices. But that's really just the first step. When you've done with the purchase, that's when the real work begins!

'Suppose it's a custom-printed circuit board. While that board is being produced, the supplier can make sure that it's going to be the right part. So there's collaboration over the internet regarding design and manufacture of components. Manufacturing entails secondary supply issues. That supplier who GM selected for boards is going to purchase raw materials and chips. Maybe that supplier is a design shop which outsources. Automation will allow both parties – GM and all its suppliers – to see where each one is in the process, to see availability of components and raw materials, to co-ordinate activities, and, ultimately, match production more closely with demand.

'Then there's physical delivery. What you really want to have is all information: when is the part available? What is the defect rate? Is it acceptable? How many parts are you going to be able to produce? Which assembly line needs it now? Is it Detroit or Mexico City?

'The exchange is where everyone meets. It is the Grand Central Station of information. But it's sad if the train leaves at lightning speed and hits a dirt road. A dirt road is when the electronic order that was processed and requisitioned on the internet goes to a supplier and then, instead of immediately going into the order inventory management and manufacturing system, it's printed out in manual form and has to be re-keyed.'

Converging on the same space from a different starting point is I2 Technologies, a logistics information software company which holds leadership position in supply chain management.

'When you look at many of the things businesses want to accomplish through exchanges, including improving relationships with suppliers, I2 has many of the solutions. It is by far and away the leader. Its products are particularly suitable for B2B on the internet, solving what we call multi-enterprise problems. Their software is optimized to analyze information generated by the different companies who form part of the supply chain – the manufacturer, the component suppliers, the trucking company – enabling an acceleration of collaboration between multiple parties across multiple organizations. I2 produces a platform for adding other services in a B2B environment while linking third parties. They recently added payment mechanisms and online credit evaluation. This is very different from the focus of traditional ERP systems which look within at one enterprise.'

Which dovetails perfectly with the seven Immutable Laws of Collaborative Logistics as promulgated by Dr C. John Langley at the

University of Tennessee. Here is one nexus where new-economy behavioural and business models reinvigorate old-economy industries.

3. Infrastructure providers or enablers

'Infrastructure companies capitalize on the inherent growth of traffic on the internet; the increasing complexity of the types of activities and transactions that corporations and individuals are trying to accomplish on the internet; and, of course, the ever-increasing competition among emerging and established companies to gain customers, market share, or competitive advantage. In this area, we think Exodus Communications, Inktomi and Vignette are potential internet-era franchises.'

And, of course, the story does not stop there. The often overused picks-and-shovels analogy is entirely appropriate. Companies enabling infrastructure improvement should generate longer-term growth.

'For all this to work well, you need good, fast networks, you need security and you need good hardware.'

> # Companies enabling infrastructure improvement should generate longer-term growth.

The list of likely winners includes the usual suspects, with Cisco, Microsoft and Sun prominent, plus a few additional names that are not yet so well known, including BEA Software and Verisign. Exodus Communications, a leader in web hosting, is another market pioneer where Alger was early to the party and also early to the exit selling out in the summer of 2000. And there will be others which are only a gleam in a garage as of 2001 but, by 2006, could be immensely important. Equally, newcomers may emerge that appear to hold great promise but turn out to be no more than a passing fad. In an era where change rules, mistakes will be made with attendant costs. But the cost from not getting aboard will be greater.

'This is the first innings of a nine-innings revolution called the internet. As a result, we can be confident of only a few things. One, that three years from now, some reader will e-mail us, perhaps via a wireless, web-surfing, voice-transcoding, America Online wristwatch, that we were fools investing in one of the companies named above. It would surprise us if that were not the case. On the other hand, we would be even more surprised if many of these companies (and new ones yet un-IPOed) did not continue to evolve and continue to transform the US economy, and, indeed, the global economy, in dramatic fashion in the next decade. So, while it is difficult to predict any of the changes we may or may not see in the next ten years brought about by the internet, we think it is very clear that investing in change, and in the companies that we believe are leading that change now, is the right thing to do.'

You can count on Chung and his colleagues at Fred Alger to lead the charge in the investment community, to embrace change, analyze new ideas to death, and unearth at least some of tomorrow's stock market stars – and certainly enough to continue to rack-up superior returns for their shareholders.

3

Wayne Cooperman

A young contrarian

One of the few to remain true to value

Ahead of the crowd in cyclical plays and sector consolidations

Successful shorting in a bull market

Compounded at 29 per cent annually since he began managing money

Excelled in 2000 with a net return of 42 per cent in one of the most difficult investment years in recent history (when most markets were down)

Value investors are a dying breed. Ben Graham would be lost in today's financial markets – his pronouncements alien and his views disregarded to the same degree as those of Rip Van Winkle. His disciples, who did so well for so long, are struggling to redefine and reinvent their methodologies. In this tech-driven environment, value is for wimps. Most of the big names in the business who made their reputations and profits espousing the creed of value are over 50. Will there be any believers left once that generation retires?

Step forward, Wayne Cooperman, who has no hesitation in describing himself as a value investor and whose career, since he struck out on his own and set up shop in 1995, proves that it is possible to make money with a value strategy – even in the twenty-first century.

It's no surprise to find Cooperman involved with investments. His father, a well-known Wall Street veteran, was Head of Research at Goldman Sachs from 1972 to 1989, so Wayne grew up with the business, and with a favourable impression of the business. Early experiences were positive. Conversations went beyond baseball and homework, as when Cooperman senior was evaluating Viacom. That research included his son's views on MTV, an area of expertise for Cooperman Junior at the time. A positive recommendation and purchase for the family portfolio resulted. Others that did well included Teledyne, bought because Wayne's dad was constantly mentioning that Henry Singleton, who ran the company, was a very smart person. Teledyne duly delivered more than a double, to Cooperman's delight.

'This seemed like a great way to make money without working.'

His initial insight was to prove half right. Making money – yes. Without working – well, maybe that was over optimistic.

This impression was reinforced at Stanford, where Cooperman's extracurricular activity included following and investing in the market. Oracle caught his eye in 1986, and proved an extremely successful purchase.

'They were growing fast, hiring a lot of people from the college, and seemed a great company. I knew people from Stanford who worked there and talked to friends who were more technically oriented.'

A brief stint at Goldman Sachs and a longer apprenticeship at Mark Asset Management confirmed Cooperman's interest in investment management rather than any other part of financial services. What he relished was the challenge of evaluating and analyzing a company, seeing beyond the numbers to the business underneath, and searching for real, rather than perceived, value.

Right from the get go, Cooperman had an instinctive reluctance to overpay. He was uncomfortable with high multiples, and was drawn, instead, to seeking a Margin of Safety in every investment. While most of his contemporaries were making big bets and not worrying about the odds, he was concerned about preservation of capital, making money without taking on too much risk, and always anxious to limit the downside. An emphasis on value was to become a hall-mark of his stock selection and continues to permeate his portfolio today, 11 years later.

Since his original investors included friends and family, a strategy that emphasized safety made a lot of sense. When Cooperman set up Cobalt Capital in January 1995, he made two commitments to his shareholders. The firm would be founded on a philosophy that called for 'knowing as much as possible about the companies and industries in which it invests', and it would invest only in companies where Cooperman could be convinced there was a genuine value proposition.

Quality value

Cooperman's definition of value was, and still is, mainstream. Forget trying to bottom fish or buying bad businesses at bargain-basement prices: what Cooperman is on the look-out for is akin to growth at a reasonable price, but with extra protection. So, unlike most traditional value investors who begin by taking apart the balance sheet, he often starts off by seeking companies with growth prospects.

'Growth doesn't get me excited *per se*. It's only companies that have the ability to show sustainable growth because they have a competitive advantage.'

And that is a question he keeps on asking every company he encounters.

'Do you have some sort of competitive advantage, whether it be technology or market position, or some kind of brand – something that basically doesn't make you susceptible to the next guy coming along and doing it better, or being subject to price competition?'

Cooperman stays away from revenue at racy multiples – especially where it is hard to see how above-average rates could continue. He is sceptical of glamour growth and one-year wonders.

'Companies growing 50 and 100 per cent a year that don't have a sustainable business model I view as more of a short-sell candidate than an investment. Anybody can be in a hot sector and grow quickly from a small base.'

The business must have the ability to grow more than just the top line. What Cooperman wants is demonstrated improvement in the

The business must have the ability to grow more than just the top line.

firm's value at above-average annual rates achieved through internal investing. Management must deploy capital so that this rate of return exceeds, by a decent margin, the cost of that capital, creating a cycle of continuous value creation. In other words, he is looking for a good business at a reasonable price. Businesses like Panera Bread, the reincarnation of Au Bon Pain, a superior sandwich chain.

'Au Bon Pain bought St Louis Bread, a suburban version with bigger stores – more of a bakery selection, and more of a sit-down atmosphere. I thought St Louis was going to be a huge home run and Au Bon Pain was a steady cash cow. St Louis continued to do extremely well, while Au Bon Pain was disappointing. Eventually it was sold and the stock became a pure play on St Louis.

'Panera Bread has one of the highest unit economics of any restaurant company I have ever seen. I modelled it out about $1.1 million in 1995, and they are doing closer to $1.6 million per unit now, while costs have remained relatively the same. They are moving to franchise units, and growing rapidly. They have about 500 franchise units in the pipeline to open over the next couple of years, compared to only 136 today.

'Having been to many of the restaurants and talked to franchisees, we were convinced that this is a great concept which has legs. They make 40–50 per cent returns on investment on a unit. If you go out a few years, you have tremendous value in the franchise royalty stream. We figured that the share, at $7, was basically the value of existing company-owned restaurants, so you were getting future royalties for free.'

Or, again, it could be a reasonable business at a good price. This second group which fall within Cooperman's value embrace may include companies with only average growth prospects, but where the discount is sufficiently compelling to compensate for lower growth.

The quality comes from the business – the value from a Margin of Safety to be found in the company, part, but not all, of which can be its relative cheapness. The tag 'quality value' seems to fit, especially when you start to delve underneath and see exactly what Cooperman has in mind. He always returns to the numbers, but there is no point doing detailed number crunching if the business cannot satisfy his fundamental requirement.

There must be a Margin of Safety

This is a refrain heard so often from value investors that it has almost become the distinguishing mantra of that community. Before disowning the concept as too vague, reconsider the importance of protecting the downside. Nor is Margin of Safety one-dimensional. As value investing has evolved, the best of the breed have refined the definition. Cooperman starts with the commonsense proposition that, rather like a loan officer at a bank, he wants two ways out of any position:

'Margin of Safety, to me, is if I'm wrong – if the company doesn't earn what I think it's going to earn – is there something there that, besides the earnings, creates a level of value?'

Assets offer one escape route.

'Is there a book value? Can the company liquidate their assets for a certain price?'

Sounds familiar, but what follows shows that Cooperman has gone beyond basic Ben Graham.

'That's mostly relevant with financial companies. It's hard to make that case for an industrial company. If paper prices are plummeting, I'm not sure what a paper machine is worth. I find the book-value argument mostly works just with liquid financial assets. Of course, in an economic crisis, or when there's financial market turmoil, then even that doesn't necessarily work.'

More important to Cooperman is to develop confidence that there is a Margin of Safety in the business itself.

'Does the company throw off significant amounts of free cash? Even if the earnings are off 10 or 15 cents, is the company still going to generate a lot of cash? Is the stock price trading at a low enough multiple of cash flow where the company is theoretically LBOable? Can you financially make it work, just by changing the balance sheet?'

Shaw Industries, the carpet manufacturer, illustrates Cooperman's point about a company where there is a Margin of Safety in the share price. A lot could have gone awry before Shaw, at $12, would have turned into a poor purchase, since it was expected to generate cash of over $1.80 per share in a normal year.

'If I was off from the earnings estimate by 50 per cent, at $1.20 of free cash flow, the stock was still incredibly attractive. Unlikely to go up a lot, but minimal downside. I think that it would be difficult for them only to earn $1.20, just to throw a number out, but even that big a difference potentially allows a high return.'

While Cooperman leans towards cash flow as a more reliable indicator of a Margin of Safety, he is a believer in horses for courses. Assets can do the job better in certain categories of business.

'With a hotel company, you're looking at assets. They're not unrelated, because an asset is theoretically only worth the cash flow it provides. If you're buying hotels at $40,000 a room and it costs $60,000 a room to build a comparable hotel in a comparable market, that's when you're looking at the asset base. But you can't forget cash flow. With a crappy hotel in a lousy market, a room may not be worth $40,000, because it's only cash flowing $1,000. So it's probably only worth $10,000. You have to look not only at the assets, and what they cost to replace, but also at the cash flow today and how could it change.'

After which there is one more filter to determine whether you may have a Margin of Safety, even if none is apparent on the surface.

'Are the assets worth a lot more to somebody else that can do more with them? That's more difficult. There are companies that have good assets where they aren't maximizing value. Maybe they lack critical mass, or their cost of capital is too high. Over time, those assets will, hopefully, migrate into someone else's hands.'

Cash is the ultimate store of value. The key determinant for Cooperman, who makes no bones about its overriding importance, is cash flow. Cash flow is a component of Margin of Safety, but it is much, much more. It is the lifeblood of every business and the primary driver of his investment decisions.

'The first thing for me is cash flow and free cash flow. That's the easiest, quickest way to understand the value of a company. You look

> ## The first thing for me is cash flow and free cash flow.

at the business, its projections. What's the cash flow going to be? What is the use of the capital? Do they earn a good return on capital or not? Are they buying back stock? Are they reinvesting in the business at a high return? That's pure, simple and straightforward. If I'm buying this company and planning on holding it for the next couple of years, what is the stream of cash flows that I expect?'

Of course it's not always that simple. Some of the most interesting value investments require more digging to establish a Margin of Safety that may, on further investigation, turn out to be equally good, or even better – just not so obvious.

'Then there's other situations where you say, "The cash flows are poor, right now, but either something structurally is going to happen that's going to dramatically improve cash flow, or the asset value of the company is a lot higher than indicated by the cash flows".

'The newspaper inserts industry was a cosy duopoly between Valassis and News Corporation. A third company, Sullivan Graphics, decided to get into that business and destroyed the whole pricing mechanism. News Corporation ended up buying Sullivan, taking out the third irrational player and consolidating the industry back to two. While there were three players, the industry went into the tank and Valassis stock got creamed. We were able to buy at a very low valuation. With the industry back to two players, prices rose and returns were restored to acceptable levels. With a time lag, Valassis was a great stock again.'

Sometimes a shift in structure affects a whole sector, making silk purses out of sows' ears. That type of re-rating can be the value investors' green light, especially for investors quick off the mark.

'When the government, in 2000, started talking about increasing reimbursement rates to hospitals instead of decreasing them, we bought a bunch of hospital stocks, including HCA and Triad, because you had a quantum change. The HMO sector suddenly started getting price increases above cost increases, and you had margin expansion.'

Even companies like Oxford, which had been dogs, took off, but not before Cooperman had tucked some away for Cobalt shareholders.

What, in summary, are the sort of characteristics Cooperman likes to see in businesses that might make suitable holdings for Cobalt? They are:

- some sort of sustainable franchise;
- lasting competitive advantage;
- a change in environment not yet factored into the stock price;
- and, of course, that ever present Margin of Safety.

Cyclical growth

One way to find value and growth in the same security is through playing the right part of a business cycle – buying and selling well-established companies in relatively predictable industries. This strategy has rewarded Cooperman on several occasions. Early on in 1995 he went big into banks, which were coming off a poor period and were out of favour.

'There were companies with over-reserved loan losses, so you had very good credit quality and excess capital that they were able to release over time. We had relatively low valuations, with companies trading at, or around, book value, and earnings were increasing.'

All of which set the stage for a resurgence of growth in a sector with a patchy record. Cyclical growth, however, has limitations. Share prices only go up so far because investors have been there before; but what can cause a breakout is when cyclical sectors consolidate. Cooperman was also attracted because, in 1995, US banking was entering such a phase.

'We made a lot of money in Midlantic Bank. It was one of the dominant banks in New Jersey. They had to be acquired at some point by somebody because of their position. The stock was cheap on its own, trading at book and around eight times earnings, so there was not a lot of risk and it was likely to be taken over.

'We had a lot of Chemical, which ended up buying Chase. You bought good consolidators as well as companies that were attractive candidates. That action was overlaid on the fact that the banks were, as a group, attractive, given low valuations and excess capital. You could buy Chemical at seven or eight times earnings trading right on book, and they were buying back stock because they were over-capitalized.'

This bifocal strategy worked because of the entry point: a sector where underlying valuations had fallen too far and where the business was capable of generating a decent return, but with too many competitors and structural inefficiencies. Similar conditions prevailed throughout the hotel industry beginning in 1995 and on into early 1996.

'We were coming off a couple of very bad years. Construction got slashed. The economy was good. You had limited new supply – actually flat in some markets – at a time when demand was growing, so there was an imbalance.'

Attractive assets at below cost

Value growth has been harder to find of late, as investors have paid up even for relatively modest increases in earnings, reducing attractive options in that category. Just as fervently as investors embraced growth at almost any price, they shunned asset-rich companies. In true contrarian fashion, Cooperman, who has always fished in these waters, has been finding more and more bargains. What attracts him is nothing so simplistic as cheap assets, but quality assets available at well below replacement cost, and especially assets in sectors where some sort of shake-up is underway. As consolidators look round and realize they can buy existing assets for less than cost, even after paying an acquisition premium, it makes sense to go down that route rather than to create new capacity.

Real estate represents a long-term store of value and is a recurring theme at Cobalt. Many of the firm's largest holdings have been backed by a sizeable property component. Cooperman spotted an opportunity in hotels in the mid-1990s, when management at a number of REITS (real estate investment trusts) were hungry to expand. At the time, there were several good quality chains at depressed prices.

'Again, you had extremely low valuations. Companies were trading on a per-key basis well below replacement cost. Even some of the best names in the industry. We owned a lot of Prime Hospitality and Promus Hotels, which is more of a franchise company.'

Another proven way to buy assets below cost is through shares of companies that trade at a discount to the sum of their component parts. This approach is easier when those components are listed, allowing Cooperman to own companies that would not normally fit his model, such as UnitedGlobalCom (UCOMA), a communications company with cable systems throughout Europe, Australia and Latin America. The company offers video, voice and internet services, and also owns a portal. While difficult to value UCOMA, stakes owned in two publicly traded subsidiaries indicated a much higher valuation than its current market.

Ogden Corp, another example, was a more complicated situation, though the asset argument was similar.

'Ogden was the quintessential, poorly managed quasi-conglomerate. The ex-chairman did the company a disservice. He expanded into water parks, into concessions at stadiums, airport privatizations, baggage handling, and a mess of other barely related businesses. At the core was an energy business, waste-to-energy plants, and a bunch of independent power plants. Those were doing well.

'We thought the energy business was probably worth over $20 a share, but the stock was trading about $10. They finally threw out the old CEO. It was a waiting game. Hopefully they could sell all the other assets and go forward with the core business. At this point, they have sold off 90 per cent of what they were supposed to sell. The stock has gone up to $16.50 and we still think the value is north of $20.'

Similar thinking led Cooperman to acquire a large position in Seagate Technology late in 1999. He is no fan of disk drives, where Seagate is worldwide market leader, nor does he expect improvement in industry dynamics any time soon, though, one day, the cycle should work for him. His investment was justified by net cash in the company and investments, notably a holding in Veritas, a software data storage company. What followed was classic. When management distributed Veritas stock and sold the disk-drive business, Seagate's price promptly soared and the valuation gap disappeared, making shareholders, Cooperman included, happy campers.

> # Value is a state of mind, more than a discipline encumbered with requirements.

All of which adds up to an approach that says value is a state of mind, more than a discipline encumbered with requirements that imposes inflexible yes/no tests and limits investment opportunities. Or, put another way:

'The one thing I try to do is not be rigid. I don't say, "I only buy stocks that trade below book. I only buy stocks below ten times earnings and five times cash." Some stocks at 12 times cash flow are better values than stocks at five times cash flow. It's all a question of the quality of the business, the sustainability of the earnings, the growth rate going forward and the free cash flow characteristics.'

Cooperman can maintain this approach to value only because upfront analysis allows him to confirm the presence of a Margin of Safety. He is fanatical about depth of research. Talk to him about any company Cobalt owns, and you can tell he knows the investment intimately. And not just the one he owns, but the entire sector in which his holding competes. The Cobalt process is depicted diagrammatically in the company literature (see Fig. 3.1). This is the essence of the investment process that Cooperman works through to identify quality value propositions.

It all comes back to cash flow

One reliable way to determine whether a cheap business is good or bad is to leave the balance sheet behind and focus on picking apart the components of cash flow. Figure 3.1 highlights cash flow more than any other characteristic. This has always been a hallmark of Cooperman's style and the emphasis has, if anything, become even more acute over the years. To Cooperman there is no other indicator of greater importance in determining value, and he spends a lot of his time looking at EBITDA (Earnings Before Interest, Taxes, Depreciation and Amortization) or EBITA, depending on the nature of the business. For many companies, depreciation is a real expense. To sustain earnings may require reinvestment at a rate equal to, or greater than, available cash from depreciation.

'I like investing in industries which are consolidating where you're taking capacity out. We made a lot of money in the clinical-lab business through Quest Diagnostics. Testing had regulatory problems, Medicare fraud and disputes with the government. Now the industry has consolidated, pricing is starting to get better. There's pretty good earnings growth now and, with a ton of goodwill amortization and depreciation, cash flow is above capital expenditure, because they were shrinking the number of labs and did not need to invest. So I prefer to look at cash flow before amortization and depreciation.

'On top of that, they bought Smith Kline labs and consolidated the industry, which gave them the opportunity to take a ton of cost out and shrink capacity further. You go to a doctor's office and they have three milk carts outside for the blood. Take one away and you cut your route and delivery costs.'

It is important that companies generate significant cash flow in relation to their market value. Cooperman also constantly makes the

Figure 3.1 | The Cobalt process

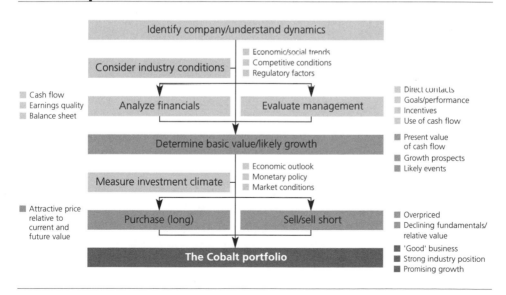

point that isolating suitable investments is not just about generating good cash flow. It is also important that companies use their cash flow for the benefit of shareholders. Which sets up the next attribute that Cooperman makes sure to analyze in depth.

Active and user-friendly management

One constant running through Cooperman's presentation of his investment approach is the need to evaluate the top people at a company. The ability of management to create shareholder value is paramount, regardless of the initial determination that a security starts out undervalued. Read every quarterly letter ever written at Cobalt and you find the text peppered with phrases such as (in July 1999): 'After having spent a lot of time with Advanta management, we see signs that they are reducing their cost structure'. Or again (in April 1996), about a merger involving temporary staffing companies: 'We like the fit between Interim's strong management and Brandon's market position … and have increased our position since the announcement'.

The emphasis is on management capable of improving operations, and also on those with a commitment to put shareholders first. This can come to the fore when a company is in play. While not his primary consideration, Cooperman makes the point that it is important to invest where management is prepared to sell at the right price and not resist all offers. This aspect of good corporate governance is often overlooked until too late. Cooperman considers sale prospects upfront, including the issue of how management might respond if approached, which is especially relevant where the rationale is that the assets are underperforming.

'If I think that a company has problems, but know it's worth a lot more to somebody else, and I feel like the company is motivated or under pressure to maximize shareholder value – that is a reason to purchase.'

Ogden proves the point, but only worked after a change at the top brought a fresh focus to the company.

Combine a Margin of Safety with good, shareholder-motivated management and you get Cooperman's version of investment Nirvana. He describes one holding that meets all these demanding criteria.

'LNR Property is a diversified real-estate company. They own securities, they own land, they own properties, they develop properties. It's a difficult animal to understand. It's not well followed. The stock price suffers from its complicated nature, and also from a general bear market in real-estate related securities, even though real-estate markets, as a whole, are quite healthy.

'Here's a company that has a stated book of $22 per share. The land is at historical cost, some of which is well below today's market. These guys were large buyers of land from the RTC in California in the early 1990s. The land they haven't sold is on their books at those prices, and is worth a lot more today than at the bottom of the cycle when buying from a motivated seller. They have conservative accounting policies. Real property is depreciated over time, even though cash flows are increasing. All of which makes asset value way above book. I would say by nearly 100 per cent. Look at their stock exchange filings: the company just filed an 8K. They state the value is north of $40, yet the share is still only $21, as of November 2000.

'That's my first Margin of Safety. I know that the assets are worth almost twice the stock price.

'Secondly, I believe management is incredibly sharp. Look at their record. They have been astute real-estate investors. They've bought at good times; they've sold at other times; they've redeveloped properties and earned high returns. This company doesn't have problems. The company's bought back shares, and they're still trying to buy back stock. The family controls a third. They're playing with their money, as well as mine. The book goes up, the earnings go up, the cash flows go up, while the stock has done nothing for two years or more.'

LNR sounds like one to watch.

Questions to ask before buying

Cooperman always asks himself two questions before pushing the button and adding a new security to his portfolio:

'Can I make a 50 per cent plus return over two years? That's sort of my bogey. I'm not looking to make 100 per cent a year, or 100 per cent in a week, like some funds. If I can make more than 50 per cent over a two-year period, 25 per cent compounded, then it's a good investment.'

And, having satisfied himself that more than 50 per cent is attainable, the second question is:

'Do I have quantifiable and somewhat limited downside risk at the same time? There's a lot of stocks where I feel I can make that much on the upside, if everything goes right, but I'm not comfortable, that, if something goes wrong, I have a Margin of Safety that there's an inherent value underlying the company that would prevent it from declining too much.'

This second question resurrects the issue never far from Cooperman's thoughts. Does an investment provide the Margin of Safety he looks for in every holding in his portfolio?

It is this constant examination of the downside and concern for what could go wrong that differentiates Cooperman from most of his peers. Up until 2000 so much went right since the early 1990s that few professionals in their thirties have an appreciation of the importance of capital preservation, nor proper respect for the market's ability to flip over and eradicate, in a handful of trading sessions, the gains of many months. High expectations, if not met, are punished severely, and the higher the expectation, the greater the risk of falling short.

> # The higher the expectation, the greater the risk of falling short.

Cooperman likes a degree of certainty that value exists at the time of purchase. He wants to buy the present at a discount, not the possible future at what may turn out to be a premium. Equally, he does not want to buy the stock with a great Margin of Safety which no-one will ever want.

Avoiding value traps

One problem when you are in the business of compound annual rates of return is an investment which, on the surface, seems to be the perfect value play: so cheap that the value investor can hardly resist. But, year after year after year, it stays cheap, maybe even gets a little cheaper, and the portfolio's performance suffers. Deceptively attractive candidates can be dangerous to value investors. Cooperman explains how he sifts the wheat from the chaff. Some companies will never earn a decent return on capital. Value investors need to sharpen their scepticism. If the rate of return is low, and likely to remain low, that is a lighthouse urging investors to stay away, however sweet the siren sounds.

Potential traps can be sprung where there is a catalyst. Here relief comes from externalities. Acquisition is the quickest and most efficient route to asset redeployment. Where existing management does not deliver and the return on capital is below par, which is one explanation for a 'cheap' price, Cooperman considers whether the company is a realistic takeover candidate. If it is a piece which fits in someone else's puzzle, then the answer may be 'yes'.

'If you think that there's a catalyst for those assets to change hands, you get more excited about it.'

The reasons why a business may be worth more to a particular acquirer than to the market can be convoluted, and do not always depend on obvious operating overlaps. Cooperman explains why one situation that the market had written off turned out to be a smart call:

'A couple of years ago we owned Continental Homes, a large home builder, mostly in Phoenix. It was doing very well, but never had a good multiple. People were wary of owning a company with very high concentration in one market.

'We figured it was worth a lot more to a more diversified home builder, which, by buying Continental, got an attractive land position, and became the largest builder in Phoenix, Arizona, but the Phoenix-based activity was now only a part of a bigger company instead of 90 per cent. Because DR Horton was diversified, they were able to pay a premium. The price was low enough that Horton could earn a good return on the purchase, and because the combined company was a diversified, much larger operation, the risk of too much concentration in one market, Phoenix, was reduced.'

Leave something on the table

The value investor's exit strategy is not to be too greedy when selling. If you are careful about entry and buy well, you can make excellent returns and still afford to miss the top. What you cannot afford to do is not sell, especially if you own cyclicals, which inevitably turn down. Cooperman closely monitors both sides of a trade.

'That's in keeping with a valuation discipline, as opposed to a momentum discipline. I'm buying because I believe the price is well below its value. When the price gets to or above what I believe the value is, it's difficult to justify owning it. There are tax implications but, at the end of the day, you have to have a view on what it's worth and be willing to sell if it's no longer trading at a discount.'

One area where Cooperman was sensible in booking profits was hotels, where he built sizeable positions during 1995 and the first part of 1996. He started to sell in 1997 and was gone by early 1998; a wise move, since prices subsequently cratered when industry dynamics entered a less favourable phase.

Cooperman owned most of the main names in the sector during this period. Figure 3.2 shows his activity in one of the largest, Prime Hospitality Corporation, with the main periods of purchases and sales

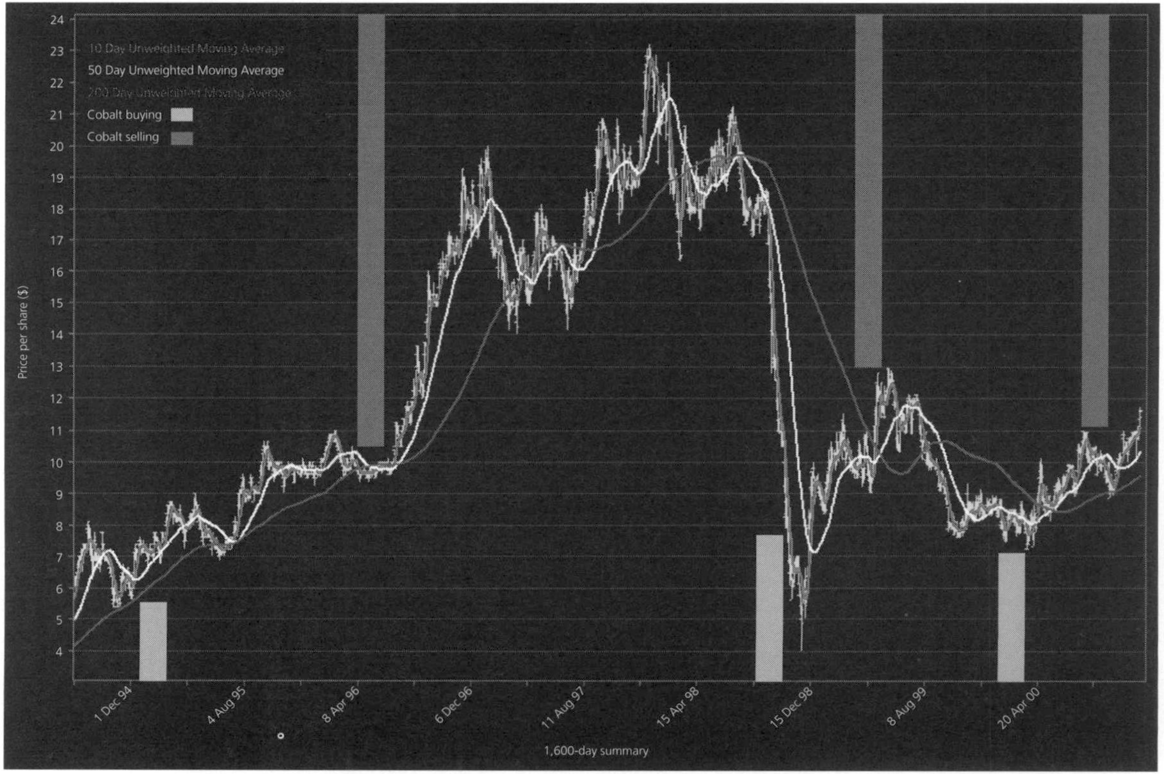

Figure 3.2 Share price of Prime Hospitality, 1994–2000 *Source:* Bridge, Cobalt trading records

marked. As is clear, Cooperman is not averse to double dipping. If he unwinds a position making a profit and the price subsequently tanks to where its value is once again compelling, he is more than happy to re-enter lower down and complete a second round trip in the same stock, or even a third! There is a lot to be said for the stock you know. It makes sense to leverage the research effort – not just with a large position, but also with multiple purchases and sales, especially in cyclical sectors.

Making money on both sides of the trade

One response, when value is in short supply, is to search for the antithesis of value and sell overvalued shares short. Cooperman has used shorts selectively since starting Cobalt. Most long-bias firms short to manage risk and hedge. Cooperman is concerned about portfolio balance, but his primary interest is to profit from inappropriate and excessive valuation anomalies. In spite of markets that have risen relentlessly, Cooperman has made money consistently through shorting. Yet most short houses lost their shirt in the 1990s. Which makes his strategy of special interest.

He displays the same caution in shorting as he does in going long; and perhaps even to a greater extent, since a bad decision can be that much more painful.

'I have much smaller positions on the short side. I tend to be more conservative. These companies trading at 100 times revenues are tempting, but it's difficult. You feel you will be right over time, but there's too much short-term pain possible to really get aggressive. You try and stay away until you get a reason for them to go down.'

Short candidates were plentiful, as of the middle of 2000. Cooperman resists high-profile candidates, where overvaluation can persist for long periods, so has not been caught out by excessive exuberance in sectors that have been pig heaven for day traders. And he does not get on the wrong side of good businesses, even when the prices seem expensive.

'I'm not going to short cable companies, even at 18 or 19 times cash flow, because that's one of the better business models, and they generate gobs of cash. You can't short just based on price. There are many companies with incredibly large market caps with what I consider to be dubious business plans. But what's to say what's overvalued? The final say is the market. The market determines what price is correct at any given point in time. Ideally stocks that are incredibly overvalued are good shorts. One day it'll change and therefore that will be the best strategy.'

An example of the sort of stock where Cooperman has conviction to short is AMF Bowling. AMF's balance sheet left no room for error and, when an unexpected externality undermined cash flow, the company was vulnerable.

'AMF consolidated the US bowling-centre industry, yet their earnings had a heavy reliance on selling bowling equipment into Asia. So when we had a downturn in the Asian market, coupled with an extremely levered balance sheet, plus you had somewhat poor results from their US bowling centres, the equity collapsed.'

Cooperman opened this short in early 1998, when the share was north of $30, before the full impact became apparent; as the situation deteriorated, he added to the position. He suspected sales would dry up as the Asian crisis hit home, with leisure as a luxury likely to bear the brunt. That proved an accurate assessment, as the stock was last seen at 25 cents and still heading south.

Take a walk on the short side

Working the short side adds elasticity to Cooperman's portfolio. This is not a token nod to hedging, but serious stuff. In early 2000 Cobalt got up to 30 per cent short, a meaningful weighting, but a natural posture for a value investor when markets are expensive. Cobalt has invested in shorts through its entire history. Even in his first year, Cooperman averaged

> By using shorts you're able to create interesting value propositions that you can't create otherwise.

between 10 and 15 per cent of his portfolio in short positions. While such exposure may seem perverse in strong markets, there is a method to his apparent madness.

'Although the indexes have done well, the average stock hasn't done nearly as well. By using shorts you're able to create interesting value propositions that you can't create otherwise.'

Cooperman's shorting strategy is multidimensional:

1. Naked shorts

These include stocks such as AMF, or what Cooperman calls the classic generic short, such as Boston Chicken.

'The whole business model was flawed. Returns on building a restaurant weren't there. You lay that on top of the way they financed the company with development loans. They were basically using accounting gimmickry to keep losses off their books. So you had a weak base business and a company whose financial results weren't being accurately reported. They were on the hook for all this money that they lent to their developers, who were losing money, but their income statement was showing interest income. The loans were really secured by the restaurants, and restaurants were doing lousy.'

2. Going ex growth

Yesterday's heroes can make good shorts when earnings momentum slows.

'We've made money shorting growth stocks that aren't growth stocks any more. I'm not sure that P&G is a growth stock any more.'

P&G tanked by nearly 40 per cent days after this conversation on a profits warning.

Adaptec makes, perhaps, a more interesting example, reminding investors that fame and fortune in the stock market can be very short-lived these days.

'They made their money selling SCSI interfaces. The technology moved more towards fibre channel. Adaptec was left behind in the technology curve.'

Cooperman banked over 50 per cent on the way down as the glamour wore off.

3. Matched pairs

These usually involve two similar companies in the same line of business and preferably in the same country.

'If I'm buying Company A, I may short Company B that is very similar to Company A but less attractive.'

In US book retail, Cooperman went long Barnes & Noble and short Borders:

'You had two companies that were, for all intents and purposes, very similar, building large superstores to sell books, and both had an installed base of mall stores. Borders was trading at twice the multiple of Barnes & Noble, because they were showing higher comparable store sales. What was really happening was that Barnes & Noble had a lot more stores than Borders. Borders would open in a new market which hurt Barnes & Noble's comparables. Barnes & Noble stores are more productive than Borders' stores, though showing lower comparables. So people were positive on Borders because they appeared to have better comps, but Barnes & Noble was a cheaper stock. The other thing was that Borders' accounting was more aggressive. Their depreciation expense was much lower as a per cent of sales.'

Neither stock has exactly been a star since Cooperman opened his positions, but their relative values reversed, allowing him to emerge with a satisfactory net profit.

In disk drives, Cooperman found value discrepancies between Read Rite and Applied Magnetics irresistible. He went long the former and short the latter, after spotting a shift in technology that was compounded by corporate action.

'Both companies make the heads that go in disk drives. Applied Magnetics had older technology that happened to be in the sweet spot at a given point and, therefore, were making incredibly large profits, but it became pretty clear that that was a three-, six-, nine-month proposition. For the next generation, Read Rite was much better positioned. Read Rite missed the current generation and instead invested a lot of money for the next. Applied had been milking the cow, but wasn't prepared for the next generation.

'These technologies have short lead times. That's why it's a really crappy business. They make money for six months and then lose money for two years. You had Applied trading at an incredibly high multiple of peak earnings. On a market cap to revenue basis, Applied was much higher than Read Rite. We thought Read Rite was going to do better and Applied was going to be in a lot of trouble. The guy that ran Applied, being pretty sharp, realized this and thought, "While my price is high and Read Rite's well positioned, I'm going to make an offer to buy Read Rite with stock". What happened was Read Rite's stock went up a lot, and Applied went down, and Read Rite said, "No way". People realized Applied was doing this because they knew they were in trouble. The deal didn't happen. Applied's been delisted.'

A success, then, but Cooperman was not entirely satisfied. Although he booked a good profit, he could have done better riding the long-term trend in what is fundamentally a bad business.

'I wish I'd stayed short. I wish I'd shorted both companies. Shitty industries are shitty industries and you want to be short. I think Applied's bankrupt and Read Rite's down a lot.'

4. Fundamental value mismatch

Shorting can emulate hedging when equities are related, especially through a cross-ownership structure that the market has not properly understood.

'There's parent/sub relationships which are out of whack with reality where the value of the sub that the parent owns is worth more than the parent.'

So you can buy the parent as a simple value play, or you can go one better by shorting the subsidiary at the same time to lock in an arbitrage profit on one stock while going long the other. Which way you go depends on the degree of discrepancy and on which is likely to rise or fall by the larger percentage. These types of trades – sometimes known as straddles – are relatively painless to put in place for US-listed companies, even for private investors, though the mechanics are harder elsewhere. Cooperman cites Williams as one such situation:

'We're short Williams Communications, but we're long Williams Energy. It's not a negative call on Communications so much as that, if I back out its value, I'm buying Energy for approximately $2 a share. Energy is a fine company and earning $1.10. It's possible that that stub will stay at $2, but not likely.'

And, if Energy goes up $1, that's 50 per cent, but the increase in the price of Communications should be a lot less. So the net gain from two linked trades should be nicely positive.

Structural arbitrage is a cute variation on the imperfect-pair shorting strategy. Such a strategy is compelling, but logic alone is no guarantee of a favourable outcome. Once you have found a suitable candidate to short, you also need a good reason to open the position. Cooperman looks for something that will trip a company up or, effectively, a reverse Margin of Safety. Structural flaws with the business model is his preferred place to start. There are other give-aways that would encourage him to consider going short – telltale signs that all is not well in Camelot and, if more widely known, should lead to a radical downward reappraisal in multiple rating. Here's where the culture of detailed analysis of the notes can pay dividends.

'Is this company inflating results through aggressive accounting? Are they taking one-time gains? Are they capitalizing things they should be expensing? Are they pulling forward business? Are receivables and inventories growing at a rate inconsistent with sales growth? Are they making acquisitions that have little chance of earning a good return? If you can overlay an overleveraged balance sheet, that always makes it just that much better.'

Any of the above can be the catalyst for a downgrade. A combination that includes deteriorating business fundamentals or insufficient cash flow of course is even better. There are several questions Cooperman asks to try and decide whether a high-flying business could come crashing down to earth and so reward a short stance.

'The first thing is, does this company have a weak business plan? Are they doing well today, but they're going to do a lot less well next year, because their product is going to be obsoleted by somebody else, or because some law is going to change or the government's going to cut reimbursement rate? Is something going to happen to make current earnings and cash flow decline? The best short is when you can see a decline in the base business. That's the most basic element. Is this a good business or not? Can this company earn above-average rates of return over an extended period? The problem now is you have many, many companies where the market's saying, 'Go ahead! Lose as much as you want – we don't care, because, one day, we'll get it back.' I think that's difficult for a value investor, because people are blind-faith investing.'

> # The best short is when you can see a decline in the base business.

Essentially, he is after the flip side of the analytical outcome that he uses to select his longs, but with a caveat.

'Shorting is difficult because you need more of a catalyst. Just because you think the stock is worth 50 and it's at 100, that doesn't work that well. You need a reason. To me the best reason to short is a poor business plan.'

Just as long-only investors can trade in and out of a stock depending on price, so thoughtful hedge managers can cover and reopen short positions as price fluctuates – especially if there is a quasi-hedge through a long elsewhere in the portfolio. Cooperman has made money several times by going in and out of his short/hedge at Williams.

'When the price went down a lot we covered Williams Communications, and when it rallied back up, we put some more out, so we try to be sensitive to the price of the sub, and pick times when it is relatively more or less attractive.'

Even with a truly dreadful business where intrinsic value may well be negative, the risk of a rebound rises, the lower the price goes. But, occasionally, there may be a way to hedge that risk by staying short the equity and going long the debt. Cooperman did well with his AMF short but, when the price was down 80 per cent or so, the temptation was to close out the trade. Unwilling to leave profit on the table, he devised a variant of pairing through separate classes of financial instrument in the same company.

'AMF is either going to zero, or they're going to have to do something. I own debt at a big discount because, at the end of the day, I think they're going to need another rights offering, or some kind of restructuring which would issue equity to the debt holders.'

Either way, equity will be diluted and the credit of the debt should improve, causing its value to increase. So Cooperman stands to win with both his short and his long!

Unlocking value: the contrarian way forward

You will not find Cooperman flocking to the latest investment fad. Rather the reverse. He is active among assets or sectors that are shunned by most: the essence of the bargain being that, if he is willing to buy what others want to sell, he should get in with a lower basis. When sentiment shifts the other way, he will turn seller and take advantage of the shift to make his holding available – for a higher price, naturally. At the start of this first decade of the twenty-first century, Cooperman is finding value in sectors that, as far as the financial media and Wall Street brokers are concerned, barely exist. Property, in particular, has repeatedly staged a comeback to prove its critics wrong, even if real-estate companies fall out of favour every so often.

'By definition as a value investor, you need to be a contrarian, because you need to be looking in sectors that are overlooked and undervalued. If everybody's saying "left", you have to look right. And, if everybody's saying "real estate sucks", that gives you the opportunity to find good players, like LNR Properties, or Newhall Land and Farming. When the whole world is saying "you've got to go in technology", it's hard to be a value investor and own technology. If I agree with everybody else, then what value am I adding?'

The trends, both macro and market, that matter to Cooperman reflect his position as a value investor. He sees several reasons in 2000 to be encouraged about opportunities for superior returns from his style of investing. This is situation-specific stuff which does not rely on a favourable market or momentum or anything other than overdue recognition of an undervalued security.

1. LBOs are dead: long live the LBOs

Equity valuations and a high-yield debt market in hibernation have limited leveraged buyout activity. There has been less of this type of financial engineering in the 1990s. Action on the street has been elsewhere and, in the second half of the last decade, LBOs have been conspicuous mostly by their absence. With many 'old economy' industries trading at depressed valuations, especially compared to their cash-generation capability, Cooperman expects a revival in LBOs, particularly once the current interest rate cycle peaks and liquidity looks for new outlets.

'In the market today, given the very low valuation on many companies, you'll see more and more LBOs or management buyouts. Once the junk-bond market strengthens a little bit, you'll see a lot of that.'

Traditional industries are where these sorts of transactions are most likely.

2. Recaps and buybacks

Companies languishing on meagre multiples may not take the market's lack of regard lying down. In addition to expecting a pick-up in LBOs, Cooperman also anticipates an increase in proactive steps on the part of management to address low ratings. Two tools that should see greater use are recaps and stock buybacks. Cooperman provides an example of how this can work in practice, using a company that he owned where he believed management would do the right thing for shareholders.

'Shaw Industries is the largest carpet manufacturer in the country. The stock is $12. Whatever they earn is pretty much free cash flow. Depreciation and amortization is roughly equal to capital spending, so take $1.80 cash flow per share and, without increasing leverage, you can buy back 15 per cent of the shares outstanding during the year and not have more debt than you had when the year began.

'They have buyback authorization for approximately 10 per cent of the shares, and bought back stock each year for the last six years. You may not have an LBO but, in effect, they're going to decapitalize the company.'

Just as happened at Seagate. Remarkably prophetic. Shaw seemed set to go down the same route, but subsequently agreed to be acquired by Berkshire Hathaway in conjunction with members of management, some two months after this conversation.

3. M&A activity to accelerate

While Cooperman does not deliberately search out takeover targets, his value approach tends to throw up companies that are attractive acquisition candidates. And it works. In one 12-month period – 1997 – companies equivalent to 30 per cent of his portfolio were snapped up, contributing to the 51 per cent return he achieved that year.

Sectors in turmoil usually experience an above-average degree of corporate activity and, when under consolidation, it is possible for both buyers and sellers to see their price rise as a result of a deal. Cooperman expects this trend to be evergreen. Both banks and hotels have been good to him in the past. In 2000, house building contained attractive assets that could be picked up for less than replacement cost. That would suggest fertile soil for a value investor looking for a Margin of Safety and angling for an early catalyst to unlock the value.

'We own Dell Webb. An investment group, Pacific Partners, which owns over 5 per cent of the company, filed a 13D and are seeking board seats to maximize value. Then a private home builder, JF Shey, came in with a $30 bid.'

Very nice, too, if you were Cooperman and paid $15 barely four months ago.

'There are other, smaller cap names in the group, like Ryland and MDC Holdings, which are potential takeovers because they trade at four or five times earnings and below book value.'

4. The internet = extra analysis

Unlike most other professionals profiled in this book, Cooperman does not embrace the internet as a stand-alone theme. That is not to say he ignores its development or underestimates its importance.

'The internet is new and exciting. It's not a fad. I don't own any internet stocks *per se*. I use it all the time. But I haven't quite figured out how a lot of these internet companies are going to actually make money, so I've not invested in them.'

One day he may find suitable opportunities that fit his criteria, but only when values return to more reasonable multiples. In the meantime, he sees the issue in terms of assessing the internet's effect on potential holdings. In addition to the financial and business environment evaluation, a complete audit must take into account the impact of the internet.

> **A complete audit must take into account the impact of the internet.**

'You have to try to understand how companies fit into the internet world. Even if you're not an investor, you can't deny its importance. Clearly people look at bricks-and-mortar retailers as losers, although that might not be the case. Some distributors may end up being suppliers to internet retailers. Then there's the whole B2B commerce phenomenon. Whenever you look at a company you just have to say, "How do they play into the internet?"'

Nor is his impact analysis confined to individual companies. The starting point has to be at sector level. Implications are not always obvious. Take real estate. Cooperman believes that the fashionable view may be too simplistic. His own conclusion is somewhat contrarian. Retail space may be in less demand, but additional warehousing will be required. So far he is in the mainstream. He also sees opportunities in office property, whereas the popular perception is that the commercial sector will suffer. His argument is that even start-ups need corporate offices: possibly smaller, but also smarter and, perhaps, more expensive, so possibly more profitable to developers and owners. And then there are hotels:

'If the internet causes the economy, as a whole, to grow, so demand for office space grows with the economy. More people will travel and go to hotels, so it's never quite as simple as people want to make it out.'

The internet is also one reason Cooperman is bullish on residential real-estate and house builders. The net explosion, with its wealth effect, raises the question of what those who have converted paper into cash will do. One likely beneficiary, and early on in the spending cycle, should be housing. The new rich usually make a more expensive piece of real estate their first major expenditure. Though his value discipline prevents Cooperman playing the internet directly, he can position his portfolio to take advantage indirectly.

'You want to be invested in the companies that will do well in the new economy, but I'm not sure if that means the new economy *per se*. We were bullish on house building and part of that, I guess, is because of all the wealth that has been created by the so-called new economy. ... At the end of the day, it's what people do with their money: they buy a new house and carpets, then a new car and a vacation home. There's a major wealth effect. I think you want to own companies that benefit from that.'

Equally, he accepts that technology will change some functions to the detriment of the current generation of businesses. Avoiding losers is just as important. Within real estate, residential house builders look likely winners, not just due to increased demand, especially at the higher end, but also through more efficient procurement of materials. B2B purchasing should be a plus for buyers, especially those who, in the past, may have been limited to regional suppliers. Realtors, in contrast, look likely to lose out, as net-based marketing facilitates the removal of agents, linking buyers and sellers directly at no, or lower, cost. All of which translates to buy Kaufman and Broad, California's largest builder, but avoid brokers.

'You can buy a house over the web, so that may hurt the real-estate brokerage business, but someone's still got to build the house. They've still got to put in the plumbing and so forth. I don't think that business will be hurt by the web. In fact, maybe large home builders will be able to leverage their size on the web, reduce distribution costs, reduce the commission they pay to sales people, and run the business more efficiently.'

Value is eternal

Value may be down as the new century gets underway, but the core philosophy is never out. Value investors revel in the unfashionable. That is how they outperform. Investors are facing a period of massive contrast. Alongside breathtaking multiples assigned to anything that has a hint of growth, unfashionable companies, even those with strong cash generation, are lumbered with miserly multiples. While there are no guarantees in financial markets, this sort of discontinuity suggests the nearest thing to a one-way bet. Cooperman is able to load up on investments that no-one wants today, but should come back into fashion one day. He may not have long to wait.

The fact that value can still work as an investment approach is clear from Cobalt's results. Since January 1995 Cooperman's partners have seen their fund achieve a gain of 198 per cent, compounding at over 25 per cent p.a. after all fees. And Cooperman achieved these results without the use of leverage and with a net long position that rarely exceeded 65 per cent, which makes his performance all the more creditable. It must also give his investors a warm feeling to know that Cooperman eats his own cooking. He has a substantial portion of his personal wealth tied up in Cobalt. His interests are exactly aligned with those of his shareholders.

The big imponderable for Cooperman, as with all value managers, is – when? Timing is impossible to predict. He can increase the odds of events occurring earlier by focusing on sectors and stocks where catalysts could kick in. And he can increase his potential for making money and reduce risk through selected shorting. Last, and perhaps most important of all, he can sleep well at night. Many of his peers must be wondering whether their holdings will be up or down 10 per cent when they wake up. The value investor who has chosen a position for its Margin of Safety may not have the same excitement but, equally, will never be a prisoner of the wall of worry. And, if Cooperman can sleep well, so can Cobalt's shareholders.

4

Katherine Garrett–Cox

Management matters most

Top peer group fund over five- and one-year period, outperforming the Micropal Index by 40 percentage points

Rated best out of 40 rivals by Combined Actuarial Performance
Services for 1999

Created one of the largest London-based managers of US equities,
growing from $800 million in 1993 to nearly $6 billion by 2000

Hailed by *The Wall Street Journal* for beating Wall Street and
confounding Bank Street

Named to the Ultimate Investment Club 2000 by *Money Magazine*
alongside Abby Cohen and Peter Lynch

Cynics may say it takes a woman to elevate the soft side of investing and place qualitative insights on a par with quantitative analysis. They have, perhaps, a quarter of a point, but are missing the big picture. A company can only perform to its potential in the hands of good management. The accounts can never tell more than some of the story. The numbers are a function of the business and the people who run it and their ability to create value. So all elements have to be in place to achieve longer-term market outperformance.

Any cynic should take a look at Garrett-Cox's numbers, after which they will have to reconsider the relative importance of making judgements about people. Both traditional investment tools and personal insights are part of her stock in trade but, because so few investors seem able to assess management effectively, it is more interesting to emphasize that aspect of her decision process.

Garrett-Cox is based in London, but her career has been dedicated to US equities. Why, you might wonder, are we devoting precious space to a UK professional covering an area where there is no shortage of home-grown talent? Two reasons: first, Garrett-Cox comes at investing from a perspective, as indicated already, which has all but disappeared within the US itself. Second, and naturally of greater importance, her record proves she can beat the Americans at their own game.

London, one of the world's leading investment centres, made a big mistake in the 1990s: nearly every major firm went underweight the US and badly underestimated both the strength of the economy and the importance of new technology. Garrett-Cox had an advantage over other managers in that she has built her reputation as a US equities expert, so arguably there is an element of self-justification in what she has to say on the subject. But, for investors outside the US in particular, her view deserves due consideration.

'The average UK investor has huge prejudice against the US as a market and it gets harder as the market keeps going up. People hate to admit that the Americans are good at anything but, ultimately, I do believe that what happens in America very much dictates what happens in the rest of the world. In global asset management, you need to be aware of what is going on there. America leads the world in so many different industries.'

This belief is reflected in the composition of a recently launched fund that Garrett-Cox and her team run. Aberdeen Global Champions is a global thematic fund but, at least initially, will be about 70 per cent invested in the US because so many themes emanate from the US. Globalization, innovation and communications are the three pillars, all of which have strong American overtones.

'For generations the United States has been a land where the opportunity to create personal wealth is unsurpassed.'

Garrett-Cox intends to make sure her shareholders continue to participate properly in that opportunity, as they have been doing now for more than a decade.

No single style is sufficient

In a world that likes labels, Garrett-Cox defies a catchy description.

'I'm naturally cautious of being boxed. Houses love to box you into small cap growth or mid cap value with an index tilt, and this sort of stuff. I have run both small and large cap money. I am generally a growth investor, but realize that cycles change and one has to be adaptable.'

Her approach to investing is multifaceted. There is no one right way, no single magic formula, no black box that tells you what to do. Yes, she has a checklist, but the hallmark of her style is flexibility rather than rigidity. In examining each security, she considers multiple factors. In part, this stems from her first days in the industry at Fidelity.

'I had one mentor who was extremely fundamental and focused on bottom-up stock picking. That was his great skill. My second mentor was a remarkable technician. He taught me the value of charts, and that has stayed with me and I think is one of my strengths: a meshing together of the fundamental and the technical.'

An open-minded attitude is almost certainly one key to her success. The investment environment is constantly changing, life moves on, and Garrett-Cox repositions her portfolio. When she talks about investment style, there is a certain softness to the delineation. Garrett-Cox does not care whether she falls into one camp or another. What matters is delivering the best possible performance to shareholders. And, if that means modifying her preferred stance from time to time and bending with market forces, so be it.

'I would describe my style as being one with a growth bias, although I'm not wedded to growth. That has historically been the style that has made me the most money. Ultimately, I would describe myself as a "relatively traditional growth at a reasonable price" investor. But, over the last few years, the way we've morphed that a little is to say that it's effectively a blend style. I know that sounds vague, but it is actually what we do. When growth is working, we'll be growth, but when the markets tend to be more value, we'll be more value. That process just means that everything is much more flexible.'

Her flexibility is a virtue recognized by the industry. Only with a flexible strategy can a manager buy oil companies such as Exxon and Apache in response to rising oil prices and put them in a portfolio alongside Yahoo and AOL.

There are even moments when she is prepared to relegate fundamental analysis to second place behind market forces.

'At times, within the market you have to be more of a momentum investor.'

Flexibility also shows in her preference to come to a conclusion and move on.

'I'm much more inclined to make a decision with, say, 75, 80 per cent of the facts rather than waiting for that additional percentage, whatever it may be, because I am decisive, and will decide fairly quickly if this is something that I want or not in the portfolio, both on the buy and on the sell side. I tend not to dither, because dithering loses you money over time.'

She has a point. To hold or not to hold is hardly the way to run a successful investment fund, nor, indeed, is it the right way for individual investors to manage their own money.

'If you make a decision, for instance, that you're going to cut your tech weighting, make it and do it today.'

By all means do whatever analysis is necessary to arrive at a decision but, once made, do not sit on the decision. Investors who fall into that trap are indulging in that most dangerous activity – market timing.

'Market timing is one of the hardest things to get right. I wouldn't claim to be an expert, but I think you become better at it if you're decisive.'

That this multifaceted approach works is confirmed when you put her numbers up against her US peer group. The Hill Samuel fund Garrett-Cox ran from 1994 to 2000 came top of its class over that period. How does Garrett-Cox keep ahead?

'The American market is the best researched and most efficient in the world, so you have to differentiate yourself from the pack.'

She has spotted a weakness about the way many of her American rivals operate. New York managers, in particular, are often insular, cocooned in their offices and lapping up the same research. By contrast, Garrett-Cox likes nothing better than getting out to see the people behind the numbers, and visiting companies to find out for herself what is going on.

Know your companies

It may sound trite, but knowing the companies in which you invest is vital, because extra information is one of the only ways for investors to gain an edge. Useful analysis, let alone accurate diagnosis, requires detailed knowledge of the company concerned. The importance of fundamental research was brought home to Garrett-Cox in her early days at Fidelity by Alan Thomas, who said:

'"Remember that the knowledge base you have on companies is the most important thing you can ever get. That is your franchise. No-one can take that away from you." He was saying to me, "You've got to know your companies inside out and develop a knowledge of as many as you possibly can".'

Garrett-Cox took his advice to heart. Knowing her companies has been key to her investment process from the first day she began to run a portfolio.

Know your management

Everyone pays lip service to this mantra, but rarely does anyone elevate scrutiny of management to such a pinnacle. For Garrett-Cox, getting to know the top echelon at a company is investing 101. And know them she does. Her team, when she was at Hill Samuel, met with over 700 companies a year. Garrett-Cox herself expects to see some 350–400 face to face.

> If we don't like the people, we don't buy the company.

'The great advantage of company meetings is that, in a relatively short space of time, you can look managers in the eye and decide whether you believe what they are saying and whether they really know what they are talking about.'

She always meets key management in person before investing, having concluded, from prior experience, that analysis is incomplete without the personal touch.

'Management is at least half of the decision-making process and would probably be *the* most important. If we don't like the people, we don't buy the company.'

And where an investment is made, she expects a minimum of one follow-up meeting a year. Talking to management, visiting the companies, consistent and frequent follow-up to establish patterns – these are all core to her decision to invest and have a strong influence on whether she adds, holds or sells a position.

'I spend an awful lot of time with management, and can't over-emphasize that enough.'

This emphasis is what gives Garrett-Cox her edge. She identifies a number of characteristics that give her a warm and fuzzy feeling about the quality of management.

1. Enthusiasm and self belief

Take Reuben Mark, Chairman and Chief Executive of Colgate:

'He's very dynamic. He's got boundless energy, talks 19 to the dozen and, most important of all, he's enthusiastic about his business. He believes that Colgate is going to be, and is, one of the best companies to work for and to own.'

Contrast that with many other management teams:

'I can't tell you the amount of companies that you meet and you think, "What a complete snore". They don't believe it themselves.'

2. Vision and ambition

Managers who achieve results usually combine a clear business focus and desire to make something happen with the ability to implement. These paragons are few and far between. Garrett-Cox cites Jack Welch at GE and Sandy Weill at Citibank as two chief executives who have a complete skill set, and whose companies are stronger down the line because of their leadership. Bill Gates at Microsoft, in the early days, was a textbook example. It is not just about being a one-man band:

'If you have these attributes you are much more likely to attract top calibre people into the business. Bright, talented individuals can be self-sustaining and ensure you have good people everywhere in the organization.'

Which feeds through to her third point.

3. Strong corporate culture

Culture has to come from within. Garrett-Cox, however, looks for out-ward signs of a common commitment, including a belief in shareholder value. She found what she was looking for at Enron.

'Go to any of their offices. They have a board at the front desk with the share price. Ninety-nine per cent of employees own stock. Almost all individuals at Enron have a vested interested in making it work.'

Naturally there is more to it than that. Garrett-Cox believes a strong corporate culture extracts extra mileage out of employees. Culture can only take hold by filtering below top management to permeate other levels. A demonstration of strength is when that culture has taken root throughout the workforce.

'I recently spoke with people who work for Enron in London. It was comforting to find that they have the same hopes and ambitions for the group as top management in Houston. I was struck by the fact that UK-based employees hold the CEO, Ken Lay, in such high regard. This unity of purpose is very important for a company to be successful.'

4. Accessibility

Here Mr Mark scores high again.

'Reuben Mark takes the time to come here at least every year and usually one of us will see him in New York at a six-month interval. He will give us his time. Even though we are, on the face of it, a lowly, UK-based investor, he will never overlook the fact that we have been long-term holders.'

Equally, Garrett-Cox has identified, over the years, several attributes or characteristics which she feels are absolute no-nos. Her danger signs tend to be outward manifestations of managers who may lack the superior ability she seeks, or who suffer from vanity or some other character flaw that could reduce personal effectiveness as an executive. Do not invest in companies where top management have:

- Beards: 'I've had really bad experiences with beards. If I invest in a company and the guy's got a beard, I almost always lose money.'
- Bad toupees: 'Americans love them. Every time I've invested in a company run by someone who has a toupee, I've lost money. I won't be doing that again.'

    For some reason, certain clusters of companies seem to attract the toupee brigade.

    'Traditionally toupees are worn by gentlemen from the funeral home business.'
- Hats: oddly enough, the same sector – funeral homes, which sounds the knell of toupees – provides examples of the kiss of death for extravagant headgear.

    'Funeral home directors are larger-than-life characters. Some wear Stetsons when they come to visit, which is rather off-putting, so you actually can't tell if they have a wig on or not.'

Sounds kooky, but nearly every company in this industry that at one stage seemed almost a copper-bottomed certainty to print money went belly up.

● Excessive jewellery: another turn-off is men who wear more jewellery than women; the more ornamentation, the less happy she is about the idea of investing. Garrett-Cox describes one visit that took place outside Los Angeles.

'The guy came towards me and he could barely lift up his hand, he was so loaded down with jewellery. It was a complete turn-off.'

Actually, the CEO of this company also failed on just about every other dimension.

'He was a wig merchant, as well.' And the surroundings reinforced her concern about the people. 'I went into the boardroom. There was a shiny glass table with really naff, but rather expensive looking pictures round it. Everything was electric and all supposedly very mod con-esque, and absolutely hideous.'

It took her all of two minutes to make up her mind. The conclusion, naturally, was 'no way.'

'I called my colleague as soon as I got out of the meeting and said, "Don't touch this with a 10-foot pole – I don't trust them".' Good call: 'It went toes up within six months.'

● Vanity symbols: none, on their own, are conclusive, but any one gives her cause to pause and too many sets off alarm bells.

'Big identity bracelets, shirts with initials embroidered on them and little pins with the company logo. All a bit strange.'

● Way-out wardrobe: casual is cool, but there comes a cut-off point at which you start to question a person's judgement. If the clothing is too inappropriate, what does that say about judgement in other areas?

'Not so long ago, the chairman of a company that subsequently did go public, came into our office. I walked into the meeting and thought, "It must be raining outside", because I could see stuff on his suit. Then I realized, to my horror, that his suit had gold thread. Both jacket and the trousers were pinstriped with gold running through. Apparently the investment banker completely freaked and said, "You can't possibly wear that". And he said, "I run this company. I'll wear what I like".

'It's first impressions. You don't turn up to London in a gold lamé suit. But apparently we got off lightly, because at one of the other meetings he wore bright red shoes.'

While this IPO was hot, hot, hot on its debut, and spiked on opening, the cold wind of reality soon set in. The price was last seen well below the peak.

Garrett-Cox also emphasizes the importance of visiting company premises. Seeing people on their own patch usually aids in understanding the culture and the character of management.

'Meeting in London, you get the corporate face. Kicking the tyres enables you to check things out. It sounds trite, but is the car park stuffed full of Ferraris, and is there fluffy, deep carpet everywhere, so you trip over it as you walk in, but the substance is relatively shallow? These sorts of things do give you a sense of where they're coming from because, ultimately, I'm trying to identify companies that are going to be successful now and in years to come. I'm not looking for flash-in-the pan sorts of things.'

In an interview with *The Daily Telegraph* in May 1999, Garrett-Cox listed six sell signals:

- so much gold jewellery, the chief executive can't lift his hands
- cowboy boots on the desk
- fifteen Mercedes in the parking lot
- shag-pile carpets in reception
- directors with beards and bow ties
- a po-faced receptionist who doesn't smile.

Any more than two strikes on this checklist and the company is out.

Of course there is more to understanding the company than assessing management, though Garrett-Cox's approach is sufficiently distinctive that this aspect deserves a disproportionate amount of space. There are other important elements and, as Garrett-Cox is at pains to point out, meetings can have value beyond sizing up the people and their immediate environment.

'One of the things we're always trying to do when we meet companies is to see what else we can find out. Not just about that company, but about their competitors, and about other parts of the industry. You usually get a fairly unbiased view as to what they think: people they respect, people that they don't think are doing a good job. Some won't say but, when they do, it's often very interesting.'

She illustrates this point with a situation that tipped the balance, for her, between two contending investments. Following a visit at the end of March 1998 to McKesson, a leading pharmaceuticals distributor, Garrett-Cox came away having decided to own more Cardinal Health, which was McKesson's key competitor in an industry where the top two were well ahead of the rest. It seemed clearer, after her conversion with senior executives at McKesson, that Cardinal was better placed, given the way the industry was unfolding. Adding to Cardinal was definitely the right decision at the time, since, in the subsequent two-and-a-half years, the price of McKesson fell by almost half, while Cardinal was up nearly 70 per cent.

Ignore qualitative insights at your peril, because they have a place in the process and rarely receive proper respect.

It is refreshing to find someone who not only recognizes the importance of impressions, but is able to articulate them in a semi-systematic manner. Too many investors feel foolish about taking decisions on anything other than a strictly logical basis – but ignore qualitative insights at your peril, because they have a place in the process and rarely receive proper respect.

'I think maybe a lot of people don't like talking about it because they don't believe it's really important and want to stun people with, "We roll out the balance sheet and forecast earnings for the next ten years". I could do that, but so could anybody. I think the ability I've developed – hopefully to sniff out a lying toad – is important because, ultimately, you have to believe in people, and I would never invest in a company where I didn't trust the management.'

It all adds up to a different approach. Garrett-Cox does not do everything strictly by the numbers. A vital part is elevating the interaction with management to an art form and putting the personal meeting on a par with the review of financial results. But it's not just touchy feely.

There is another absolute no-no for Garrett-Cox. If ever the numbers are called into question, she is out the door and does not look back. Once again, funeral homes rear their ugly heads with this deficiency – the final nail in the coffin, as far as she is concerned.

'We made money very briefly in Service Corp, going back about five years ago. The reason that we've steered well clear of the group of late is that it became beleaguered by various accounting issues. That is a big red flag from my perspective. Once that goes up, forget it. I don't care about the fundamentals – I'm gone. I'm a big believer in where there's smoke there's fire, eventually.'

Other examples, interestingly enough, emerge in industries that are just a touch distasteful.

'The waste management industry is another classic case in point, where there have often been rumblings of accounting irregularities. These things can go on for years and years.'

And since they cloud the stock, these companies are best avoided.

Know your corporate vision

Garrett-Cox is also looking for a business that knows where it is going. Her reasoning is straightforward.

'If you have a company trading, say, at a 20 per cent premium to the market, but you think they've got no vision and you just can't see where future growth is going to come from, that multiple is going to contract.'

However good the environment, if management is unable to explain its strategy clearly and demonstrate how all the pieces come together, then they probably won't. Which is one lesson Garrett-Cox learnt the hard way.

'We bought Petsmart in March of 1997 at about $19. Dogs and cats and pets. People have them. Petsmart was going to expand the store base. I felt this was an interesting retail concept.

'Then we met management. They could not articulate their strategy. I was asking about projections and couldn't make their numbers stack up. They were saying, "We think we'll hit earnings for the quarter", but everyone looked around with nervous glances. Then they started talking about the flea and tick season. Because there hadn't been a problem, important products hadn't been selling. It seemed to me that sales were going to fall short of estimates.

'I thought, "This doesn't look very good", and sold at about $10. Which was a fantastic decision, because now it's $3.'

Another company that came up short was Rite-Aid, a drug retailer.

'It had done quite well, but one of the question marks was over management, because people believed, quite rightly, that Walgreen and CVS are the quality operators. Was there really space for a third? I became increasingly uncomfortable that their strategy wasn't going to pan out.'

Which leads into a related point. In most sectors, the market leader is the company with the best management. This can change, of course, but on the whole an investor is more likely to be rewarded by sticking with quality.

'I've found that if you go for the number-two player, it never does as well as the number one, because, ultimately, people want the quality company. I can sleep better at night if I've got the quality names in the industries I follow, as long as they are not too stretched on a valuation basis and there's upside for outperformance. Generally, going down the quality scale has been one of my Achilles' heels.'

If you have confidence that the company has a clear vision, that allows you to hold winning positions a little longer than investors who lack the same understanding.

'One of the reasons that we did relatively well over the past few years is that we were happy to run some of the larger cap stocks, even though, on the face of it, they appeared to be trading at multiples that were at significant premiums to the market. Historically, that would have meant that one shouldn't own them, but we are not frightened of paying up if the growth is there. We did so much work on the companies in terms of trying to understand their corporate vision, their culture, and where they were taking these businesses, that we actually ran those companies, as far as I can tell, for far longer than a lot of our competitors in London and in the States, for that matter. Detailed knowledge allows you to be a little flexible.'

Know your markets

Here we mean financial markets. That involves charts, trading volume and all the other stuff that most managers look at, but few are prepared to admit can make or break decisions. Garrett-Cox is not so reticent.

'One of the key factors that distinguishes me from my peers is that I employ both fundamental and technical analysis. I rarely buy a stock if the technical picture does not confirm the fundamentals. It's better where the two mesh.'

Again, you can argue this is the softer side of investing, as we are dealing with sentiment. Sadly, sentiment can often overwhelm fundamentals. Which is one reason the perfect market remains a myth. Shrewd investors look for what charts can tell them about market perception of a security, as well as what analysis reveals about the financial performance, and try to reconcile the two or exploit a mismatch.

> ## A chart will tell you something is going wrong very often before the fundamentals really deteriorate.

'Charts confirm, one hopes, what you believe will happen and I think, from a timing perspective both on the way in and on the way out, can be remarkably helpful. A chart will tell you something is going wrong very often before the fundamentals really deteriorate.'

Garrett-Cox recalls a situation that illustrates her basic premise, prompting both her entry and her exit.

'One of my early successes was Micron Technology. They make memory chips. I went to visit them in Boise, Idaho. The industry appeared to be turning, but sentiment on the group, at the time, was very, very down. The numbers stacked up. I looked at the charts. Everything felt right. I bought Micron at about $20.

'This stock more than doubled on me big time. It got to $90. At that point it was one of those charts that was clear that this wasn't going to continue for ever. On the basis of the chart and a chat with management, I felt it was time to take my profits and leave. Very shortly after that, the air got completely pulled out of the semiconductor cycle and it collapsed back down to $20 again.'

Micron illustrates both the attractions and perils of cyclical investing. Clearly there have been opportunities both to make big profits and to lose all that and then some. So how did Garrett-Cox decide to call time out?

'I'm looking for relative strength more than anything else. On a technical basis I'm looking for relative strength against the index. It's all very well having an absolute chart but, unless it's compared against an index, it tells you nothing.'

Relative strength is a relatively easy concept to grasp. Most charting software now comes with graphics that allow individuals and professionals alike to call up comparative history with a single keystroke.

There are two other technicals she watches closely:

1. Moving averages

The assistance they provide is worth more elaboration. One signal in particular causes Garrett-Cox concern.

'We are looking at 50- and 200-day moving averages. On the downside, if the stock crosses below its 50-day, nine times out of ten it's likely to head back down to its 200-day, so that's usually quite a good sell signal.

'We owned Motorola all through 1999 as the price ran up from $16 to over $50. Then, in March 2000, the price had been hovering around the 50-day moving average. When the stock crossed back through, we sold. Shortly thereafter, the company was hurt by adjusted earnings expectations and questions over the quality of earnings.'

As Fig. 4.1 shows her timing was excellent. While not capturing the high, she nailed down a gain of over 150 per cent. Had she held on, ignoring the signal, almost all of that would have evaporated, with the stock now back below $20 again. Nor is she in a hurry to buy back without chart confirmation.

'Effectively we are looking for inflection points, although, having said that, the way I describe it is that if a stock was on a sharp, downward path and then it bounces – because of a change in strategy, a positive earning surprise, a change in management, whatever it is – I would much rather wait for the stock to bounce 5 per cent off the bottom than try and buy on the downward trajectory.'

2. Money flow

Garrett-Cox wants to compare buy and sell orders to get a sense of which way the market is leaning.

'One of the interesting charts you can get on Bloomberg is money flows plotted against price. Very often a jaws pattern opens up. Money flow has been steadily going into the stock, but the stock has been trending down. Nine times out of ten, the price will snap back, because it's still got institutional support.'

Equally there is one signal that usually calls her to pick up the phone and sell.

'The thing to avoid would be where you've got the price rising at an exponential rate with money flows falling off the cliff. That is a big, big no-no for me.'

The best use of charts is not, however, to rely on any single signal alone. If only life were that simple. A combination of indicators either confirming or questioning price direction is usually what works best.

Chart inconsistencies enabled Garrett-Cox to stay out of Coca-Cola in 1998 when the stock was being tipped as overdue for recovery.

'People were trying to talk the fundamentals up, saying trends are going to be good; the rest of the world is going to be strong. A number of people were buying and money flows were starting to pick up. There was upward improvement in money flow, but the relative strength was not confirming it. And you have to have all the boxes ticked. The chart told me that this was a head fake. Very shortly after that here was an announcement. They changed the chap at the top because the strategies he had been trying to implement hadn't worked. The stock has relatively underperformed big time since.'

An additional point that acts as a sanity check on price action is not to hold losers.

'If the stock disappoints once, sell. It's going to take more than a quarter to fix any problem. You're far better off leaving, than waiting for management to sort out the mess.'

Figure 4.1 Motorola share price and moving averages, 1996–2000 *Source:* Bridge

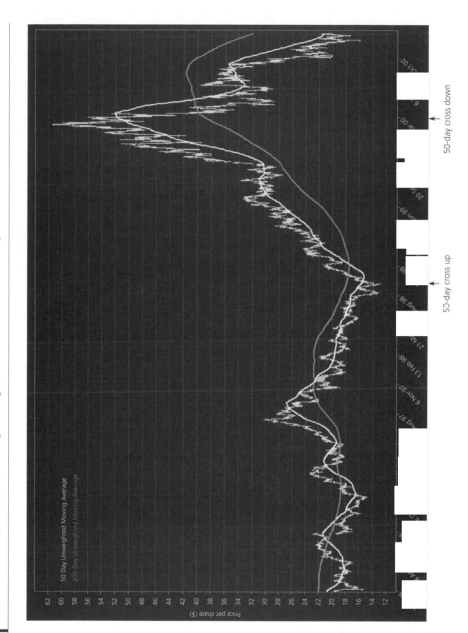

Know your brokers

Garrett-Cox believes that an ability to get the best out of brokers has been one of the cornerstones of her success. The broking community has come in for a lot of stick of late, and online trading enables investors to bypass brokers, but for individuals and professionals alike, the right relationship can be a valuable asset. A good broker should increase a portfolio's return.

'Brokers – love 'em or hate 'em – are helpful if one can use them right. The way I saw it was that I was trying to establish relationships for the long term, not for a quick turn on a couple of IPOs. I wanted to identify people that had an investment philosophy akin to my own.'

This was a matter of necessity when Garrett-Cox took on her first solo responsibility in charge of a small US portfolio for UNI Storebrand, the Norwegian insurer, since she did not have resources in-house to do her job effectively. She had no choice but to look outside. It was a struggle to get attention when funds under management were modest.

'I needed to draw on other people to get ideas and see companies. At that point, a lot of people thought, "UNI Storebrand. We don't need to talk to them." I was never able to get one-on-one meetings, but I was able to identify people at some of the bigger houses that I wanted to talk to, some of whom I still talk to now and, as I rose through the ranks, they equally have been elevated to where they're running teams at broking houses.'

She has no problem talking to whoever she chooses these days. More to the point, Garrett-Cox, through a degree of trial and error, has organized the interchange so as to extract the best of what brokerage houses have to offer in an efficient manner.

'I take most ideas to brokers, because we see so many companies. I'll say, "I was talking to Boeing the other day and met the new CFO – this is what she said. Can you check it out with your analysts? Because I'm not sure the numbers stack up, or that she had the credibility needed, or whatever."

'I was able to cross-reference the numbers she gave me with Wall Street sources, but still did not end up having confidence from those conversations, so avoided the stock. Boeing underperformed the market for well over a year following that exchange, though it did rally in late 2000, along with the defence sector.'

It is not just an efficient interaction that is called for. Time management requires focus in Garrett-Cox's relationships, just as she focuses her portfolio.

'When I moved to Hill Samuel, we spoke to over 60 brokers, which is crazy. One of the first things I did was to cut down dramatically the number from 60 to about 20, of which eight were mainstream houses that I felt we should talk to on a day-to-day basis, with the balance being specialist or regional houses, because there is a need for both. One does need to talk to Goldman Sachs, Morgan Stanley and Merrill Lynch but, equally, you need to have people on the ground in places like Chicago, Nashville, the Carolinas. They are often the people that find ideas and bring them to you early.'

This approach works well for her – and she believes investors could benefit by spending more time on maintaining a constructive dialogue and less on carping about the shortcomings of brokers.

'I'm horrified, to be honest, by the extent to which a lot of my peers in London look down their noses at the broking community.'

She has her own stars and is not reticent about praising two individuals in particular who she sees as the cream of the crop: Adam Glinsman at Lehman Brothers and Vicki Aston Duff at Bear Stearns. But it's not all sweetness and light. Garrett-Cox has a very defined view about why many brokers are not helpful.

'Over the years I've tended to shy away from people that all they're interested in doing is stuffing the next idea down my throat. I instinctively recoil. It doesn't work if they call up and say, "Well, the idea of the week is – whatever it is – Safeway. So I'm going to give you five minutes' pitch and then I expect you to buy half a million shares".'

Garrett-Cox has been more than usually systematic in how she decides who to deal with.

'Twice a year, all our brokers get rated on a number of different things. The first is the broker, him or herself – to what extent do they understand what we're trying to do, and to what extent do they add value to our process? Second, we rate them on research. Obviously, that is very dependent upon the house they're at. The third element is trading. It's all very well to have a fantastic idea, but I cannot afford anything on the trading side to impact negatively on an investment decision.'

She has nothing but scorn for the back-scratching syndrome.

'We're hard to entertain. There are people I know that operate on the basis of "We want a box at Covent Garden for the opening night of *The Magic Flute*". I am very much the other way. What I want is partnership. I expect to be the first call on breaking news. I expect one-on-one meetings with companies or analysts when they come through.'

Developing productive relationships can be extremely helpful, though obviously it is more difficult for individual investors, especially with the virtual demise of the private client broker. Garrett-Cox describes how she was able to leverage her involvement with Glinsman to improve the performance of her portfolio.

'At CJ Lawrence, their strategy product was very good. They also had well-known economists, Ed Hyman and Nancy Lazar. One of the things Hyman brought to my early learning experiences was a good understanding of the macro picture. It's all very well finding great stocks, but if they don't fit into the sorts of things that people want to buy at that point, because of the economic cycle or whatever, they're not going to work. We did very well in basic material stocks and capital goods companies such as Eaton, a capital goods conglomerate, and Minerals Technologies, a chemicals company, which were in vogue at that time, and where CJ Lawrence had good analytical strength.'

> **There is a pay-off for both parties when brokers take time to understand their clients and build relationships.**

There is a pay-off for both parties when brokers take time to understand their clients and build relationships. Adam Glinsman has been a broker to Garrett-Cox almost since she started. They have been to the US to visit companies together, and he believes their partnership enables him to assist her more effectively, as he understands what she expects before introducing an idea. Glinsman's view mirrors that of Garrett-Cox.

'She treated me more like a team member trying to pick the best stocks for the portfolio rather than as an adversary from the other side. She is receptive to ideas, excellent at simplification and has a very good intuitive sense of a recommendation.'

Garrett-Cox has ended up doing well with several of Glinsman's suggestions. One that worked was Travellers, in part because it fitted with what he knew she liked to see in a stock.

'We were recommending it at Wertheim Schroder in the mid-1990s. She was one of the quickest to pick up and run with the idea. She identified the strong management, their vision for the company and clear-cut acquisition strategy, so saw this as a stock she could hold for a long time. She is good at holding her winners. Too many managers cut and run too quickly.'

So a fruitful two-way street and a model more professionals on both sides of the street might find instructive.

'I do regard the relationship that I have cultivated with brokers as very much one of a partnership. They know exactly where I'm coming from and, equally, I know exactly where they're coming from.'

This is an eminently pragmatic solution to a problem that Garrett-Cox has learnt to live with. You can never have enough resources. You have to pick your spots and also pick people elsewhere in the community whose coverage complements your own.

'If an analyst at Goldman Sachs is being paid $10 million to look at Microsoft's balance sheet, he is going to have a much better idea as to what's in there than I am, so why replicate something when we are talking to the best people in the industry?'

Sentimentality has no place in this system. When brokers muck her about, they are history. She recounts a warning war story.

'The day the merger was announced between CUC and HFS, which subsequently became Cendant, we had the chairman in our office. He pretty much had his feet up on the table telling me that this was the best deal since sliced bread. I was deeply sceptical. He couldn't articulate why they were getting together. If you merge two companies of that size it is usually problematic in one respect or another, whether it's culture or strategy. So we sold the stock. And – this is how crass the broking community in London can be – they would come on to me and say, "You know, you're the only person in London that doesn't hold this stock". And I would say, "Great! What a bunch of sheep out there!" But that was their top selling point, which I think is appalling, so some brokers got axed as well as the Cendant holding.'

Cendant subsequently came apart at the seams, losing the sheep a ton of money.

Another American decade ahead

Up until 2000 Garrett-Cox concentrated exclusively on the US, but, as an outsider looking across the Atlantic, she has a slightly different perspective. So what does an Englishwoman, whose numbers are better than most US managers, see as investing hot spots for the future? Technology is inevitably first up.

'Like it or love it, it is 30 per cent of the index now.' And there is a second reason that relates back to her search for sustainable earnings growth. 'Technology multinationals have pricing power.'

Garrett-Cox feels investors ought to concentrate on identifying companies that should continue to have pricing power in what is essentially a cost-driven world. Partly because there will be so few, their value should be that much greater. Some brands may still command respect, such as Colgate. Selected product categories where cost is low on the list of consumer priorities, can also flourish.

'Estée Lauder has pricing power. It is high-margin stuff. Men don't really understand how much money women spend on cosmetics, but I understand. This is a very, very profitable business. Tiffany, too, is an interesting name, and should do well, especially if Japan comes back.'

Garrett-Cox, unlike many others in her age bracket, is less wedded to the supremacy of technology as stock picks than to the importance of using technology as a tool: both at the corporate level and to support an investment thesis. Eaton illustrates how old-economy companies can contain operations that deserve new-economy multiples.

'Eaton has underperformed the market for the last four years. But, prior to that, I made a lot of money in it, riding the cycle because of its semi-equipment business. Now they're talking about unlocking value to shareholders by selling off 20–25 per cent of that. Obviously they're seeing what sort of multiple these stocks can trade at. So that's the sort of company I'm interested in buying. It has a technology spin, but buried within a company that is predominantly perceived to be a sleepy old capital-goods company.'

Equally, old-economy companies can flourish and merit rising stock prices if they change their approach to business.

'Colgate is a good case in point. They were one of the first companies of that type to roll out SAP systems throughout their global universe and, as a result, are able to reduce their cost structure significantly.'

> **Investors need to think creatively about where to find value that can benefit from change yet to come.**

This approach is interesting, because even the best technology companies tend to overstretch in valuation terms. Investors need to think creatively, or maybe laterally, about where to find value that can benefit from change yet to come.

Garrett-Cox makes a fairly bleak assessment of what is happening, but can still find bright spots from the way certain companies have adapted technology to benefit their customers.

'Technology is all about making people's lives better and improving the speed with which we can do everything; but one of the unfortunate things is that it makes our lives much, much more competitive. There is free flow of information – everybody knows everything – so, in order to make a difference, your cost structure has to come down. Companies which saw that early on – Colgate, or GM or Ford re-engineering their manufacturing lines in order to pump cars out more quickly and far more cheaply – can be opportunities. You don't have to be invested in Yahoo in order to participate.

'Costco is one of the most impressive retail concepts and is very much on the forefront of using technology in a retail environment. They are able to reduce their cost structure significantly because everything has gone to just-in-time inventory. And, on their internet site, they are selling slightly different things from in the stores. One of the reasons the internet side is doing well is because it has things on there that people can't take home, like greenhouses, or pool tables.'

Management is alert to how technology can be harnessed both in terms of increasing sales and cutting costs. The insight for investors is not to buy technology blind, but to find companies that exploit technology to improve performance.

The other big theme for Garrett-Cox is healthcare, which was largely in the investment doghouse for most of Clinton's two terms as President. The political environment has been a problem for companies in almost every area of that industry.

'The spectre of government regulation sat on this group for a number of years to the extent that, having traditionally sold at multiples well in excess of the market, many of the big pharma names were trading at market multiples or lower. 'I saw huge value there, because a lot of these companies, like Bristol Myers, have product pipelines, and real growth. They also have, in many cases, other businesses. J&J is a drug company, but also has an enormous consumer products business. What we're trying to do is to identify areas and companies that can grow regardless of what happens on the legislative side.'

She remains somewhat sceptical over intentions of politicians towards pharmaceutical companies. Both parties claim they want to extend Medicare, which means pressure on drug prices is likely to continue. Nonetheless, revolutionary developments will continue to generate commercial success for particular players such as Pfizer.

'Healthcare is a good place to invest long term, but it is not enough any more just to be in the big pharma names.'

Healthcare is a huge portion of GDP and the demand for better healthcare unremitting, so investors may want to revisit the sector. An ageing population is also positive for the industry, but investors need to be selective. Garrett-Cox's approach here, as elsewhere, is very much bottoms up, considering each company on its own individual merits. One product category that has caught her attention is instrumentation.

'The whole area of medical devices is a story with legs. Leaders in the field represent potential investments that can be attractive for years. Medtronic is designing more and more implantable devices to help people live longer and enjoy more healthy lives. Their products will have increasing demand.'

Patient care, at the point of delivery, is also an area that may get respect once more.

'For the first time in a long time, HMOs are not beating up hospitals. There seems to be a recognition that they can live alongside each other. And the pricing environment is much better than it has been for a long time. Companies like HCA and United Healthcare should start to do better if this climate holds.'

And to end on one to avoid: anything to do with litigation, of which there is too much in the US. Tobacco is obviously out. She also steers clear of companies that run the risk of being contaminated or even destroyed by contingency lawyers. So selected utilities, companies with exposure to asbestosis claims and most waste-management companies are out of bounds, as far as Garrett-Cox is concerned.

Valuation has its day in the sun

All the emphasis on analysis and building relationships cannot bypass the valuation question. Garrett-Cox looks at several parameters, but one sways her much more than all the others.

'I understand that, in some industries, price to book is important, cash flow multiples and the rest of it; but, in terms of what is probably the single most important valuation measure, it's P/E to growth rate.'

This is no surprise, given her preference for growth, so what is more interesting is how she has operated in an environment where growth has been rather highly valued. Investors, especially in the last couple of years, have found that many growth companies are fully priced. Garrett-Cox has, as is natural for an investor who is able to turn change to her advantage, adapted to prevailing market conditions.

'We don't say, dogmatically, we can't hold stocks if they have a P/E to growth rate bigger than 1.3. Each company has to stand on its own merit. In certain industries you can justify holding companies at higher multiples. Technology is a classic case in point where, if there is a compelling secular growth case, you can pay more.'

Having understood the complexity and comprehensive research that characterizes her approach, it is a useful counterpoint to listen to her scepticism about the way investors tend to get carried away with fads or stretch to justify decisions by changing parameters.

'I think people have developed all these different methodologies because the one they were using first looked too high. EVA [Economic Value added Analysis] is a classic case in point. Everyone talked about EVA about two years ago. Do you hear anyone talking about it now?

No! It's died a complete death. And I think one of the reasons is because no-one can really understand what it is, and no-one can really measure it. So it's a fat lot of good to the average investor. Maybe I'm being too simplistic, but I do think there are many people in this industry that try and over-complicate our business.'

Hardboiled quant jocks glued to screens may be tempted to write off this critique, but they should think twice. Garrett-Cox makes a convincing case for the importance of the personal side of the investment calculus. There is no point crunching numbers if the company is fundamentally flawed or the management is unreliable. Her holistic approach has led her to side-step some real turkeys.

'It sounds silly, and it's touchy feely, but part of asset management *is* touchy feely, because you're never going to know 100 per cent of the facts when you make a decision.'

How true! Anyone still sceptical only has to look at her results. Since she has outperformed almost all her peers, many of whom have many years' more experience, maybe more investors should brush up on the touchy feely part of the process if they want to improve their results.

5

Roger Guy

Ten golden rules

Ranked top out of 1,500 UK unit trusts by Greig Middleton in 1999

In top quartile of European unit trusts each year since 1993

Investment Week Fund Manager of the Year for Europe in 1998 and 1999

Won Standard & Poors Micropal Award for Europe in 1998

Rated the Man for the New Millennium by a *Financial Mail* poll of advisers

Making money is a habit for Guy, who managed to make a nice profit on his first ever investment.

'When I was 14, my father got me to buy shares in Woolworth's with my savings and I made quite a lot of money. Throughout university, I used to apply for all the privatizations, and was one of the few students who made money. I put my grant into them. In those days, it was like a free cheque. And I used to open up building society accounts to try and make money.'

With that provenance, perhaps it should be no surprise that Guy's primary vehicle, Gartmore Select European Opportunities, has racked up a net gain of 475 per cent to December 2000. Since he took over in March 1993, that 22.4 per cent compound annual rate of return works out at over twice the growth in the FT-Europe ex UK Index over the same period. Why work if you can be one of Guy's shareholders?

A programme in European financial analysis at Newcastle University, which turned out to be more of an introduction to fund management, clinched his career choice and turned his attention to a region which, in 1989, lacked market cachet and, in his words, 'wasn't treated desperately seriously'. Which may have had something to do with why he ended up running a portfolio within two years of entering the investment profession. But, if luck played a part in providing an early breakthrough at Eagle Star, Guy moved swiftly to consolidate his promotion through performance.

'All the senior people either left or got fired in 1991. My boss said, "Take over for three months and then we'll get someone in". The fund started to do well, so he said, "We'll give you another three months". At the end of the first year, it was the number one unit trust in Europe.'

Guy has never looked back, neither has he faltered once in producing superior performance each year since his career got its kick-start ten years ago. One reason for this initial success was making sure the portfolio had an overweight allocation where the action was.

'When I first started in the early nineties, it was all about top down. You used to ask, "Do I want to overweight France or overweight The Netherlands and underweight Germany?" That was the important call. Probably 60–70 per cent was getting the country right. The icing on the cake came from picking the right stocks.'

Times have changed – in a big way.

'But European markets have evolved. Whilst they're still not completely efficient, they're more efficient. Markets have become differentiated much more by sectors and stocks. So, over time, I've evolved from looking top down to almost entirely bottom up. I guess

I've evolved with the market. I don't ignore countries, but they're secondary these days.'

Guy, too, has come a long way in a short time. At only 34, he runs several portfolios for Gartmore, including the flagship European Select Opportunities, and the Capella hedge fund. He still likes to focus on where the action is, but a guiding philosophy, an evolutionary development during a decade of outperformance, acts as an overlay and has been codified into his ten commandments of investing. They glory in the title of Gartmore's Golden Rules and contain a good deal of Guy's own influence:

1 Do not fall in love with companies: you buy the share price.
2 Keep an open mind: fight fund managers' prejudices.
3 The price paid for a stock is irrelevant: do not be afraid to close at a loss.
4 Be careful when bucking a trend.
5 Do not get into a position you cannot get out of.
6 If company earnings disappoint and stock does not go down: strong buy signal.
7 If company reports strong numbers and stock does not go up: strong sell signal.
8 Do not make a short-term idea into a long-term holding.
9 When IT/concept stocks go wrong, cut the position.
10 Never stop looking at the portfolio!

Any analysis of why Guy has been so successful needs to start with Golden Rule Number 1: 'Do not fall in love with companies', but one particularly strong stand recurs as an overriding imperative.

If you don't like something, sell

Most managers emphasize the investment decision. The Golden Rules emphasize selling. Golden Rule Number 9 is 'When IT/concepts stocks go wrong, cut the position'. Guy enforces the rule across the board. Referring to his early experiences, he made the point:

'My old boss said a very good thing to me, and I always say to anybody, "if you take over a portfolio and you're not comfortable with a position, get rid of it straight away".'

Golden Rule Number 8 is 'Do not make a short-term idea into a long-term holding', a variant on the same theme. Here, perhaps, is one – if not the major – point of difference between Guy and the way most investors operate, as he himself recognizes.

'So many people concentrate on the buy side. Obviously you've got to pick good stocks, but where I differentiate myself more is that we're aggressive in cutting things when they don't work.'

He refers to constant pruning as one of the keys to his success, an insight, interestingly, that was first pointed out to him by the financial community.

'Brokers say that I'm the best at selling shares, and not holding on to deadwood. I am, by far, the most aggressive when it comes to cutting positions.'

Of all observers, brokers should be in the best position to know, so this endorsement has a ring of truth. Selling is hard. Parting is such sweet sorrow. Cashing in winners is easier than weeding out losers; but it is the latter process that is more urgent and a trickier task. Taking a loss is an admission that the original decision was wrong. The temptation is to revisit the analysis, justify the purchase and hang on, or even average down – which can work, but Guy strongly espouses an opposite view.

'The market is normally right. If you sit there and say, "No, I'm right and it's going down," well, you're not right, because the market is telling you you're not.'

Disciplined selling is core to how Guy manages portfolios and juggles individual positions to maximize his returns.

'One of my biggest passions is not having dead wood. Why do you own something? A lot of managers buy and then forget about it. I'm always questioning "why is that stock in the fund?"'

Anything that disappoints is out the door. The 1999 Managers' Review of Gartmore European Investment Trust plc is typical: 'In contrast, Banco di Roma was sold following its decision not to merge with IMI-San Paolo, and Bayerishe Hypo Vereinsbank was sold after it made unexpected provisions against East German real estate exposure, which rendered it unlikely to achieve its targeted returns to shareholders'.

This commitment to selling reflects the composition of holdings and portfolio construction methodology employed by Guy.

'I've always managed funds 50 per cent, roughly, in longer-term positions, and 50 per cent in shorter-term positions. The longer-term positions are conviction holdings. If they start to go wrong, I typically do reduce, but don't get rid of them until I'm absolutely convinced that something's gone wrong.

'With short-term positions, I set a target. Typically I buy on about a three- to six-month time horizon and, if they haven't gone up, I get rid of them; and, if they start to go down before that, they're gone. I'm a big believer that if it doesn't work out, you get rid of it.'

Clinical, efficient and easy to execute. Naturally, there is more to it than that. The decision to sell usually ties back to the reason Guy purchased a position in the first place.

'Let's say I bought thinking there's going to be a management reshuffle and new strategy. Let's say they have the reshuffle and launch a new strategy. Two weeks later the stock hasn't gone up. Well, to me, that was the catalyst. It hasn't happened. Or it has happened, but the price hasn't moved, so you get rid of it. You don't wait around.'

Not merely efficient, then: relatively ruthless, too; but, and this is all that should matter to shareholders, also right.

Out it goes, even if at a loss: which is Golden Rule Number 3. Guy does not waste emotional energy fretting over his original decision. Failure to perform triggers a trade. Equally, it is important not to get sentimental over successes. Just as bad companies can be attractive if oversold, so the best business in the world should be sold when overbought. Guy has no patience with investors who forget the goal of investing. Professionals, in particular, have no excuse for failing constantly to assess and reassess their holdings.

'A lot of fund managers fall in love with companies. They've done well over the years, and think management's fantastic, but, at some point, it's expensive and you've got to get out.

> ## You're not buying the company, you're buying the share price.

I'd like to think I'm a bit of a butcher. I'll sell anything, however well it's done for me in the past, however good a company it is, because you're not buying the company, you're buying the share price. And that's very, very important to remember.'

There is a touch of the trader about his style, but who would want to argue with the results?

'So many managers end up with stocks that are dead. To me, you should know why you own every stock in the fund. All the time.'

When I wrote *Investing with the Grand Masters*, highlighting the most successful UK fund managers of the 1980s and early 1990s, one key insight to emerge was that there is no room for romance in the market. This philosophy proved its worth at the AlphaGen Capella hedge fund in mid-2000. When Philips and ST Micro kicked off the tech reporting season and their prices did not go up on good numbers and upgrades, Guy cut all long exposure to semiconductors and telecom-equipment stocks. This meant that, although he had faith in the long-term prospects of favourites such as Ericsson and Nokia, he went through the period of the release of their figures with no net exposure, as he felt the short-term risk/reward profile was unfavourable. An inspired move, as Nokia's price slumped nearly 35 per cent in under a month on apparent moderation of its near-term growth prospects.

If you agree that constant pruning is essential for consistent performance, the next step is to ensure sales happen when they should. Without discipline the portfolio drifts and deadwood pollutes. For Guy, the discipline is derived in part from value shifts and in part from price movements. One useful signal can be what happens when a company releases results.

'If a company has very good numbers and the price doesn't go up, that might mean that all the good news is in the price. So that's when I'll start to trim.'

The converse can also be a good guide.

'If a company has poor numbers but the price doesn't go down, that's interesting. LVMH, when the Asian crisis hit, had awful numbers. The stock had been a terrible performer. And the price didn't go down. I thought, "Maybe all bad news is priced in". We bought. LVMH tripled in the following seven months.'

As important as knowing when to sell – and actually selling – is knowing when not to sell. Price targets are soft rather than absolute.

'I have a mental target, but don't always stick to it, if a stock does well relatively. Let's say the market has gone down 10 per cent and this stock has gone up 5 per cent. It might not have gone to the price, but it's outperformed by 15 per cent. I might think, "Well, that's OK". So a combination of relative and absolute.'

Guy is prepared to hang on when the message from the market is that there is more upward movement to come, and will bend with the market when the trend is his friend.

'So many shares go beyond fair value that, if you immediately cut at a rigid price target, you can miss out on an awful lot. I might set myself a price. But when momentum gets with a stock, then part of the art is to say, "It's reached my target, but there's so much good news, strong momentum, people upgrading", you have to hold beyond where you thought you were going to sell.'

It is worth remarking on the use of the word 'art' in this context. Guy talks about the 'art' of selling several times. When he discusses his decision to buy, the tone is different. In judging when to trigger a sale, he seeks input avidly from the market. Unfortunately, few individual investors will be able to replicate his methodology.

'I talk to brokers all the time to find out: is it in the price, what have other people done? Is everybody underweight or overweight? If everybody's been buying for the last six months, you're probably right to be selling, because the stock's unlikely to keep on going up. Whereas, if brokers are saying, "We've had a lot of phone calls about that stock. A lot of people are asking about it", you think, "There's probably more to go for".'

Many people set a target price. Guy also sets a time target. A stock should do what it is supposed to do *and* when it is supposed to. Failure on either count is reason enough to part company.

'If, in my time horizon, the stock hasn't moved, it goes; or if the good news has come out, but the stock hasn't gone up or even has gone down, then I'll get rid of it straightaway.'

Given this mentality, you would expect Guy to pay a great deal of attention to a stock's liquidity. And you would be right. Golden Rule Number 5 says 'Do not get into a position you cannot get out of'. This is sage advice if you plan to trade, but is also relevant if you believe, as Guy clearly does, that you need to cull losers fast.

'Look back to the market fall in March 2000 when tech stocks blew up. Large stocks you could still get out of. Small stocks you couldn't sell, even if you wanted to.'

For this reason, you will not find other than the odd small cap anywhere near his portfolio. The top names in Select European, as of 31 December 2000, in descending order of significance, were:

> Total Fina
> Nokia
> Royal Dutch
> Vivendi Universal
> Roche
> Zurich Financial
> Aventis
> Astrazeneca
> Fortis
> Christian Dior.

What they have in common is that all are large companies with big market caps and sufficient trading volume to enter and exit with ease. This emphasis effectively drives a cut-off point in size below which Guy does not bother. He trawls the top tier.

Golden Rule Number 8 at Gartmore is so embedded in the culture that it is appropriate to repeat it again; and Guy does, frequently. 'Do not make a short-term idea into a long-term holding.' One of the classic traps into which many investors fall is to allow the price at which they bought to influence their thinking. Guy concentrates solely on the question, 'Should I own this share at this price today?' and, in doing so, breaks with common practice in a way that has helped his performance.

'The price you pay is irrelevant. I've always been really rigid on that. It's the price today that matters. Would you still buy, or would you sell? A lot of managers buy a stock, lose money, and say, "I can't sell, because I've lost money. I'll wait for it to get back to the price that I paid". As soon as you start doing that you end up holding on to dogs. The price you pay is irrelevant. The price today is what matters. And that stops you selling things too quickly, too. Would you still buy the stock at this price? Forget the fact that you've doubled your money in it.'

> # The price you pay is irrelevant. The price today is what matters.

Fine-tuning a fund

Given all that has gone before, it is inevitable that turnover is well above average, with a holding period under four months, which is on the short end of the spectrum. Tracking back to the way Guy groups stocks into two camps – core positions and what are essentially opportunistic trades – turnover is not only healthy but also necessary.

'There's two ways turnover comes. On the short-term holdings, the time horizon is three to six months so, obviously, that part of the portfolio should get turned over quite a lot. With long-term holdings, there is a very thorough process that helps choose them but, if you just buy and hold, you miss out on so much. What I try to do is fine tune positions.'

Active management means a somewhat different approach than day-to-day monitoring. A daily diet of challenging yesterday's decisions, whenever fresh information breaks, dovetails with Guy's desire to reassess constantly every stock he owns.

'I'd like to think I'm very market aware; very on top of what's going on – what news is coming out. I'm passionate about being at my desk all day. I hate being at meetings until at least 4 o'clock. A lot of fund managers spend a lot of time in meetings and probably are not quite as on the ball. A bit of news comes out and you're there, able to react very quickly. If you can react quickly to news, often that gives you a real advantage.'

This level of hands-on management reinforces the requirement for stocks with liquidity where money can be switched in and out relatively rapidly. Individuals have many more options if they want to initiate such a strategy since the sums involved will be smaller. Guy has far fewer, but one stock that illustrates perfectly what he is on about is Nokia, the Finnish cellular phone company.

'We've owned Nokia for seven years. That's probably one reason why the fund has done well, but we haven't just bought and held. There's been times when I think the stock's really going to do well when we're aggressively overweight. Then I might say, "The stock's had a great run; let's take a third of the position out". Then we'll buy it back three months later. We're very active within the core holdings. That can add a lot of value.

'There's no stamp duty in Europe, so a round trip is about half a per cent. If you're switching into something that's going to do better, you've only got to make half a per cent to make it worthwhile. Anybody who says that turnover's bad is crazy.'

He has a point. Of course you need to get this right. Guy does more often than not, so is able to outperform managers who simply sit tight. Even if a long-term trend is up, the trajectory is normally punctuated with pull-backs. By adding or subtracting, Guy can mitigate down phases and exaggerate the impact when the price goes up. Many commentators pooh-pooh trading or find the subject distasteful in some way but, while it is hard to time markets, timing a specific stock is a different proposition.

'Turnover is only bad if you're bad at your job, and if you're not good at short-term timing, which some people aren't. I think turnover is a real positive. That's probably one of the key areas where we add value.'

If you can plug yourself into 'the market' for a particular stock with an internet chat forum, perhaps, as a potential substitute for broker nods and winks, then it may be possible to enhance total return through turnover. Guy has.

There is no better way of getting to grips with what is going through his mind as he fine-tunes core holdings than by repeating verbatim his history with Nokia, a long-time favourite.

'Nokia had been a glamour stock and then had a profit warning in 1996. They had growing pains but, at the time, everybody thought it was pretty much the end of the world.

'If you get a bit of bad news, you get out quickly, because you know that, particularly with a stock like that, you have committees that take a couple of days to meet and get the analysts in, and then make decisions. Whereas if you can get out, normally you do. We reduced the position very substantially. We took a bit of a hit, but the stock halved fairly soon after.

'Then Nokia started to perform a little better, but I couldn't see any reason why. I met a couple of analysts who said they'd been to see them and the company was saying a lot of the problems were from growing too quickly. They hadn't been able to ramp-up production, and were overpaying for components. They had started to sort that out.

'Consensus was still that it was an awful company. So we went aggressively overweight.'

The stock has risen roughly eight times since Guy made Nokia one of his top five holdings; but, at its nadir, Select European Opportunities was never completely out and, even on its best day, he is always prepared to top-slice, if news flow suggests a haircut, and especially if charts indicate a turn.

'I look at relative performance statistics. If Nokia has done way better than Alcatel and Ericsson over a one- or three-month period, I might think, "Let's take a bit of the money out of Nokia and put it into Ericsson". Maybe all the good news is in the Nokia price. It's had lots of upgrades. Maybe Ericsson is due a bit of catch up.

'Or you might think that the sector as a whole has had such a strong run. Maybe they've all done well compared to the market. And you think, "That's probably all they're going to do for the short term, so let's take the weighting down". And put it back up when you think there's going to be more good news.

'It gets to a point on the chart where you might get to real resistance and I might think, "We'll take it down a little bit". And then, if it breaks through, you think, "OK, I'll buy it back again".

'One of my favourite sayings is, "Don't be afraid to buy and sell a stock", because if you sell something, you can always buy back. I've always believed in that. If you reduce Nokia and get it wrong, you can always buy it back again.'

> ## Don't be afraid to buy and sell a stock, because if you sell something, you can always buy back.

In and out is not an approach that comes easily to most investors, in part because a spate of buy and sell and buy decisions suggests inconsistency. Which most people find difficult to live with. Guy is totally relaxed and up-front about changing his mind, and thinks investors must come to terms with that aspect of investing life.

'I frequently admit I'm wrong. If you sell something and you buy back 10 per cent up or 20 per cent higher, it doesn't matter. The important thing is you buy it back. Having the ability to admit that you're wrong is one of the key things that you need to be a fund manager. So many people have sold and think, "I can't buy it back: it's higher than where it was when I sold". That's ludicrous. You can be wrong, and shouldn't be afraid to admit it.'

Buying and selling can be driven by other market-related factors. Guy is constantly combing sectors to spot a stock where price behaviour has resulted in an unsustainable variance, because that could be an opportunity to make money as the outlier reverts to the mean – which generally occurs.

'I'm very conscious of picking out anomalies. Let's say the steel sector has had a great run and you feel "I've missed that". Normally, in Europe, there are always one or two stocks that have lagged. Perhaps Usinor hasn't moved and all the others have. You look into it and find there's been a huge seller. Maybe they've got a million shares left. And you think, "If I clear those out the way, chances are the stock's going to have a bounce, because everything else in the sector has gone up", and the overhang is gone.'

Catalysts at a company could also be a trigger to a trade both on the buy and sell side. Guy lists some of the indicators that at least get him to look and, in many instances, to act.

'If you get a change of management, of strategy, or a significant broker makes a really significant move – let's say Goldman Sachs has been negative – then they turn from being strong sellers to buyers. That is often an interesting catalyst to make me want to look at a stock. It's upgrades, it's downgrades.'

This approach allows Guy to buy – and, of course, to sell quite quickly – stocks that are not suitable as long-term holdings.

'You are only buying the share price – you're not buying the company. How ever bad a company, unless it's going bankrupt, at some point there's going to be an opportunity to make money. Nothing goes down in a straight line for ever.'

Guy gives this example:

'Olivetti in Italy was run by not the best management in the world. It was a restructuring story for ever. They were always going to sell off their loss makers, and didn't. I think I got sucked into it three times. Each time I lost at least 20 per cent.

'Then they got the mobile phone licence. That changed the company. It went from being this awful computing and typewriter manufacturer into a telco play. They were very successful when they launched. I spoke to so many people who said, "You can't buy Olivetti. It's a terrible company". I thought, "I know it's a bad company and I know I've lost a lot of money in it, but I think it really is changing this time". Many people in the market said they'd never buy, because it was Olivetti. I quadrupled my money in 18 months.'

This is by no means a unique story. Guy constantly keeps an eye out for turnarounds, especially in companies that have a history of disappointing the market. When the turn comes, it can be huge and the impact of re-rating can transform a perennial loser into a standout winner. Guy found a not dissimilar situation in Germany.

'Mannesmann changed itself from being an awful engineering stock into a completely wonderful telecom operator. If you say, "I'm never buying it because it's rubbish", then you miss out on opportunities.'

One market-driven dynamic is also on Guy's radar as potentially important and worth watching: index changes.

'If a stock hasn't been in an index, but they're going in, you get index-fund buying. We did well two years ago with Deutsche Telecom, when fundamental people said, "Its a crazy valuation and I wouldn't touch it with a barge pole", but its weight in the DAX was going up. Then Europeans started to use a different index – the Euro Stoxx Index – where it had a huge weighting. And I thought, "This stock is going to go up, whatever happens. It doesn't matter what the valuation is".

'So we took a big position in Deutsche Telecom. I think it went up 35 per cent in January 1999 – purely on a technical squeeze. People that did things just on fundamentals got killed against the index, because they said, "It's overvalued, therefore we're not going to own it". I was more pragmatic, and thought, "Yes, it is expensive, but, with this index squeeze, it's going to go up".'

Seeking the unexpected

The chapter would be incomplete without some discussion of how Guy selects stocks. He falls into the growth camp, but through default rather than conviction; in fact, he is somewhat scathing of so-called growth investors.

'What moves share prices in the long term, and it's important to differentiate between long and short term, is unexpected growth. Some people say, "We buy growth companies". To me the market should be relatively efficient so, if something is expected to grow at 15 per cent a year for the next five years, and it does, then presumably the chances of getting abnormal returns from that are fairly low.'

That said, he prefers growth over any other attribute, but looks to blend in market inefficiency to extract superior returns.

'I've always felt that you need to buy a stock that's going to surprise. That could be through earnings, or sales, or winning new contracts, or from moving from being poorly run to a company that transforms itself into a market leader. The main one is unexpected earnings growth.'

His logic leads to companies with certain characteristics as most suitable for the longer-term core component of his portfolio.

'In order to get that, it's got to be a company that's well positioned within its industry. Normally, I've tried to buy the leader, or the number two, or somebody where there's a really strong niche. If you buy those and they're well managed and in an industry that's growing, that's where you'll get surprises.'

That aside, in European equities, finding the potential to surprise on the upside is increasingly tough. So how does Guy manage?

'You get so many bits of research. "Hold" or "10 per cent upside" or whatever. I chuck them all in the bin. What I look for is somebody that comes up with an idea that is different. Something

> **What I look for is somebody that comes up with an idea that is different.**

new. They've been to the company, they come back, they're excited. They say to me, "I've just seen this company. We'll have to upgrade earnings. Things are going much better".'

Which sparks off an investigation into a possible opportunity for outperformance.

'I phone around and ask, "Have you looked at this company recently? What are your thoughts?" If other analysts say, "Yes, we've seen them. We've been upgrading", it's probably in the price.'

Guy uses analysts to root out these truffles of the market. He is the arbiter who tests ideas and makes sure any insight does differ from general perception and could, therefore, cause a company to exceed expectations.

'My job is to work out who the good people are, and then make sure that, if they are excited, other people in the market haven't quite realized that yet. It's so important to know people's expectations.'

Guy gives a couple of examples of how his approach can work. One way is when a company is small and largely unknown, yet has an interesting business that deserves wider recognition. Kudelski, a Swiss maker of encryption software for digital TVs, was just such a company.

'Kudelski was a small cap in 1998. Merrill Lynch was the one that was up on it. Even the local brokers did not seem to know much. When people don't really know a company, you need to see that there is going to be some sort of catalyst that will change things. In this case, management was planning road shows to meet investors so other people would hear the story and start to look at it. But the key, when a stock is not widely covered, is to make sure you're not buying something no-one will ever find out about.'

In the event, a lot of people learnt about Kudelski and liked what they heard, causing the price to increase fivefold in just two years. Undiscovered gems are always of interest to Guy.

The other way that works is when the market cannot agree about a company and there is a divergence between what Guy is able to glean from his own research and analysts' estimates. This was the situation at ASM Lithography.

'A manufacturer of machinery usually lags the semiconductor cycle. I met the company in early 1999 and felt they were being conservative in their presentation because of what was happening to their customers. So I called around analysts following the stock, who felt my estimates were high. But when I asked how recently they had met ASM, none of them had seen the company for months. Then I found one who had just been. Andrew Griffin at Merrill Lynch agreed with me that the market's numbers were too low. He said that he expected to see forecasts upgraded.'

So here Guy was able to spot something ahead of the crowd. As the market came round to his point of view and estimates were, indeed, adjusted upwards, the stock flew.

One other place where potential surprises can sometimes show up is in charts. Given Guy's thirst for superior market intelligence, it is natural he should play that source off against price action in arriving at an assessment of whether what he is hearing is new or stale.

'If the chart looks nice – it's forming a base and you think it's on a tick up – that is the final confirmation. If an analyst comes back and says, "I've just seen this company and what a great story", and the stock's gone up 30 per cent in the previous month, then you're probably not the first person to hear about it. So charts are very useful in trying to work out whether you're relatively early or whether you've missed it.'

Positive surprises are close to Guy's heart. His understanding of the dynamics of the telecom sector has been a critical contributor to his outperformance, since he anticipated exceptional growth ahead of the crowd. Both cellular and equipment manufacturers have delivered positive surprises.

'We've been in Nokia and Ericsson for years. I always felt that people's forecasts for penetration of mobile phones was far too low. Even though the stocks performed strongly, you looked at where expectations were, and thought, "They're too low". When I saw good analysts saying, "We went through the numbers and forecasts are too low", you had confidence in holding on.'

And, more importantly, so have traditional telecoms.

'Everybody thought they were going to get killed when markets opened up to competition. That was the European Union's big thing a few years ago. These stocks were trading on incredibly low valuations. Then you had this huge boom in mobile use but also in fax and data. Forecasts were far too low. When you talked to analysts they said, "Most people don't like telecoms". I felt very confident that people were going to be consistently surprised by the numbers, and they were.'

Sounds simple, but you need reservoirs of self-confidence to swim against the crowd. So how was Guy able to spot what so many other observers missed?

'Finland and Sweden were the earliest adopters of mobile phones, and were used as a test-bed, really, by Nokia and Ericsson. When you looked at penetration rates five or six years ago, they were at 20 or 30 per cent. The rest of Europe was at about 2–3 per cent. Analysts like to forecast linear growth. They like to say, "It's 30 per cent this year and 30 per cent next year". Finland and Sweden were having exponential growth. Once mobile reaches this critical point, it moves from being a specialist tool to mass market.

'Everybody was forecasting straight line growth. I could see no reason why the rest of Europe wouldn't follow Finland and Sweden. Analysts privately said, "Yes, but we can't put in that kind of growth". It's all about picking out privately from analysts that "Well, actually, my numbers maybe are too low". But they won't go into print, because they couldn't forecast something up 100 or 150 per cent.'

It is in his willingness – even eagerness – to take a stance apart from the consensus where Guy can score big. So his approach to research, especially his use of broker reports and his attitude to their earnings forecasts, is instructive.

'One of the things that I look for is analysts that go out on a limb. Because most don't. You can ignore most sell side analysts. They are sheep. They know that if they have roughly consensus forecasts they're safe – they're never going to lose their job. You phone up a company and they tell you what to write. Anybody can do that. Ninety-five per cent of research from brokers I throw straight in the bin.'

The Holy Grail is an analyst with a well-researched opinion at variance from the crowd. Guy gives an example made more relevant because he acted on the information and made significant amounts of money.

'Chris McFadden at Merrill Lynch was always way more bullish on telecom stocks than anybody else. He had very aggressive price targets based on greater usage, but also was arguing that telcos were far too cheap, because they were growth stocks. Three or four years ago, everybody thought they were utilities. It was controversial, but he was very passionate, and turned out to be exactly right.

This success was not a one-off, since Guy was able to reach into his repertoire and recount several other, similar stories.

'I rate very highly Marc Giapazzi, who is at Schroders in Spain. He had forecasts for a sausage-skin manufacturer called Viscofan four or five years ago, which I think were treble the next in the market. He knew the company backwards. Saw them five or six times. Was absolutely confident his numbers would come through. I phoned up a few other analysts who said, "No, he's absolutely crazy". And I asked, "When was the last time you saw the company?" "Oh, we haven't seen them for a while." It turned out two years down the road that he was exactly right, and I think the stock more than trebled.'

Surprises can be good or bad

Guy pays particular attention when any broker puts out a sell note, especially one with ties to the company, and even more so where a reputable house is first to break ranks. Investors may also want to pay more attention to sell notes in the light of his comments.

'Integrated houses don't like cheesing off their clients. They very rarely put sells on stocks. Equally, they often don't like going out on a limb on the upside, because companies like to keep expectations manageable, and don't like aggressive forecasts, because then they've got to live up to those numbers. They like to keep everybody in a pack and pleasantly surprise. Most analysts seem willing to play along.'

Unfortunately, by the time a sell note hits the street, the bad news may be in the price. Institutional investors, especially those who work hard at cementing broker relationships, can expect a full explanation that puts a hold recommendation in perspective. Guy believes the investment he makes in talking with analysts and cultivating individuals at the best brokerage houses pays off in spades for his shareholders when faced with a hard call.

'If you have good contacts with the best analysts, whilst they may not publish a sell note, if you talk with them enough, they may say, "Well, I would downgrade this, but we've got a corporate relation-ship", and it's difficult to do it.'

Guy remembers a position in Man, the German truck manufacturer, which he felt could go either way.

'One of their analysts called and said "Truck sales in Europe are starting to slow down. I would downgrade the stock, but it's difficult for me." So we sold and it was off 15 per cent the following month.'

You can detect a contrarian streak in this line of thought. Guy does not call himself a member of the club. Indeed, Golden Rule Number 4 at Gartmore is 'Be careful when bucking a trend'. Not, however, 'Don't buck a trend' – and that is a key distinction.

Guy's whole approach is peppered with contrarian flavour.

On swimming separately from fellow professionals: 'When you talked to people about telecoms, everybody was so negative. That to me is a great combination, when you really believe in something but everybody else is very negative.'

> **That to me is a great combination, when you really believe in something but everybody else is very negative.**

On using analysts: 'When one of them really goes out on a limb and says they've got a forecast that's way different, either positive or negative, that's when I call them in, because they so rarely go out on a limb that, when they do, they normally have something interesting to say.'

His decision to go back into Nokia big time was a classic contrarian call. Having hit an air pocket due to excessive growth, Nokia's price halved and the company was out of favour at many firms. Guy began to get a sense that the situation was improving, so called his contacts at brokers and other investment houses to gauge sentiment in the market.

'When I phoned around, people said, "We wouldn't touch it with a barge pole. They've disappointed. It's a terrible company." Typical closed mind stuff. So I thought, "This is interesting".'

Which was, itself, one reason for Guy to go aggressively over-weight again, searching for a positive earnings surprise that duly arrived, and leaving consensus seekers to play catch-up.

Charts for confirmation

Guy is up-front about admitting that charts play an important role.

'I never buy or sell a stock unless I've looked at the chart.'

He does not allow charts, on their own, to drive the investment decision, though where the chart is awful, that would veto a proposed purchase. But, as to the question of when, then charts become the dominant influence.

'The chart is crucial in timing purchases or sales.'

The good news for the less numerate is that Guy's approach is not demanding. Most critical for him are the 50- and 200-day averages and resistance levels.

'Occasionally I look at relative strength to see whether a stock's overbought or oversold. But really it's absolute price and key resist-ance levels. I like to look at the range where the stock's been trading.'

What attracts his interest is when a stock strays outside its range, in either direction, or when the price bumps up against a resistance point.

'Once we decide to purchase, we take a position but, if the price breaks the resistance level, then we'll take a big position. When the chart starts to look right, that would be a catalyst to increase a posi-tion. On the sell side, when a stock approaches a key resistance level and you don't know whether it's going to break out, I may reduce.'

Guy elaborates on the interpretation appropriate to an exceptional chart pattern: 'If a share is on a big spike, I would be very reluctant to buy. If a share has formed a base and is starting to turn up and the moving averages are starting to turn up, that is lovely, and I may think, "Yes, this is a stock that probably is turning, and now is the right time to buy".'

But woe betide a share that slips.

'If a stock dips down below a key level such as the two-year low, or even worse, the all-time low, then I'll just cut and get out entirely.'

Back on the sell side, Guy constantly consults charts as he tries to decide whether to hang on or get out: especially when he is running a profit.

'If a stock is going up and keeps on going up, then there's not a lot of reason to sell. I'd rather wait for it to start to turn over and sell 5 per cent below the top rather than trying to call the top and be proved wrong when it keeps on going up.'

While he tries not to act prematurely, he is also anxious to act quickly when the chart turns nasty.

'There's always key levels where a stock breaks up or down. And if a stock breaks down, I would automatically reduce if it's a long-term position and, if it's a short-term position, sell straight away. Chart breakdowns are very significant.'

Given the importance Guy attaches to this signal in particular, it is useful to understand in more detail what he means.

'You can get a golden cross or a death cross. The 50-day average is moving around much more, while the 200-day is relatively stable. When the 50-day falls through the 200-day average it's a death cross, and if it has been below for a while and breaks above then that is a golden cross. Many chartists would say when either one happens it is significant.

'I don't follow these crosses religiously but, when the 50-day average has been above the 200-day for, say, three years and it suddenly turns down, and relative strength turns down as well, that can be horrendous. Where the averages have been moving in and out of a range, this move may not be significant. Conversely, when it moves up after having been below for a long time, that normally signals a price going higher.'

Guy cites the leading French telecommunications manufacturer, Alcatel, by way of illustration.

'We've been pretty negative on Alcatel over the years and been right. It's hugely under-performed Nokia and Ericsson. Very bad management. Always number four or five in the world. Not what we tend to look for. But, since 1999, Alcatel's been transforming itself, getting exposure to high growth areas. So we took a small position. And then the price went through its all-time high in the fourth quarter, which, for that stock, was very significant [*see* Fig. 5.1]. This was an all-time high from many years ago. That move was the final bit of the jigsaw. We went big in Alcatel on the back of that. We thought this break probably confirms that the stock is turning around. It went up 40 per cent in the following six weeks.'

Guy took a big position in Alcatel in early 2000. The price rose to 90 euro, close to a doubling. At which point it seemed to have got ahead of itself. Also, the valuation on optic stocks in general reached extremes. Guy was further concerned by what did not happen.

'A couple of big brokers upgraded the stock at around 90 to a strong buy, and the price did not go up. The stock was forming a top. If a stock does not go up on good news and it's struggling on the chart, it's probably a good time to let go.'

Figure 5.1 Alcatel share price history, 1996–2000

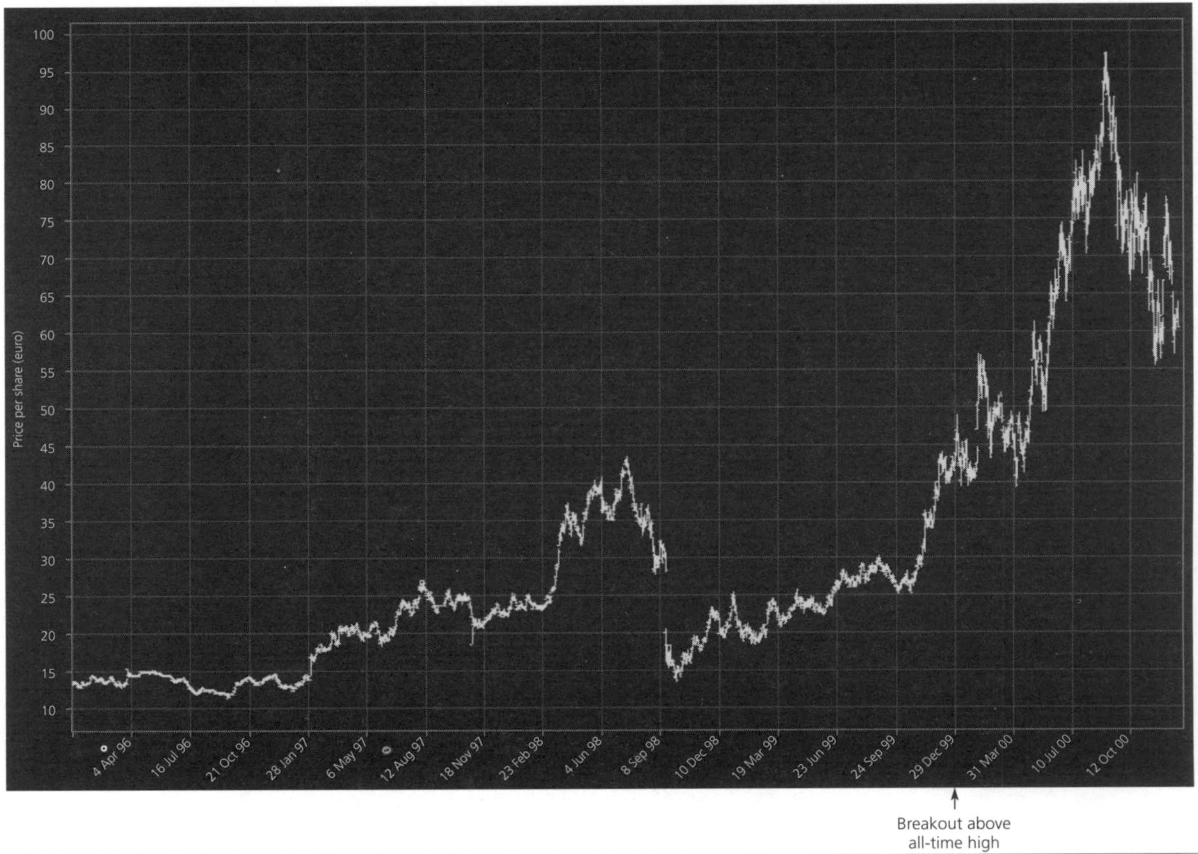

Source: Bridge.

The stock that did not bark was the clue that good times were coming to an end. He sold half within weeks of the top, locking in an excellent return for his funds.

Guy is categoric that, however enthusiastic he became about chart action, he would not act on that alone. Charts cannot substitute for analsis. They can only confirm.

'If I had hated Alcatel and thought it terrible, then I wouldn't have bought even if the chart was good. But because I'd been warming to the idea anyway, then that really was the final push to take a position. I would never buy a stock just because it had broken up. You've got to actually like the stock, or not like it, if you're looking to sell.'

Charts, then, are an auxiliary in the armoury of an investor, but they should be constantly checked. If price movement confirms other analysis, that strengthens the likelihood of making the right decision. Conversely, where the chart goes against the analytical outcome, that is reason enough to pause and review the analysis again. Trying to explain why this seems to work is counterintuitive and lacking in a firm logical underpinning. Still, it is hard to argue with empirical data. Guy is pragmatic about what he has witnessed.

'As long as there's enough people around who look at charts, and a lot do, then that may be the reason they work. You have to respect that. People set absolute levels on stocks. If the all-time high is 400 euros and we've bought it at 300, I'll let a third go when the price gets close to the all-time high. As long as enough people think like that, the resistance level becomes a self-fulfilling prophesy.'

Since the market reflects the people who participate, it pays to remember that price action is every bit as behavioural as analytical.

Never say never

Many investors, individuals and professionals alike, find comfort in a loosely defined set of benchmarks – often quantitative – which work for them. Then they stick by these through thick and thin. And since markets are constantly on the move, and rarely linger for long in the same place, there is often more of the thin. One of Guy's most disarming characteristics is his willingness to accept that what once was right might now be wrong. Rules, like stocks,

> **Rules, like stocks, constantly need reassessing and can be changed.**

constantly need reassessing and can be changed. He has no absolute investment mantra other than always to keep an open mind; and, perhaps, a bias to taking the contrarian point of view. So he has no specific style as such. Essentially, his is an approach where flexibility rules, where the only important thing is to be in tune with the times so he can chop and change without prolonged soul searching. This flexible attitude embraces sectors, such as his decision to overweight telcoms when all around were sceptical, and also specific stocks.

'In the early nineties, people hated Philips. They'd almost gone bankrupt. Many investors said, "I'm never buying that share again. It's always disappointed for the previous 15 years." But we bought it when they brought in a new manager, Mr Boonstraas, as Chief Executive. He talked about restructuring the business and came across as very credible. You sensed he meant business. He was not just reading the script. If there is reason to expect change and everyone hates a stock, there should be a lot of upside. It's gone up about ten times since.'

And, again, in his approach to the duration of a holding. Take his sell targets. These are a moveable feast.

'I've always regarded targets as not fixed. You can sell before it gets there, if you think sentiment is getting negative. I don't hold because something's showing upside on the price target. If you think that sector's been downgraded or that this stock is not behaving as you'd expect, then you want to reduce. If you're getting bogged down insisting it's still got this much upside, that's when things start going wrong. Equally, you're going to hold on to a stock that you think is expensive when you can see that there is a lot of momentum behind it.'

You can tell that Guy practises what he preaches simply by reading past fund managers' reviews. Each year, in the European Selected Opportunities fund, his emphasis alters and he homes in on different themes to play or avoid:

- 1996: high-quality growth – stay away from financials
- 1997: quality cyclicals and corporate restructuring
- 1998: pharmaceuticals
- 1999: telecommunications and more telecommunications, plus oil
- 2000: telecommunications once more, and corporate restructuring comes round again.

Themes recur, but anyone who can revolve from high-quality growth through to quality cyclicals and on to oil definitely operates with an open mind; and, given Guy's results, perhaps more investors should refresh their own thinking and re-examine their own degrees of flexibility.

Europe's hot spots

With his European brief, Guy's perspective has a particular slant, but it is perhaps no surprise that in a period of relatively open markets and increasing globalization, in financial markets in particular, his focus on growth areas for the future is broadly similar to his peers in North America and, to some extent, in Asia also. The themes that excite him have a familiar ring.

1. Telecom equipment manufacturers

'I think you're going to see tremendous growth over the next five to ten years or so, in particular at Ericsson and Alcatel, and Nokia as well, to some extent.'

Guy contrasts the position of manufacturers with where he sees operators and raises questions about whether growth for those companies will reward shareholders.

'Telecom operators themselves are more fully valued. Whilst revenues will be very significant – you've got ADSL and also, via mobile, you've got 3G and 4G, probably, in about eight years' time – competition is definitely increasing. Also it's hard to predict revenues. They will be there, but very, very hard to predict. To me, at the moment there's too much uncertainty to want to be aggressively overweight in that sector.'

This doubt represents a break with the past. Since Guy did so well for many years by being overweight in operators, his reticence for the future is all the more interesting.

2. Digital television

'I think digital television will be one of the absolute growth themes for this decade. At the moment, television is dumb. You can do very little with it. Over the next ten years you'll get huge advances in interactivity. People involved in that have huge potential. That would be companies like Kudelski in Switzerland, Open TV in Amsterdam, Philips, even, because it's involved in making digital television sets. And also companies that provide content. Clearly, there's going to be huge choice over the next ten years in what you can watch so, obviously, people that have the right content will do very well.'

Guy sees several subsectors under this umbrella, all of which look poised to experience high growth.

'What I like about digital television is that it *is* still early days. I think people are, a bit like they did with mobile phones, underestimating the potential growth. There's no reason at all why, in ten years, everybody shouldn't have digital television. You should be able to do a lot of interesting things over it. You should be able to pay per view so you never have to traipse to the movie store again. You can download as you want; stop and play. There's so much value-added. Also can you order things. You will be watching something that says, "Would you like to order this CD? Press 2 to order." I think growth from that is going to be huge.'

There can be caveats even in those areas that should outperform. Not all content is equal and, certainly, different strategies will produce different financial outcomes.

'Film is a very dangerous area. Senator Films has a very clever strategy where it doesn't invest much money itself but, when you look at where Vivendi is going at the moment, buying into Seagram, that's empire building.'

And on the back of this growth could come other value-added services.

'I saw a very interesting company – not quoted yet – called Future TV. They get you to put in a card, so they know which member of the family is watching. They build up, over time, a profile of what programmes you watch. Then they can work out what sort of person you are, and tailor adverts to you. Obviously they can charge a premium, compared to normal advertising, because the message is reaching the right sort of person.'

Guy will be watching the whole digital arena closely for other good ideas to emerge and, when they do, he is likely to pounce.

3. Semiconductors

'Over the ten years, there will be a whole host of new electronic gadgets and instruments. They get ever more complex, and that means you need more complicated semiconductors and also more of them.

'There is likely to be a blurring between personal organizers and mobile phones. With the 3G phone and their ability to transmit data, that will increase demand.

'Cars are getting much more sophisticated. Satellite navigation should be standard in five years, even in a Fiesta. Smart credit cards and intelligent cards that hold all your financial information will need a lot of computing power. And, of course, digital television will need an enormous amount of computing power, and more sophisticated set-top boxes.

'I think companies like ST Micro Electronics in France and ASM Lithography in The Netherlands will be real winners.'

The two examples Guy gives are very different, even if they fall under the same general heading. Each deserves elaboration as separate companies with strategies that should enable them to take advantage of a favourable trend.

'ST Micro makes the chips. It's been good at predicting areas that are going to grow rapidly and not getting involved in commodity semiconductors. ST Micro has been positioning itself in value-added areas. It's a very large player in mobile phones. It's a very large player in smart cards, and it's a very large player in digital television, so, to me, it seems to be very, very well positioned in all the right growth areas and also is in value-added.

'ASM Lithography makes the equipment that makes semiconductors. There's only about four companies globally that are heavily involved. There's a new line of machinery coming out now that's more powerful. ASML has always been well positioned, but it's never been number one. Now it seems to have a lead, and it's just starting to win orders. It's never been used by Texas Instruments or Intel. I think that they've got a good chance of being picked by these two companies as a supplier for their new generation of machines.

'Semiconductor use will probably grow at 30–40 per cent a year, so people have to invest in new capacity all the time. ASML are well placed to benefit. On top of that, I think they're well positioned to take market share. The chances of unexpected growth over the next two to three years is huge.'

4. Asset management

There is one trend arising from changes in investing culture and attitudes to equities, in particular in continental Europe, that Guy believes could have a dramatic impact on the sector in which he himself operates.

'Europe is still in its infancy when it comes to people owning shares and buying funds. It's started to take off in the last 18 months, but they're way behind the US and UK. Where you can find good asset gatherers on the Continent, they are interesting plays. AXA in France has been very successful. In Italy, although I've had to sell it, Bipop has been incredibly successful. They just got too expensive. Swiss private banks are interesting. Julius Baer has very strong growth in assets under management. Historically, Europeans have been bond orientated. Typically, their savings were in bonds. They are moving towards equities, now. On a ten-year view, I can't see any reason why they wouldn't be up at our levels, which creates huge demand for equities over the next ten years in Europe.'

And, of course, any such shift potentially has beneficial implications for equity markets on the Continent as a whole. Assuming a huge influx of new money, liquidity should provide the momentum to move prices up, especially in those markets that are least mature, such as Germany, Italy and Spain.

'The pension markets are still very immature. Most people do not have a personal plan and, typically, those that do have only 30–35 per cent invested in equities. There is going to be huge growth all across Europe in personal plans and equity ownership.'

These are examples of themes where Guy expects to find sustainable growth that will allow him to hold companies in the longer-term core part of his portfolio. But he will watch over his choices like a hawk and move in and out on an opportunistic basis with one eye on the chart and one ear always to the market, judging when to be overweight or underweight. And let a favoured stock show the slightest sign of weakness and it will be history. For however open he is to new ideas and new ways of improving his excellent record, one thing will never change: Guy will cut dead wood ruthlessly. So should you.

6

Bill Kennedy

Matching Asia with the world

Achieved a no load cumulative return of 42 per cent through year end 2000 compared to 17 per cent for the MS Pacific Basin index during the same period

---

In 1999 outperformed the relevant MSCI index by 55 per cent, while managing a $1 billion portfolio

---

Beat Lipper Pacific Region comparable peer group fund average by 21 per cent

---

Achieved the highest one-year no-load return in the ten-year history of Fidelity Pacific Basin in his first year of management

---

Tracks global trends to highlight regional winners

To start a new career on Valentine's Day seems like a good omen. For Bill Kennedy, joining Fidelity in Hong Kong on 14 February 1994 was the consummation of a career-long love-affair with the investment industry. Still, it is worth noting that his fascination with Asia began before he realized that financial markets was the field that fascinated him. The Asian economic miracle and that period in the 1980s when Japan could do no wrong caught his attention.

'When I was in high school, the Japanese were beating the Americans at everything: cars, computers, steel – you name it, they were taking the market. I became fascinated with how they managed their businesses and grew globally. You used to read about how Japan was going to take over the world. I began to look at Asia, taking Asian studies, and spent quite a lot of time studying Asian history.'

So it was no surprise that, when the opportunity arose to get over to Asia with Prudential Investment Corporation, where he first worked after graduation, Kennedy did not need to be asked twice. Once there, he was hooked. Hong Kong became his home for the best part of five years, following from a two-year stint in Singapore, and he is now a resident of Tokyo.

Kennedy has crammed a lot of experience into less than a decade, starting with venture capital Asian style, then covering emerging markets in Asia with an initial emphasis on India, later adding to his brief by becoming regional power-sector specialist before progressing to head of research for the region. Finally, he took over direct responsibility for the Fidelity Pacific Basin Fund and also recently added the role of manager of the Fidelity Advisor Japan Fund.

An eight-year stint in the analytical trenches gave Kennedy a solid grounding. Kennedy looks back on this time as one of ideal preparation for his current career:

'Being an analyst teaches you to role up your sleeves and analyze companies backwards and forwards to appreciate what is driving earnings and, more importantly, what drives the stock price.'

In some respects Kennedy was fortunate, since he transitioned to fund management at a time when the Asian crisis was drawing to an end, but before recovery was in full swing. Still, his arrival, in January 1999, does coincide with a marked upturn in results. From 1990 through to the end of 1998, Fidelity Pacific Basin beat the MCSI Index, but merely matched its peer group average. Since Kennedy took charge, both absolute and relative outperformance have rocketed, with a gain of nearly 120 per cent in 1999, beating 80 per cent of its Lipper peers for the period and placing him at the front of the pack.

In part, this outperformance has been a function of the focus in Japan and Kennedy's emphasis on larger, forward-looking companies. As the dominant economy in the Pacific Basin, with an 80-per-cent-plus weighting in the MSCI Pacific Index, how a regional fund approaches its Japanese allocation can be the decision that drives relative performance. Kennedy believed that Japan's time had come again. Both macro issues and company-specific events have reinforced his belief.

Change in the air

What excites Kennedy most is that, after a long period of moving sideways, a number of important developments in the financial landscape are starting to come together. Collectively these suggest that investors could be about to witness a second golden age in Japanese equities. It is possible to isolate several separate trends, each of which is potentially positive.

1. Light at the end of the economic tunnel

First off, the overall economy seemed to be stabilizing. Official figures continue to flirt with recession, and some sectors remain in decline, but others show signs of life. The year 1998 began badly.

'Things were still pretty bad. Every time you talked to companies, earnings would be a down tick from what we had previously discussed with them. Every time we walked out of a meeting, our analyst tended to revise down estimates.'

But, by the middle of the year, Kennedy sensed that the tide had begun to turn.

'Slowly you started to feel things get a little better. The Asian crisis was easing up. A lot of companies had taken their lumps. Things were not deteriorating any more. That alone, going from a decline to stabilizing is the most important thing to look for. Throughout the fourth quarter of 1998 into the beginning of 1999, every time you went to companies you walked out feeling a lot better.'

This was not just about Japan as a stand-alone economy. There were also early stirrings of recovery elsewhere.

'One of Japan's biggest customers is South-East Asia. That customer was starting to import more, and starting to spend a little of the money that disappeared in 1997 and 1998.'

With home and abroad both beginning to perk up, Kennedy was able to find specific companies that showed evidence of a resurrection.

'In the middle of 1998, most of Sony's businesses were under intense pricing pressure. Demand was weak, because emerging markets in general were very weak. Korea had just had a huge currency devaluation, as had Thailand. Sony competes with Koreans in displays for PCs, and in TV sets. The Koreans had become a lot more competitive and were facing problems in their banking system so needed cash. They became very aggressive in pricing to gain share and get cash in the door.

'Every time you talked to Sony, pricing was bad. Then you sensed things start to stabilize at the end of 1998, beginning of 1999. Pricing wasn't such an issue because the won had started to strengthen and Korean companies had less pressure from banks, so stopped the market share game.

'Sony did a lot of restructuring. They closed a plant in the US which was high cost and moved production to China, and also sold a major plant to a contract manufacturer which will produce products outsourced from Sony. Eventually, every time you spoke to them the electronics business was better and the game business was better. You felt demand picking up and prices stabilizing.'

If Kennedy is correct, and the jury is still out, then the next step is to home in on sectors likely to pick up first as conditions improve. Kennedy noticed that the economic malaise of the 1990s had made Japan somewhat of a laggard among developed economies in certain product categories.

'One of the big reasons why the US had phenomenal PC penetration is because the economy's been great. Look where there has been good penetration. It has been in good economies. Japan is behind. Asia fell behind because of the crisis. When these economies get better, they're going to buy PCs; they're going to buy consumer electronics, and cellular phones.'

If you believe that this is a good space, then Japan provides the investor with plenty of choice. You can own companies such as Sony or PC makers like NEC and Toshiba and the folks who supply the parts, or even electronic retailers like Yamada Denki.

Another key development was wholesale change in the banking sector. Accumulated problems and practices rooted in the past were preventing banks from playing their proper part in revitalizing the economy. Kennedy believes that, while problems persist, recent changes are positive.

'Banks needed to be recapitalized because their non-performing loans placed them in such a dire situation. The government agreed to put in capital, but this capital is coming with a lot of caveats and requirements to change. The SSA, the financial supervisory authority, was aggressive getting in there and saying Japanese banks must change, and quickly. When the government recapitalized the banking system in 1999, they said, "We demand that you focus on lending to projects that make sense, rather than lending to affiliated companies or typical relationship lending".

'Companies all of a sudden realized that, "Hey, if we want to build, they are going to have to be projects that are economically viable and earn a return, not only to pay investors but to pay shareholders". Capital became more scarce. You couldn't rely on the banks. You had to rely on shareholders.'

Revamping and reorienting banking is a precursor to a full-fledged recovery. If revitalization is, indeed, underway, then, as it feeds through the system it will

> # Revamping and reorienting banking is a precursor to a full-fledged recovery.

provide a vital boost and reinforce other positive trends: not just aiding the economy, but also shareholders in Japanese companies.

Whether or not the economy in general is on the mend, there is no dispute that certain sectors are demonstrating growth.

2. The Japanese new economy

Much of what is encouraging about new corporate Japan can be understood by looking at selected leading-edge companies. Softbank, for a while, seemed the very essence of an outward-looking, forward-thinking company. Kennedy used to cite Softbank as a model and, even after recent reversals, still finds things to admire about its approach.

'Softbank was very radical in the way they thought about things and I think that was very important for Japan. This company is changing every day. You have highly skilled management that is not only savvy operationally. They have continued to make good, smart, astute investments that have contributed phenomenal returns for shareholders. They are a bit like venture capitalists. These guys find management that has a vision. They find aggressive management that's highly incentivized to make things work in the shareholder's favour, and buy stakes in those companies. One is Yahoo in the US, another is Yahoo in Japan. They also have stakes in most of the Yahoos around Europe.'

Kennedy is careful to temper his enthusiasm for management with the importance of not getting carried away over multiples. He made a ton of money in the stock, but cut back when valuations became uncomfortable. The environment has changed dramatically, but Softbank led the way in 1999 in exploiting emerging technologies.

Trying to anticipate how Japan might attempt to regain technology parity was Kennedy's key to choosing the right 'new-economy' companies for his portfolio.

'One reason why the Japanese don't access the internet that much is because PC penetration is so low. Why is PC penetration so low? The economy has been really bad for a long time. The software hasn't been very good. Software spend in Japan has been very low, relative to the US and Europe. If you don't have the software, people don't buy hardware.'

But Kennedy observed that everyone was carrying cellular phones.

'If they can get the internet on the phone, cellular is going to be very powerful.'

That suggested one cluster of potential investments. Content, too, needed improvement.

'Internet use has not been very good because you haven't had a lot of content in Japan. It is developing now but, two years ago, you didn't have much. You had Yahoo and a few others, but it was slim.'

So companies with content are addressing a potentially high growth market. The importance of going overweight in these types of businesses cannot be understated. Following this trail, Kennedy found winners such as Softbank during 1999; and Kyocera, which had a good run, in part due to strong demand for mobile phone components; and Yamada Denki, which rode increased retail interest for its product categories.

3. Sector-specific modernization

Within 'old' Japan, attractive investments can also be found when a sector commits to change. Winners are likely to be one of two kinds.

First, there are the companies driving change who will emerge as leaders when the dust settles. The banking industry is one among several set for a shake-up.

> **Within 'old' Japan, attractive investments can also be found when a sector commits to change.**

'You've had a system that's been so concerned about bad debts that they've neglected customer service. They've neglected everything. When Japanese banks were recapitalized, the government made itself a shareholder, but provided a buyout option. Since banks do not want the government as a long-term business associate, there is a strong incentive to earn enough money to buy the government out. Right now, banks are putting ATMs in 711 convenience stores, for instance. Two years ago most ATMs in Japan closed at 5 o'clock because they were inside the bank! You couldn't just walk down the street and boom, there's an ATM. I remember seeing a woman in the office running out, and I asked, "Where are you going?" and she said, "Oh, I've got to get to the ATM before 5". But that's going to change.'

Front-line beneficiaries are companies that make component parts for ATMs, including NEC and Oki Electric. Ultimately, the big beneficiaries will be the banks themselves as their costs come down. And this could only be the beginning, since Kennedy believes a number of positive developments are in the offing that will bring Japanese banking into the twenty-first century.

'There is a lot of low-hanging fruit. Some day they are going to get it right and put in Customer Relationship Management Systems [CRMS] to cross-sell products. When a customer walks in you should know not only how much that customer has in the bank, but also what his or her spending patterns are on the credit card and on insurance. Japanese banks have no idea. They are starting to implement CRMS. That has been very powerful in the UK and the US to get more of the customer's wallet.'

While it is still impossible to predict the eventual winners, Kennedy spotted one that he believed was an early adopter.

'Suruga Bank was among the first to put in a customer relationship management system. They have a joint venture with EDS of the US. They seem to be way ahead of the curve. As a result, their return on equity and earnings growth has been far superior to the average Japanese bank.'

Regional banks also intrigued Kennedy.

'They were cheap compared to UK building societies. They were very cheap compared to US Savings and Loans on a P/E basis and also on price to book.'

Which indicated that the whole sector might be a good place to look for bargains. There is a second attractive area: those providing the tools and services to enable change to occur. Bankers are behind the times, but a modern economy demands streamlined financial services. *Ergo* Kennedy believes software support should be a great place to invest, particularly where improvement is overdue.

'Talk to an average Japanese company and ask, "How much have you spent upgrading your systems, and is that a growing or declining percentage of your sales?" Look at banking. Look at a Japanese manufacturer. They haven't spent much money, partly because of the recession. Take the ERP trend. It hasn't really hit.'

Knowing the huge numbers companies have sunk into systems elsewhere is an indicator of the immense profit potential still to come in Asia.

'Y2K made them focus and say, "Do we just want to fix this, or do we spend more and buy a system that is not only Y2K compliant, but, more importantly, is going to add better value for the customer?" Japanese companies started to say, "We can execute a transaction a lot cheaper, more efficiently, with a lot more customer service, by spending more on software". Software companies see orders accelerating. I think the next couple of years are going to be very good for them – with internet changes and moving from a COBOL-based platform, the old mainframes, to a web-based platform.'

Kennedy had his eye on a couple of companies likely to benefit from a pickup in expenditure.

'The biggest is NTT Data, which is a general-applications company. There's also Nippon System Development, a software company that has the highest exposure to banks, and Fujisoft ABC, which has middleware as its main line, with a corporate focus.'

4. The land of the rising shareholder

Perhaps the area of change easiest to embrace is early indications of a shift in sentiment in respect of shareholder value. Shareholders' interests traditionally came a poor third after employees and corporate relationships. The low priority most companies in Asia historically gave shareholders and, specifically, minority or non-family owners, may have hurt stock performance and deterred potential foreign investors.

It was early 1999 when Kennedy sensed the possibility of a market revival after what had been effectively an eight-year slump. He noticed that some Japanese management began to talk the talk and, in a few instances, even to take concrete steps to enhance shareholder value. Among the earliest to get religion were new-economy leaders such as Sony, which rewarded management in ways that made them pay more attention to the impact of their decisions on the stock price.

Kennedy is keen to see more of this. As he says, 'I think that is by far the most important thing that has happened in Japan. It aligns shareholder and management interests, and is bringing a lot of reorientation of management to the interest of shareholders. Stock options are very important. People suffer financially if they don't hit their targets.'

The impact can be seen beyond internal improvements at one or two leading-edge companies. Opinion leaders can influence thinking across whole swathes of society.

'Softbank has changed younger business people in Japan. Now they think about equity, about stock options, about a variety of things that are taken for granted in Silicon Valley.'

Sony comes up trumps, too.

'Sony has a stock option programme. They are compensating most middle and senior management on performance, which is becoming a bigger portion of overall compensation. You are starting to see benefits accruing. That shows up in operating efficiencies and execution. Sony fit my investment criteria with regard to highly incentivized management that builds value for shareholders.'

> # New-economy companies that are shaking up not just the business environment but the whole way corporate Japan used to conduct business.

It is primarily the new-economy companies that are shaking up not just the business environment but the whole way corporate Japan used to conduct business. Kennedy identifies other pacesetters.

'Trend Micro makes anti-virus software. Many employees have stock options. It's been run like a Silicon Valley company.'

And not just in staff motivation, but also in business management.

'It is a globally competitive business operating in Japan, but with support staff in the Philippines, where it is easier and cheaper to employ people. Most customers are in the US. If you have a virus problem, you call and people who speak English fix your problem over the phone.'

Other changes in the way incentives are paid are welcome. Kennedy points to an extreme example of where one company has added an intriguing twist to the normal menu. Senior management at Matsushita Electric Works (MEW) can potentially be asked to pay the company up to ¥100,000 or approximately US$1,000 if they do not meet their minimum performance goals. In some areas it would seem that Japanese respect for the shareholder has leap-frogged into leadership. It is not difficult to think of companies in the US or Europe that might do well to emulate this practice.

Kennedy also sees improvements in the way Japanese companies communicate with their shareholders and in the use of technology to facilitate that exchange. A leader in improving standards is Sony.

'When I was in Boston, Sony came every quarter. Disclosure improved dramatically over the last couple of years in terms of how it break things down. It has an investor relations department that exists to increase disclosure.'

Others are making strides to become more open and accountable.

'MEW historically rarely earned its cost of capital. A new president, Kazushige Nishida, was shareholder friendly. Now MEW has broken out a level of detail that it never used to. You have a company that takes everything out by division and measures it on an EVA [Economic Value Added] basis. It made sure to communicate that to shareholders and show how each division is doing.'

A growing awareness of the importance of stock prices is expressed not only through greater emphasis on the shareholder and corporate governance, but also in structural changes. Mothers market, the Japanese response to AIM in the UK, and Euro.NM provides investors access to a category of company previously not available due to listing restrictions, enabling individuals to participate in some of the more exciting new-economy businesses. There is collateral advantage to established listed companies who have a new route to create share-holder value via Mothers. Kennedy was ahead of the crowd in realizing how the existence of an additional exit strategy might play out through unlocking value previously hidden within relatively opaque conglomerates.

'JAFCO is one I owned in the past. It's basically a venture capital company which has a bunch of investments ripe for IPOs but, in the past, they couldn't list in Japan because of regulatory requirements. They weren't eligible for the main markets because they didn't have the track record or profit history needed. Now they can go on Mothers or NASDAQ Japan, which are more relaxed. That should crystallize value in the underlying portfolio.'

JAFCO has benefited from the flotation of Softbank and other IT companies in Japan, as well as blue chips within the region such as Singapore Airlines. Even conglomerates like Sumitomo Precision Products Co have spotted the advantages. The company recently floated 40 per cent of its Surface Technology Systems (STS) subsidiary. STS, which makes machines that produce parts for micro-electro-mechanical systems, has ended up listed on the UK's junior AIM market.

5. Increasing corporate activity

The concept of value creation carries over into another area that has, until recently, been more or less off-limits: mergers and acquisitions, particularly of the unfriendly variety. An increase in these sorts of transactions can only improve the prospects for superior returns.

'Historically there weren't hostile takeovers. As Japan liberates, you're starting to see foreign companies buy out Japanese companies. For example, Cable and Wireless taking over IDC in 1999. Here you've got a foreign company buying a telecommunications company from NTT, of all people. That was unheard of only a year or two ago. Things are changing very quickly.'

Creating value through M&A is catching on around Asia and likely to be a more potent force for crystallizing shareholder value in the future than has been the case in the past. Kennedy has seen the first signs within his own portfolio.

'DDI announced a merger, in December 1999, with KDD, another holding, and IDO, the telecom subsidiary of Toyota. This made obvious sense, given the fact that each has different types of assets. Now they can rival NTT. That's something that would not have happened in Japan maybe even two years ago.'

DDI's stock price did very well on the back of the merger and also, to an extent, in anticipation of an announcement. Stock movements driven by the possibility of deals is a recent phenomenon. Kennedy was one of the first to spot the possibility. He was buying when locals were sellers: a brave move, but one that paid off.

'I was nervous for a while because the sell side was very negative. I bought and it kept on going down. Management was not executing according to expectations – DDI had a few down earnings revisions, and disappointed investors – but there comes a time when value is compelling.

'We did a lot of research on what companies were ripe for consolidation and what made sense. DDI, IDO and KDD together had synergies. A lot of cost could be ripped out, so they seemed logical partners.

'We had owned DDI. Based on our mosaic principle of putting pieces together we were able to say, "If KDD and IDO aren't going to buy these guys out, some big international carrier will. It's just a matter of time, given where they are strategically positioned and how cheap the stock is".'

This sort of analysis would have been a waste of effort as recently as 1998 in Japan. Now it is worthwhile, as Kennedy's experience shows. Expect more of the same in this sector, but also elsewhere. One industry where Kennedy sees conditions as suitable for M&A activity is banking.

'Some day Japanese banks could make very attractive investments though there are many risks associated with this sector. Banks have started to look at their balance sheets, address credit quality problems and make fundamental changes. If you strip out bad debts and shrink the balance sheet a bit, they have franchises that can be very attractive. But there's a few issues and, if these problems aren't addressed, they are going to continue to weigh on the entire system. Non-performing loans, obviously, lack of investment in IT, and management that doesn't really care about its share price.'

Which is where mergers or acquisitions could come in. Whereas before the idea was a non-starter, now it is on the radar screen, and a stronger banking system might result, as well as value creation for long-suffering shareholders.

Another area where Kennedy believes corporate activity could occur is pharmaceuticals. This follows from what has happened elsewhere – developments he has monitored as possible precursors to what may occur in Japan.

'You've seen a lot of M&A globally in pharmaceuticals, but you haven't seen it in Japan yet. Pharmaceuticals is an industry which is ripe for consolidation. There is M&A to buy drug pipelines and to buy distribution. Not many foreign companies have distribution in Japan. Japan is big drug market. It is an ageing market. You've got to think somebody's going to come in.'

And there are candidates aplenty, perhaps too many to predict where the call will come.

'Companies like Takeda Chemicals or Fujisawa Pharmaceutical have their own drugs and license them to companies in the US or Europe. They do not represent logical candidates. There are other smaller companies producing drugs, which have distribution domestically, that license from foreign companies and distribute on their behalf. There is a whole host of these that could provide what a foreign drug company wants by way of access, and so any of them could be an attractive target.'

All these improvements came at a time when prices in Japan were as low as they had been for a decade. Even relatively modest improvements can make a big difference when a market, sector or company are relatively bombed out – as was true almost across the board for Japanese companies in late 1998.

'Valuations were cheap. You were looking at stock prices that have been beaten up and earnings multiples at the low end of historical trading ranges. Things weren't really getting better, but they weren't getting worse.'

So, on top of a more benign environment for fundamentals and corporate behaviour, investors could overlay more enticing entry prices to attract acquisitive predators. All the ingredients appear in place.

Far from the madding crowd

With so much change at the local level, what is a *gaijin* to do? Kennedy has found an edge for himself and for Fidelity through identifying themes that transcend national borders. When he took over Pacific Basin he was located in Fidelity's US headquarters, which had both pluses and minuses. One plus of being Boston based, but having lived in Asia, was that he could see the big picture and, at the same time, set global trends in a local context. Building on this distinct advantage, Kennedy concentrated on areas of the economy and on specific companies where cross-border analysis was appropriate. Taking a top-down perspective, interesting ideas emerged.

1. Cross-border technology transfer

This can be as simple as a single product suitable for transplanting, or as complex as the adoption of a new business model with, of course, the need for local modification for the graft to take. Kennedy operates all along this spectrum.

'I try to spot a theme in the US and see how that's going to affect Japan and South-East Asia.'

Japanese companies, which historically have exhibited a tendency to overdo the 'not invented here' syndrome, now seem ready to be regional pioneers and early adopters of new technologies innovated elsewhere. Or even promoters. Softbank has been a leader in technology transfer.

'They have enough vision to look down the road and say, "A lot of the stuff that we buy in the US has scaleable business models that we can move to Japan". Where the real value comes is bringing technology to a new place, adapting it to a new culture and building from the ground up. That's where they get their big bang for the buck.'

Other areas of opportunity were influenced by personal observation *à la* Peter Lynch, the *eminence*

> **Where the real value comes is bringing technology to a new place, adapting it to a new culture and building from the ground up.**

grise of Fidelity, but with one important difference. Twenty years later, Kennedy did not have to go to the shopping mall: the shopping mall came to him.

'Before Christmas 1998, friends were telling me how they would notice all these boxes that would show up at their offices every morning. It was colleagues buying gifts online. You hadn't really heard of this before. Secretaries, executives – they obviously didn't want them to go home, because they didn't want their spouse or kids to see, so purchases were shipped to the office instead. That's what made me realize the power of the internet. The year 1998 was the first e-Christmas.

'But you hadn't seen any of that in Japan. You never see Japanese secretaries on the internet. I knew that that was going to change. Nobody really understood, in Japan, how powerful that was, and how quickly companies are going to change.'

Internet proliferation was one development that Kennedy pursued as likely to lead to profitable investments. That road led him to buy Softbank early. As one technology started to lose its lustre, a new one began to burn brightly.

2. All things cellular

Cellular is one of Kennedy's big themes for Asia: 'The way that Asia's going to adapt to the internet is over cellular phones.'

The superior investment calculus requires digging a little deeper, following the food chain, and trying to spot, ahead of the crowd, which sectors, and which specific companies within sectors, will gain most.

'If you spot a trend, you always try to scratch your head and think, "Who else is going to benefit?" Kyocera produces a lot of parts that go into high-value-added cellular phones. They have subsidiaries in the United States and in Japan. They have a cellular handset business in Japan. They also own a pretty large stake in DDI, which is the CDMA operator in Japan, and that provides the platform to internet access.'

Whichever way the cellular theme plays out, some part of Kyocera should do well.

3. Telecommunication infrastructure

It is not difficult to conclude that another area that will be hot all around Asia is telecommunications. Kennedy wants to own businesses that will facilitate this explosion. So he had a large holding in NTT Docomo, in part because it owns the infrastructure for cellular internet access, and in part because it is by far the leader in cellular. An even bigger holding has been Furukawa Electric.

'They produce WDM [Wide-band Division Multiplexing]. Data traffic in general is going over fibre optic now, because fibre optic is a lot faster. But you have band width constraints. Furukawa produces components that split light into its spectrum. Basically you take a prism and split a beam into every colour of the rainbow. That allows you to open up, in a sense, this wave of light and multiplies the amount of data you can send. Instead of sending one pure wave, it splits the wave open so you can send more data on each wave of light. This is very cost effective, because it allows you to get more out of what you have in the ground. Your sunk cost. Telecommunication companies can dramatically increase the capacity of their existing network to meet demand.'

4. Outsourcing

Here Kennedy isolates a trend that, within this region, originates in Japan, but has implications – overwhelmingly positive – for the whole Pacific Basin.

'Japan is restructuring, which is going to benefit South-East Asia. Japan historically believed that all products should be made in Japan to employ Japanese people. But as the labour force ages and people retire, Japan can downsize, and get rid of expensive production. They're starting to move more to Taiwan, to Korea, and to Singapore, outsourcing to countries with cheaper labour, but, more importantly, places where things can be done on a mass scale.'

The immediate impact is to improve the efficiency and potential profitability of those companies in Japan that lower their cost in this way, and so become more attractive in their own right. 'Mitsubishi Electric outsources a lot of D-RAM production to Powerchip in Taiwan.'

The flip side is companies elsewhere that benefit from this new business.

'Look at some of the foundry companies in Taiwan. Taiwan Semiconductor Manufacturing Company and United Micro Electronics Corporation are the two big ones. 'Their government has provided cheap loans to build infrastructure. They have talented engineers they can hire for a lot less. They've also had the advantage of scale. They've had very large foundries that can lower the average unit cost. If they are producing a chip for one customer that's similar to a chip for somebody else, they've been able to take advantage of using the same equipment and the same fab. The capital cost is spread over multiple products. If you can do that in what is a high-fixed-cost business, you are going to be the cheapest.

'They have had American customers for years and can produce a chip a lot cheaper than in the US or in Europe or, for that matter, Japan. The Japanese are starting to outsource. You can see these trends in the order books at the Taiwanese foundries.'

This trend can stimulate a virtuous chain, enabling investors to predict where and, better yet, who the beneficiaries will be, so pinpointing potentially attractive candidates for investment. Kennedy sees areas, beyond Taiwan, with potential to deliver superior returns as those companies expand.

'Natsteel Electronics is a contract manufacturer in Singapore which produces motherboards. Its customers have been mostly US companies like Apple. Now they're starting to get Japanese orders. They're not only expanding in Singapore, but are moving production to China. And they opened factories in Mexico to assemble the final PC and ship to their US customers.'

Natsteel is covered by the investment community but, in mid-1999, Kennedy was able to look beyond the numbers, because his knowledge of trends in the region gave him a better appreciation of how outsourcing elsewhere should feed through to greater growth than consensus analyst predictions, which led him to anticipate higher earnings than the market was expecting.

'A lot of people were saying, "Hey, Natsteel's pretty expensive. They're only going to increase at a certain rate." Everyone was looking at this industry as driven by US demand, and Natsteel and its competitors as being US customer-centric. But I was comfortable that the sector was going to grow a lot more because, in speaking to companies in Japan such as NEC and Toshiba, I'd understood that they were starting to outsource more to Singapore and Taiwan. Japanese companies would be another source of customers providing the next leg of growth. This type of business can only go to a fairly small group of people, one of which is Natsteel.'

In due course, orders did come through and Natsteel began to beat its forecasts.

To follow the chain to the final link, if contract manufacturers are going to satisfy rising demand, they, in turn, will need to expand and upgrade their facilities, which should feed through to increased demand for certain categories of machinery. Kennedy identifies not only the intermediate beneficiary, but also the second order effect; and the trail loops back to where he started, providing verification of the original analysis and further confirmation of the original rationale behind his decision to own Natsteel.

'The other way to look at the sector is to look at their suppliers, such as Fuji Machine and Matsushita Electric Industrial, which provide chip-mounting machines to contract manufacturers. Their orders were off the charts, so you've got to think that business must be pretty good for these guys down in Singapore. There's almost 360 degrees that you can cover in looking at a company, because there are so many different ways to get information and put the pieces together.'

This all played out in 1999 and 2000 just as Kennedy had anticipated, though with one minor glitch.

'I think the story hasn't changed, but business was so good for contract manufactures that they had problems getting parts. Margins got squeezed.'

Another area of outsourcing is software. India is a thriving centre for this activity and one company caught his eye early on.

'I want to own globally competitive businesses that are going to benefit from global trends. Infosys is into high value-added outsourcing. If a company wants an inventory system installed, they just say, "You do this is project. Our IT department will work with you, they'll provide information. But, at the end of the day, you can do it more effectively and cheaper in India".'

> **I want to own globally competitive businesses that are going to benefit from global trends.**

These companies have performed exceptionally for investors such as Kennedy, who first recommended purchase back in 1994. Individuals will find direct access to domestic Indian equities difficult. A few better-known names are available on overseas markets. Even though the price enjoyed a dramatic rise before its debut on the New York market, the Infosys ADR did very well.

Going global

If there is one overriding theme, it is the search for companies that are actors in the global economy rather than companies whose fortunes are hostage to primarily local concerns. Kennedy sees himself best placed to assess Asian businesses that are international in scope rather than domestic. This point of view has to be correct, and was prominent in his approach even as an analyst back in 1994.

'One of the things that has always directed my research and how I manage money is to find interesting global themes and apply them locally.'

As Kennedy goes shopping for stocks in Asia, he tries to make the most of differing national strengths that he has identified in the 11 Asian countries he covers. By focusing on sectors that play to the strong suit in a given country as an overlay to rigorous analysis, he increases the odds of his chosen company performing well. Which is why his Indian portfolio contains companies markedly different from his Korean holdings.

'In India, I own a few of the software names. These companies are export-oriented, selling mostly to the US. They are so competitive because India graduates more engineers than any other country that speaks English fluently, and a software engineer in India costs about one-tenth the price of a US software engineer.'

Indian investors are best placed to assess a Calcutta-based retailer, but international investors should be able to see more clearly how software companies based in India, but serving a worldwide clientele, deserve to be rated. Kennedy confirms this hypothesis.

'I'll tend to stick to companies that are benefiting from some global trend, and are globally competitive. I don't want to own a company in India just because I feel the economy's turning and we'll get a nice little pop. I'm not going to be able to second-guess the turnaround in the Indian economy.

'A great example is Infosys Technologies, which was a Fidelity holding more or less continuously from late 1994 to early 2000. Almost every software company around the world that you talked to, even back then, had problems finding good people, well trained, that aren't demanding outrageous sums of money. Indian graduates tend to have a very solid background in engineering and mathematics.'

The *prima facie* case for owning Infosys was clear.

'US companies needed to find people to lower their software costs. They go to India because India has a huge pool of talent and it's cheap. Given the change in technology, particularly with the internet, you can have somebody sitting in Bangalore doing your work at a tenth of the cost, and it's almost like they're in the next building.'

Not that his investment decision was driven simply by sitting in his office and concluding one country had a certain comparative advantage. Having decided on an area such as software, Kennedy went to see companies operating in that area in India. He liked what he saw at Infosys.

'I was one of the first foreigners to visit them in Bangalore in 1994. The president was very humble, but dynamic, and a smart individual. He was global in his outlook. Most Indian companies at the time didn't think globally, but here you had a young manager with IT experience who was trying to take advantage of India's inherent competitive energies and bringing them to the global marketplace. I fell in love with the story and consistently recommended it as an analyst and consistently owned Infosys as a fund manager.'

Going global attracted Kennedy to some of the largest blue chips, such as Samsung Electronics, which combined some of the best attributes of what Kennedy wants to see in a business with an undemanding rating.

'Samsung has been one of the most competitive D-RAM makers in the world. They also make cellular handsets – taking something that's a commodity business, D-RAMs, but then looking at other areas to become globally competitive. Labour's relatively cheap in Korea, and you have a lot of talented engineers, so they have benefited not only from a broader technology theme, the use of D-RAM in PCs, but also, more importantly, they've benefited from the cellular trend. They've beaten Micron – in the US – at their own game. And they have been a lot cheaper than Micron, however you look at it, on EV/EBITDA [Enterprise Value divided by Earnings Before Interest, Taxes, Depreciation and Amortization] and on a P/E basis, or price to cash flow.'

The strategy of building upon global strengths within Asia drives the weighting towards countries that have a more open and integrated economy and industries that draw on local competitive advantages to compete globally. Kennedy's filter explains why China has yet to figure in his portfolio.

'I find Chinese companies to be inward looking. Most haven't had to compete in the real world. It's been difficult to find a globally competitive business in China.'

Even in outsourcing, where one might expect China to feature, since the country attracts considerable inward investment for component manufacture.

'There are not many listed companies in China that take advantage of outsourcing. The ones that do are very expensive and very small.'

Kennedy does not dispute China's growing importance, but has found a way to play the China card that he believes should be more rewarding.

'China has very cheap, but skilled, labour. You have a lot of well-educated engineers. The way I played that is through Natsteel Electronics. They're moving production out of Singapore and into China. I'd rather have them do it for me as opposed to me trying to find a company.'

While Kennedy is chary as to the upside in Chinese equities, he is more upbeat about prospects for Hong Kong, which he sees as the back door to China, with better corporate governance and transparency.

'When you think about it, the Chinese don't like foreigners coming in to run their companies. Especially things that have strategic sensitivity, like telecom, airlines and power. China needs foreign expertise and capital. Hong Kong has what China needs. China thinks of Hong Kong as part of its own. I'm convinced that, longer term, it's going to be Hong Kong companies that benefit most.

'The CEO at Hutchinson Whampoa, Li Ka–Shing, is very well connected, and has the most expertise of doing business in China. He has international knowledge of telecommunications through Orange, through investments in wireless in the United States, through investments in Australia and Israel. He's also one of the most shareholder-friendly managers in South-East Asia. He has a lot of cash and expertise in telecoms so, as opportunities in China open up, he could benefit.'

All of which goes to explain why Hutchinson Whampoa has been one of the top holdings at Fidelity Pacific Basin.

Even though direct investment is likely to increase, Kennedy does not perceive this as a threat, but more of a new opportunity.

'More foreign companies will move to Shanghai instead of using Hong Kong as a base, or they'll move right into Guangzhou, but I still think capital's going to go through Hong Kong and through Hong Kong corporates, because of the legal infrastructure and because of the knowledge a lot of Hong Kong companies have about the outside world and about China. It's a good marriage.'

Again, it's that engagement of global competition with local strengths that Kennedy seeks to exploit. So who will benefit most?

'Companies that have international expertise in telecommunications, aviation, and power infrastructure; most importantly, telecommunications.'

In addition to Hutchinson, with its expertise in the telcom field, the list could include Li and Fung, which should be a big beneficiary from the general increase in trade by providing procurement and sourcing expertise with their local knowledge of logistics and subcontractors; or Cathay Pacific, simply through the increase in traffic in and out of China.

Lessons to learn about Asia

Themes are fine, as far as they go, but you still have to do the spadework to pick individual stocks, and it is as a stock picker that Kennedy excels. That, at least, is the verdict of *Smart Money* in its regular annual roundup of the world's top fund managers. Tricks of the trade that he has used to improve performance are:

1. Buy one, get one free

Kennedy identifies companies where ownership in other businesses accounts for most, or even all, of their market capitalization, effectively giving him the core business free. This line of reasoning has proven particularly fertile in Japan, where several such situations found a place in Fidelity portfolios. Kennedy profiled a couple that have worked for him.

'I try to find companies that have an underlying asset that gives support to their valuation. CSK was cheap at one point, if you stripped out its internet assets. Furukawa Electric has a stake in JDS Uniphase,

> # I try to find companies that have an underlying asset that gives support to their valuation.

which is one of its competitors and also a customer in the US. That stake, as of December 1999, was worth more than Furukawa's market cap. So you were buying, at that time, one of the best businesses in the world for nothing.'

Shuttling between Boston and Asia, using his local knowledge and tapping into Fidelity's global network, Kennedy is ideally situated to spot these opportunities.

'I try to look for something that the market isn't fully valuing. Most people in Japan didn't know Furukawa had this asset. You looked at JDS and said, "It's amazing how much this company's worth if you put JDS Uniphase's multiple on the underlying business, after you've stripped out the stake in JDS".'

2. Stay clear of debt-laden balance sheets

Excessive leverage can be a problem anywhere, but in Asia, in particular, it brought down high flyers following the currency crisis in 1997/8. Balance sheets that looked stretched to start with deteriorated dramatically where loans were dollar denominated. Kennedy managed to miss the fallout. Avoiding losses is every bit as important as making gains. This awareness of the perils of too much debt arose, in part, from Kennedy's first encounter with financial markets as he entered an environment in 1990, when the hangover from excessive financial engineering in US markets during the late 1980s came back to haunt over-enthusiastic deal makers.

'I started with Prudential's leveraged buyout group just when the Gulf War started. Oil prices shot through the roof. The economy slowed. I became, in a sense, part of the workout group.'

An experience he has been anxious not to repeat in Asia, which was one of the main reasons he did not recommend popular stocks such as Hyundai Electronics, which has always been heavily leveraged and which is heavily into D-RAMS, a very price sensitive industry. Commodity products where companies are price takers, and balance sheets with too much debt, do not make a good mix. Hyundai Electronics, given its poor balance sheet, was vulnerable to a downturn. When a downturn duly arrived in 2000, Kennedy saved himself and his shareholders a lot of grief by having passed on Hyundai.

3. Back only proven management

This sounds so obvious, but one of the easiest mistakes to make is to get seduced by a story and forget about implementation. The key question always is 'Can the team deliver?' Kennedy learnt this particular lesson the hard way.

'Consolidated Electric Power Asia [CEPA] had independent power projects in China and Indonesia. Asia needed power, and demand was growing. Things looked great. You figure somebody could negotiate with governments, tie up with the right people to facilitate negotiations, put in power plants and that should be a big winner. CEPA was trading at a huge discount to its global peer group on price-to-replacement cost, or enterprise value to EBITDA, or on price to cash flow. No matter how you looked at it, it was cheap. And it seemed a compelling story.

'But the reason why it was cheap and why there can be a fallacy doing global comparisons is that execution risk was very high. Management was weak. They overpromised and underdelivered. Looking at experiences elsewhere in the world, companies had been very successful. American companies went into Latin America and Eastern Europe, put in power plants, executed quickly, and got superior returns. So the mistake was that on paper, CEPA looked great, but it all boils down to execution.'

Which, at CEPA, went AWOL.

'They were a Hong Kong company. They didn't select, in some cases, the right local partner. They often didn't manage relationships with governments that well. So you had problems. And you also had a company that didn't have a heck of a lot of experience building power plants. They built one in China which was successful, so everybody thought they would be able to replicate that, but CEPA weren't able to repeat that success.'

The company was eventually bought by the Southern Company, a US utility, that paid a premium to the then market, but the bid was well below where the price had once been.

4. Stick with companies that practise good corporate governance

Poor profitability has, in the past, been an area of vulnerability for many Asian companies that focused on top-line growth. Less attention was paid lower down the income statement. Reported pre-tax profits were often static, even as sales romped ahead. Little interest was shown in the share price. Multiple share classes and discriminatory voting rights could divorce economic ownership from corporate control. These are negatives for equity investors, especially outsider minority investors.

There have been patches of improvement, and Kennedy has seen equity ownership assume greater importance, though change in outward appearance does not necessarily mean a conversion of Pauline proportions in underlying attitudes.

'Companies in Singapore are talking about return on equity, and managing their capital more effectively, but a lot of that's because the government told them to do so. Take Singapore Technology Engineering, where the major shareholder is the government. The management now measures itself on ROE [Return on Equity] and also uses EVA [Economic Value added Analysis]. Those drivers were put in place by the president, who has firmly grasped the idea that shareholders own the company. Divisional presidents are all measured on their performance against those targets and also are incentivized by options. The number of options they get is a function of how well they do against their targets.'

All good stuff. Once again, Singapore is among Asia's leaders in this, as in other capital-market improvements.

Corporate governance has a direct linkage to the efficiency of financial markets and an indirect impact on values. Asian companies have typically not placed a high priority on corporate governance, but there is a growing acceptance of its role. Kennedy ranks the degree to which countries have started to embrace corporate governance. Australia is in a class of its own. Next comes Hong Kong; after that, Singapore, followed by Japan and Taiwan, though both are a bit more patchy; Korea moving up into tier two; with the rest, India, Indonesia,Malaysia, The Philippines and Thailand, in tier three. However, as Kennedy is at pains to point out, there are specific exceptions, such as Infosys, where disclosure is superior to that at most US companies.

One positive outcome of the 1997/8 crisis was to force corporate governance and concern for shareholder value up the agenda, even in the face of cultures that found the concept alien. Kennedy has seen encouraging signs in Japan and contrasts the more positive response in Korea to the lack of progress in other countries.

'A lot of companies are family run. They disclose the bare minimum that the stock exchange requires. After the Asian crisis, Korean companies changed very quickly. The government came down with a heavy fist and said, "Go bankrupt if you have to". Thailand and Indonesia had greater problems than Korea, but the government didn't want their companies to go bankrupt, and the banking system kept them going. In Korea, a lot of companies had to do rights issues to stay afloat. They needed shareholders to bale them out. Hopefully, with the economy improving, these things won't get thrown out the window.'

This is not a trivial issue. Particularly for European and US investors, who may have less familiarity with the personalities and management, corporate governance can be key to determining whether a particular company is attractive, adding another layer to the analytical process. Kennedy points out both the positive rewards and negative penalties.

'As corporate governance improves, multiples expand. Companies oftentimes are cheap because they have done something to the detriment of minority shareholders in the past. You have to look beyond the numbers and say, "Maybe this company deserves to be cheap". I do think you can make money if investors get more confidence in management. We are starting to see that in Korea. Korea, historically, traded at a big discount to global peers, but, with more corporate governance, you're seeing Korean valuations start to converge.'

Kennedy provides an example of how adoption of greater access to the investment community and improvement in transparency has helped the share price at one Korean company.

'Samsung has gone from being incredibly cheap, by any measure on international comparison, to merely cheap, in part because it has increased disclosure and has started to organize global road shows. It has also improved the quality of its annual report. This seems to be going 50 per cent of the way, but there is still a way to go, particularly in respect of providing details about some private holdings. If Samsung can complete the process, I believe it could become more competitively valued in comparison to international valuation levels.'

The implications are huge, both for companies, because their weighted average cost of capital could come down, and for shareholders, because stock prices should rise. Improved corporate governance can create a virtuous cycle, particularly when a business that has neglected its responsibilities starts to reform.

Investors require a certain comfort level about basic corporate governance and minority protection, as well as an assurance that management places some priority on shareholder value. This is equally true of a US-based investor considering India, or a Hong Kong resident wondering whether to invest in France. The share prices of companies that lead their region in matching international best practice should outperform. One more aspect, if you will, of the search for globally competitive business.

This potpourri of insights from someone who is a veteran of the Asian investment scene at only 32 should help other investors interpret regional opportunities. These, though, are more icing than cake. The key, for Kennedy, lies in trying not to treat the region as odd man out, but as integrated into the world economy. Then you either buy leaders capable of competing globally, with the edge being where local expertise improves their global competitive position, or you invest in companies capable of harnessing global trends to their advantage in their home market. To the extent that the US or Europe is ahead in some aspect of financial market discipline or technical innovation, you look for relative local position. Where Asian companies are in front, or at par, the emphasis shifts to one of relative valuation. A portfolio positioned to outperform in Asia, such as Fidelity Pacific Basin, will contain companies from both categories, and both categories can produce winners.

7

Sam Lau

A young China hand

Hong Kong China Fund outperformed Lipper Asia, Micropal Hong Kong and Hang Seng every year since 1995

Greater China Fund beat the MSCI China Index by over 10 per cent annually since 1995

Won *South China Morning Post* Award in 1999 as first in category over five years

Rated five stars by Standard & Poors

Lau has a rather different perspective on investing, and indeed on life, than most investment professionals. In part, that stems from his early years, which were far removed from capitalism – or anything remotely connected to financial markets.

'I was born in China and came to Hong Kong at the age of 12. In China the economic system was completely different. The structure was basically allocation by the state. When you go to the shops, you don't buy what you want. You ask for what you have been allocated. That was the way.'

Once in Hong Kong, Lau did not take long to make up for what he had been missing.

'One thing that amazed me is how the market works. You go to a supermarket and pick things that you like. And people serve you. That made me think about how the economy works in different kinds of systems and that's when I became interested in economics.'

An interest in economics was but a short step away from an interest in finance. Lau's first exposure came at Sanwa Bank, where he performed company credit analysis. He found this work a worthwhile experience, but incomplete.

'Banking is about trying to reduce risk. Everything else is given. Analyze the balance sheet and cash flow and, if in doubt, ask for collateral. That's how to reduce risk. It's not about increasing return. I found that a bit boring.'

People who find returns more stimulating tend to gravitate to the investment end of the finance spectrum, which is precisely where Lau went next, joining Baring Asset Management in 1993. He has been there ever since.

China: the investment case – a long march …

Lau began in the business at the time when investing in Chinese equities first became feasible. This new cultural revolution was an eye-opening experience on both sides. Investors and management of companies that listed had a lot to learn about each other. Expectations were largely unrealistic, as Lau recalls.

'People made very simple assumptions about China. There were 1.2 billion people and, if each one of them consumed so many cans of Coke, it would mean so much in sales for Coca-Cola. If each person consumes one packet of noodles a day and there are 365 days, then you will have enormous sales of noodles. That's why people were excited about China, but I think this is a bit simplistic, in the sense that such a view has not taken into consideration the potential for competition.'

But, of course, capitalism comes to China was a two-edged sword. And rosy forecasts overlooked the fundamental dynamics of free markets, as Lau was one of the first to observe.

'There is only one Coca-Cola, but there won't be just one drink company in China. There won't be just one noodle company. Also, there are differences in taste across the country, and also different systems and practices. What works in the US or in western countries may not work in China.'

Investing in China has been something of a roller-coaster ride. The right approach for those first few years no longer applies, but it is educational to start at the beginning, since to track the market's evolution requires looking back less than a decade.

In one sense, the early days were easy. Chinese equities were new and exciting. A lot of people wanted a piece of the action and there was not a lot to go round. The correct strategy was to buy everything that moved; or, at least, almost every new issue as it arrived. Which was, in any case, almost the only option open to investors. China itself was still at the first stage of development, with its industry pretty much protected, so where there was a choice the best strategy was to own the leader, because that would be the company reporting the most profit. In reality, buying what was on offer was largely how decisions were made at that stage, akin to the system of state-controlled shops. Initial public offering documents and company visits were among the few ways of introducing an analytical element to the process.

Lau recalls an early encounter with Beiren Printing, a company that manufactured machinery for newspaper production or applying print to packaging material.

'It was very interesting to be able to go into the factories, to visit and to talk to management and get information. Beiren had a huge market share in China, a very good margin, and was growing rapidly. We did buy shares in the company after that visit. It was priced at quite a low valuation. Only a seven times P/E.'

Profits came thick and fast. In the case of Beiren the price tripled in little over a year. This period was almost fish-in-a-barrel time for investors – but the trick was to remember to take profits. Which was where professionals such as Lau scored over the average punter. He did not allow himself to get carried away by all the excitement. Barings banked a good profit across its accounts, selling precisely because the share had been so strong. Not only that, but the climate in China was about to change for the worse. Lau saw a deteriorating environment coming.

'Later on you had the problem of competition from foreign enterprises, as well as increasing competition from imports and other domestic ventures. Beiren had a product they had invented and all their so-called domestic competitors actually were Beiren's offspring. They never really had to compete. They had a dominant position. But with foreigners coming in, they started to feel competition and I don't think, at that time, they were equipped with the knowledge of how to compete.'

Lau timed his exit well; but what was true for Beiren was true elsewhere, which meant the investment climate in China quickly became much more tricky.

... but on a fast road

The economy evolved more rapidly than most people had anticipated. Investors had to reposition portfolios and also become more selective. Lau was one of the first to take on board the need to reappraise and differentiate. In this second phase, he started to select based on positive characteristics he wanted to find in a company and also he identified negative factors that might indicate potential problems.

> # Growth alone was not good enough. Growth had to be profitable.

The first, and perhaps most obvious differentiator, was growth. But upside was everywhere, so growth alone was not good enough. Growth had to be profitable. High margins were best of all. Few businesses combined all three characteristics. Lau went big into Shanghai Dazhong Taxi because it was one of the few that did.

'Shanghai Dazhong owns a fleet of taxis and rents them to drivers. It makes very high margins. They had cash payback within two years. It's highly cash generating and was growing because, at that time, Shanghai's taxi market was far from mature. The base was small, so the scope for growth was enormous.'

What Lau prefers is not a business that takes off like a rocket, since such a trajectory is unlikely to be sustainable. He goes for companies that have identified a growth market and expand from a solid base at a pace consistent with the company and, indeed, management's ability to control growth. In short, conservative growth.

One company that fits his preferred profile is Ng Fung Hong, a food distributor (Hong is Chinese for 'trading company').

'Ng Fung Hong was expanding, but it was very gradual, even sustaining a net cash position.'

Of course conservative growth in a Chinese context can look pretty lively. Ng Fung has been increasing earnings at around 15–20 per cent per annum. It could have expanded even faster, but preferred not to stretch its resources. Management's game plan was longer term, which allows Lau to invest for the long term. In keeping with this philosophy, Lau stays away from one-month wonders.

'So many companies were changing their names to .com, especially in the fourth quarter of 1999 and the first quarter of 2000. There were a lot of speculative buys in the market. But there's no business model, there's no earnings, there's no cash flow in the company, and you would not expect this fund to hold that kind of stock.'

Arguably, he may have missed easy profits, but the pedigree of his portfolio stayed intact and, given a strong performance from the core holdings, why muck around with a winning formula and run unnecessary risks? Lau manages his fund as he would like managers to run the businesses in which he invests.

There is another attribute that Lau learnt to appreciate early in his forays into China and that was rather a rarity in the mid-1990s: management that cared about outside investors and their share price. Shanghai Dazhong had solid shareholder friendly management.

'This management is quite different from state-owned management. They are very innovative, following a new business model. The management set up this company after gaining special approval from Zhu Rongji, who was the Mayor of Shanghai. They own shares themselves. They were one of the first to treat the company as if they were owners as well as managers. They were focused on making a profit, not on scale.'

The China syndrome

Emerging markets appeal to investors looking for exceptional growth, and China is no exception. Inevitably Lau's first focus is on growth and, to attract his interest, a company must have good growth prospects.

'We look at growth of the company: how sustainable is the growth? How strong is the growth? How visible is the growth? How certain is the growth?'

Certainty must include some assurance about the financial condition of the company, because, without a decent balance sheet, growth could be jeopardized. Having assured himself that growth can be expected, Lau then draws on his banking background to confirm that the finances will permit growth to occur. He is a cautious investor.

'We would not buy a company that could be going to go bankrupt. Throughout my investment life we have not bought any company that has gone under, even during the Asian crisis.'

This may sound like back to basics, and, arguably, the problem does not arise to any great extent in mature markets, but in China a lot of companies came to market seeking solutions to financing problems and with a very real risk of failure. Assessing bankruptcy risk was essential.

'We looked at cash flow. We looked at how much they spent and how much they planned to invest. If they had negative cash flow, how did they expect to find sources to fund that? If through debt, for how long could that continue? We also looked at interest cover to check for any immediate risk.'

Guangnan, a food distributor, had negative cash flow when investments were included. Yet all their growth came from these investments, so they needed to continue making acquisitions to show growth. Lau was uncomfortable about their plans for future funding, and he was right to be concerned, since Guangnan went to the wall.

The final area of focus is management. Here Lau has several concerns: the people themselves, but also how they present their company and their attitude to financial markets.

'We look at the management. This is a bit qualitative, but management needs to demonstrate their strategy, vision and also a track record of caring for shareholder value.'

> **Management needs to demonstrate their strategy, vision and also a track record of caring for shareholder value.**

More recently there has been an additional element of risk assessment that has achieved greater prominence in the equation. Following the Asian crisis, Lau now places equal emphasis on currency risk.

'Later on, our criteria also expanded to currency, and how changes would impact the company. We look at the sensitivity of the earnings and the balance sheet to devaluation or depreciation. It's not a very big issue for Hong Kong and Chinese companies, because their currency tends to be much more stable. It's a big issue for Korean and ASEAN companies, because they suffered a lot during the financial crisis.'

Given the focus on growth, the initial issue is whether valuation, relative to the growth potential, is attractive.

'We look at the P/E compared with the earnings growth. If a company is growing at 25 per cent and it is trading on a P/E of six to eight times, that looks very reasonable.'

Or perhaps a less stringent test would suffice, though investors do still expect growth at a discount in China.

Lau then would compare the absolute multiple to those awarded to companies as similar as possible elsewhere in the world to decide whether the relative rating was attractive.

'We also looked at the sectoral global comparison. I remember when we bought China Telecom, which became China Mobile. We were saying it was cheap relative to its counterparts in Asia, and also to its counterparts elsewhere in the world. We looked mainly at Vodafone and NTT Docomo. China Mobile was trading at eight times EV/EBITDA while Vodafone was around 14 times. That's why we were comfortable. Now it is at a slight premium, around 15 times, which is probably deserved, given the growth prospects.'

Equally, just as is best practice elsewhere, the financial criteria vary depending upon the business which is being evaluated. So far, the emerging cellular sector has placed most emphasis on EV/EBITDA. Other industries rely on earnings growth, and that makes up the majority in a Chinese context, while a few turn to asset-based measures.

One country: two sets of valuation criteria

For the individual investor converted by the investment case, there are two separate routes into China: direct investment in Chinese companies, whether through class B shares or via Red Chips quoted in Hong Kong; or indirectly through Hong Kong companies that have the bulk of their business in China.

A little history is again helpful. When China first opened up, everyone was effectively taking part in an experiment. That is a normal pattern for a new market. In the initial stages, no-one really knows what anything is worth. Valuations vary wildly. Usually the first few issues come cheaply. Being able to buy is what counts. That seems to have been true here, and Lau, who had an outsider's perspective coupled with an ability to interpret the business, bought a lot of shares on low valuations. Multiples during this period were low, given the upside on offer.

'Six to eight times was the yardstick for the P/E. Towards the end of 1993, early 1994, they were re-rated to around 20 times, which I thought was more sustainable.'

The rising tide meant that almost everyone who invested did well.

'Basically whatever you bought went up by two or three times.'

Still, few people had been willing to do the work and decide to go in early when the easy profits were there for the asking. Lau was one of the few who recognized that the first Chinese companies to come to market were cheap and should be bought, almost irrespective of the underlying quality.

'The key was really to buy something.'

In the next phase there is lots of excitement. Word gets around. Speculators pile in. Prices tend to run up and markets become overextended. That is usually the best time to take profits. Which is, by and large, what Lau did. He was astute enough to get out of at least some positions when the going was good. In addition to Beiren, he took profits in Maanshan Iron and Steel and Guangzhou Shipyard, all of which looked toppy.

'The key was a disciplined approach and knowing when to sell at the peak.'

Inevitably reality asserts itself. Investors revert to fundamentals. Often businesses do not stand up to scrutiny. In China, that turned out to be true at many of the companies in the first batch of listings. The search for quality growth threw up a depressingly short list.

> **Even though many of the stocks were a story of boom and bust, instability in individual shares does not negate the underlying investment thesis for China.**

Even though many of the stocks were a story of boom and bust, instability in individual shares does not negate the underlying investment thesis for China. Here was the largest market in the world opening up and that should mean massive growth in certain sectors. But once initial optimism disappeared the smart investor needed an alternative to the Shanghai Stock Exchange to benefit from these developments. Lau looked closer to his new home and found another way in.

If most Chinese domestic companies did not meet his criteria for longer-term investment, there was a larger number in Hong Kong that could. Their involvement in activities in China allowed Lau access to its potential, but through companies where he could have greater confidence over issues that concerned him, such as sustainability of growth, balance-sheet strength and the mentality of management.

'In Hong Kong, a lot of companies pass. We always had a very significant weighting in companies like Hutchison and HSBC. Those are companies that have been demonstrating very good management quality, and strong growth in terms of visibility and sustainability.'

Hong Kong has long been seen as the back door to China and, oddly enough, that proposition may never be more true for international equity investors than in 2001. Other cities may be assuming more importance as China opens up to direct investment, but the role of an intermediary is alive and well, as illustrated by the success of Johnson Electric, a core Lau holding. Johnson is quoted in Hong Kong, but the engine room is in Guangdong, and, effectively, all its earnings now come from Chinese operations exporting all over the world, with Hong Kong merely the corporate headquarters.

'Johnson Electric is one of the largest micro-motors producers in the world. These are motors that scroll car windows or kick-start vacuum cleaners. Those kind of applications. Eighty five per cent of their production is now located in China, taking advantage of the low cost of land and labour there. They have been in China for nearly 20 years and had 50 per cent five years ago, but the percentage has been steadily increasing.'

These are the kinds of stocks that allow Lau to enjoy the best of both worlds – the most efficient operating base, combined with all the accounting and governance advantages of a Hong-Kong-based company.

Currency: an ace or a knave?

The Hong Kong dollar may be linked to the US dollar, but Lau still has to contend with currency as a critical added variable in his analysis. In 1997 and 1998 investors received a pointed reminder of the importance of understanding a company's foreign exchange position and the impact exchange rates can have on profits. The volatility was more than anyone had anticipated and had a huge bearing on returns,

Investors should devote considerable time to assessing currency risk before buying a stock.

especially for dollar-, euro- or sterling-based investors. Investors should devote considerable time to assessing currency risk before buying a stock. Lau makes currency one of his key considerations.

Part of the solution is simply to go overweight on the strongest countries and companies.

'Hong Kong and Chinese companies experience less impact, so we went to the strongest in those countries. We invested in the best companies, which should not be affected so much by the currency impact.'

Another answer is to emphasize sectors where the business could gain from the shift or where currency has less of an effect, or at least a limited direct effect because of the nature of the business or its financing structure.

'We went to utility companies like China Light and Power. We went to companies with net cash such as Hong Kong & China Gas. We looked for companies with net foreign income. That's why we bought companies like Li and Fung, which acts as procurement agent for multinationals and retailers such as Marks & Spencer. They also had net cash. We went to exporters like Johnson Electric. They have almost 100 per cent US dollar income. If there is any depreciation or currency devaluation, they are going to benefit, because their cost base in local currency is going to be lower compared to the currencies in which they invoice.'

The point Lau makes rather well is that investors have blown the currency risk out of proportion. While real and intensely damaging for certain companies, astute investors can find ways to protect themselves, and even profit from the problem by selecting companies where a falling currency has a favourable impact.

All change

A challenge for investors in China is the similarity, in one respect, to the environment faced by investors who specialize in technology. Change is pervasive. The pace of change is rapid, the extent of change is profound, and also the direction – and its impact on existing businesses – is not easy to predict. Something that seems safe may not be so.

'In China, industry regulations can change. Go back to 1993/4. There was a shortage of power. To attract investment, the government gave agreements to guarantee a fixed return. Later on, by early 1999, there was surplus power. So the government then asked companies to auction and bid on the price at which they were willing to sell, and the network would only accept the lowest price bidder. The new terms of business were much less favourable.'

Lau returns to an early investment and company he followed thereafter to illustrate the point in a private-sector context.

'When Beiren Printing came to the market it had an operating margin of about 25 per cent. So a lot of people were attracted to the business, but the competitive landscape changed quickly. In two years' time margins became single digit.'

That profitability should have gone south is no surprise, though perhaps the speed with which it collapsed caught investors by surprise. Beiren's story was not a one-off. The pattern was repeated for many companies and across whole industries in equally rapid fashion.

'Another example would be the home-appliances market. When Guangdong Kelon Electrical Holdings came to the market, their return was quite high, with return on equity around 25 per cent and net returns around 15 per cent. But, later on, there were a number of foreign joint ventures like Sharp and Matsushita which built new facilities and, within two or three years, the whole profit picture changed. There was excess capacity. Margins just went. Kelon survived, but a lot of the other domestic manufacturers of home appliances barely made a profit. Shanghai Shangling Electric became loss making two years after it came to the market.'

All of which underscores the need for investors to be nimble and book profits when investing in Chinese equities. The environment can change equally fast for old-economy companies when the competitive landscape is in transition, or if the regulatory regime reverses itself. China has yet to come close to a settled state.

A trader's territory

One has to be careful about generalizations, but the data so far suggests that the right strategy for Chinese stocks is not buy and hold. To make money, investors have to behave more like traders. Turnover of holdings should be higher than in many other equity markets, and timing the market may be as important, maybe even more important, than searching for specific shares that should outperform. Lau has noted the gyrations.

'For Chinese companies, every year there tends to be two or three moves in value, and the key is to try to sell at the peak.'

The performance of the Shanghai B Share Index (*see* Fig. 7.1) shows how an astute trader could have done rather well by moving in and out of the market over the past seven years, having no less than

Figure 7.1 Performance of Shanghai B Index, 1993–2000

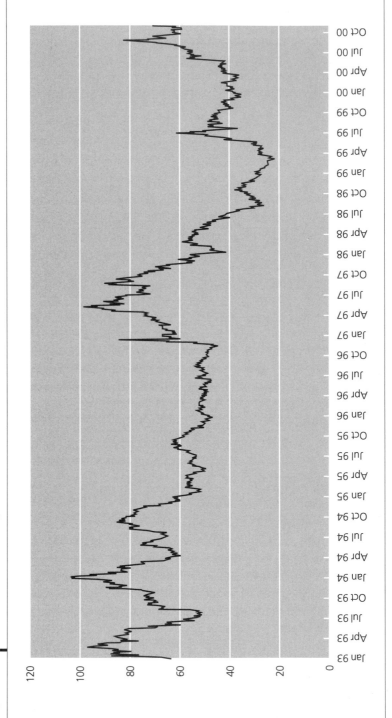

Source: Exshare via FactSet Research Systems.

four opportunities to secure a double, and each within a 12-month window. By contrast, an investor who stayed in and rode out the volatility would have ended 2000 barely above the January 1993 starting point.

So as Lau acknowledges, one way to prosper in Chinese markets is to trade, though there are inherent risks as well as costs in following that script. Trading is not for the timid and requires a strong stomach.

'What you have to do is either to buy when people are saying that it's not the time, or to sell when everyone is jumping in. We bought Yanzhou Coal Mining and Shanghai Petrochemical and Yizheng Chemical, all H shares, when the market was near the bottom and H shares were out of favour. China, as a market, was out of favour because of a number of corporate failures. This was in the early part of 1999. They more or less doubled in less than six months.'

At one level, the insight is to say the Chinese market is a company and treat the index exactly like a stock – which, in one way, it is, though a corporate with chameleon-like qualities. In a sense, you are into index territory, but an index that demands active management.

'What I'm looking at is the valuation. When it becomes very, very cheap – when the world is saying that these stocks are dead, these stocks will never come back – it's probably the time. What we do is look at the absolute valuations and, if we feel comfortable with that, then we buy the stocks.'

But here is where the chameleon confuses. Since China is in a state of turmoil arising from massive structural shifts, you cannot, as is sometimes possible in mature markets, simply play a countrywide cycle. Lau faces a tougher environment.

'In China various fundamentals cause companies to change often. That's why I rarely go back to the same stocks I sold.'

Witness the Beiren and Kelon sagas. Both had their day in the sun, but that happy period did not last long and it is doubtful whether either can ever regain their former position.

So trading may suit some, but not Lau, who is at pains to stress that he disagrees with this attitude on several occasions during our conversations. Early on, when conducting triage among his inherited holdings after appointment as sole manager of his first portfolio, the axe fell selectively.

'I kicked out a lot of the second or third liners which I believed were there for speculative reasons or for trading purposes, rather than for a long-term hold.'

And, again, when describing his approach to management of the portfolio on an ongoing basis.

'Normally we don't trade a lot. We don't participate in spivvy issues.'

Which left Lau to look elsewhere to ensure outperformance within his portfolio.

An investor's alternative

Trading requires a different temperament and the aim of *Investing with Young Guns* is to unearth strategies with durability. Lau has used three filters to weed out the weaker brethren and concentrate on long-term winners. None is revolutionary, but all are of especial relevance in the context of Chinese markets as of 2000.

1. Buy only the best management

'Focus on companies that have proven management ability, or potentially have management ability, or have demonstrated their track record to ride through the cycle. We try to identify the best managed company.'

Characteristics that Lau is looking for in an environment that is exceptionally dynamic are adaptability and flexibility, virtues which have relevance elsewhere, but which assume greater prominence in Chinese companies.

'Management may have to change the strategy. They may have to change their product mix. They often adjust the marketing side of the equation quite quickly to cope with the market and survive.'

Lau cites Kelon, the home appliance manufacturer, as a company whose management has shown an ability to adjust to changing circumstances.

'They cut costs aggressively to respond to competition. Then they did not try to keep prices up. They cut prices to meet competition, and could do this because they had been successful at cost control.'

Given the importance of finding the right people, you would expect Lau to spend a disproportionate amount of time in face-to-face meetings with management – and you would be right.

'Normally I go to see around 20 companies a month, so around 200 a year.'

We did a quick back-of-an-envelope trying to figure out the percentage of his time absorbed by meetings, including preparation. It appears to be about half, which is high, but reflects the relative importance he attaches to people, as opposed to analyzing accounts. Lau explains what he wants to get out of these meetings.

'We try to understand the background of management. What have they been doing in the past? What are their past experiences and track record? If we understand that, it will be easier to understand their future strategy. For example, if someone used to work for Microsoft, we probably would assume that their management would be American style. If someone who has been active in

> ## We try to understand the background of management. If we understand that, it will be easier to understand their future strategy.

investment banking became the financial controller, we might assume that the company would be involved in a lot of corporate deals.'

Background intelligence helps form a picture of the key executives and how their personalities and histories may affect the companies where they now work. Prior experience can also suggest a couple of red flags.

'If investors have been misled in the past by this management, that obviously would be bad. We look at where they were before. We want to know, were they government officers, or are they important people's sons and daughters? We would be careful if the latter, because it may mean they are there because of connections rather than because of ability or experience.'

Potentially, prior experience can be an indicator of management's likely attitude towards investors as well. Knowledge of what they have done in the past is helpful, though it cannot always be conclusive as to how management may approach their new business. Which is one thing Lau really wants to know.

'I always find it interesting to talk with them about their targets. The management's mandate. What are they trying to achieve. Some tell you that, "We want to be number one in the world". I think that's ignoring the shareholders' interests. Some tell you that, "We want to expand capacity by so much … We want to be the biggest." I think these are grand statements, but they are not necessarily profitable for shareholders. They seldom tell you, "I want return on equity of how many per cent". They seldom have that kind of target. But if they care about margins, about the market, about pricing, about the opportunity cost of funds, then, usually, from my experience, those kinds of management tend to do better.'

Here, then, is a key part of Lau's filtering. This sounds fairly simple and, in the sense of identifying the most useful questions to ask, that is so; but arriving at the right judgement is another matter entirely. Deciding how people will behave and whether they are likely to do things to help or damage their share price is hard. Encouragingly, Lau has seen a material change in the nature of conversations he would have had nearly ten years ago and the typical interchange of today – and the movement has, in his view, been mostly positive.

'In general, Chinese managers have become more and more focused on profitability and return to shareholders. You see that from their capital expenditure plans. In 1993 or 1994, when they came to you about financing, they talked about grand plans of expansion, how much of the money they raised would go into capital expenditure, that they would create all this capacity and then would sell it. That's a very optimistic assumption. Nowadays they talk about the return that they could get from additional investment. They have become more cautious in expanding capacity. That's a good sign. Some still lack vision or concern for the shareholders, but others have been changing slowly towards a more entrepreneurial style.'

There are sinners and saints. Zhejiang Expressway, a toll-road company, is one of the saints.

'Zhejiang Expressway came to market in 1996. They have focused on return to shareholders. They do care about how much return they are going to get from additional investment. When they planned new investment into other toll roads in the region, they did calculate the internal rate of return. They did talk about what kind of payback they wanted and compared that with their existing investments. They also compared return with the cost of funds.'

It is not just a case of looking at the type of measures likely to lead to creation of shareholder value. There is also the issue of visibility, a virtue that was in somewhat short supply in the early years, but where things are getting better, as Lau has witnessed at Zhejiang.

'This company has been very transparent in terms of its culture. They tell you traffic expectations so you can track company performance. This is the kind of example that shows management is trying to do its best.'

So far, virtue has not received the right reward, and the performance of Zhejiang's share price has been disappointing, but Lau places blame firmly on the macro environment and changes in market sentiment, absolving the company from any error.

'Overall return in China has been declining, especially on infrastructure, and the multiples people use to value toll roads has been coming down because of assumptions on these kinds of cash flow.'

In addition to learning about the business he is visiting, Lau also uses the conversation to gain useful market intelligence about the industry, especially helpful where official statistics are not always available or current.

'I always welcome the opportunity to meet with management, because not only do you get a feeling of how they see things, you also tend to get more bits and pieces about the industry, and about the economic environment. If you talk to a textile manufacturer, you probably understand the upstream and downstream situation.'

2. Avoid companies that look too good to be true

In an environment that is more wide open than Europe and North America, some managers are tempted to go too far too fast. Lau looks for warning signs that something is not as it appears and was fortunate enough to see beyond the numbers at Guangnan, a red chip listed in Hong Kong which was reporting fantastic results for a time in the late 1990s.

'This company was expanding very aggressively, going into joint ventures to get into the food business in China. They bought a large number, and quite a variety, of businesses from canned food manufacturing to eel farming.'

So far, so fine; but Guangnan's strategy had a peculiar twist to it.

'What they normally did was to ask for a guarantee from the Chinese partners for the first two years. They got a guaranteed profit so they could show a price earnings ratio of a single digit on that acquisition. It seemed that they paid a good price. They've got guaranteed profits. It's certain. It's sure. Things are looking very good. Because of the acquisitions, earnings seemed to be growing very fast.'

All of which looked terrific, as long as investors did not look too closely. Lau was sceptical about the long-term sustainability of their business model, however exciting the near-term earnings over the next year or two.

'I didn't buy any Guangnan, because I had doubts about these investments. It's nice: for two years you've got a profit guarantee – although I still would attach a risk to that guarantee, to the honourability, or credibility of that guarantee. I have more doubts on what would happen after two years. I have doubts on how management can manage all these businesses they acquired in a short period of time and whether they can derive synergies from that.'

His doubts were well founded, since Guangnan was unable to maintain momentum, and the company is currently on the edge of bankruptcy.

'In 1997/8 the company was in trouble, partly by what some observers suspect could turn out to have been management fraud, and partly because it was acquiring companies using debt, so its debt grew to a level that was unmanageable. I think it's now under custody by the banks.'

The contrast to Ng Fung Hong, in a similar business that has done well for Lau, could not be more clear cut.

'I saw two styles of management. One was aggressive and the other conservative.'

The lesson must be do not get seduced by seemingly superior growth without looking underneath to examine what is fuelling that growth. The answer, in the case of Guangnan, could turn out to be something a trifle unorthodox.

3. Treat accounts with caution

While the amount of information available is increasing, there are still concerns over consistency and comparability. Lau sees certain similarities to his home-turf regime, but the differences are more revealing and more relevant to potential investors. There are at last three areas where it is worth drawing a distinction.

'When you ask for gearing ratios, Chinese management gives you total debt over total assets. Here, in Hong Kong, when you ask companies about gearing, normally they give you net debt over shareholders' equity. 'When you ask for margins in China, they tend to give you pre-tax margins. In Hong Kong they tend to give you operating margins.

'When you ask for capital expenditure in China, they only regard new investments as capital expenditure. In Hong Kong and most other places, capital expenditure often includes some maintenance that can be capitalized as well as the new investments.'

These are non-trivial distinctions, so it pays to be clear where you are, particularly before moving on to cross-sector and cross-country comparisons using ratios that must be calculated on the same basis to be meaningful. To take but one relatively obvious point without adjustment, you might conclude gearing is higher in China than is strictly correct if fixed assets are understated, and even more so if there is also a cash balance on the books.

In part these variances stem from tradition, but also there is, understandably, a gap in the knowledge base that makes communication of financials more complicated.

'A lot of them still don't know ROE, and aren't familiar with return on capital. We have to calculate our own numbers.'

Which makes extra work for analysts, who often have to come up with restated versions of reported numbers and may have to recast the financials presented to the public. Investors need to be alert. You may not get exactly the answer to the question you had asked or you may end up with a statistic that is not strictly comparable. In addition, since accounting conventions are not identical, computation of important analytical aids may vary.

> **Analysts often have to come up with restated versions of reported numbers and may have to recast the financials presented to the public.**

This is something that Lau has learnt to come to terms with over the years. Novices accept these discrepancies as part of China's rich and changing fabric, and take comfort from the fact that international investors are no longer pioneers on a foreign frontier.

GLCMV

Lau, along with his colleagues at Baring Asset Management in Hong Kong, has refined a firm-wide approach to portfolio management that rejoices in the acronym of GLCMV. This stands for:

- Growth: in earnings must be sustainable.
- Liquidity: in the balance sheet and also in the stock's trading.
- Currency: exposure and risk profile has to be acceptable.
- Management: which has great significance in a country where connections count.
- Valuation: which must be right in the context of the company and its sector.

To see the approach in action, Lau offers Hutchinson Whompoa as a company that meets all the criteria.

'Financially it is very healthy. Management has been delivering value in the past year, particularly the winning bid for a third generation mobilephone licence. I think mobile phones will be a long-term growth engine. Near-term growth is visible with China recovering, ports recovering and the retail business also recovering. So, as of May 2000, the valuation looks very reasonable.'

Another Hong Kong based business that came through all tests with flying colours is Li and Fung.

'Growth – it has an excellent record. The outsourcing trend will ensure growth. Liquidity, again a net cash position, so no problems here. Currency. They use the US dollar as their base currency, so no risk. Management has delivered and the business model has been excellent. As they add more multinational corporations to outsource, they increase their buying power, which in turn increases their competitive position. Valuation. We went into Li and Fung big time early in 1999, when it was at a 12 times P/E multiple with growth of around 35 per cent.'

As of the end of 2000, its valuation has largely caught up with events, so Lau began taking profits, even though the company still meets all the other criteria.

Lau fits comfortably within an essentially corporate framework and a collegial investment approach. GLCMV ties together several separate strands of his thinking about individual holdings in China, Hong Kong and, indeed, elsewhere in Asia. Once all the analytical bases are covered through this shared methodology, then Lau has an overlay of his own.

One of the insights that emerged from *Investing with the Grand Masters*, a book I wrote in 1997 about Britain's top fund managers, was that nearly all of these successful professionals ran large positions. The top ten holdings in most portfolios would usually amount to 40 per cent or more of the total portfolio and the top 20 usually exceeded 60 per cent. Lau is of like mind. Sadly, he had not read this earlier book, but had arrived at the same conclusion independently. Indeed, one of the first things he did on taking over the Hong Kong China Fund at Baring was to reduce the number of holdings to 35.

'I have the belief that you have to understand a company very well and then you invest. So I like to take concentrated bets. It would be a waste of effort if you study a company, understand a company, and then take a bet of 0.5 per cent or 0.2 per cent. Either go positive or negative. I'm taking bigger bets on individual companies that I have more confidence in.'

Some things are the same, whether you are investing in Asia, Europe or the US.

The barbell theory of portfolio management

A bottoms-up stock picking system has meant Lau is agnostic over issues such as sector weight or industry composition in creating a portfolio. In terms of the new versus old economy debate, he is prepared to recognize virtues in both camps, allowing for the balance that has served him well. Thus the barbell analogy.

Focusing on fundamentals has been central to Lau's style since he started managing money. What has changed since 1995 has been the composition of the portfolio and the types of companies that fit his steadfast parameters.

'One obvious change would be the weighting of property and banks, which used to be a big part of the fund and is now a small part. Industrial and manufacturing companies are getting more weighting, because they've been able to deliver quite well in terms of earnings and return on shareholders' equity.'

That translates to specific companies that he likes in 2000 which, in turn, points the way towards areas of the market that he expects to reward investors in the opening decade of what may turn into China's century.

The first to spring to mind is China Telecom, a clear-cut growth situation about which Lau is extremely enthusiastic.

'An idiot would be able to run this company. You just sit there waiting for subscribers to come and pay money. You count the money, put it in the bank and buy the equipment, install equipment, and go home. It's simple because penetration is so low that growth is going to be enormous, which is what we're seeing. Nowadays the company adds about 800,000 subscribers a month on a base of about 10 million. Eight hundred thousand subscribers is equal to about one operator in Hong Kong. So this company is adding one Hong Kong operator every month.'

Another sector where Lau has placed a relatively large bet in the accounts he manages is in semiconductors, where he likes ASM. This subsidiary of a Dutch company is not a name that features among the top ten holdings at many other funds.

'ASM is a typical cyclical play. We bought at the bottom of the cycle in late 1998 because we believed, even at that time, that the company was undervalued, trading at a low, single-digit P/E. We compared that value with competitors such as Kulicke & Soffa of the US and ASM was priced at around a 50 per cent discount, yet gaining market share.'

Lau is more sanguine about the prospects for the old stalwarts of the Hong Kong market.

'Government policy has changed. No matter how good the developers, if the rules of the game change, you have more uncertainty. The rules have changed to the extent that the property companies are not going to enjoy the margins they used to. On the banking side the same. The environment has become more competitive in Hong Kong and the margin has come down quite a lot. I don't think the kind of return they enjoyed in the past could be repeated.'

A new China for a new century

The macro-economic environment that caused all the original excitement when China first opened up still makes a compelling case for investment in 2001. This extract from the August 2000 report of the Greater China Fund contains several encouraging observations:

The Chinese government remains committed to SOE [State-Owned Enterprise] reform through privatization of state-owned assets, restructuring, and forced closure of inefficient operations. The pace of SOE reform is likely to accelerate, given China's expected WTO [World Trade Organization] entry. More aggressive activities such as mergers and acquisitions, deregulation of protected industries (such as the telecom sector) and introduction of share option schemes can be expected. This will create investment opportunities to equity investors, as such reforms should lead to accelerating industry consolidation in which strong and efficient players will emerge.

There are encouraging signs, with corporate profitability displacing historic priorities of maximizing production at all costs. Industrial consolidation is taking place, and the banking system is being recapitalized through the establishment of asset management companies.

The quality of economic growth is improving. Unlike previous cycles, which have been led mainly by government and SOE-related investment spending, recent growth has been broad based. Demand side factors were the key drivers, including revised domestic consumption and strong trade performance. Overall, the sales/output ratio has been improving, meaning less build-up of unwanted inventories. Higher productivity is also reflected in China's exports to the USA which have taken market share from ASEAN [Association of South-East Asian Nations] countries despite a strong renminbi. These encouraging secular trends are partially the results of restructuring, which is finally bearing fruit. The current recovery is likely to be more than just a cyclical phenomenon and should be more sustainable.

The successful listing of large capitalized stocks like China

Unicom and PetroChina, coupled with the increased China weighting in MSCI [Morgan Stanley Capital International] indices, has helped raise the international profile of China stocks. These are long-term positive measures to improve the liquidity and will lead towards re-rating of China shares.

That said, prior investment experience shows the need for careful interpretation of favourable macro factors. Lau's knowledge of China and his expertise in an area that will grow in importance should make his observations of particular interest to any global investor. His first observation is not the obvious one.

'I think the overall structure of the Chinese economy is changing from a pure export-led economy to a domestic-consumption and services-led economy. Services will be especially important. Services are now less than 20 per cent of Chinese GDP. It's a country of 1.2 billion people, so if you develop that part of the economy, it could become very significant. Services, I think, are 80 per cent of Hong Kong GDP. Probably 70 per cent in the US economy. Twenty per cent for China means one thing: scope for growth. I think that's why Europe and the US are so interested in the WTO. Their interest in WTO is not about exporting their machinery to China. It's about opening banking, insurance, finance or telecom services in China. The WTO is all about services. That part of the economy is going to grow very significantly.'

Lau identifies a couple of companies whose prospects should improve if the WTO implementation proceeds to plan.

'China Mobile will be able to team up with foreign companies and to get expertise from foreign telecom operators. China Everbright currently owns a bank in China. With the opening up of the services industry, they will be able to expand their business more aggressively, in particular if they will be allowed to raise capital overseas. Which means they could increase their market share substantially.'

His second topic is one that covers familiar ground, where transition is already well underway.

'What Asia *is* good at today is manufacturing at a very competitive cost. I think the manufacturing base in China is going to go up the value chain. What do I mean by that? We've seen the outsourcing trend from the US and Europe to this part of the world. The Japanese haven't started yet, because of restructuring. They will need to outsource their manufacturing to Asia. What that

> **I think the manufacturing base in China is going to go up the value chain.**

means is a significant amount of demand for Asian companies. The next question is who is going to benefit most from that kind of demand? Obviously it will be the lowest cost manufacturer in their respective industries.

'Taiwan became a dominant player in the world's PC and electronics market. Korea as well. But low-cost production is now migrating to China and I see that trend continuing, because China is low cost in a number of factors of production: labour, land, materials are cheapest. I believe Taiwan will go up the ladder, in terms of the value chain. China is going to pick up some of the space. Probably, a few years from now, you will see China having a dominant position in electronic component manufacturing or PC manufacturing. Although you may have Taiwanese companies running those operations.'

Chinese companies are already responding to the challenge. Legend is leading the pack.

'Currently they have about 25 per cent of China's PC market. Their market share has been increasing. Two years ago it was only 15 per cent. They are facing competition from Compaq, Apple and IBM, all major vendors, yet were able to establish a brand name in China. One of the reasons was their successful marketing campaign and the other was their production base, which was 100 per cent in China, and very cost competitive.'

So how should an international investor take advantage of these trends? On one level, there are still areas of the economy that are not open.

'China is not going to give away its telecom franchise to foreigners easily. Domestic companies will continue to dominate.'

Here likely winners will include China Telecom, covered earlier. Legend looks to be in the inner circle for reasons mentioned above and, in the world of banking, China Everbright. Outsourcing is likely to see a separate group that may not include so many domestic names.

'What I'm looking at is companies that have expertise in their own industries and good connections with China; that have the ability to access the China market, and the financial resources and product. So what are these companies? Firstly, Hong Kong corporates. Secondly, the Taiwanese manufacturers. They speak the same language, have management expertise, and understand the Chinese mind. Hon Hai makes PCs and connectors for PCs. In semiconductors, it's going to be people like Taiwan Semiconductor, or Charter Semiconductor in Singapore. They provide foundry services. In the area of trading or procurement, it's going to be Li & Fung. In the area of electrical motors, it's going to be Johnson Electric Hong Kong.'

Further down the road, the list of possible beneficiaries could become much larger.

'If China opens up more, a lot of people will benefit. Even banks in Hong Kong will benefit. HSBC and Hang Seng Bank. The market's not open yet, so they are there, in symbolic terms, but not really doing a lot of business, just corporate banking for foreign joint ventures. If allowed, they should be able to wean a lot of human resources from existing banks, because people are paid very poorly. The general manager of the Bank of China is only paid around $200 per month. HSBC should be able to pay ten times that without any problem, and so get the best people.'

And there are other areas for improvement.

'I don't think Chinese banks are competitive enough in customer services, or in their products, or in terms of cost control. Chinese banks don't know how to price products relative to their cost, because they don't really know how much their products cost.'

In spite of obvious benefits to the local economy, Lau suspects it will be at least five years before foreign banks, even Hong-Kong-based, are granted licences for consumer banking. Other aspects of financial services may offer more immediate opportunities.

'Insurance will be another big area. This will be *the* market for global players. AIG, from the US, is doing very well in Shanghai selling life and general insurance. They have well over 3,000 agents already in Shanghai, and are gaining market share. They came from a competitive background. They know marketing tactics, while Chinese insurers, their competitors at the moment, were basically monopolies. They only know how to open a door and wait for people to come, rather than getting out and getting the business.'

So the battle is barely joined, let alone complete, with today's winners possibly eclipsed by names no-one yet knows.

There are other changes in the structure of the economy that Lau believes could be positive for China and its future growth. Although barriers remain to some steps that might promote greater efficiency, he is optimistic about the direction of change.

'Public companies should be privatized. They are not efficiently run. They have conflicting interests. The government is both regulator and operator and, a lot of times, also the judge for any conflicts. If they are privatized, and if the government becomes a regulator instead of an operator, efficiency will be improved. In every industry the government is trying to separate the state from the business. It's a big step for them, and this step is not complete. It takes time.'

Lau believes that this is one of the areas of greatest potential and that Initial Public Offerings are one of the three legs to the Hong Kong China investment story. He recently participated in PetroChina and liked the look of Unicom, the cellular company, and Bank of China.

'IPO activity will provide improved depth to the market. An exciting stream of privatizations is underway.'

Lots of ways to play China, then, coming soon. But not, it seems – though with a small number of exceptions – through buying equity in domestic Chinese companies that are listed and available as of 2000. Which begs the question, 'Why not the most obvious route of all?'

'I think the B-share market has failed. It's not workable. The key difference is regulation. Regulation in terms of participants, in terms of company disclosure and, more importantly, in terms of which companies can list. State planning decides which companies get listed. They give you the company that needs money. What's happening in the western world is investment banks or the market itself are looking out for the candidate that will be liked by the market, and by fund managers, and list them. It's a different structure. I think that's key.'

This drawback does rather complicate the China play for investors, who may see inviting opportunities but not a clear way to purchase a piece of the Chinese dream and profit stream. The only answer for now may well be to rely on professionals like Lau to navigate these tricky waters and unlock the enormous potential that waits to be tapped directly or indirectly. And when the next wave of change comes, Lau will be there to make sure his shareholders participate, intending, as he does, to maintain the pole position he has achieved in China over the last five years.

8

Barbel Lenz

European equities come of age

Rated top of her category for 1997–9 by *Smart Money* – nearly 10 per cent p.a. above the second best fund

Achieved over 35 per cent compound annual rate of return since taking charge of Dresdner RCM Europe in 1996

Received top five-star rating from Morningstar

Consistently outperformed the Dax while running a Germancentric portfolio – by over ten percentage points in some years

Also outperformed the MSCI Europe benchmark in every period

Barbel Lenz has come a long way – literally – since she started in derivatives with Frankfurt-based BHF-BANK in 1989. She still works for a German firm, but now covers equities all across Europe from a San Francisco office, following a spell in New York. This chain of events began with migration into fund management, when her particular expertise was in demand as one plank in a comprehensive investment strategy. Head-hunted into DIT, a subsidiary of Dresdner Bank, Lenz quickly gained a wider brief: initially equities in Germany, then the Scandinavian component of equity portfolios. Ultimately, her remit expanded to include Europe as a region.

A slumbering giant stirs

While the focus here is Germany, what has happened in that country was pretty much mirrored in most of continental Europe, if to differing degrees. The following commentary could apply to France, Italy or Spain, albeit with minor modifications and staggered timing.

Equity investing, as practised on the Continent ten or so years ago, was rather limited, with heavy emphasis on quantitative and structural disciplines for allocation. Lenz had a background in business and finance and studied under Professor Doctor Uhlir, who was an unusual academic in that his speciality was equity derivatives. This gave her a good grounding for a career choice that was considered unusual at the time.

'From the German or European perspective there was a very risk-adverse perception of equities. The interest in equities was very little – totally different to what was going on in the US. My guess is not more than 5 per cent of the population was interested, probably even less. Hardly any of my friends knew anything about mutual funds. Investing in equities was considered risky.'

The performance of shares generally reflected their second-division status. Few people were exposed to equities early in life, Lenz being one of those few. When she began at Dresdner, there was only a handful of investment professionals. Now the bank employs 190 worldwide. The scope of activity has also expanded. Back then, such equity investment as existed was almost exclusively home grown, with an emphasis on big blue chips. Lenz cut her teeth on household names such as Mannesman and Veba. The goal, which was more or less to mirror the market, left little room for individual initiative.

'We had model portfolios based on quantitative analysis which gave guidelines about where to be positioned. Our goal was to outperform both the benchmark and the model portfolio. Having said this, we had a range and couldn't deviate too much. The approach was controlled by staying quite close to the index, trying to over-weight or underweight where we thought stocks might outperform or underperform, but we were not allowed to risk any huge deviation from our benchmarks.'

The restrictive mandate within which decisions had to be taken was, to a degree, mirrored in a limited menu of potential equity investments and the ability of professionals active at the time to venture much beyond basic desktop analysis, was constrained by custom and culture. Research was largely confined to published accounts, which did not always provide the most useful information, and to staged and symbolic Q&A sessions where protocol often prevailed over substance.

'When I started it was hardly possible to visit a company. Management was not open to investors. When you called and asked, "Can we meet you?" they came up with all sorts of excuses and referred to their public releases or conferences. It was difficult to get information on companies. The only sources were newspapers, business magazines and broker reports. There was no way to do the work we are doing now.'

Thoroughly frustrating. And when the first cracks began to appear in the façade, that still did not provide much of an opportunity for out-performance through superior research – an aspect of her present approach on which Lenz places great stress. Listed companies were large, well-known names for the most part. They tended to have tight relationships with the main banks, their primary source of financing. The overall relationship, often involving share ownership, was a higher priority than maximizing returns in the relatively less important invest-ment departments. Analysts could not, therefore, rock the boat. And there was not much of an equity culture in the country at large, so little to no external pressure on cosy arrangements, which had benefits to both sides, but relegated market returns as a less important priority.

Shareholder value German style

Change came not from shareholder pressure, but caught up with companies when they became interested in finding sources of financ-ing beyond bank loans. Once businesses began to explore other avenues, they were embarked on a journey that required greater transparency. Lenz believes the US model was helpful.

'Companies saw that they could use the capital market in different ways and did not need to be dependent on their bank for loans. I think this realization was the first step in becoming more investor-friendly and shareholder-value-friendly.'

All of which led to change both internally and externally. For Lenz, by 1995 ensconced in New York and in charge of a publicly listed closed-end fund, Dresdner-managed Emerging Germany, the key to superior performance lay in identifying companies where top management truly took on board the 'new' philosophy. Paying lip service was not enough. She staked her fund on CEOs who genuinely believed that courting the financial community was the right way to go.

> # The key to superior performance lay in identifying companies where top management truly took on board the 'new' philosophy.

The first challenge was to find right-minded management. One-on-one meetings were now possible, and Lenz took full advantage. The key was how shareholder value would manifest itself. Lenz waited to see talk translate to action. She bought those businesses that began to restructure. Lenz identified four that were among her favourites at the time: Hoechst, the chemicals giant; Hugo Boss, a clothing company; Mannesman, an engineering and machinery company with telecom interests; and the utility Veba. Just the green shoots of restructuring was usually sufficient to spark interest.

'At this point it was unheard of to start to divest non-core businesses and to focus on a core area.'

But longer-term stock price outperformance required more than merely embarking on symbolic divestitures.

'We had to believe in management: that they were able to do this.'

Lenz found the right combination of people and programme at Hoechst in 1995.

'Jürgen Dorman, the CEO, was a great manager. He realized that you can't have multiple divisions in totally different business areas. You have to emphasize a core business. What he set out to do was impressive. The plan was to build up pharmaceuticals and list it as a separate company in 1997. Dorman received an award in 1995 from a business magazine as Manager of the Year because of his commitment to shareholder value and focus on profit over other things. I felt confident that he would be able to execute what he was promising.'

Hoechst demonstrated commitment to the new culture in more ways than one. Restructuring was for real. The company also improved communications with the investment community which, for Lenz, was an important indicator that here was a company she could make a large holding.

'They started at a very early stage to release frequent information about progress in their restructuring. When they sold Uhde, an engineering company, to Thyssen, there was complete disclosure of the details of the transaction. They set up an investors-relations department, which was unique at this time.'

That was the spin side taken care of, and no-one should be under any illusion that spin matters in markets. Performance is only sustainable, however, with substance, and Dorman did well on that dimension.

'The company delivered, getting rid of unprofitable areas and redeploying money raised into core business units to increase profitability. The cosmetics business was the first to be divested. Uhde was the next major operation to be sold. SGL Carbon was listed and some of its shares sold. Capital was invested in pharmaceutical businesses with higher margins.'

Almost regardless of the rights and wrongs, while a restructuring was in full flow, Lenz observed that it was a good time to own a stock, even if earnings in the short term took a knock.

Another encouraging sign was the spread of equity ownership among management. Lenz felt, rightly, that this would make a difference to how the company performed and consequently how the share would perform. Sitting in New York, she understood the impact option programmes could have, so was one of the first to buy shares in continental businesses that were early adopters of stock-related incentive schemes. At SGL Carbon, a Hoechst spin-off, most of these elements came together, which made it a buy.

'I think SGL Carbon was probably the first company that was vocal about stock option plans. On the day of the US listing, Robert Köhler, the CEO, made a speech at the New York Stock Exchange. He was very Anglo-Saxon in his approach. He started to build around technical carbon products, using graphite electrodes as a cash cow to finance investment in niche growth markets of carbon fibre. He restructured business units and incentivized management to focus on their core activity.'

This behaviour was rewarded by the market, which also rewarded Lenz for her insight as one of the first big institutional investors to back SGL.

'Prior to the spin-off, it was a boring division, but SGL Carbon was probably one of the most successful IPOs at this time. Listed at around

DM55 in 1995, by late 1997 the price was approaching DM300. They exceeded expectations for several quarters in a row.'

The mid to late 1990s was a peak period for equity performance as investors started to take notice of what was going on in Germany. The Dax rose 28 per cent in 1996 and 47 per cent in 1997. Increases in certain sectors such as banks and insurance was even larger – which was exactly where Lenz was invested, as she saw a market structure in financial services that was incompatible with the changes taking place at the top of the largest corporations. Incompatibility seemed likely to lead to merger and acquisition activity. Her reasons for anticipating activity were straightforward.

'Europe was over-banked. There were far too many financial companies. There was a need for consolidation.'

The situation was complicated by the cross-holdings in the sector, which she felt should be unwound as part of a process of increasing efficiency and improving return on capital employed.

'Munich Re, Allianz, Dresdner Bank and all large German financials had huge cross-holdings. I think the first important move was when Munich Re merged two of its subsidiaries, Hamburg Mannheimer and DKV, with Victoria Holdings to create a new group, Ergo, which is now Germany's second largest general insurance company with a focus on life and health.'

As earnings visibility improved, the market was able to award higher multiples to companies such as Munich Re, which were leaders in rationalizing their sector. Lenz did well owning that stock in 1997. The price rose 7 per cent on the day of the announcement alone, showing that pioneers were recognized for making the right moves.

> **Nothing suits shareholders of a target company better than a spirited bidding war.**

The flip side also provided opportunities. By owning a number of the names in an area of intense activity, she could win whether her holding was a consolidator or takeover candidate.

'The consolidator and the acquisition target both benefited. The French insurance company, AGF, had a nice run when it attracted interest from other countries. Generali, the Italian insurance company, opened up with the first bid. Then Allianz came in as a white knight and offered a higher price.'

Nothing suits shareholders of a target company better than a spirited bidding war. But spotting an active sector is easier than selecting the right individual holding. So it was sensible for her predecessor portfolio to end 1997 with a 23 per cent concentration in banking. Corporate activity was already underway with a number of names in play, and aggressive companies such as Allianz also attractive. The AGF deal was something of a watershed, as the original offer triggered a spate of takeovers within countries such as France and Italy, and also cross-border. BNP of France, Hypobank of Germany and UBS of Switzerland were all active, doing deals that created shareholder value.

These developments were overdue in the context of global equity markets. It was only in 1993 that Jörg-Matthias Butzloff at Deutsche Bank had asked awkward questions, in public, of Hoechst at the shareholders' meeting. As recently as 1995, Munich Re did not even use the word 'shareholder' in its annual report. Glasnost came late to corporate Germany, but come it did. Following companies once they first began to pay greater attention to shareholder value – either through corporate restructuring, or through introducing a new approach to management motivation, or, better yet, both – worked well for Lenz from 1995 through to 1998. By 2001, however, if the transformation has not run its full course, much of the benefit to shareholders has already been garnered, largely by managers such as Lenz who backed the early wave of converts.

Having ridden the transition, she now believes her only error was not to sell more quickly. In future, when Lenz sees a company deviate from its announced strategy, she knows it is time to exit. Slow to pull the trigger on Hoechst, she regrets the delay.

'It was a big disappointment when Hoechst seemed to make a U-turn. In November 1996, Hoechst announced its intention to combine all its pharma business under the Hoechst Marion Roussel banner. The plan was to raise cash by selling shares in the unit by June 1997. This decision was welcomed in the investment community, since it was a big step in the move to reorganize Hoechst into a holding company and to focus on its most profitable businesses. In March 1997 Hoechst announced disappointing numbers and, at the same time, postponed the listing of its pharma unit, placing the whole restructuring and shareholder value strategy in doubt.

'This deviation was a wake-up call to watch for backtracking at other companies. In 1998 Veba started to disappoint. They came out with a profit warning due to huge start-up costs in their telco business. In addition, they owned a silicon wafer company in the US no-one really knew much about, which lost $161 million totally out of the blue and in contradiction to guidance management had given earlier in the year.'

Having learnt the lesson, Lenz did not hang around when she saw similar symptoms. Out went Veba. Companies stuck in a time warp stay out. Unfavourable competitive conditions or market dynamics count for more than the best efforts of well-intentioned managers. As of early 2001, Lenz avoids the whole automotive sector, other than Porsche, because of concern over over-capacity and the trend towards commodity status as consumers become more price conscious. RWE, the other big German electricity generator, is off limits on the basis that 'They're entrenched businesses being challenged by upstart companies with lower prices.'

No amount of good corporate governance can overcome bad markets, especially when most positive mileage from basic blocking and tackling is behind you. To succeed in the first decade of the twenty-first century, something extra would be essential.

Back to the grassroots

Lenz has access to a unique asset that has helped propel her performance to the forefront of all equity investors, and not just among those whose attention is concentrated on Europe. Dresdner RCM has a division called Grassroots Research. Grassroots is a network of approximately 300 independent researchers in over 35 countries, supplemented by 40,000 industry contacts, which gives Lenz the sort of firepower individual investors can only dream of. The group can unearth the onset of trends before they become readily visible to Wall Street, thus allowing managers to make decisions ahead of competition, and also acts as a reality check when issues arise with existing or potential investments through its proprietary and often unorthodox field research into products and markets.

The genesis of Grassroots Research some 18 years ago is relevant to certain calls Lenz made so successfully in 1999 and 2000.

'During Christmas 1982, personal video games were the rage. Atari, the industry innovator and leader then owned by Warner Communications, was rolling out its latest offering, Pong. The certainty of strong year-end sales for Atari had Wall Street analysts and investment managers convinced there was only one direction for Warner's stock. They were all very wrong. The game was a bust. Atari had to take back inventory or compensate dealers for losses incurred from selling at mark-down. By year-end, Warner's stock had slumped 56 per cent and the following year's second quarter was the company's worst ever.

'Dresdner RCM's portfolio managers reflected on what they had missed. Discussions of their own holiday toy shopping suggested that, if they had only asked salespeople a few simple questions, the lack of consumer interest would have been revealed.'

As a result of this experience, Dresdner started Grassroots Research to obtain information directly from the marketplace.

'This type of face-to-face qualitative research had never been available within the investment community. The response: formalize a new approach and apply a "grassroots overlay" to investment ideas.'

The basic methodology of Grassroots is very much in line with the way Lenz has always wanted to supplement information from brokers with primary research. Grassroots emphasizes direct interviews at the coal face in person or by phone, often developing hundreds, even thousands, of relevant data points to test conventional wisdom through research which is integrated into the stock selection process used by all investment professionals at Dresdner RCM, including Lenz.

Some suggestions originate with Grassroots, but, more often, the request for research comes from portfolio managers. Lenz has used this tool with great success on more than one occasion. It works either way, both for potential purchases and in deciding whether to sell a holding. Insights from Grassroots have helped Lenz stand firm and not follow the crowd into costly errors when sentiment obscured reality.

'Roche Holdings, the Swiss pharmaceutical company, came out with Xenical, an anti-obesity drug. Among the first countries where they launched were Argentina and New Zealand in spring 1998, followed by Europe towards the end of the year. At the start of 1999, the investment industry was convinced that Xenical would be very important, with a market potential of several billion dollars. We had feedback on how this drug was working from doctors and patients. Grassroots found out that the drop-off rate was extremely high. Many people didn't get a second prescription.

'It was not the wonder drug everyone was hoping for. You couldn't just take it and lose weight. You had to be on a strict diet to avoid unpleasant side effects, and also you didn't lose weight quickly. The other big issue was you rarely were able to get reimbursed by insurance. I think it's about $120 a month: a pretty significant amount, if you don't get reimbursed, and if you don't see immediate effect. Grassroots' studies indicated that market expectations were probably too high. We sold our Roche position. In June 2000 Roche lowered revenue guidance for Xenical and its price came off.'

So Lenz was out before the crowd and her portfolio suffered no ill effects. In contrast, she stayed in Nokia and even increased her position on the back of superior market information about consumer anticipation of its data-enabled phone.

'We commissioned reporters to compare Nokia, Ericsson and Motorola, the main handset manufacturers. We learnt, through numerous studies which began in early 1996, that Nokia was gaining share. This caused me to do more work on Nokia, which became one of the largest holdings. And then, once the first Grassroots study was complete, we continued to do follow-up research to stay up to date in terms of "Is Nokia able to continue to gain market share?" and "Can Nokia maintain technological leadership?"'

During the summer of 1999, Nokia's quality was called into question.

'People in our office were complaining. We heard comments that their cell phones didn't work. Grassroots called repair centres and phone dealers to check if a lot of Nokia handsets had been turned in and if there were problems. The answer was "no".

'The second step was to find out what was going on. The situation arose because of migration from analogue to digital in the US. Nokia was producing new handsets when a lot of the infrastructure was still analogue. Phones didn't work in all areas. We heard that some users had two handsets to make sure that they were always covered. So this was a problem that was not Nokia-specific.'

> # Investors who understand end-users have an edge over those who merely read brokers' research.

Lenz held on when others sold, and enjoyed further gains due to using the Grassroots capability to find out facts rather than rush to act on rumour. There is no substitute for firsthand research. Every investor has their own mother-in-law sample. How much better when you have data *en masse*. Instead of analyzing only financials, you can assess whether market expectations are likely to be high or low and act accordingly, going long or short. As Lenz points out, investors who understand end-users have an edge over those who merely read brokers' research.

Getting to grips with what is happening in the marketplace for the product or service remains a priority for Lenz.

'We want to find out what consumers are buy-ing and where trends are going.'

The process works equally well in a corporate environment. Again, she was ahead of the pack getting into SAP in 1996:

'We got positive feedback from Grassroots that SAP had started to penetrate the Enterprise Resource Planning market and was gaining share. They did interviews with purchasers, with companies who had started to implement systems, and with third party companies which installed systems, like Arthur Andersen. That's when I began to buy.'

But she trimmed the holding significantly in late 1998 because of worries about a possible slowdown in ERP demand ahead of Y2K issues and also a change in market perception captured by Grassroots.

'There was frequent monitoring of the technology capabilities of SAP compared to its major competitors. One competitor was beginning to overhaul SAP and gaining share back.'

Lenz booked a healthy gain, missing the whiplash in SAP. By autumn 1999 Lenz was back in again because the outlook for ERP companies became brighter and SAP's share price fully reflected worries about the sector, only to bank another profit early in 2000 when she sold again this time due to concerns over increasing competition. With market intelligence to supplement standard broker fare, this sort of measured trading is possible. Individuals who know a sector intimately can also use that knowledge to make exceptional profits in similar fashion.

The pyramid approach

The overall approach at Dresdner RCM and the approach adopted by Lenz in her portfolios is captured in Fig. 8.1. Idea generation lies at the heart of the process, which is where Grassroots makes an important contribution. The base is raw data. The emphasis Lenz places on detailed and direct research gives her an advantage when it comes to evaluating the data, which is a key input to prioritizing specific stocks. The ranking then comes up against the next tier of tests.

'The most important building blocks for this pyramid are quality and growth. There's not a shortage of idea generation. The key issue is how do we define growth and quality? Our focus is quality of management and the quality of their business plan, market positioning, technology lead, and their ability to sustain market share to sustain earnings growth and any unique franchise.

'Often, if you look for quality and growth, there is a justification for valuation even where companies trade at higher multiples than competitors, if they are in a unique position, if they are market leader, or if they are continuing to gain market share. We are willing to pay up for this and stick with companies where we have the highest convictions

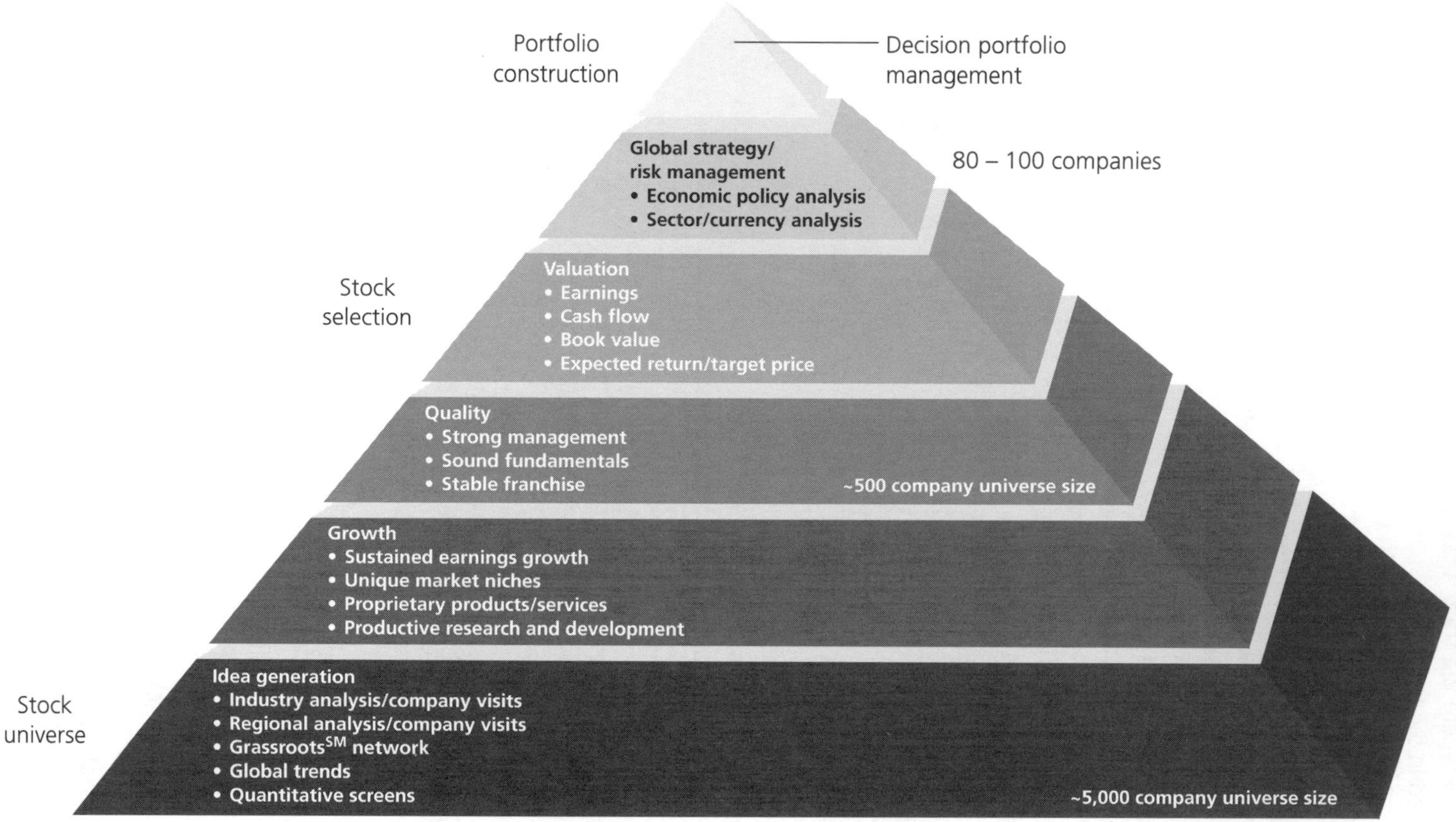

Figure 8.1 The Dresdner investment model *Source:* Copyright © 1997 Dresdner RCM Global Investors LLC, San Francisco, California 94111

and where we think they are able to stay on the growth path they had in the past.'

In short, Lenz places a premium on growth and is willing to pay a premium for growth that is relatively reliable and likely to continue into the future at an above average rate. Some prefer growth at a reasonable price, but Lenz elevates quality growth and is less concerned about the price aspect. Which is why her portfolio is full of the highest quality companies, even if these top tier names are apt to trade on multiples that look full. And also explains why leading-edge technology companies are over-represented. They combine the highest potential growth with a lower likelihood of disappointment. Among her top ten, in the third quarter of 2000, were ST Microelectronics, Ericsson, Vodafone Air Touch, Siemens, Alcatel and, naturally enough, the number one holding was Nokia, which slots right into this model.

'One of the best examples is Nokia, where we have strong views and conviction on management execution. There might be some little clouds right now, since Nokia is not able to produce its CDMA chip sets, and is not clear enough in terms of what they are going to do going forward. But I would say, in terms of execution in the past and in terms of market, or in terms of their sector position, market niche and technology lead, Nokia has proven to be one of the leading companies in this area.'

Lenz elaborates on how Nokia passes all the tests to emerge at the pinnacle of the pyramid.

'The handset market is growing across the world, and subscriber numbers are growing fast. Last year I think there were 275 million telephones produced. The consensus estimate for this year is 450 million. Nokia has about 30 per cent of the market, with a high likelihood that they are going to expand their share again. If you break this down and take the number of handsets Nokia is probably producing, you can come up with a growth rate and an earnings model looking forward from here justifying valuation multiples with a premium to companies like Motorola, Philips and Siemens.'

There comes a point, however, where even the highest quality companies are caught by the final filter in the pyramid, because they get too expensive to own.

'We invested in Sonera, the Finnish telecom service provider, in 1999. I liked its strategy to position the company in cellular, where they were one of the early leaders, and also in other potentially high-margin, high-growth industries. They developed Zed, a mobile global portal, and Smart Trust, a wireless secure-payment system. They were among the first to see the opportunity in global portals, and also to identify m-commerce security as an attractive business.

The price was in the low 20 euros. I felt this was not expensive for the core business and put hardly any value on the new areas. When markets got excited over wireless e-commerce, the shares soared, reaching nearly 100 euros. We started to trim around 80, because, at that price, if you did a sum of the parts valuation, then the market was paying more for Smart Trust than for Verisign, which was a substantial and established competitor. We were completely out by July 2000.'

Valuation is an issue that can never be ignored, however compelling the fundamentals for both the business and its marketplace. Here Sonera swung from undervalued to overvalued and is considered by some analysts as undervalued again after it plummeted all the way back to 20 euros in November 2000. Lenz combines her proprietary research with financial filters, supplemented by a conclusive value overlay at the peak of the pyramid with metrics that would be more or less standard at most leading investment houses. Take her approach to telco candidates.

'It is important to look at numbers like enterprise value to EBITDA or to compare price per subscriber or price per population. With these valuation parameters, we compare companies on a global basis. This helps us to identify stocks that might be overvalued or undervalued.'

However compelling everything else all the way up the pyramid, unless valuation confirms a buy indication, Lenz will not act. And the same dynamics operate on the way down as well.

Parting is such sweet sorrow

Since Lenz will not compromise over quality before opening a new position, it is no surprise to find that the one thing guaranteed to trigger a sale is any sign that her quality standards may be compromised.

'Because there are so many great companies we can own and quality is very important for us, if the quality of a company deteriorates, this is a clear sell signal.'

Quality can come into question along a number of dimensions. If a proprietary product or service edge erodes, or competitive pressures increase, or if barriers to entry in the market start to come down, any of these negative developments could undermine the quality of the earnings stream and its future growth. Even the firm's favourite, Nokia, has been trimmed recently because of concerns over increasing competition in the core handset business emerging from Asia. The final verdict is awaited, but any cloud over quality at least leads Lenz to lighten, if not to sell a position in its entirety.

Baltimore Technology, a UK pioneer in encryption, provides a more clear-cut example of a company that was once a top-ten holding. Lenz grew concerned when its business edge began to blur in 2000.

'All of a sudden there were a couple of other companies where we felt they are equally well positioned in this field, like Verisign and Entrust.'

To check out her concern, Lenz called in Grassroots and got almost more confirmation than she bargained for.

'We found out a lot of companies do their own encryption or their own security, as opposed to using an outside provider like Baltimore.'

The story was not sounding so strong after the results of the research were reviewed. Baltimore peaked at 1480p in March 2000. Lenz was out by the end of April, missing the top, but locking in a gain comfortably in excess of 200 per cent for a six-month hold. By December, Baltimore had sunk to 365p.

There are other reasons to close out a position. Foremost among these is any question over the integrity of the balance sheet; and, specifically, since her main orientation is growth, any doubt about future cash flows. Lenz needs confidence that a

> # Where a great business concept collides with questionable financials, she sides with the financials and sells.

company can fund all steps necessary to generate growth. Where a great business concept collides with questionable financials, she sides with the financials and sells.

'We experienced this with a couple of companies which we thought had great positioning, but were facing higher risk because they had to go back to the market to finance their capital expenditure. We used to own Global Telesystems [GTS]. When we acquired the position, we thought it had a superior strategy, building a fibre-optic network across Europe. But it kept coming back to the investment community to fund expansion. There were three secondary offerings after its initial listing.'

This was the warning signal that led Lenz to reopen her file on GTS. Financial pressures often detract from business quality; as proved to be the case here on further examination.

'We found out that the quality of their network was not entirely as we expected and that's why they were facing difficulties in the market.'

Here she was helped in the decision by networking with other users to validate customer perspective of alternative carriers, and also by talking to the competition. One company that potentially fell into both categories was Colt.

'We found out, by meeting with other companies in the same business like Colt Telecom, that the quality of GTS's network was not great and that Colt had started to build up their own network instead of using the Global Telesystems network.'

GTS also manages to illustrate the third main reason Lenz will rush to unload a stock: when any kind of question mark arises over management.

'Management did not give good guidance on revenue numbers. They never emphasized that they had not hedged their exposure, even with more than 90 per cent of the revenues in Europe, and did not highlight a potential negative translation effect. When the euro weakened against the US dollar GTS got hit by the currency.'

When she decides to sell, Lenz does not agonize over irrelevant issues such as the price she paid. This hang-up frequently interferes with sensible selling and allows dead wood to clutter up a portfolio. If in doubt, sell. Lenz took a loss on part of the position, netting $20 in late 1999, having paid around $25, but that shortfall was small compared to how much she would have lost had she hesitated, since the share price now languishes below $1 and the company defaulted on a bond payment on 15 December 2000.

Lenz works with the relevant internal research analyst to set price targets. She takes a disciplined approach when those targets are reached. Either sell, or justify a new and higher target.

'If we buy a stock we are looking for a certain upside potential. If there is no further catalyst, if we don't expect any valuation extension, then we sell. But often the fundamentals come much stronger than earlier anticipated. Companies surprise on the upside and this triggers a review and revision of the share price target.'

ST Microelectonics shows how her philosophy operates in practice. Dresdner RCM initiated a position in February 1999 at $14.50 (split adjusted price). The share price target, at that time, was $25. In July, STM released their second quarter results. Earnings and revenues came in higher than expected, and the order backlog was substantially larger. Consequently, Lenz revised her price target to $35, based on higher forecasts and strong fundamentals for the semiconductor industry. STM passed the price target again in November 1999. Again Lenz reviewed the file, finding stronger than anticipated industry fundamentals, continued strength in end markets such as wireless

handsets and set-top boxes, improvements in margins and, to reinforce her own analysis, higher guidance from management. So she set
a new target of $50.

When STM broke that barrier, Lenz took another look, but the picture was less conclusive. High expectations for STM were in the
market because of management's guidance, but she saw an earnings
risk because of a slowdown in parts of the end-user market such as
digital consumer electronic products and the car industry. So this time,
in early 2000, Lenz began to trim as the price rose and, for these
same reasons, sold much of her position later in the year.

Europe's next revolution

When it comes to the question of an encore for the next five years,
Lenz places her faith in the continued expansion of technology.

'The reason I am still excited about technology is that, if you take
IT spending as a percentage of GDP in Europe, compared to the US,
it is far lower. We are talking, in Europe, about 6 per cent of GDP for
IT spending compared to about 10 per cent in the US. However,
growth is accelerating in Europe. To catch up would require about
$250 billion of spending each year, which means that IT spending
has to grow about 11 per cent each year for the next five years to
match the same level as we have in the US today. That's why I feel
there is still a lot of potential.'

For her, the only qualification is to find the point of maximum
impact and greatest growth. That is where she will want to be. Lenz
identifies three areas that she believes are already important, but
which should assume greater importance.

1. Compound semiconductors

Lenz likes to find subsectors or niches concealed within a large category
that can be expected to grow at significantly greater rates than the
market as a whole, due to enhanced performance, new technology,
substitution, or some other inherent competitive advantage that should
stimulate change. Semiconductors overall may deliver respectable unit
growth over the next five years, but the market is cyclical, and some
core products are approaching commodity status. Not so compound
semiconductors, where penetration should ensure sustainable and
superior growth for some time.

'Compound semiconductors are different to silicon devices. They
combine different elements of the periodic table, usually gallium

arsenide. Compound semiconductors offer unique properties which can't be matched by traditional silicon.'

This cluster of relatively new products is enjoying exceptional growth due to a number of characteristics that make them superior to traditional silicon.

'They are five to eight times faster. They offer optoelectronic properties. This means they are able to admit and absorb light. They have much higher power efficiency and internal and external performance in the field of light and magnetic field detection. So they can be used for applications like LEDs, solar cells for consumer electronic products and mobile phones, for radio frequencies and for optoelectronic components. These advantages make compound semiconductors an exceptionally fast growing area. And all these applications are enjoying strong secular growth. They are less cyclical than the silicon world.'

The declining cost differential should usher in more opportunities to replace existing silicon-based products.

'They used to be considered a niche market because production costs were significantly higher than silicon. Now they are penetrating large volume applications.'

Explore the reasons for conversion, especially in terms of end-user economics, and you quickly understand why the cost barrier is coming down.

'The state of California started to replace traffic lights with LEDs. They need much less power consumption than regular lights, and also maintenance is lower. LEDs last for at least ten years, whereas regular light bulbs have to be changed all the time.'

Then there are applications related to optoelectronics where compounds are the only game in town. This combination of new markets, replacement in existing markets and end-user product substitution supports the case that usage of compounds should grow very rapidly for several years. The natural next question is which companies are best positioned to benefit? Her favourite name in this sector, as of December 2000, is Aixtron.

'Aixtron is a German company traded on the Neuer Markt that develops and produces equipment for production of compound semiconductors. They are market leader, with a share of over 50 per cent. Aixtron uses metal organic chemical vapour deposition. Their technology is superior to that of Emcore in the US, their closest competitor. Manufacturers using Aixtron machines achieve a higher degree of homogeneity of the individual crystal layers, a clear separation between individual layers, thinner layers, and a higher degree of process accuracy and stability.'

Leadership has been cemented by acquisitions and there are high barriers to entry. All of which translates to strong earnings growth and positive cash flow, even in a capital-intensive industry. A formidable competitor with proprietary technology addressing high-growth end-user markets is the type of package that appeals to Lenz.

Competition is bound to increase as compounds raise their profile and gain a greater share of total semiconductor production, but companies like Aixtron which have emerged as early pace setters are likely to capture and hold investor interest. Clearly an area to watch – though with a wary eye, given rapidly changing conditions.

2. Optical networking

The whole communications field should continue to flourish, but the subsector that is expected to enjoy exceptional expansion is everything to do with optics, fibre-optic networks or related component manufacturers. The particular problem that Lenz sees as most relevant in a European context is network congestion. Old-fashioned existing infrastructure is cumbersome and unable to cope with growth in traffic volume or the changing nature of the traffic. Yesterday's network is a roadblock to the ability of telcos to maximize revenue generation tomorrow. Yet, at the same time, existing problematic infrastructure is extremely expensive to replace.

'Because of the structure of European cities, it is very difficult to lay new fibre. You need technology that increases capacity so that you can send more data and information through what is already there, thus multiplexing the capacity of existing fibre.'

Which is precisely why any process to enhance fibre is likely to be huge, as enhancement of the existing structure is the most logical way forward. Lenz has alighted on another Neuer Markt name that seems perfectly positioned.

'Adva develops, produces and markets systems for fibre-optic technology, mainly dense wavelength division multiplexing (DWDM). This increases transmission capacity of fibre-optic networks and allows them to be intelligently managed by large enterprises or ISPs. There are a number of companies, like Nortel and ONI, also offering this kind of technology, but Adva is offering solutions that have a lead in the short-distance segment, especially for Metropolitan Area Networks. The key advantage is its lowest total cost of network ownership, due to its technological expertise and broad product portfolio.

'Adva has signed distribution agreements with Alcatel, Cisco and Siemens. I think it means a lot when a company like Cisco deals with someone the size of Adva. Cisco had already acquired Qeyton, which was trying to develop a similar solution, but that product was inferior. Cisco signed this distribution agreement to be able to offer a product for its enterprise customers immediately.'

A ringing endorsement, then, for Adva from a source, Cisco, which is second to none and confirms her assessment. Superior solutions to network bottlenecks will be hot for years to come. So far, DWDM seems the best answer and Adva is well placed to exploit the opportunity, though that, too, can alter rapidly.

3. Asset management

The third theme is somewhat of a step change from the previous two. Technology may be the source of greatest growth, but money makes the world go round. The current boom in financial services looks set to continue, not only because of well-recognized demographic trends, but also due to the likely result of recent political initiatives, especially in Europe. The growing realization of the need for alternative pension funding should bring into existence new and larger pools of savings. A more prominent role for private providers, as against government schemes, is also widely accepted.

> **Technology may be the source of greatest growth, but money makes the world go round.**

'We see an ageing population in Europe. Except for the UK, countries have to do something. The German government has started to acknowledge the need to make changes. The population will probably decline by about 15 per cent between now and 2050. This demographic shift will put a strain on the system, because benefits are financed by current tax payers. The government last year proposed comprehensive reform, with the introduction of private pension funds. I think that's a trend we shall see, sooner or later, all across continental Europe. Private and company schemes will become similar to those in the UK and the US, like 401K plans. At some point, everyone has to take care of their own retirement, because the government system is not efficient.'

The impact of moving pension provision from the public to the private sector could be massive, both in terms of those companies involved and the impact on the mix of asset classes. In the front line will be big money managers. Banks will be beneficiaries, among them Dresdner, where Lenz works, which is emphasizing its asset management activities. Important as this is likely to be for her employer, Lenz is looking for smaller pure plays. There the impact should be more dramatic, translating to very high earnings growth over a prolonged period.

Not just the obvious asset gatherers, then, but also those who offer help as well as structured products; or, better yet, both. Lenz has identified one company she thinks should prosper.

'German-based MLP started as an insurance broker, but now offers the whole spectrum of financial services. They package products into tailored solutions for individual customers. MLP uses a wide range of sub-providers. They primarily focus on high-net-worth individuals such as lawyers and physicians. Physicians often have a lot of money, but are not familiar with financial services, and lawyers are in a healthy business.

'Their strategy has extended into the graduate population. MLP goes to universities to introduce their services. As soon as students start a job, MLP helps them with insurance and financing needs. Then, the more experienced and the more wealthy they become, the more products MLP are able to offer, like asset management.'

There should also be side effects from a boom in individual investment. Changes in the pattern of financial services could cause an upsurge in what is generally regarded as a more mature, even cyclical, industry, leading Lenz to highlight the prospects for personal insurance providers such as Ergo.

'About 70 per cent of their business is life and health. Life insurance will be one of the major beneficiaries of pension reform. The current draft of legislation requires that lifelong payments of pensions will be assured.'

Good news, then, for Ergo if the final version contains similar language, as it has the expertise and experience to handle the type of long tail risks which arise with liabilities that last a lifetime. Whatever happens, consumers are reappraising their own requirements, so the sector should expand.

Outside Germany, Lenz points to Julius Baer, a Swiss private bank; Unicredito, an Italian bank that has a high level of fee income from asset management; and Banca Popalare di Verona, also of Italy, a regional bank that is rapidly increasing its exposure to managed savings. These are all organizations that are well positioned to exploit developments in personal pensions leading to more emphasis on building nest eggs. Not everyone in this field is equally well placed. Nor does it follow that every company in the right space will be a good investment. Lenz contrasts Skandia with some of her aforementioned preferences.

'I think it's a great business model, but they have suffered in 2000 because of their high exposure to the US mutual fund market where their funds were heavily slanted towards technology. There was a slowdown in their main sector with the tech connection and also competition is picking up, so the environment is not favourable. With competitors offering products that had a guaranteed return, Skandia lost share.'

4. Mergers and acquisitions: revival or reincarnation?

In addition to highlighting three specific categories of company, Lenz makes an interesting observation about how certain attributes of the technology arena could cause an increase in merger and acquisition activity. M&A, in the past, has largely been driven by two goals. Companies, especially industry consolidators, combined in the belief that they could achieve operating synergies; or deals were done by conglomerates or financial buyers on the lookout for cheap assets, some of which are often restructured and sold on. Investors wishing to benefit from M&A activity through finding the targets of the future should consider a change in focus.

'We all know that there's a shortage of talent. Technology companies face difficulties in hiring enough talented employees to continue their growth. What often happens in this context is that they acquire other companies, first of all for their technology, but also to acquire the people.'

Proprietary intangible assets – perhaps patents or even processes, and, increasingly, skilled employees – are likely to be what attracts the more active acquirers in the decade ahead. Even in sectors such as financial services, assets are now only part of the equation. Top managers have value. Indeed, stars such as Lenz are valuable corporate assets in their own right. Lenz sees US corporates as leading this trend.

'We have seen acquisitions from big US players like Cisco which bought several companies including the optical systems part of Pirelli, the Italian tyre and cable manufacturer, and a number of optical-related businesses, including Cerant, Qeyton and Monterey Networks. Uniphase has also turned to acquisitions, buying E-TEK and SDLI, which are optical component companies.'

These are more traditional transactions, though with an emphasis on technology and future potential. Prices paid reflect strategic rather than short-term financial benefits. Cisco paid Pirelli $2.15 billion in stock to broaden its line of fibre-optic products, so strengthening its challenge to Lucent and Nortel Networks in the fast-growing optical network market.

The natural extension is where companies buy early stage enterprises to capture key people, who may be more important even than intangible assets. Lenz refers to an example of a company that fits this model. Brokat, a German entity develops and markets software for e-business and e-banking. It has been on the acquisition trail specifically to solve a shortage of qualified personnel in this specialized area where demand is exploding but there is a talent deficit. Among recent transactions were MeTechnology, a German company, MyAlert.com, a Spanish start-up, and Fernbach Financial Software, a Luxembourg-based company. These acquisitions brought Brokat good people with scarce expertise.

This trend to buying human resources may generate two-way traffic, with more activity originating in Europe.

'You also see European companies buying US start-up companies, either to gain access to the US market or to get a foothold in their technology. Nokia, for one, has been actively acquiring companies with interesting new technologies and competencies. All acquisitions were designed to enhance Nokia's ability to help create the "mobile information society".'

Among those coming into the Nokia fold were Network Alchemy, which develops infrastructure solutions that advance the use of the internet for secure private communications and commerce, and Ramp Networks, a leading provider of internet security and broadband access for the small office and enterprise remote office. These companies are now part of Nokia Internet Communications, run by Kent Elliott, who himself arrived with an acquisition, Vienna Systems, where he was president and CEO. So Nokia benefited both through acquiring technology and the addition of strong people when it bought that Canadian software company.

For this, and for all the other reasons articulated in this chapter, if you look at Lenz's portfolio in 2005, you are likely to find the concentration on technology intact, though individual positions will almost certainly have changed. Names not even on the radar screen in 2001 will have replaced today's holdings. What will remain the same is the importance Lenz places on growth. Equally, her emphasis on extensive research to identify a company with an inherent advantage – through proprietary technology or a superior business model that should sustain growth – will continue to act as the primary driver to portfolio selection. All of which may be a little easier now that her area of expertise, European equities, has come of age. And with all the changes and an apparent commitment in Europe to catch up with the US in certain high potential areas, maybe Lenz will find herself in the sweet spot. Investors should consider carefully the possibility that the greatest global growth will occur in a revitalized European equity environment over the next five years.

9

Chip Morris

Technology investing is a science, not an art

Returned 1,089 per cent in his 10-year tenure, nearly triple the increase in the S&P 500

Ranked number-one out of 691 equity mutual funds by Lipper through year end 1999

Rated Best Buy by *Forbes*

Awarded five stars by Morningstar

Named by *Money Magazine* as one of the top ten fund managers of the 1990s

Arguably Chip Morris is out of place in a book about the next generation of top investment professionals, since he is already established as one of the world's best fund managers. More than ten years of top-tier performance running T. Rowe Price's flagship Science and Technology Fund has won him accolades at only 37 that most managers never receive in their lifetime.

His barmitzvah stimulated Morris's interest in the investment world. He received cheques adding up to around $1,000. His father suggested that he should save, rather than spend the money, and that he should try to grow his savings by buying shares rather than letting cash just sit in the bank. Between them, they settled on Wendy's International and AH Robbins, picking up 100 shares in each. Morris liked Wendy's hamburger best over other fast food and, due to a cold at the time, he was using a cough syrup manufactured by Robbins. Hardly scientific, but the outcome was eminently satisfactory. Within a year, both shares had doubled in price.

Morris was hooked.

'I thought to myself, "Gosh, what a great job this is. You don't have to do anything and you double your money in a year! Why work, when you can do this?"'

Unlike many students, Morris had a clear sense of where he wanted to be. Finance was his undergraduate major, and then an MBA from Stanford provided his entry ticket into the profession. Even though he made sure to nail down good grades, his focus during college years continued to be on the market.

'I spent a lot of time at Indiana and at Stanford investing what little money I had and looking for companies to invest in. I owned Apple Computer and Centocor, a biotech company which was bought by Eli Lilly in the late 1990s. It never felt like it was truly work.'

A summer job at T. Rowe Price proved a positive experience for both sides. Morris accepted a full-time offer and has been in Baltimore ever since.

His initial apprenticeship was under Roger MacNamee, one of the stars who helped cement T. Rowe Price's reputation as a tier-one player on the US mutual fund scene.

'He was great to work for. Unfortunately, he taught me everything I know, but not everything *he* knows.'

Four years' pupillage and Morris was ready to go to the plate himself when MacNamee moved on in 1991. Following such a successful manager was no easy challenge, especially for a novice. As Morris describes his inheritance:

'I'm the guy who batted clean up after Babe Ruth retired. I was filling such huge shoes that my strategy was to make sure that no-one remembered my name, because I could only be remembered as the guy who messed it up.'

Fortunately Morris hit a few home runs of his own, even in his initial innings, as Science and Technology rose 18.8 per cent in 1992. He has never looked back. A new Babe was born. Now, after a decade in charge, during which he racked up an increase in the fund's Net Asset Value of over 1,000 per cent, and having steered Science and Technology from $150 million under management to over $14 billion, Morris is batting as close to a thousand as any manager can.

He has already won plaudits from the press, his peers, and even competitors. Accolades and awards have come from *Forbes, Money Magazine* and *Technology Investor*, to name just a few. Commenting on Morris's overall record, Paul Wick, manager of Seligman Communications and Information Fund, a firm that has a fine record in this field itself, said, 'He's the best. He has the courage of his convictions.'

The next generation arrived early at T. Rowe Price.

A culture of growth

T. Rowe Price was a good fit for Morris. The firm has its origins in its founder's appetite for buying growth at a reasonable price, a variant of value that was considered revolutionary when initially employed as a stock selection technique. Not for nothing did the *Financial Times* select T. Rowe Price over every other firm to write the chapter on growth in the *Global Guide to Investing*.

'My summer project at T. Rowe Price was the home building industry. After working on that for three months, I was pretty convinced that I didn't want to do anything that was so economically cyclical that the only question you had to answer correctly was: which way interest rates? I wanted something that always grew, no matter what. So that put me in technology.'

Morris fitted right in, but he nearly missed out on the chance to take over Science and Technology because, in the late 1980s, there was scepticism at the firm, and elsewhere in the industry, as to whether technology was a viable sector for fund management companies. Strange as it may seem in 2001, this choice was a contrarian stance when Morris began his career in 1987. What a difference a decade can make!

'The sector had been through such a gut-wrenching two years in the 1983–4 period that hardly anyone wanted to cover technology. It was a disaster. By the summer of 1986, a lot of the large cap hardware companies like Digital Equipment and Data General, Unisys or Sperry Burroughs were rolling over as the personal computer was coming on to the scene. Most people hated technology. It was extremely volatile, you never grew long enough before the company lost its reason to be, and somebody else had a better mousetrap. Then the stock got creamed and never came back.'

How fast and how far have things changed when, a mere 15 years later, technology is *the* place to be, and Science and Technology is one of T. Rowe Price's flagship funds. It would never have reached that position if Morris had not made changes, even in his first year.

Early insights

What worked so well was really not so much what went right as what did not go wrong. Morris had observed closely the stock market demise of DEC and IBM in the late 1980s and learnt the appropriate lessons for a technology investor. The structure of the portfolio was one starting point.

'We had a small cap and mid cap bias. We looked at the large cap stocks of the day which had come through the minicomputer era, and said, "That's yesterday's news". That was one of the key drivers of the early success of the fund, to ignore all these legacy companies whose best times were behind them.'

> # Ignore all these legacy companies whose best times are behind them.

Sometimes it is an advantage to be a relative novice.

'I had no experience with these legacy companies, so I didn't know that you were supposed to own Digital Equipment. I just said, "Who cares? They make big, ugly minicomputers." I think that helped a lot.'

So he was able to avoid the dinosaurs that dragged down the performance of peer group funds.

One rule which served him well from day one was, 'Dying companies almost never come back.'

Selecting the most promising technology companies

Most obligingly, Morris set out his guiding principles in a special supplement for the *All Canadian Mutual Fund Guide* as recently as June 1999. Five factors guide selection at Science and Technology, and each is worthy of more detailed explanation as, in aggregate, they provide a structured understanding of the analytical process employed by Morris.

'There are about 3,000 technology companies. We look at the universe and the first thing we do is try and identify secular themes that drive the technology industry.'

Perhaps of even greater importance to investors is that Morris expects to use these same determinants to winnow out winners from losers for at least the next five years, even if his preferred and by derivation his priority investments are likely to shift. Certain underlying characteristics are constant, and can be used to identify areas and stocks with potential. The most promising technology companies are those that have:

1. Strong intellectual property

This allows them to maintain high profit margins and market share. Morris points to several which pass this test.

'We look at the level of intellectual property. It's hard to put your finger on what that is, but it usually manifests itself in very high gross margins or very high share of market. Microsoft is probably one of the best examples: they have 90 per cent market share in desktop operating systems and 92 per cent gross margins. Texas Instruments would be another, because they dominate the cellular handsets' chip market with a 70 per cent share. EMC have at least half the market for high-end storage and their gross margins are probably in the mid 60s, which is very high for a peripherals company.'

One interesting attribute is the differing valuation that can emerge as a result of corporate transactions. As Morris points out, intellectual property is often worth much more to a large company with resources to exploit its potential right away than to a small, early-stage entrant struggling to create the infrastructure needed for expansion. This variation is particularly pronounced when sectors are fashionable and paper highly priced, though even favourable stock market conditions are no guarantee that the right deals will get done.

'It's very hard to predict M&A activity, because things can make sense, but egos get in the way and managements don't want to sell –

they'd rather build and buy – so we don't really make a lot of investment decisions based upon potential acquisition targets. But, obviously,
we know what's in demand at the moment, and we're never disappointed when somebody we own sells out at a fat premium.'

The insight is that the range of possible values is often greater than
appears from analysis of intellectual rights on a standalone basis.
Acquisitions can accelerate the process of realizing value even more
rapidly in businesses where intangibles are the drivers of future growth.

2. Sustainable business models

Morris looks for companies with the potential to grow between 20
and 30 per cent annually over an extended period of time through a
business cycle. He also wants to see an acceptable level of profitability
consistent with the type of business.

One cluster of companies that illustrates the case is analogue
semiconductors.

'The thing that makes the business model sustainable – that is, prevents competition or prevents other technologies from usurping it – is
that the value drivers are the human capital in the form of analogue
chip designers. There aren't a lot of analogue chip designers coming
out of schools. Most people that major in computer science or chip
design want to build digital processors.

'Analogue chips basically take the outside world and convert it into
digital 1s and 0s, so it allows you to speak into a telephone and have
someone at the other end hear exactly what you said. They do all the
processing between the wires. It's probably among the most sustainable businesses, because you had tons of customers, each accounting
for less than 2 per cent of sales, selling chips that cost between a
buck and five bucks, on average. So there wasn't a lot of individual
value ascribed to the chip. Once you were designed in, you could stay
in that particular product for seven or eight years. You never lost a
customer. You never were designed out. And the whole gating factor
to competition was the number of analogue designers, of which there
weren't that many.'

These sorts of businesses are very powerful and, unlike some technologies, have tremendous staying power, which means investors can
buy without having to worry about watching developments as closely
as is obligatory elsewhere in the sector. Morris amplifies such desirable
characteristics with a study drawn from the service arena.

'The other area where this really comes into play is in data services.
And here we're talking about companies that use technology to provide data services to other companies: credit card processors would be

the foremost example, companies like First Data Corp, which is something we've owned in the fund for a long, long time. They authorize credit card transactions. It's a recurring revenue business model, fairly predictable on a statistical basis. The company's had its ups and downs, but they've never shrunk. They've always grown at between a 10 and 25 per cent rate. The margins have always been very good. And they've always had good visibility on next year's revenue base.

'If you look at that business, these are companies that generate 20 per-cent-plus profit margins and average growth at roughly 15–20 per cent a year over a cycle, some years higher, some years lower.'

3. A major new product cycle

Software is an industry that is constantly reinventing itself, creating a plethora of investment ideas for people such as Morris who keep a finger on the pulse of the sector and can spot what is about to be hot ahead of the market.

'Electronics for Imaging provides software on a board that you put into high-end printers and copiers that allows people to network that copier or printer, which means you don't have to walk down and put something on the copier bed and scan it in and copy – you can just send it from your computer. This is a market that they dominate, but one of the reasons why the stock has fared so well in the last two years is that they had a brand new product cycle in the digital black-and-white copier space. They started out with Canon. I think sales went from scratch to $120 million in 18 months. The other businesses were doing OK, growing at a 10-15 per cent rate, but this extension really turbo-charged growth.

'For better or worse, momentum investing underscores how people look at the technology space. Companies that have strong, new product cycles are more likely to provide upside earning surprises than those that are mired in transition.'

Finding companies that fit here is a result of sweat as much as technology savvy.

'We spend a lot of time visiting companies and attending road shows, and going to investor conferences. It's about kicking the tyres and asking what's

> **Finding companies that fit is a result of sweat as much as technology savvy.**

new, what new products are coming out and when. It can be as simple as knowing a ship-date of a product, or it can be as difficult as trying to anticipate industry or market demand for a particular technology.'

4. Strong management

Analysis of the business cannot be complete without a thorough examination of management. Morris is looking for one that has both a solid vision for the business over the next three to five years and has a history of effective execution.

'Even if you have a good business, you need a solid management team to seize the opportunity.'

Are those the guys who can make it work? Back-testing against previous accomplishments is the most reliable indicator.

'The other thing that we like to see is a past history of executing to a business plan. In these days of rapid-fire initial public offerings, a lot of times we have to go back to the previous employer and ask, "What did they do for them?" It helps to have history. If you know that this person was the sales person at company xyz and xyz mucked up their sales strategy, you have to be a little bit suspect; or this person ran the R&D team for this company and they brought out a lot of good products on time, it usually means that he or she knows what they're doing.

'When there were a number of management changes at Adobe Systems during the late 1990s, I immediately met with the existing Chief Operating Officer, along with the new Chief Financial Officer and new Senior Vice President of products. Since the old CFO and SVP had done a terrible job, new people in those key positions ought to be a positive. It was important to find out what they felt was wrong. I wanted to know how they would change it, and when the impact would be felt. Then it was a matter of closely monitoring new management against their stated objectives.'

What Morris is looking for is not necessarily management that agrees with his view of the world, but management that presents a view of its world that makes sense, that has a credible plan, and appears capable of carrying that plan through.

'We like to see management that has a good vision of what the next three years hold. And it doesn't really have to be a vision that we agree with. It just has to be plausible. We are not locked in. If we ask, "Gee, how do you view the world?" and, if it's different from our own, we don't just walk out and say, "Forget it". We're not as brash as to think that we know a company's business better than they do. We just want management's view to make sense.'

Morris's opinion of management may be the single most important determinant in choosing one counter over another. For technology, as elsewhere, in the trade-off between management and business quality, it is still the quality of business that comes out on top.

'We would rather have a good business with mediocre management than a mediocre business with strong management, because we definitely want to be where the tide is rising the fastest.'

That said, a really classy team of managers can be counted on to come out on top against comparable companies.

'One of the teams that has probably done the best job of any I've seen in the internet is Yahoo. When Yahoo started out, it was one of a handful of search engine companies. They really morphed themselves into an open-access, AOL-like platform. I give management a heck of a lot of credit. They've really done the most with the least in the shortest amount of time I've ever seen. That's one where, if you believe in the industry, they were the appropriate management to bet on. Clear leadership of that category.'

But, in technology, there is an additional consideration that makes the answer more clouded.

'I guess it's very tough to know the difference between market evolution and companies just being there at the right time versus companies where management has really done something.'

After all the analysis, where there is residual uncertainty about which individual stock is best but the space is hot, the best answer for a port-folio manager may well be to buy the entire sector. Which is what Morris did for the three main players – Maxin Integrated Products, Linear Technology and Analog Devices. Here he found an example of a niche with a powerful, sustainable business model. If in doubt about the likely winner, buy 5 per cent of each. Not, perhaps, an option for an average investor, but the solution, if on a smaller scale, has merit in days of *de minimus* dealing costs.

5. Attractive valuations

This last sounds simple but is hard to put into practice. How do you decide if a technology stock is attractive? This is where difficulties really begin, because traditional techniques, by and large, do not work.

One method that still seems valid and seems to have weathered the transition from an old-economy context is to adopt a contrarian stance. As long as the underlying technology retains validity, it has value, so, if other factors depress a stock, that can be a good time to get in. Morris cites America Online (AOL) as one which worked for him.

'We were fairly early investors in AOL. Especially in 1996, when they were having all sorts of problems with people not being able to get access and calling their State Attorney General and threatening to sue. We just looked at this rather simply and said, "They have 70 per cent share of consumer internet access. That's got to be worth something. It's probably going to be worth a heck of a lot more than it is today." The stock had at least halved, and we made our initial purchases at that time. Not a very high gross margin, but a huge share of market and very strong intellectual property.'

Beyond that, current conditions present a challenge to traditional valuation levels and measures alike, as Morris openly acknowledges.

'Valuation is a real tricky one in today's market, because valuations are so high. You've really been penalized for looking at valuations. Historically, in technology, as in other sectors of the market, there has been a reversion towards the mean, where investors would ultimately sell expensive merchandise and buy cheaper merchandise; but there's been a diversion towards extremes over the last two years, and people have actually sold cheaper merchandise to buy more expensive merchandise, and so our valuation bias and adherence to some valuation discipline has probably served us poorly in the last 18 months.'

While recognizing the distortion, Morris has no intention of abandoning a discipline that had served him well for a lot longer than 18 months. What he did do was adopt, on an interim basis, alternative tools.

Valuing the unvaluable

How does one of the most successful professionals deal with an era that defies the textbook?

'If you're smart, you ignore traditional valuation techniques.'

Arguably, anyone attempting to apply any kind of rational valuation has been penalized during much of 1999 and the first part of 2000. Momentum took over from valuation metrics, in large part due to the rush of retail investors who prefer action to contemplation.

'All the financial analysis I learnt has really become a burden in the last 18 months. So I have often, tongue in cheek, thought that maybe I'd write to Stanford and ask for my money back, because obviously what they taught me hasn't been working.'

> # All the financial analysis I learnt has really become a burden in the last 18 months.

But investing in a vacuum is extremely uncomfortable. Suck it and see what happens hardly seems like an adequate substitute for EV/EBITDA or P/E ratios. While most floundered, Morris came up with a concept which, if not the Rosetta stone to internet investment, at least provides a benchmark for comparative valuation across companies that often have minimal tangible assets and negative earnings.

'There's got to be a fundamental underpinning for stock prices. They're grounded in reality, ultimately, and our attempt at valuing internet companies addressed the heart of what we thought was a sort of conspiracy by bankers, managements and Wall Street to convince people to value things on the basis of revenues only; without any regard to how profitable the revenue stream might be, or how risky, and volatile, that revenue stream may be. Our approach was to say, "You tell me this thing's worth 20 times sales, and we say, 'No way to that', because we're going to take that price to sales multiple of 20 and, for a company that only does 15 per cent net margin, you're asking us to pay 150 times earnings if it were at full profitability level, which it's not. What we're telling you is no-one in their right mind would pay 150 times for this company".'

Morris's response is the Practical P/E Ratio, a four-part process that individuals can replicate in the safety of their own homes. The example in Fig. 9.1, based on Amazon's most recent available public information, shows how four relatively simple steps produce the Practical P/E Ratio. If 7 per cent is a good ballpark estimate, then investors are able

Figure 9.1 | Illustrative calculation of a Practical P/E

The steps	The maths
Find the company's current market value – the number of shares outstanding times the price per share	356 million × $14* = $5.0 billion
Multiply the most recent quarter's sale by four to find a current annual 'run rate'	$638 million × 4 = $2.6 billion
Divide the market value by the annual run rate to get a price-to-sales multiple	$5.0 billion ÷ $2.6 billion = 1.9
Divide this by your estimate of the biggest net profit margin the company may enjoy, say 7%	1.9 ÷ 7% = 27
Were Amazon.com profitable now, its 'Practical P/E' would be 27× (based on the quarter ending September 2000)	

* as of January 2001

to evaluate the stock based on a prospective 27× earnings multiple to decide whether it is attractive or expensive. Of course computation is the easy part, and the ratio itself can be no more than one input into a very complex decision process. But when you are in a valuation swamp, every island of dry land is welcome. Morris describes how Practical P/Es fit into his stock-picking framework.

'What you're doing is converting companies that are promising profits and saying this is going to compute your future promises into current profitability. That takes a lot of the mystery out of it.'

Transforming data into new formats should not encourage investors to give up on the accumulated wisdom of the past 30 years. Many virtual corporations trading today at stratospheric valuations will metamorphose into recognizable companies that will then be capable of being valued using more objective benchmarks. Morris elaborates on how he decides whether established growth companies are trading at attractive values.

'Price to earnings is the primary valuation driver; then enterprise value to cash flow; with price to revenues as a backdrop. I don't really pay a lot of attention to book value, or dividend yield, because, a lot of times, companies take one-time charges that wipe out book value for acquisitions or restructurings, and rarely is there any substantial dividend.'

So, in due course, technology investors should be able to revert to a more familiar analytical landscape. For now, excitement is found elsewhere.

'You can still calculate those multiples today, but they're more a residual. People today are buying purely at price momentum. If a company trades at a 50 P/E or a 20 P/E or a 100 P/E – that's the residual of what happens when you take a stock price and divide by earnings. No-one has looked at that saying this is *worth* a 100 times or 50 times earnings. Where the fundamentals of this sector are very good and there's global growth and not much else is working, in terms of other sectors of the investable economy, people pile more and more money into the tech base, which takes valuations higher and higher.'

As of 2000, the specific areas Morris highlights as hot, and which filter through his five screens, include:

- the build out of corporate internet infrastructure
- broadband networking
- the proliferation of digital wireless communications
- outsourcing.

Enjoy the boom but plan for the bust

Morris is sanguine about the current climate, accepting that this is
how his patch behaves for now, but looking ahead, he positions
Science and Technology to minimize the impact of any fallout.

'At some point, we all have to pay the piper. But the big question
is, "Is it today, next week, next month, next year, in three years ...?"
Don't spend a lot of time thinking about it, other than that we know
that the environment we are in right now is unsustainable. It just is.
It's too crazy to last.'

A lot of pundits agree. And between the time of our initial interview and the publication of this book, much of the froth did, indeed,
evaporate in short order, as Morris had predicted. In technology, the
issue of overvaluation is not so much subsector as stock-specific.
Obsolescence strikes in ways that are hard to predict, and the drivers
of longer-term market position are less obvious, so picking winners is
that much tougher. Morris underscores the validity of this observation
throughout the sector.

'What's most interesting is that Digital Equipment was not the first
minicomputer vendor to arrive on the scene. Dell was not the first
personal computer company to arrive on the scene. For years, people
thought Lotus would eat Microsoft's lunch, because there was no
value in operating systems. When Sybase came public, it was thought
to be the heir apparent to the database kingdom. SAP came out of
nowhere to steal the applications business from domestic players.
Nokia was long thought of as a middle-tier handset manufacturer of
no great importance until it drove to leadership status in that marketplace within a period of two years. There have been such huge,
monstrous market shifts that people forget that it's not that obvious
who the kings are, unless you look at it retrospectively.'

Even so, Morris still keeps the faith. Opportunities exist and the key
is to stay alert to emerging new companies. Take the internet stock
valuation oxymoron that manages to confuse most investors.

'We continue to believe that the market value opportunity presented
by the internet is much greater than the sum of the market caps of the
public companies that play today, but we're not sure if the market capitalization of any one company, today, is justified by the market
opportunity for that company.'

For now, the biggest problem in dealing with apparent overvaluation is not on the buy side, but on the sell side.

'The errors we made were taking profits too quickly. We were a
victim of our own success. You buy something at 50 and, 17 trading

days later, it's 120. We're motivated to sell. That same stock could be at 250 today. So we leave a lot on the table.'

Sell some, but let profits run is one dictum that does carry across from traditional growth investing. Indeed, this time-tested homily has never been more true – nor more difficult to adhere to.

You also have to factor in activity in a stock, since sentiment can shift rapidly, as can reality. Investors have to be fleet of foot if they are into technology. Even the best professionals have problems, as Morris acknowledges.

'If we would find out that a stock we owned 8 per cent of was going to miss its numbers we couldn't get out in time. We'd sell 20 per cent of our position and then we'd take a full hit on the other 80 per cent.'

The compressed window of opportunity creates a handicap, but does not necessarily mean that the right course of action is to increase turnover. Day trading is not what Morris has in mind when he extols the virtues of liquidity, which is another lesson he learnt the hard way. Describing a period of high turnover in 1998, he observed:

'We could have held basically everything that we bought and sold several times during those 18 months and would have been better off if we had just stuck it out.'

That may be so, but staying put requires constant monitoring and a strong stomach, especially since, in technology, it is absolutely essential to prune losers.

> It's very important, in the technology game, always to keep a portfolio fresh and full of new companies in the most vibrant areas.

'It's very important, in the technology game, always to keep a portfolio fresh and full of new companies in the most vibrant areas. Look at our portfolio and you won't find a lot of yesterday's news. We get out of companies that were heroes of the last technology cycle or that have fallen on hard times, or are mucking through a very ugly company-specific transition, or where the end market that they play in has slowed quite a bit.'

The structure of science and technology

The honest manager must admit that no-one really knows for sure which will be the *big* winners or losers – and there are plenty of both. The rewards for getting it right are highest in technology. Equally, a bad selection may produce a serious wound, not a scratch, if the position is too large. One or two sector funds achieved exceptional numbers, especially in 1999, by making huge bets. But that is precisely what they were. Bets. Great, if you can afford to lose, or do not care about investors, but are only focused on a one-off chance to take home a massive bonus.

Morris has different motivation. He is concerned about shareholders whose pension plans and future retirement payments depend upon his performance. Capital preservation ranks alongside capital appreciation as an important objective.

'T. Rowe Price, as an organization, wants to be in a position to make good on our promise of investing the way people expect, without taking undue risk. And the last thing we want to do is have 80 per cent of the portfolio doing really well, and then 20 per cent get wiped out because we own two very large positions that, for whatever reason, got damaged. We try and keep positions less than 4 per cent of assets but we like to have anywhere between around 60 names, plus or minus 15, in the portfolio. The average position size is about 1.5 per cent. We don't make big sector bets. It's all pretty balanced.'

His current portfolio reflects dual aims and it shows in the structure. Nothing over 5 per cent. Concentration is relatively low, too. The top ten usually add up to around 35 per cent, a level Morris finds comfortable. Technology is not a sleep-well sector, so diversification, to a degree, ameliorates risk. This may mean Morris will not appear in the top five performers in any one year, but you will see him right up at the top in the five- and ten-year tables. His worst performance was 1.7 per cent in 1997, while his best, in 1999, was an increase of over 100 per cent. It is the result over time that matters. If you compound at over 30 per cent p.a. for more than a decade, everyone is a winner.

Balance is not just an arbitrary preference. The year 1997 was a year that hurt, in large part due to weightings that got out of whack and to three stock-specific situations – sadly large holdings – which went wrong and were linked to the problem sector. Morris is determined not to repeat that error.

'The fund, historically, had emphasized small- and mid-cap companies and had emphasized companies in two segments: software and communications. Both of those sectors underperformed the overall industry and large caps beat the pants off small- and mid caps.

'Two stocks received bids, ironically both from Cisco, and turned them down, and one also received a bid, we believe from Compaq, but turned around and made an acquisition itself in order to stay independent. If these management teams had just decided to cash in, instead of going it alone, the year might have had a different outcome.

'Shiva made a box that allowed you to access your work computer from your home: one of the first remote access devices. Its stock had been at $70, but went to $50. It received a generous offer. Management wanted more. It eventually got bought by Intel for, like, 10 bucks. Anyway, if management had just said, "You know what? That offer from Cisco is pretty good", Shiva's share would probably be worth $300 in Cisco stock, because Cisco's more than quadrupled since then.'

Leaving on one side the lesson that ended any interest in excessively large stock positions Morris's preferred themes mandate a degree of concentration in favoured sectors.

'If you look at how we position the fund now, software, semiconductors and communications are the three linchpins.'

One aspect of the fund which, at first blush comes as a surprise, is how little was outside the US, in Q2 2000.

'Foreign companies comprise about 17 per cent. We have about a 3 per cent position in Nokia, a 4 per cent position in what will be the combined Vodaphone Mannesmann, and almost a 2 per cent position in Softbank, a Japanese internet company, and Ericsson.'

Yet it is easy to understand Morris's stance.

'With Silicon Valley and what's going on in Boston and down in Austin, you haven't had to venture overseas to look for good investment ideas. And, for the longest time, the personal computer industry, at least in the era of client servers, was dominated by US companies. You haven't had to stray.'

He does see certain exceptions that suggest areas of expertise where international investors should concentrate their search for non-US gems.

'If you look at wireless, Europe definitely dominates. In semiconductor manufacturing, Asia dominates. So the US's role in some technologies is probably receding.'

Or, then again, maybe not, because valuations matter everywhere, at the end of the day, and, with a shortage of local product, technology stocks outside the US have not only caught up but, in many cases, gone beyond multiples for US competitors.

'We are now at a point where the valuations on the foreign companies are actually much higher than they are in the US, for the most part. SAP is much more expensive than Oracle on a price-to-growth basis. Ericsson and Nokia are more expensive than Motorola.'

That said, Morris expects the number of attractive non-US opportunities to rise, with significant new technologies such as wireless assuming more prominence, and believes that his international weighting is likely to be higher one year from now compared to the current portfolio composition. In anticipation of an evolution in emphasis, T. Rowe Price recently launched a Global Technology Fund to exploit innovations occurring outside the US. Needless to say, Morris will be at the helm.

Devolution, evolution or revolution? A century of change in a decade

Harking back to the early days when the technology sector was in its infancy, there are a mere eight stocks surviving from 1990 in the portfolio of 2000. Even so, Morris believes his strategy has not changed significantly. What has changed most is that he has to concentrate on big caps, as a small cap position is not meaningful to a $12 billion fund.

The other differences result from externalities. The environment for technology managers has become extremely competitive, with many more involved and all looking for an edge, at a time when management at investee companies is less accessible and often reluctant to disclose anything useful for fear of regulatory criticism or law suits.

'Because of legal issues and full disclosure mandates by the SEC and the conference calls after every quarter, things get disseminated pretty broadly, and it's the rare exception for a company with strong momentum that you can really gain a ton of insights.'

Such a climate makes his job harder. So how is a manager to beat the crowd? Try and stay off the well trodden paths, for starters.

'Most of the companies that will talk are going to be the ones where no-one has shown up in a while. And that won't be that they would not tell anyone else, but it's the fact that you're there and no-one else has been for six months that's your real advantage.'

The other big change is in the importance of technology, now 30 per cent of the S&P, compared to less than 10 per cent back then, and 15 per cent of most mature foreign exchanges as against a minimal percentage in 1990.

The effect shows up everywhere, not just in financial markets, but in capital investment, personal income and major economic indicators. Technology is, in the view of many commentators, the main driver of global progress. Investors have to be part of the key trend, or suffer. Many have taken the message on board.

The increasing power of the retail investor has also changed the game, at least in technology. Morris recognizes their impact.

Technology is the main driver of global progress. Investors have to be part of the key trend, or suffer.

'You are, perhaps, dealing with a less informed, less educated technology investor, and what is happening is that first, they would always get burned, but now there are so many of them, and they dominate the trading of a number of stocks that they have reset the ground rules.'

So much for the past and the present.

Secular themes for the future

As someone who lives, breathes and occasionally sleeps technology stocks, Morris is well placed to see, in advance, trends of importance that are likely to attract the market's attention. Stocks in these sectors, all other things being equal, should trade at higher multiples than those not in the sweet spot. Morris has identified several he expects to shape his portfolio selection over the next three to five years, and which serve as supplements to his five main themes explained earlier.

1. Retooling of information architecture

For the most part retooling involves the transition from a client/server model to a web-based model. This transition is playing out along separate lines for corporates and consumers. As the impact is immense it represents his most significant theme.

'It means less processing power on the desktop, and more power in back-end servers. It also means that you don't necessarily have to be resident at your desk to access your applications. It really means Oracle running on Sun, stored by EMC, and routed by Cisco. There are competitors, but generally those four are retooling corporate IT. On the consumer side, it's all about access, both wireless and broadband wire line. It means fatter pipes to homes, and mobility.'

2. Wireless data access

Here the answer is murkier and the outcome may be different for America as against Europe and with minor variation as against Asia as well.

'I think Europe is a little bit more advanced than the States in wireless access, and is a little bit less PC-centric, so it's probably going to be different. I have a hard time thinking someone's going to stare into a 1-inch by 2-inch display on their phone and do a whole lot on the internet. You want to check a stock quote? OK. You want to get weather? Go outside. Or you can check your phone. But, in a lot of respects, we have to wait for new form factors and third-generation digital technology to see the promise of wireless internet access.'

3. Outsourcing

Nothing new here, rather a continuation of a 1990s trend, though potentially with acceleration in certain areas where outsourcing has not been so pronounced in the past. Morris highlights three areas of special interest in the context of technology investing.

'Manufacturers deciding to subcontract their manufacturing; or companies deciding to run applications in a remote fashion, in the old time-sharing fashion. The use of consulting firms and systems integrators to help applications get up and running has been a theme that has been playing out for the last eight years, and is going to continue. We still see increased outsourcing of all types. It's really just a specialization of companies doing what they do that generates profit margins as best they can, leaving all the other stuff that's tertiary to their business.'

4. Upgrade of semiconductor capital equipment

Where Morris expects most activity is in semiconductor manufacture and the greatest impact is likely over the next couple of years.

'Right now, you've got the size of a chip, which is 8 inches, and they're going to move to 12-inch size wafers and, when you do that, you need to upgrade most of your production equipment. And that means that there's a bubble of demand in the 2002 and 2003 period. Semiconductor equipment manufacturers of all types will benefit. Applied Materials spans the gamut. Companies like KLA Instruments and ASM Lithography should also be among the beneficiaries.'

5. Entertainment and information convergence

Looking even further out, Morris is already anticipating the next big trend where he expects investments will arise to the advantage of T. Rowe Price shareholders. To explain what he sees ahead, he sets the next leap forward in its historical perspective.

'If we think back to the personal computer era, the reason people bought faster processors in the old days was to stop the Lotus 123 red calc light from flashing. For anyone that's an old PC user, you would hit the calc button and it would seem minutes before it would calculate. The process was mind-numbingly slow. People wanted to upgrade just to get rid of that flash. The next generation was to add graphics, and the generation after that was to permit multiple applications to run simultaneously.

'I think that the first wave of broadband access will be a function of getting rid of the wait – the world wide wait, where you click on a web page and it takes for ever to load, or you're downloading a file and it takes half an hour. That will allow people to download movies and spawn video on demand platform proliferation.'

Convergence is also on the cards. Once PCs and TVs merge, almost unlimited personal gratification is possible.

'Imagine if it's 9.45 at night, and you've worked a full day, and you're coming home, and you want to watch something that was on the television at 8 o'clock, and you don't want to wait 26 weeks for the reruns. You should be able to log on to your TV and pay $1.95 and have that show broadcast to you in its entirety. That is probably coming. I don't think it happens until we get 40 per cent of phones hooked up for broadband access, which probably puts us in the 2004–5 time period.'

More shifts are likely to be seen in the mobile arena.

'I think the other interesting thing is going to be when we get to 3G wireless technology, which provides broadband data capability through a cell phone. The internet speed in your handheld would be roughly the same as what I'm getting through my corporate computer. Here we're probably in the 2004–6 time frame. I think you'll see a changing form factor for cell phones. People will carry a receiver with them. If they want to talk they'll pick up something that looks like a phone today and, if they want to access the internet, they'll pick up something that looks like a thinner palm pilot. You can do a fair amount of surfing on a 3-inch by 6-inch screen, but you can't do it looking at the current size. Five years from now, your receiver will know whether it's a voice or data call, and will alert the appropriate viewing, or interaction, device. If it's a data blast, it will ring your pilot, and, if it's a voice blast, it will ring your phone.'

One specific use of technology has also caught his attention. Morris expects an explosion in online gaming.

'I mean both gambling online and the actual playing of traditional games online. An online lottery makes extraordinary sense, and online gaming is a lot more fun than playing the computer. Again, it's got to wait until you've got about 40 per cent uptake of broadband access, so those are things that happen at the midpoint of the decade.'

Talking to Morris about technology is a bit like watching the scenery out of a window on a bullet train. Ideas rattle out, along with investment insights, at such a speed that it is hard to capture all he has to offer investors. He is a man very much in tune with the dynamics of his sector. Amateurs who want to play in the space will need to emphasize the same attributes: flexible in analysis, alert to new ideas, comfortable with change, sceptical and enthusiastic at the same time. Selecting good investments is tough, and never tougher than in technology. For the rest of us, you can always buy T. Rowe Price Science and Technology and let Morris do all the hard work. He so obviously enjoys his subject, and it shows in his results: which are worth repeating. Up over 1,000 per cent in ten years.

Technology investing can deliver that sort of exceptional return, but only if you master some of the most complicated investment challenges: Morris is clearly a master.

10

Dave Nadig

Internet savvy meets institutional experience

A pioneering Interactive Mutual Fund

Up 101 per cent in its first full year

Continuing to more than double NASDAQ through January 2001

Digital civilization collides with the fund management industry

Nominated for Finance Oscar-for-the-Web in 2000

Click on the website www.openfund.com and you will find the investment professional's worst nightmare: a totally transparent mutual fund. MetaMarkets.com, adviser to the fund, has ushered in a whole new level of service by creating a virtual community devoted to online investing which combines internet savvy and institutional expertise, all operating in an open environment – hence the name: OpenFund.

Investors can log on at any time and see exactly what their manager is up to, trade by trade, tick by tick, and comment, criticize or congratulate by leaving messages. Congratulations has been the most frequent form of communication since Nadig started this new venture as, worst of all, from the standpoint of the old model of fund investing, this new style works extremely well. In its first year from 31 August 1999 to 1 September 2000, OpenFund gained a spectacular 100.6 per cent, and that enormously encouraging debut compared to 54.5 per cent for the NASDAQ, its most relevant benchmark, over the same period.

Give the investing public what they want

The driving force behind this revolution is something of a surprise, since Nadig, although a nine-year investment veteran, never ran a portfolio prior to OpenFund. He and co-founder Don Luskin came out of Barclays Global Investors. Once upon a time trading as Wells Fargo Nikko, the firm is the largest institutional investment manager.

Luskin had been vice-chairman at Barclays. H. Davis 'Dave' Nadig, as chief strategy officer, spent most of his career concentrating on product development and marketing. Among earlier achievements, he helped develop a family of products called Life Path, while Luskin is one of the people named on the patent by Barclays. Innovation was not confined to a unique structure, but carried over into an allocation strategy tailored to the expected change in risk profile as investors age.

Similar lateral thinking underpins Nadig's new venture now that he operates outside a large corporation. What differentiates the OpenFund team is the amount of effort that goes into the front end: first and foremost figuring out the customer and only then on to conception, design and structure of a product. As an interesting aside, at Barclays Global they do not have managers. They have portfolio engineers whose job is to execute a pre-defined strategy.

'This isn't two people sitting in a room and coming up with ideas about stocks. You sit down before you launch the product and figure out how to select stocks for the portfolio. You build the methodology, and the methodology is more important than the execution on the first day.'

This affinity for new products is one reason Nadig spotted the gap in online funds before anyone else. Enter MetaMarkets, the brainchild of Luskin and Nadig, combining the former's extensive investment management experience with the latter's insights into what investors wanted – and, up until August 1999, had not been getting.

MetaMarkets represents the next generation of investment product and the first of breed. Its structure and process take full advantage of available technology in reaching out to a community that was one of the first to embrace, at an individual level, the power of the net. The name was not chosen late at night in a bar in Palo Alto, but sprung from a desire to describe the essence of the new firm. A meta market is where information about a market is exchanged. In contrast, a market is a place where goods are exchanged.

'Official markets, such as the New York Stock Exchange, are not about insight – they are all about transactions. Usually, when you're talking about a meta market, you're talking about a market of information about an underlying market. If you like IBM, you can go buy, say, Solomon Brothers' report for $10 from Multex.com, or someone similar. You're a participant in the meta market for IBM. You're not doing anything with IBM. You're exchanging information about it.'

While the term may not be widely familiar, academics use meta markets to describe information flow such as reports on consumer products like cars and electricity. Nadig took the term beyond the theoretical and into the financial community for the first time. He expects to hold the trademark. His application is pending. Needless to say, his firm also owns over 70 permutations of the term, along with .com, .net and .org, making sure every relevant domain name is sewn up. Harking back to his marketing roots, Nadig had his URL strategy in place before bedding down his investment strategy.

'You need to be able to assert global dominance in a word in order to get a brand name for anything.'

MetaMarkets is likely to become well known. Nadig et al. have staked out the

> **You need to be able to assert global dominance in a word in order to get a brand name for anything.**

space and embraced technology to a degree almost unimaginable before they began to blaze the trail. While most firms merely improved access to dealing information or account administration, or focused on cutting transaction costs, Nadig hardwired technology into the heart of his business, taking the transformation of fund management to the next logical level.

'Traditional mutual funds are old-fashioned, exclusionary and non-participating. OpenFund offers diversification and professional management, combined with all that's good about online trading – the empowerment, the excitement, the immediacy and the interactivity.'

This concept had been germinating for the best part of five years, ever since Nadig, in his capacity as an involved individual investor, became a frequent user of the net.

'Back in 1995 I started using a service on AOL called Motley Fool, and caught their first success, which was Iomega.'

Nadig was intrigued when Fools began to get excited about the stock. He watched. Iomega started to move, first from around $1, on a split-adjusted basis, to about $2. He decided to test the waters. Shortly after he bought, Iomega went bonkers. Nadig hung on as it flew all the way to $27. And then began to collapse. He got out around $11; nowhere near the high but, even so, a fantastic run producing a return of over 1,000 per cent in under a year. The power of the Motley Fool community to move prices impressed. Nadig was hooked, not by his extraordinary profit, but because of his realization that an entirely new investment force was emerging that would be incredibly powerful and maybe he could figure out a way to be part of the first wave.

'The lesson of the Motley Fool experience was that there's a real revolution in the industry. Because I didn't come from a traditional analyst background, and came at everything from a marketing perspective, to see individual empowerment was incredibly exciting.

'Yet it also made me realize that the process was flawed. It was purely "go find something" and, once you've found it, that's great, but then how do you decide when to get out? Motley Fool still holds Iomega in their portfolio, despite serious signs that that company has been in trouble for a long, long time. It's not news that this company has seen better days. But they had the classic investment problem of falling in love with the stock.

'I had this binary experience of incredible euphoria and, at the same time, realizing you have to apply discipline. Those two realizations are what eventually led to the creation of MetaMarkets.com.'

The other element that makes MetaMarkets so unique from the standpoint of a retail investor in collective investment vehicles is the degree to which the firm embraces disclosure. OpenFund is well open.

'In the institutional market you have transparency that doesn't exist in the regular investment management industry. Layer that on, and you've really got the three legs of the stool that build our business: transparency, involvement and discipline.'

So how, exactly, does OpenFund operate? It could hardly be simpler. You click through and there it all is – the entire portfolio in real time, with a delay of as little as 10 seconds after entry, plus key information about performance, and a series of strings on each company including analysis, commentary, feedback and write-up of conversations or meetings with the management. And, if that still does not satisfy your curiosity, try this on for size:

'On the website of MetaMarkets Investments LLC, the fund's adviser, you can see the latest trading activity in OpenFund updated in real time. And you can point and zoom our live remote-control TraderCam, focused 7 by 24 on our trading desk in south San Francisco.'

Truman eat your heart out.

Openness is not a cute marketing ploy. The team at MetaMarkets is truly committed and believes disclosure is morally right. In May 2000, Nadig was a signatory to a letter to the Investment Company Institute, along with representatives from Morningstar, the fund-rating agency, and the National Association of Investment Clubs. A brief extract shows just how serious he is.

> Even as we marvel at this tremendous long-term success of industry, we should also feel a sense of shame that investors, advisors and third party watchdogs have only a pittance of information available to them if they are interested in knowing exactly what fund managers are doing. The ICI should establish a committee immediately to examine disclosure policy, focusing on the following points:
>
> What is an acceptable minimum portfolio disclosure standard for the entire industry?
>
> What exactly should be disclosed and with what time-lag should it be revealed?
>
> What will the timetable be for rolling out this new policy?
>
> In the final analysis, we can never forget that it is the shareholders' money that we are managing, and it is, therefore their right to have as much information as possible about how it is being cared for.

Ouch. Openness is a genie that is out of the bottle. Nadig is leading the charge for change.

A couple of other operating dimensions help to set the context. First off, Nadig reiterates, at every opportunity, that MetaMarkets is a team effort. The three principals have different backgrounds, experience and expertise which collectively gel to cover the diverse skill set needed to run a successful fund management company – and, arguably of greater interest, to pick a top performing portfolio.

Nadig emphasizes the top-down element of structuring a portfolio, focusing on stories and strategies that will drive a company's success. Don Luskin is quantitative and analytical. He has set up a series of real-time spreadsheets which calculate every matrix you would ever want, to facilitate their buy/sell/hold decisions on individual securities. Luskin approaches securities, using option theory to test stock prices. He is always asking what is the upside, and what risks are you protecting? This relatively unorthodox approach has particular relevance for new-economy companies which come earlier to market. Luskin is also a chartist. Maurice Wedgedar is head trader. He focuses on the market and is momentum driven. He is quick to realize the opportunity for short-term gain. This divergence in approach stimulates lively group discussions.

'If Disney is on the table, I'll be talking about management changes, performance of the last movie and strategic alignments, Maurice will be talking about how it's been trading for the last three days, and Don will be looking at the chart, shaking his head and saying, "Looks like its sticking in a trench around here", and focusing on the resistance point. Our conversations represent three very different disciplines. Consequently, when all of us get on board for a stock, it is something we, as a firm, really understand and can have belief in.'

Figure 10.1 (pages 234–5) depicts the portfolio as of January 2001. Delve a little deeper and you find daily NAV performance, ranking versus the S&P 500, or NASDAQ and, of course, you can download the prospectus. Well, why wouldn't you, when a product is made this easy, and also delivers such a stunning return? No wonder money is starting to flow in.

Once invested, it's time to join the party, because you are now a member of the MetaMarkets community, a vocal and highly interactive group of shareholders. Nadig receives more than 100 messages daily. How many other fund managers could cope, let alone would want to open themselves up to this sort of traffic? Yet two-way communications is at the heart of the philosophy that underpins MetaMarkets and makes Nadig and his colleagues potentially so influential: small, thus far, but thought leaders in the industry, nonetheless.

Investment management is a content business

In addition to portfolio demographics, the site is rich in information. Sign up for MetaMarkets Info List and you will get a weekly download of ideas and market highlights (MetaMemos). There is also the opportunity to contribute to any thread that tickles your fancy and rate both stocks and member contributions. Before market opening, members can tune into a real-time half-hour chat. There is always at least one live forum for interactive debate on a hot topic, such as internet security or 'The End of the Brand As We Know It'.

The structure is not designed merely to lock in shareholders – although if you feel like one of the owners rather than a pain in the ass with a pin number, you are more inclined to stick around and contribute. Which can also be a bonus, because no-one has a monopoly on good ideas and Nadig is very open-minded.

'The MetaMarkets.com community is a great resource and competitive advantage. Traditional mutual funds make investment decisions based on Wall Street research and internal staff. Our community of visionaries and online investors is a powerful analyst pool that can add great value to a fund focused on the New Economy. You could say we have the Earth's largest research department.

'OpenFund listens to its customers. We think we're the first mutual fund ever to do that. The management team participates in discussion boards, chat rooms and online polls. We don't act on every opinion – how could we, considering the diversity of opinion! But if you say it seriously, we'll take it seriously.'

Participation must be positive for performance, not a distraction to consistent management.

'Participation doesn't mean some shareholder having influence just because he or she was a shareholder. Participation means that information that generates superior return is no longer what Wall Street thinks. It has moved to a higher plane.'

That caveat aside, Nadig's enthusiasm for input from informed shareholders and other active market players is genuine – it is another degree of openness.

> **Information that generates superior return is no longer what Wall Street thinks.**

'We want opinions about the stocks in OpenFund. We want new ideas. And we want macro views on trading, technology, business, the

Figure 10.1 | OpenFund portfolio positions

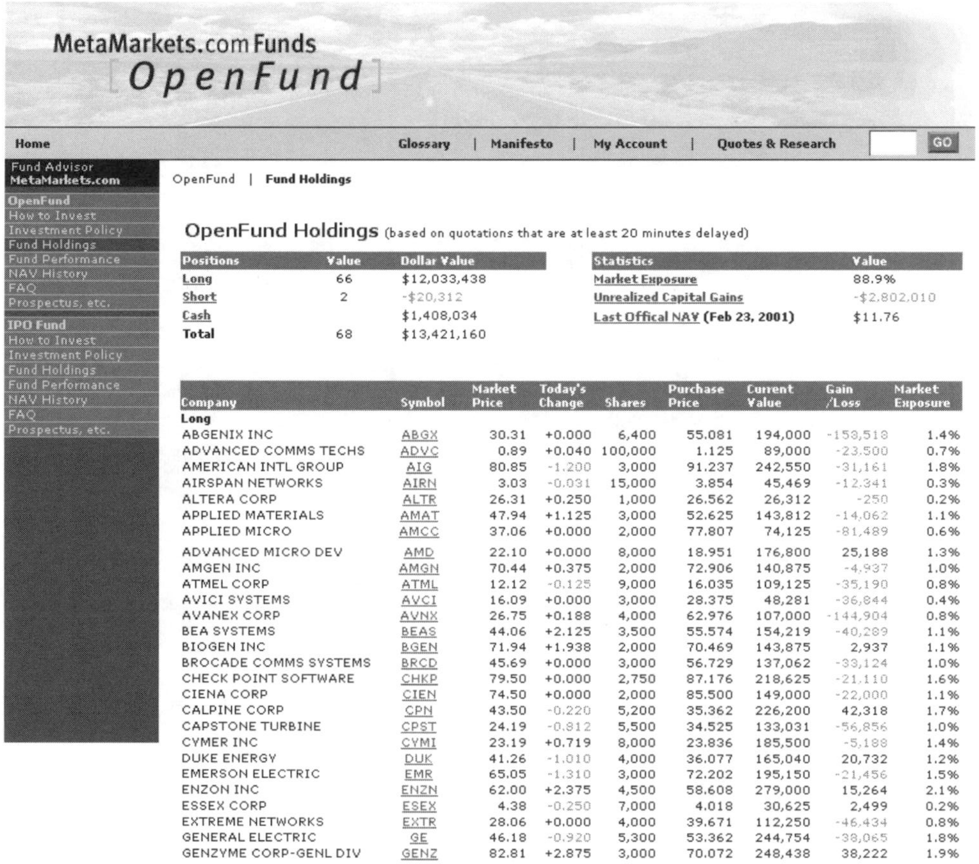

MetaMarkets.com Funds [*OpenFund*]

Fund Advisor
MetaMarkets.com
OpenFund
How to Invest
Investment Policy
Fund Holdings
Fund Performance
NAV History
FAQ
Prospectus, etc.
IPO Fund
How to Invest
Investment Policy
Fund Holdings
Fund Performance
NAV History
FAQ
Prospectus, etc.

OpenFund | **Fund Holdings**

OpenFund Holdings (based on quotations that are at least 20 minutes delayed)

Positions	Value	Dollar Value
Long	66	$12,033,438
Short	2	-$20,312
Cash		$1,408,034
Total	68	$13,421,160

Statistics	Value
Market Exposure	88.9%
Unrealized Capital Gains	-$2,802,010
Last Offical NAV (Feb 23, 2001)	$11.76

Company	Symbol	Market Price	Today's Change	Shares	Purchase Price	Current Value	Gain /Loss	Market Exposure
Long								
ABGENIX INC	ABGX	30.31	+0.000	6,400	55.081	194,000	-159,518	1.4%
ADVANCED COMMS TECHS	ADVC	0.89	+0.040	100,000	1.125	89,000	-23,500	0.7%
AMERICAN INTL GROUP	AIG	80.85	-1.200	3,000	91.237	242,550	-31,161	1.8%
AIRSPAN NETWORKS	AIRN	3.03	-0.031	15,000	3.854	45,469	-12,341	0.3%
ALTERA CORP	ALTR	26.31	+0.250	1,000	26.562	26,312	-250	0.2%
APPLIED MATERIALS	AMAT	47.94	+1.125	3,000	52.625	143,812	-14,062	1.1%
APPLIED MICRO	AMCC	37.06	+0.000	2,000	77.807	74,125	-81,489	0.6%
ADVANCED MICRO DEV	AMD	22.10	+0.000	8,000	18.951	176,800	25,188	1.3%
AMGEN INC	AMGN	70.44	+0.375	2,000	72.906	140,875	-4,937	1.0%
ATMEL CORP	ATML	12.12	-0.125	9,000	16.035	109,125	-35,190	0.8%
AVICI SYSTEMS	AVCI	16.09	+0.000	3,000	28.375	48,281	-36,844	0.4%
AVANEX CORP	AVNX	26.75	+0.188	4,000	62.976	107,000	-144,904	0.8%
BEA SYSTEMS	BEAS	44.06	+2.125	3,500	55.574	154,219	-40,289	1.1%
BIOGEN INC	BGEN	71.94	+1.938	2,000	70.469	143,875	2,937	1.1%
BROCADE COMMS SYSTEMS	BRCD	45.69	+0.000	3,000	56.729	137,062	-33,124	1.0%
CHECK POINT SOFTWARE	CHKP	79.50	+0.000	2,750	87.176	218,625	-21,110	1.6%
CIENA CORP	CIEN	74.50	+0.000	2,000	85.500	149,000	-22,000	1.1%
CALPINE CORP	CPN	43.50	-0.220	5,200	35.362	226,200	42,318	1.7%
CAPSTONE TURBINE	CPST	24.19	-0.812	5,500	34.525	133,031	-56,856	1.0%
CYMER INC	CYMI	23.19	+0.719	8,000	23.836	185,500	-5,188	1.4%
DUKE ENERGY	DUK	41.26	-1.010	4,000	36.077	165,040	20,732	1.2%
EMERSON ELECTRIC	EMR	65.05	-1.310	3,000	72.202	195,150	-21,456	1.5%
ENZON INC	ENZN	62.00	+2.375	4,500	58.608	279,000	15,264	2.1%
ESSEX CORP	ESEX	4.38	-0.250	7,000	4.018	30,625	2,499	0.2%
EXTREME NETWORKS	EXTR	28.06	+0.000	4,000	39.671	112,250	-46,434	0.8%
GENERAL ELECTRIC	GE	46.18	-0.920	5,300	53.362	244,754	-38,065	1.8%
GENZYME CORP-GENL DIV	GENZ	82.81	+2.875	3,000	70.072	248,438	38,222	1.9%

INTERSIL HOLDING 'A'	IBIL	18.12	+0.188	9,500	21,668	172,188	-33,656	1.3%
JUNIPER NETWORKS	JNPR	74.75	+0.000	2,000	105,056	149,500	-60,612	1.1%
KLA-TENCOR CORP	KLAC	43.38	+0.000	3,000	44,308	130,125	-2,799	1.0%
LORAL SPACE &	LOR	4.20	+0.000	45,000	5,557	189,000	-61,065	1.4%
MCK COMMUNICATIONS	MCKC	3.97	-0.094	10,000	4,312	39,688	-3,432	0.3%
MEDIMMUNE INC	MEDI	43.88	+0.000	2,000	42,938	87,750	1,875	0.7%
MIRANT CORP	MIR	25.49	-0.460	6,000	25,202	152,940	1,728	1.1%
MILLENNIUM	M_NM	30.56	+0.000	5,000	58,164	152,812	-138,008	1.1%
MICROSOFT CORP	MSFT	56.75	+1.562	8,500	66,412	482,375	-92,127	3.6%
NDX100 FUTURES 03-01	NDH1	2,056.00	+6.000	6	2,704,795	1,233,600	-369,277	9.2%
NETWORK ENGINES(IPO)	NENG	1.69	-0.125	31,000	2,952	52,312	-39,199	0.4%
E-MINI NAS100 03-01	NQC1	2,083.00	+25.500	33	2,723,545	1,374,780	-422,760	10.2%
NETWORK APPLIANCE	NTAP	33.94	+0.125	4,000	53,081	135,750	-76,574	1.0%
NEUROBIOLOGICAL	NTII	3.16	-0.156	25,600	8,371	80,800	-133,498	0.6%
NORTHERN TRUST	NTRS	71.75	+0.375	3,000	84,992	215,250	-39,726	1.6%
NEW FOCUS	NUFO	30.00	+0.000	5,000	43,162	150,000	-65,810	1.1%
ONI SYSTEMS	ONIS	39.25	+1.625	4,400	44,020	172,700	-20,988	1.3%
ORACLE CORP	ORCL	22.00	-1.375	7,500	28,555	165,000	-49,163	1.2%
O2WIRELESS SOLUTIONS	OTWO	6.62	-0.125	19,000	9,572	125,875	-55,993	0.9%
QUALCOMM INC	QCOM	61.81	+0.000	1,500	59,438	92,719	3,562	0.7%
QQQ 03-01 54C	QQQCBO	2.10	+0.103	200	1,825	42,000	5,500	0.3%
QQQ 03-01 56C	QQQCDO	1.50	+0.103	200	2,350	30,000	-17,000	0.2%
QQQ 03-01 59C	QQQCGO	0.80	+0.253	100	3,000	8,000	-22,000	0.1%
QQQ 03-01 62C	QQQCJO	0.40	+0.103	100	2,569	4,000	-21,690	0.0%
RATIONAL SOFTWARE	RATL	36.94	-0.125	2,000	50,281	73,875	-26,637	0.6%
RED&ACK NETWORKS INC	REAK	34.75	+0.000	4,500	29,772	156,375	22,400	1.2%
RUSSELL2000 03-01	RLH1	479.75	-0.400	2	500,346	479,750	-20,596	3.6%
SEITEL INC	SEI	17.95	-0.050	6,500	18,904	116,675	-6,201	0.9%
SONUS NETWORKS	SONS	25.94	+0.000	6,500	28,487	168,594	-16,572	1.3%
S&P DEP RECEIPTS	SPY	124.96	-0.850	2,400	139,273	299,904	-34,351	2.2%
SUN MICROSYSTEMS	SUNW	20.81	+0.000	4,500	37,177	93,656	-73,640	0.7%
TERADYNE INC	TER	35.83	+0.000	4,000	41,507	143,320	-22,708	1.1%
TARGET CORP	TGT	35.74	-0.060	3,000	34,982	107,220	2,274	0.8%
TRANSMETA CORP	TMTA	30.94	+0.312	5,500	25,945	170,156	27,461	1.3%
TRIQUINT	TQNT	22.69	-1.625	7,000	40,751	158,812	-126,444	1.2%
TITAN PHARMACEUTICALS	TTP	31.03	+0.000	6,600	38,468	204,798	-49,091	1.5%
WASTE CONNECTIONS	WCNX	30.75	-1.375	1,500	30,388	46,125	543	0.3%
WEBMETHODS INC	WEBM	48.75	+1.625	3,800	81,113	185,250	-122,979	1.4%
WELLS FARGO	WFC	48.47	+0.320	3,500	48,890	169,645	-1,470	1.3%
Subtotal (USD)						**12,030,138**	**-2,854,635**	**89.7%**
Short:								
MU 04-01 35P	MUPG_Q	3.80	+0.000	100	3,500	38,000	3,000	-0.3%
TIBCO SOFTWARE INC	TIBX	19.44	+0.000	-3,000	34,879	-58,312	46,325	-0.4%
Subtotal (USD)						**-26,312**	**49,325**	**-0.7%**
Cash (USD)						**280,064**		
Total						**2,136,533**	**-618,275**	**86.9%**

market and the New Economy. Every subject is potentially grist for the investment mill, so nothing is off-limits.'

They get their fair share of net chatter, self-promotion and garbage, but also the odd nugget, as Nadig recalls.

'There have been times that we've bought something that somebody in the community pointed out to us. Not *because* they did, but because we also ended up liking the stock. Harris and Harris Group was the first. A very frequent member of our board system, Ed Spiegel, saw we were interested in internet incubators like CMGI or Safeguard Scientific. Public private-venture capital is a business model we believe in. He said, "Here's one you probably haven't seen. It's only got about $30 million invested, but it's public, so there's an opportunity to access its portfolio." We got SEC filings and did quantitative analysis. You need to understand exactly what's in there, and how it's doing, to get any sense of real value. We made an investment because we thought it was undervalued.'

Suggestions come in all shapes and sizes – buy, sell and trade.

'We run a separate part of the board called "under the radar", which is where people fill up and say, "Hey, buy this!" And, most of the time, we say, "Why?" And most of the time we don't get an answer. But, every once in a while, somebody comes back and writes this epic, and we go and do our own work on it. A lot of the ideas that get shown tend to be, "I hear this is going to run up. I'm getting into this this morning." We're much more interested when somebody believes in a company and wants to talk to us about it.'

Insights are welcome, and Nadig recalls instances where suggestions from community members have benefited the portfolio – as where one post pointed out that, if you bought Cell Genesys, you got a stake in Abgenix, a stock they already owned, plus another business effectively for free. But the buck stops with Nadig and his colleagues. MetaMarkets is a community, not a democracy.

Not just technology

Presentation and process count for nothing unless the substance stands up to close examination. OpenFund scores well on that dimension, too.

It's important to understand what OpenFund is not.

'While it's managed on the internet, it isn't an internet fund. It isn't a sector fund at all. It's a paradigm fund. The paradigm is that we are in a new economy. We believe real growth, surprising growth, will come from companies defining the new economy, changing the way information is used, products are sold and innovation is fostered.'

The 'New Economy' is a term widely used and rather less widely understood. Worse, it can mean different things to different people or, at least, reasonable investors can disagree on its definition. Here is what Nadig has to say:

'Companies participating in the New Economy are companies that are changing the fundamental way business is transacted, leisure time is spent and information processed. Fundamental is a really big word that you can toss around like hyperbole, but we use it literally. We literally look for companies that are reversing, or so altering, the course of a particular segment of a particular industry that they'll be unrecognizable in the future.'

Which introduces the second style twist in defining what is inside the open fund universe and what is excluded. Nadig will consider any business that can meet this fundamental test. New Economy is not used narrowly at MetaMarkets, which is one reason he feels they have an edge over pure technology funds.

'The mistake a lot of people make when they look at us very quickly is to say, "Oh, these guys are just in tech". We have a lot in tech, but so does the whole market. If we had less, we would actually be anti-tech. And technology is, of course, a huge part of what drives fundamental change. It always has been. You can go back to the invention of the lever.'

Nadig offers an example of what he means by more than just technology.

'Let's look at movements that are changing things. Companies that go beyond simply winning customers can take the next step towards making them addicts, participants, tribe members, evangelists. Those companies get rewarded by stock growth, by influx of capital, by whatever measurement you want to apply to a company's success. A lot of times that has nothing to do with technology.'

Take the prospectus for OpenFund: in fact, take the very first three sentences. Technology is mentioned twice, but Nadig has much more in mind:

The Fund invests in securities of companies which ... are innovative growth companies at the leading edge of technological, social and economic change. They demonstrate the ability to continuously learn and productively change. Through innovative use of technology or the imaginative use of organisational techniques or marketing methods, they are redefining the way goods and services are provided.

Domino's Pizza is a disruptive innovator that fits into the paradigm through state-of-the-art application of systems to a time-sensitive product, effectively extending the life cycle of a mature category. Even fast food can be part of the New Economy, as defined by MetaMarkets.

Buy the future today

Luskin and Nadig have defined a trilogy of themes that drive their investment process. While each is a separate, standalone strand, at the same time these themes are complementary, even additive, and, for the most part, fuse together within the technology tent. Summarize their common essence and it comes down to this: buy the future today.

'You start with the big idea: the New Economy. You slice this up into meta themes; then you start slicing themes up into smaller and smaller divisions, and say, "OK, which really matter? Which one is a theme that's going to play out for a long time?" Then you start looking at the company stories underneath.'

Essentially the philosophy is as extracted from the OpenFund Manifesto:

> The key to successful investing is original insight – the idea that is not generally accepted in the market consensus.
>
> We believe that the most important insights are those that operate at the most macroscopic level of analysis: understanding the great trends – the MetaThemes – that drive the new economy. As a general proposition, we argue that the importance, impact and scope of the dynamics of the new economy are not fully understood or appreciated by the market.

Each theme deserves to be explored in detail.

MetaTheme 1: InfoGenesis

Nadig defines InfoGenesis as 'building out the infrastructure to transform the entire world into an information economy'. He believes that InfoGenesis 'will be the great industrial task of the new century, comparable to the creation of factories, railroads, highways and power systems of earlier times. Companies engaged in InfoGenesis are the brightest blue chips of the new economy.'

For the investor in 2001, this is familiar territory which includes fibre optics, telecommunications, hardware and networking.

MetaTheme 2: Corporate tribalism

'From retail to high tech, competitors can only excel (or, in some cases, only survive) by transforming customers into "tribes" – communities of interest that bind a company to a loyal constituency. Innovative techniques of market segmentation, branding, immersive marketing and customization not only lower sales costs, but also erect significant barriers against competitors, as well.'

Here you have a much more varied group which has, as commonality, no industry or even sectors affiliation: rather the reverse. These businesses are likely to be the leading representatives of a whole host of essential subsectors, including everyday services as well as leading-edge consumer companies.

MetaTheme 3: Innovate or die

'Capital markets and customers demand innovation, and woe to the company that disappoints. In many markets today, stagnation truly means death. But innovation is a tricky thing – the most valuable innovations are so disruptive that established market leaders often find them too heretical to internalize.'

The buzz word here is 'disruptive innovation': it's disturbing, it's uncomfortable, in many respects it's counter-intuitive and it's difficult to sustain, but it's absolutely essential.

Putting theory into practice

Fine, so far, but how do ideas translate into investments? Remember, Nadig was discussing these examples with me throughout 2000. Since revolutions are open-ended, continuous and ever more rapid, companies cited here may no longer be leading edge. His methodology and thought process is what matters. That aspect of meta investing is more robust.

It is easier to take each theme in turn:

1. InfoGenesis

According to Nadig:

'The tools to process, store and communicate are the defining technologies of the new economy. In developed countries, these technologies form the backbone of well-established but sill rapidly expanding and evolving information economies. But in the developing world, the opportunities are even more enormous: more than half the people alive today have never even made a phone call.

'Qualcomm is a perfect example. Qualcomm's core technology is Code Division Multiple Access (CDMA), an encoding system that vastly multiplies the efficiency of both wired and wireless communications. Terayon cable modems use CDMA to increase the capacity of legacy coax systems to deliver broadband services into subscribers' homes. Virtually every major mobile phone manufacturer uses CDMA to increase the number of wireless calls that can be made simultaneously using limited radio spectrum – and, at the same time, increase the clarity of the call and life of the battery. Nations around the world are adopting CDMA as their next generation cellular phone standard, and Globalstar Communications has adopted CDMA to enable its global network of low Earth orbit satellites.

'Qualcomm is the leader in CDMA, in terms of both manufacturing and pure research. It holds over 250 patents. Qualcomm's dominance and CDMA's centrality to InfoGenesis has been recognized by the market. Yet we believe that the best is yet to be, for InfoGenesis is still in its infancy. In a few short years, CDMA will be standing at the centre of a global central nervous system enabling voice and broadband data communications via handheld wireless devices from anywhere on the surface of the planet.'

Equally, it is important to understand the boundaries of InfoGenesis – what is excluded and which sort of technical innovations Nadig considers as decoys luring unwary investors on to the rocks.

'Underlying technologies change so rapidly. It's easy to get seduced by something that's solving today's problems. I just saw this article, "Fast Forward TV Through the Phone Line". M-phase is building this technology to push television signals down copper wires. Most people are going to put that into InfoGenesis. I immediately want to excise and put it somewhere else, because that's throwing good money after bad.

> **Underlying technologies change so rapidly. It's easy to get seduced by something that's solving today's problems.**

That's falling into the trap of saying, "How do we maximize this bottleneck?" which is this piece of copper going into houses.

'They may do very well in the short-term, they may be able to build a lot of buzz, but I'm not particularly interested. The real play is getting around that altogether; figuring out what's going to happen once people get beyond this bottleneck. Who's going to deliver fibre? Who's going to put a fixed wireless antenna on the house? That gets around these issues of how do you cram information down this tiny pipe.'

Nadig is after earthmoving and irreversible shifts, not a nice new idea that excites only to disappoint and does not offer substantial quality of life improvement. InfoGenesis is about value creation on a global scale through fundamental change. He invests in businesses that are creating tomorrow's solutions today.

'Northeast Optic Networks is not even worrying about what to do with their infrastructure today. They are basically just digging ditches and laying down fibre. They are fibre-ing up the corridor between Maine and Washington. Fibre is cheap – it's only going to get cheaper. Band width in general is cheap and only going to get cheaper, but it's always going to be expensive to send some guy out in a truck and dig a ditch. So they're putting as much thought into ditches as possible. They're buying ditches. They're buying rights to railways up and down the New England coast; they're buying little plots of land that get in the way; they're doing everything to free this ditch network and put as much as they can in today. The limitation on what you put in a ditch is the limitation on your imagination of engineering.

'The value in the company is not that they're going to have fibre from Portland, Maine to Washington DC: the value is that they own the ditch all along the way, or own the way along the way.'

2. Corporate tribalism

Nadig's definition of the second MetaTheme, corporate tribalism, represents a synthesis of his experience as a marketing professional, together with hands-on knowledge of technology reworked into an investment context.

'Hyper competition is the defining ethic of the New Economy. The number of trademarks filed annually has increased tenfold since 1975, and over 50,000 new products are now introduced in the United States every year. Branding has evolved from a system of marking goods to become the primary asset of many companies. As a tribe unto themselves, individual investors in the new economy are in an excellent position to forecast winners and losers.

> **Branding has evolved from a system of marking goods to become the primary asset of many companies.**

'Dell Computer is an outstanding example of a company that has built a dominant brand in a hyper-competitive market by creating intimate bonds with customers – all the more intimate, ironically, because customer interactions are not face-to-face.

'Dell was an early adopter of e-commerce, and has led the way in demonstrating that it can be used to empower customers by lowering the cost of customization. A sceptic who thinks that e-commerce is nothing more than a way to sell commodity goods at a discount – for example, books on Amazon – should visit Dell's website to experience the empowerment of designing your own one-of-a-kind computer online. And it's at a cost that competes aggressively with the one-size-fits-all computers you find at a big-box reseller.

'More important, Dell collects detailed information about customers' product configurations and uses that information to handle service problems. A sceptic who thinks that e-commerce can't compete on service and maintenance with store-based resellers – such as CompUSA – should call Dell's toll-free army of friendly and knowledgeable service representatives to experience support 7 by 24 without waiting in line and without having to either physically transport your computer or leave it behind.

'Dell's designed an experience to go with the product. An experience that seeks to make the individual consumer a member of the Dell tribe for life, recruited by customization and price and retained by excellent service. Dell's model is even more attractive for the corporate buyer. Dell becomes the buyer's partner in reducing the total cost of ownership of computers by maintaining rigorous inventory configuration records.'

Demonstrating that this theme is not necessarily tech linked, Nadig turns to a company that almost every analyst would accept as old economy for his second example of the second MetaTheme.

'Home Depot has restructured their industry. They've said "What is home improvement about?" And, from first principles, they rebuilt a company when, five years ago, a lot of people were thinking they were crazy. Like, "You'll never make money doing this!" But they created a tribe of customers that are totally loyal to this new way of doing business. They create environments that suck people in, so that they feel like they're on tribal territory. It's almost … evangelical is a word I use, precisely because of its religious connotation.

'The guys behind Home Depot realized that home improvement is not about fixing things. It's about enabling the imagination. When somebody walks into a hardware store, they generally have a task. "I need a hammer." Something very mundane, very boring. And you can go to the store and buy a cheap hammer. But the real reason Home Depot was successful was because while you are buying the hammer, you look around and, through helpful employees, through extremely good inventory management, through extremely good display management, you see things that are far more important that actually seem within your grasp to do.

'Spend ten minutes walking the aisles and you'll find everything you need to re-pipe your house for gas! Nobody is going to re-pipe their own house for gas, but Home Depot is asserting, over and over again, "You can do it. And if you want to do it, we'll show you how. We'll be here, we'll help, we'll answer your questions, we've everything you need. We'll tell you whether or not you need a permit," the whole nine yards. So the Home Depot experience isn't buying hardware, it's almost like tripping through a theme park.

'They are the only people in their industry who've realized that, if you create this positive experience, (a) you sell stuff that people don't need. Somebody will say, "Hey, maybe I *will* re-pipe my house with gas some day, and I've always wanted one of those funky little monkey wrenches". And (b) people will also linger.'

Another way, perversely, to create and maintain tribalism is through brand development. Nadig believes branding is part of the new economy, but is merciless in his exclusion of names that have no meaning. Take banking. He excludes Citibank. Sure, everyone knows the name, but he does not see depth.

'Everyone knows it. That's just because they've advertised like crazy. But what do they stand for? What is the difference between Citibank and Chase?'

Nadig claims there is only one bank in the US that has a truly valuable brand. Wells Fargo's goal is to go way beyond name recognition and to create a sense of community.

'Generally, when they do US surveys, Wells Fargo is one of the top five recognizable brands. They protect that brand: they don't just say, "OK, we'll just use the crap out of it this year and see what we can get". They are religious about it. There's a Wells Fargo museum where they've got stagecoaches and people taking kindergarten children round. The chaps and the white gloves and the bull whips and the whole nine yards.

'That sounds hokey, but it creates an anchor point in a brandless sea of opportunity. At least you know Wells Fargo's been around. They've never let the brand get polluted, even when they've made huge acquisitions like First Interstate. In the long term, and even in the short term, the market rewards that because, when things get ugly, it becomes a safe harbour. People understand it. It's the same reason money flows back into heartland companies and Coca-Cola when the market goes down 20 per cent.'

3. Innovate or die

This is the most disturbing, but possibly the most powerful, of all three MetaThemes. Nadig explains the context in which it becomes so vital an ingredient of a sustainable business model.

'Rapid innovation is the defining value of the New Economy. The number of patents issued annually has doubled since 1985. Average new product development cycle time has reduced by one-third since 1990. Successful investors must learn to identify those rare companies with the unusual

> # Investors must learn to think like venture capitalists.

ability to nurture innovation within the context of existing franchises. But more important, they must also be willing to invest in innovative but immature companies without well-established earnings records or business models – in other words, investors must learn to think like venture capitalists.

'Lucent Technologies is a company that thrives on unceasing innovation. Lucent was created three years ago when AT&T spun off its manufacturing and research division, including Bell Labs. Bell Labs has been celebrated for decades of "pure science" research that produced breakthroughs like the transistor, the laser and the Unix operating system. But research doesn't easily translate into true innovation – even world-class research. Under AT&T, Bell Labs was captive, and its best ideas were wasted. Most of its breakthrough technologies were commercialized in other companies – often start-ups founded by people who left in frustration. Liberated, Lucent is free to commercialize its technologies itself – and does so with a vengeance. Lucent is now a lead in almost every technology that motivates InfoGenesis: Wave Division Multiplexing (WDM), fibre optics, wireless networking, switches and routers, high-end chips and CDMA.'

Rather than equating New Economy exclusively with technology, and assuming only leading-edge technology companies know how to innovate, Nadig offers an example of a well-established conglomerate which he believes captures the essence of the new economy.

'I see General Electric as a truly innovative company, because Welch [the CEO] realized that the only way to get this big, mainstream company to stay at the front of its individual markets was to separate businesses, and to completely empower them. GE Capital is one of the most innovative financial companies in the world. Operating under the same umbrella as white goods, you've got the innovative imaging business which is at the forefront of many developments in medical care.'

Inevitably, technology companies will be heavily represented in this category. Nadig returns to an old favourite for his third example.

'Cisco Systems has found a way to institutionalize innovation, despite its size and market dominance. Cisco bows respectfully to a universal law of business discovered by Bill Joy of Sun Microsystems: most of the smartest people aren't in your company. In other words, the best ideas are "not invented here". Cisco's answer has been a programme of innovation by acquisition. Past acquisitions of Cerent Corporation and Monterey Networks are but the tip of the iceberg. Cisco made nearly 50 major acquisitions in the last six years. Additionally, its venture-capital arm invests in complementary businesses with emerging technologies – creating strategic relationships early and hedging against the risk of a wildcard competitive innovation coming out of the blue.'

Change winnows the winners from the losers

There is a flip side to the innovation theme – indeed, to the other two themes as well. If you identify businesses that have not taken this message on board, then what you have is an eroding franchise. The only question is whether shareholder value will erode slowly, or come crashing down when an event focuses the market on its vulnerability. From among those companies that have not got the message, or have failed to respond fast enough to obsolescence in their business model, Nadig *et al.* unearth suitable short candidates.

'A classic for us is AT&T. AT&T has shown over and over and over again that when it tries to innovate it beats itself from the inside out. It's a company that needs to innovate desperately. People talk about AT&T rebuilding itself into a new economy company. We just don't buy it. Every time they try they've failed miserably, so they keep buying innovation. They bought McCaw Cellular. Yet, with the first business that got successful – that's a real innovation business, wireless – they spun it out into AWE. They can't tolerate innovation in their own business.'

Shorting is part of an integrated trading strategy. Talk to Nadig and he uses the word 'trade' as often, if not more frequently, than the word 'investment'. Portfolio turnover is high. The team discards losers ruthlessly. Fall short and that holding may be out the door in minutes. The list of stocks on almost any day contains only a handful of names that were there 12 months ago.

The Fund reflects its frenetic environment. Change is everywhere, affecting everything that goes on internally and externally. Nadig is attuned to change – he is comfortable with change. The portfolio responds to change; the manager tries to anticipate change, even when experts in the field have a hard time identifying precisely how or what will happen. The one certainty is change, and the investor who wants to win has to cope.

'Investors always think that you've reached as far as it can go. You see some innovation and say, "Wow, it can't get any better". Lucent announces that it can get three times as many signals down a fibre. It has just tripled band width. It's really hard, as an investor, not to say, "Well, that's it. Nobody can do better". But the bottom line is there's always somebody right behind who's going to figure something else out.'

Once in tune, you should be able to spot suitable buys and also detect companies likely to suffer. If you are open-minded, you can make money from both the creative and the destructive impact of technology. Which is exactly what Nadig aims to do.

'The New Economy produces great winners, and great losers as well. By selling short, we create the opportunity to profit by identifying those losers – and potentially reduce overall portfolio risk at the same time.'

Technology is not a one-way ride. It is possible to apply the brakes every now and then. Nadig and his colleagues are not long fanatics. They try not to fall in love with a story. They understand the disconnect between exciting concepts and value creation. The bad news is that all those blue-chip certificates you could put in your drawer and forget about – well, forget about doing that. Passive investing is a shortcut to poverty. The share everyone was once supposed to own for life is where Nadig is short.

'InfoGenesis is a rising tide that will lift many boats. But, at the same time, it will sink others. Once all-powerful, AT&T is held captive by the legacy of an obsolete network infrastructure and a corporate culture built on a century of monopolistic privilege. It finds itself a clumsy giant stumbling amidst the technological and competitive whirlwind, without a compelling reason to continue to exist, and yet too big to die.'

This can even apply to companies that, only a year before, were, themselves, viewed as part of the New Economy.

'While Dell has built its tribe, Compaq has seen its once mighty franchise evaporate. Compared to Dell's ability to give each customer exactly what they want, Compaq offers only pre-configured commodities in shrink-wrapped packages. What's worse, those packages are sold by resellers who control the customer interaction both at purchase and in after-service.'

For trading to enhance performance demands discipline, a favourite Nadig word. Discipline is at the core of trading activity. Active, yes, but only subject to relatively tight parameters defined in advance. First you think, then you act.

'We're fond of saying that you can get an incredible amount of performance simply by not screwing up – by not letting anything get out of control. Where a lot of investment managers lose performance is that they don't have rigorous buying disciplines; they don't have rigorous selling disciplines.'

Lack of innovation can infect whole sectors, throwing up clumps of candidates which, at some point during their decline, become interesting shorts: such as the whole B2C group in 2000.

'We've been shorting the internet sector and specific stocks. Everybody thinks of them as being out there on the innovative edge, but they've actually been among the slowest to adopt some forms of innovation. Most internet retailers built their business models in a very narrow silo. They buy goods, stick them in a warehouse, sell online, pay UPS or Fedex for shipping and become low-cost providers. What has happened over the last year is that folks like Amazon have realized that that by itself isn't a powerful model. There have been some great short candidates among internet companies that simply couldn't realize they had to broaden their model.'

MetaMarkets tends to treat short sales as an integral part of its trading strategy. They spot weaker brethren but, rather than sit and hope that shorts implode, they look to catch a moment and then close out positions, taking a smallish profit, but in a very short timeframe. E Toys was one model where Nadig was far from convinced and was short more than once, making 10 per cent during just five business days, even when dot coms were still in fashion during the last quarter of 1999. As that fad faded, he focused on the sector and used HHH, a basket of internet holdings, as a proxy to go short for March and April 2000, during which time the fund recorded 50 separate transactions as the synthetic stock slid from 189 to 102.

> # Shorting, almost by definition, is a short-term strategy. You are always fighting against the tide.

Before rushing out to short, readers should memorize Nadig's closing comments.

'Shorting, almost by definition, is a short-term strategy. You are always fighting against the tide, because, year after year, the stock market goes up on average.'

The reason is self-evident and incontrovertible.

'Stocks don't go down for ever: they either bottom or they go bankrupt. Whereas some stocks do, in fact, go up for ever.'

A true community

Nadig and his cohorts understand the concept of investing on the net. Even if you are not a shareholder, their site repays time spent visiting, because the content is fascinating. MetaMarkets has created the classic sticky website.

One draw is the discussion, a cut above the usual chit-chat. Another dimension is provided by the MetaMarkets Think Tank – a panel of experts. Nadig calls them visionaries, which might be over-egging the pudding, but certainly contributors include extremely interesting individuals, all of whom made their mark driving new technology during the past decade. You will find the views of Nicholas Negroponte, founder of the MIT Media Lab and author of *Being Digital*; David Isenberg, author of *The Rise of the Stupid Network*; and Peter Sprague, Chairman of Wave Systems and former chairman of National Semiconductor.

The purpose of the community is clear. In Negroponte's words:

'The divide between the information rich and the information poor is being levelled by the internet. Traditionally, mutual fund shareholders have been extremely information poor, with only minimal insight into how their fund is managed – while managers were information rich. OpenFund tears down the wall between rich and poor: suddenly fund holders have as much information on their investments as the managers. This leads to greater insights not only for shareholder, but for managers as well.'

The topics covered are fascinating and the commentary relevant. Recent themes include the importance of the Microsoft anti-trust appeal, the débâcle of the US presidential elections, and appropriate strategies for gaming the additions and excisions of companies from the S&P 500.

You would have done well to read Nadig's insights into the genome project written in December 1999, shortly before prices in biotech stocks – especially those that could claim any relationship to genome research, however tangential – went bonkers.

> Biotech is in the middle of a boom. Companies like Celera Genomics have jumped into the limelight from relative obscurity. The limelight is well deserved: genomics stands to change the world as profoundly as the information revolution.
>
> Genomics tosses me into a totally unfamiliar world of new ideas expressed in a new language. Without further ado: I went off to answer all the stupid questions I could ask.
>
> OK, so what does genomics do for us? A lot, but it mostly comes down to five things:
>
> **1** It lets you discover genes associated with certain diseases, and then test for those diseases by screening people's genes.
>
> **2** It lets you make old drugs better.
>
> **3** It lets you treat genetic disorders.
>
> **4** It lets you treat diseases by making antibodies specific to certain diseases.
>
> **5** It lets you invent new forms of life.
>
> What? New forms of life? It's true. You see it in agriculture, where mutant corn and tomatoes are invented to be resistant to diseases, grow faster, etc. ... There are folks making new forms of bacteria to do things like eat radioactive waste and PCBs.
>
> New companies, like Abgenix, have bred special mice that are now so close to human that the antibodies they produce actually are biologically human. Your body, theoretically, has no way of knowing that they are just cops in mice clothing.

Heady stuff, and a few weeks ahead of the crowd. In the current environment, weeks are what count. The fewer the better. That gap is what ratchets up the all-important annualized rate of return.

In early 2000 the firm was asking the question 'What is an internet company, anyway?' Here are a few of the most pertinent observations:

> Unlike traditional media, such as book publishing or radio broadcasting, you can't actually invest in the Internet itself. Like human

language, the Internet is intangible, evolving, and pervasive. Many companies are enabling the Internet, and still more are enabled by it …

Some companies commonly regarded as 'Internet companies' are part of InfoGenesis. Other companies who conduct business on the Internet are engaged in history's fastest, fiercest hyper-competition, where the loyalty of their corporate tribe is measured not just in sales or profits, but also in new metrics such as eyeballs, click-throughs, and hang-time. Still other companies are using the Internet in strikingly innovative ways to create entirely new businesses, or breathe new life into old ones.

If you want to stay ahead of the investing crowd and seek access to a body of thought-provoking, leading-edge commentary, you could do a lot worse than to become a participant in the MetaMarket community.

Information alone is not enough

It is almost too easy to forget that the grunt work has to go on. Even MetaThemes require research the old-fashioned way. As in identifying the degree to which corporate tribalism really had caught on at Home Depot. Nadig went to see for himself.

'Stand and watch people go through the checkout counter for an hour. It's fun. For some, that seems alien. You grab a coffee on the way, some guy shakes your hand, you go to the book section. You're browsing. Home Depot has created an environment where the home improvement fanatic, the hardware guy, the gardener, can basically hang out.'

Nadig hung out there long enough to confirm the hypothesis and got hooked. Among other things, he bought the tools, plastic covers and cable to network his home, and also built a wine rack in his basement.

'It's impossible to leave Home Depot without spending at least $100. If I had spent less time at Home Depot seeing ideas to improve my home, I could have bought a second house by now!'

When not hanging around the checkout counter at Home Depot, Nadig finds time for company visits, though his attitude to management meetings is different along a couple of dimensions. He tries to spend as much time or more with the chief technology officer or head of R&D or SVP of engineering as with the CEO or CFO; and, if he likes what he hears, then MetaMarkets spreads the word to the community, which can be helpful to the companies concerned.

'Take Viisage. They make facial recognition technology, hence the two Is. You go to their offices and, if you've been there before, when you walk in, you are greeted by name. But, at the same time, it's difficult to get a handle on how applicable the technology is. How economic is this going to be? It's very expensive and still in development.

'The core business is producing drivers' licences. As old economy as old gets. If you look at the books, it looks like a licence plate company. But there is this cool technology.

'The CEO and chief engineer spent half a day with us. I asked the CEO why and he said, "I know you don't have a huge amount of money in us. Hopefully you will, some day; you'll be successful, still like us, and you'll put more in but, more to the point, I know that you guys are going to tell everyone. If some other investment manager shows up, it's never going to leave the house. They keep it quiet. Everything I say to you you're going to write about. How I treat you is going to get written about, so I have to pay attention." We get access ahead of what we deserve because of the way we do things.'

Nadig wants to understand management. He places even greater importance on personal goals in new-economy companies than investment professionals generally assign to manufacturers or other more stable businesses. Hence the need to eyeball key people. The decision to invest in Harris and Harris Group came only after a face-to-face encounter.

'We phoned New York and spent half a day with management. We talked to them about their investment philosophy and prior wins, prior losses, and tried to generate a comfort level with how they were doing things.'

Ironically that meeting meant the company was destined to be only a shorter-term hold.

'In getting to know Charles Harris, the CEO, we came to understand that being public wasn't nearly as important to him as doing his job well. That has benefits and disadvantages. The benefits are that he runs a very good company; the disadvantages are he is not particularly good at convincing the public that his company should be worth more.'

The virtual way forward

MetaMarkets is already at the forefront of the investment industry, so Nadig's thoughts on what could come next are more than usually fascinating. He is a fountain of ideas. They cascade out at a pace too rapid to include all of them in one chapter. I have selected those that seem most immediate. Some readers will be euphoric, others suicidal, over his observations.

1. Review every investment you have all the time

'The half life of competitive position and innovation can be quite short in the New Economy, so investments should be understood to be in a status of continuous review.'

This applies not just to individual holdings but to the whole process of portfolio management. Evolution is never ending.

'Markets are dynamic, and so is OpenFund. Policies will evolve; in fact, they'll evolve right in front of your eyes.'

2. We are all citizens of Day Trader Nation

This has nothing to do with market timing, but everything to do with the way MetaMarkets manages individual holdings.

> **Market cycles that used to take years to play out can now happen in months, sometimes even in a single day.**

'We have a long-term vision of the growth of the New Economy, but within that we recognize that the landscape changes very rapidly – and so do swings in investor psychology. Today we are all citizens of Day Trader Nation, because market cycles that used to take years to play out can now happen in months, sometimes even in a single day.'

It is almost inevitable that an online investment fund would trade actively. Nadig is not defensive about turnover. That, too, is part of the culture and a facet that adds to excitement and keeps investors interested. There is no room for sentiment on the new frontier of fund management. Anyone inclined to argue should peruse their performance and weep.

'The nature of what we do tends to attract traders. We trade extremely aggressively for a US mutual fund. We are more like a hedge fund. We're not interested in grabbing another random play out of the air, but we'll turn a quarter of the portfolio in a day, if we think it makes sense.'

Buy and Hold is for wimps. Only supersensitive investors are able to keep up with the pace of change that drives today's markets. Index managers are those who find the whole thing too awful and have given up. Trading strategy should be an integral part of the investment strategy.

'There are so many opportunities around today that a fund that does not do this is leaving money on the table. We track, in real time, our intra-day trading activity so that we stay in control. We can maybe make 10, 20 basis points a day for our shareholders that way (25 per cent p.a.). Our trading activity always helps more than it hurts.'

Easier, of course, during a bull phase, but this approach can work in down periods as well – as long, of course, as you are on the right side of the trade.

3. Let's hear it for the futurists

'There is another valuable source of original investment insight that tends to be overlooked by traditional fund managers. Futurists look beyond next quarter's earnings estimates to forecast the surprising forces that will shape the world. These are the forces that contain the greatest risks and opportunities for investors.

'Who was talking about the enormous possibilities of the internet a decade ago? Who foresaw the coming of the bandwidth revolution? It wasn't the traditional securities analysts! It was the futurists.'

Another worry for Wall Street. Why pay analysts huge salaries if they only know how to look backwards? People are willing to pay less and less to understand the past. Insights into the future are priceless. You can find futurologists such as Negroponte acting as discussion leaders on the MetaMarkets site. Others who Nadig believes have ability to identify forward-looking trends and predict the way the world is going include Peter Layden, author of *The Long Boom*, and David Isenberg, the telcom heretic who predicted the decline of AT&T and the rise of the 'stupid network' paradigm.

4. Jurassic investing

Avoiding shares that fail to meet Nadig's tests and could drag down performance is only half the story. Go one better and stake out a short position, as Nadig did in AT&T and E Toys. The fund has been up to 10 per cent short at times. Dinosaurs can provide a reverse profit opportunity.

'Can Dinosaurs Dance?' is a recent thread. This topic stimulated a heated debate between experts and the MetaMarkets community. One contributor, Mcarman concludes:

> Dinosaurs can waltz, but they can't cha-cha.
> Innovation comes in two flavours, revolutionary and evolutionary. The cassette was revolution, the VCR was revolution, the PC was

revolution. The Walkman was evolution, the remote control and Picture in Picture were evolution.

Sony did not invent any of these technologies, but has dominated the design and feature aspect of the business. Sony became one of the dominant consumer electronics companies following this simple strategy. Don't get me wrong, the Walkman is a great product, but it was only evolution of portable cassette players. Sony can waltz. Its industry is evolutionary. Sony is now facing the MP3 challenge – let's see how it faces up to that assault.

Peter Sprague injected definition into the debate:

I don't believe that there can be any doubt that the scale of an organisation inversely affects its capacity to innovate. I once had a conversation on this subject with Dr Carver Mead, a legendary figure in Silicon Valley. I asked him why he left Intel, where he had been one of the founders. He answered that it had 'gotten too big.' I asked him how big it was when he left. He answered '200 employees.'

Nicholas Negroponte underscores the problem facing large corporations:

There is a class of basic research and innovation which is best outsourced. It is commonly called 'thinking out of the box.' Doing it inside risks being too incremental and almost always lacks the broad range of people needed.

Still, innovation does not necessarily translate to profits, let alone strong stock price performance. Back to Mcarman: 'Pioneering small companies don't always survive. Most pioneers end up face down in the mud with arrows sticking out of their backs. The trick is to dodge the arrows.'

The astute investor needs to be positioned somewhere in-between. There's no point owning shares whose day is done, but investors should not be overeager to embrace the new model until it has served an apprenticeship.

5. It's the 'New' Economy, stupid

'Pessimistic pundits call the New Economy a "fad", and the bull market of the 1990s a "speculative bubble". They ignore the great trends that define the New Economy and have impelled the stock market of the 1990s to "crash up", as inevitably as the depression caused the stock market of the 1930s to "crash down".'

A brief résumé of the many positive events that occurred during the late 1980s and 1990s to liberate billions of people and enable them to begin taking part in economic development leads Nadig to conclude:

'When before have such colossal forces of transformation converged at a single moment in history? Can there be any doubt that this is a new economy? It's a great time to be alive, and a great time to invest. The pessimists are missing out on one of the most exciting periods in history – and potentially one of history's greatest investment opportunities. Realizing the continued explosive growth potential of technology and global enterprise in the New Economy will require lots of capital and lots of risk-taking, and will offer the potential for extraordinary rewards for sophisticated investors.'

If the digital revolution really is over and the age of digital civilization has commenced, then you will soon see clones of MetaMarkets; but Nadig was first. No-one can ever take that accomplishment away. And, as long as his returns continue to outpace more pedestrian managers, he will not only go down in investment history as a pioneer, but also as someone who made a lot of investors very happy. MetaMarkets fits the same mould as its portfolio companies.

> ## Trying to solve tomorrow's problems is a pretty good way to make money.

'History shows us that trying to solve tomorrow's problems is a pretty good way to make money.'

11

Mark Slater

Growth on the cheap

Won *The Wall Street Journal* award for Europe in 1996, his first full year of management

Ranked fifth out of all UK investment funds tracked by *The Investors Chronicle* over five years

Up more than 2.5 times the average UK unit trust since June 1995

Top decile over every period from six months to five years

Achieved superior returns while still holding high cash balances

A famous name can be a mixed blessing. Mark Slater has not wasted much time stepping out of the shadow of long-time stock market guru, Jim Slater. He has established a very distinct presence, founding an investment boutique that bears his name. Slater Investments Ltd advises offshore funds and manages portfolios on behalf of wealthy individuals and pension funds. In addition, for five years it ran one of the most successful unit trusts in the UK – Johnson Fry Slater Growth. Until recently, the company was also investment adviser to Internet Indirect plc, a quoted vehicle focused on private technology businesses.

Naturally, Slater is happy to acknowledge a familial influence in steering him towards the investment scene, but points out that he alone, out of four siblings, ended up in the profession.

'I've always been interested in numbers and business for as long as I can remember. My father encouraged that. He didn't force it. It wasn't foisted upon me. I've got a brother and two sisters and none of them were terribly interested.'

His style incorporates the analytical insights laid out in Jim Slater's *The Zulu Principle* and further popularized through the publication REFS (Really Essential Financial Statistics), but the second generation of Slaters to make its mark in financial markets has taken all his father's work and gone on to develop the next stage of growth investing, as well as finding interesting new ways to exploit exciting new economy markets, both on the buy and sell side.

Interestingly, Slater first entered the world of investments through writing. He helped edit *Analyst* magazine and *The Investor's Stock Market Letter* in the early 1990s, put in a stint at *The Investors Chronicle*, initially on the smaller companies team, and also worked on *The Zulu Principle* with his father. These experiences gave him a number of insights into the working of public markets and the linkage between analysis and investing, which he was able to draw upon later when he made the move to managing money professionally.

'Helping on *The Zulu Principle* was very valuable. We were forced to analyze everything from first principles in a pretty rigorous way. What makes a share price move? What do we really think about this?'

At *The Investors Chronicle* it quickly became apparent that Slater knew how to pick stocks. Over his 18-month tenure, his average recommendation – and there were about 50 separate suggestions – rose approximately 50 per cent. The annualized rate of return was even higher. He was also doing rather well with his personal investments. When his portfolio returned the equivalent of five years' salary in the space of one week, he decided to go off and form his own firm, even though he was only 24 at the time.

The rules of thumb that served him so well as a financial journalist during 1992 and 1993 were relatively simple, but the process of sifting through the entire UK-listed universe enabled Slater to develop practical guidelines he would use to great effect when it came to placing real money on the table.

'At that time it was quite easy. There were phenomenal bargains around, after smaller companies had been out of favour for four consecutive years. You'd find a company with a P/E of eight growing very, very quickly and it was a good business, throwing off cash.'

The sell side was a little more complicated, but here, too, he started to formulate strategies that made sure profits would not remain merely on paper.

'So many shares were cheap, yet the magazine had a policy of having sell recommendations as well as buys. I became acutely aware of the importance of timing on the sell side – even when you found an overpriced company, it could become far more overpriced.'

Which meant not rushing to dump winners. The biggest profits generally accrue when you let the best performers run, an approach that is easier to maintain when the underlying business itself is growing.

Growth to the core

Slater has a range of investment interests and runs several portfolios, but the main thrust of all his efforts is an emphasis on the importance of growth. To understand the philosophy that has made him so successful so quickly, it is hard to improve, by way of summary, on the stated investment policy for the Slater Growth Unit Trust:

> The Trust will … focus exclusively on shares which qualify under several *growth* criteria: namely, strong earnings *growth* prospects, reasonable price earnings ratios in relation to that growth, healthy cash flows and robust financial positions.

Hard to argue against a policy that weeds out stagnant companies and concentrates on growth, as that focus must turn up fundamentally decent businesses with good prospects.

> We are looking for shares with low PEGs [Price to Earnings Growth], in other words, *growth* which can be acquired cheaply, with sustainable earnings. We're looking for companies with very strong cash flows.

The PEG calculation is relatively straightforward. Slater selected SFI Group, the UK themed pub and bar operator which has already

| PEG Computation for SFI Group (data as of 29 December 2000)

Share Price: 176p

Key Financial Parameters: based on a prospective 12 month rolling basis looking forward two periods. SFI has a 31 May year-end.

Historic normalised EPS were 14p. Recent forecasts for the current year (ending in 5 months) range from 18.2p to 19.7p. For the following fiscal year, the range of recent forecasts is from 23.3p to 26p.

- Prospective earnings per share (EPS): 18.9p and 24.1p (mean concensus estimates)

Based on the above numbers and its 31 May year-end, the time weighted rolling Price Earnings Ratio for the next 12 months using 21.9p, which is a blended average of the fiscal 2001 and 2002 forecasts, comes out at eight.

Prospective Price Earnings Ratio = Current Share Price ÷ Prospective EPS
$176 \div 21.9 = 8.0\times$

- Prospective EPS Growth Rate: 34.3% and 27.3% for fixed 2001 and 2002

Using the same period, the 12-month rolling Prospective EPS growth rate works out to 30.5%.

The PEG Ratio = Prospective P/E ÷ Prospective EPS Growth
$8.0 \div 30.5 = \boxed{0.26\times}$

established an excellent track record and is an old favourite to illustrate the mechanics.

A green light then for PEG lovers everywhere for SFI. The most volatile variable is the prospective EPS growth rate. Arriving at that number involves both art and science. For SFI, the range of available analyst forecasts of earnings growth for the year ending May 2001, taken from the January issue of REFS is relatively narrow, with a low of 31.4 per cent and a high of 42.9 per cent. Even at the bottom end of this spectrum, you arrive at a PEG well below 0.4× indicating a Margin of Safety sufficiently wide to give growth investors comfort. It would require a massive shortfall against consensus forecasts to push the company over to the wrong side of the PEG divide.

Of course raw numbers are just the starting point, and a necessary, but not complete, condition for investing. Each investor will want to test the consensus forecasts against a knowledge of the business position, which is where the art comes in.

Slater pointed to other reasons, both quantitive and qualitative, behind his selection of SFI Group for the PEG *pro forma*. The company has

1 a five-year EPS growth record of 34 per cent, 56 per cent, 65 per cent, 36 per cent and 33 per cent;

2 a strong trend in sales per share, healthy margins and reasonable cash flow;

3 is rolling out two formats: Bar Med and Litten Tree – both now well established;

4 has excellent, experienced management;

5 retains scope for acquisitive growth as well as organic expansion as the industry in the UK consolidates.

Even good companies with an attractive PEG are bound to have the odd wart. Slater highlighted a couple investors need to consider in respect of SFI Group. The tax charge is gradually rising (going from 9 per cent last year to 14 per cent, and 15 per cent next year) as the company matures and capital allowances and the like offset a lower proportion of the tax charge. Also, gearing of 111 per cent at the end of last year is high.

Slater elaborates on his philosophy.

'The bare numbers are just a means to create a shortlist, at which point I start looking at more qualitative measures – does the company have strong barriers to entry and a strong market position? Is it in a growth sector? Have directors been buying shares? All the dynamics for a very, very sound company.'

This formidable set of criteria forms a filter that winnows out a small, exclusive group from a large available pool. Slater makes the point that most listed companies cannot make it through his screens.

'There really aren't that many companies that fit the criteria. At Slater Investments we are looking for 40, 50 companies, tops. There are an awful lot of good companies that are too expensive which we just don't touch. We're looking for genuinely exceptional companies with exceptional prospects, but with a significant margin of safety.'

So what do some of these paragons of investment virtue look like?

'We were very early investors in technology, but not in conceptual technologies. We invested in technology companies with real earnings and a bit of a record, in most cases, which we were acquiring in 1995 and 1996 on P/Es of eight or twelve, but with growth rates of 30 per cent. Generating cash. Back then, DCS, a specialist in software systems for car dealers and distributors, was growing at over 30 per cent, but traded on a P/E of six times for much of the first half of the year. Its PEG was only 0.2 times, obviously much too low.'

And within 18 months that divergence largely corrected, with the stock price up nearly 400 per cent. But winners came not just from among technology investments. One company that passed all Slater's tests with flying colours and delivered what he had hoped for, and then some, was Black's Leisure.

'It didn't have the earnings growth record that I'd normally look for. It had a torrid recession and took quite a long time to come round, like most retail turnarounds. At the beginning of 1996, I noticed heavy directors' buying, so I rang them up. Things were improving. They had cleaned a lot of rubbish out of the company over the previous couple of years. The main business was doing very well indeed.

'At the time it wasn't obvious but, at 60p, they were on a P/E of about two. They were on an aggressive recovery track. Blacks had results a bit later that year which were very, very good. I added aggressively to the holding when they reached about £1.50 after their results. The price was higher, but the margin of safety was far better, because those results confirmed that things were going extremely well.

'There was a lot more meat on the bone. They had eliminated loss makers and focused on First Sport, a sports retail format which they were rolling out and which was enjoying significant like-for-like sales growth. In addition, Blacks also ran the UK licensee of FILA, a sports brand that was going great guns and, by itself, underwrote the bulk of the earnings upgrades that came through.'

Black's went from 60p to £5, nearly a ten bagger, and did not take that long to get there. Slater waited until the price passed £4 before starting to sell.

Reliability of earnings is one, and possibly the key, characteristic of a company that appeals to Slater. Stop/start growth is of less interest; growth caused by a bounce back is of less interest.

What he wants is regular, consistent, sustainable growth.

What he wants is regular, consistent, sustainable growth. Companies that can deliver are golden, and those are the stocks Slater chooses for his portfolios. However, he recognizes that such companies are few and far between.

'In the UK it is very hard to find the equivalent of Coca-Cola, Microsoft or McDonald's. British companies in most sectors tend to run up against geographical restrictions before long. Often, the best you can hope for is a few years of rapid growth, after which you should probably sell up and move on. However, those companies that go on growing relentlessly remain the Holy Grail.'

Panning for gold

Given the sort of growth which Slater demands, researching for prospects can be made more efficient by separating businesses into two groups: those containing companies that are capable of passing the growth test, and those where such companies rarely, if ever, exist. From his experience over the last few years, Slater has identified a few sectors that are fruitful waters to fish, and others where the lack of suitable candidates makes them less interesting.

'There are certain sectors that I rarely ever go near, because they tend not to offer the reliability of earnings growth. Construction, metal bashers – those sorts of companies. It's very unusual for companies in these sectors to produce consistent earnings growth. You can get a great year one year, and give it all back the next.'

There are good reasons why Slater stays away from these areas.

'Take a metal basher. One's looking at a commodity business that probably competes on price, which is tied to a cycle. There are no barriers to entry of any consequence, in most cases. It should never have a high P/E, so there's not much scope for a re-rating. All you're really hoping to do is to finesse the timing, which is very difficult.'

Another area that he finds suspect is distribution.

'A lot of distribution companies, depending on what they're distributing, tend to compete on price. There's not much value-added in most forms of distribution. There's not a great deal of reliability, in my view, in earnings of those sorts of companies.'

The prohibition is not absolute. Within the worst sectors, Slater sometimes finds the odd diamond: even in construction, which is his number-one bugbear because 'construction companies so often end up cutting their own throats in the name of competition'. One of his top performers proves that every rule has its exception.

'I'm in a share called Peterhouse, which has done very well over the last couple of years. It's up two and a half times. Over 10 per cent of profits come from a strong environmental monitoring division which, in my view, is not tied to the construction cycle in the same way as other parts of the business and is worth a much higher multiple. Another 50 per cent comes from services to the industry. Only a third comes from straight construction. Peterhouse is well run and management owns plenty of shares. Also, it's growing at 30 per cent per annum, but trades on a P/E of about 11.'

So much for the pans. Now let's turn to sectors that are some of Slater's picks.

'In the support services sector, in IT, in technology, in some parts of retail – although they tend to be quite specialized – in the leisure sector, or in areas where there's a rollout going on, you at least have the dynamics that make consistent earnings growth possible. Those are the sectors where the investments I make do tend to pop up.'

Slater strongly believes that consistency deserves a premium. He had this to say in his March 1998 report, where he was concerned about whether analysts' forecasts might prove over-optimistic: 'In these circumstances, *reliable growth* will be crucial and may attract significant P/E premiums'.

Growth stocks provide investors with two particular and related benefits which are not necessarily present in any other classification of company: benefits that can make life a lot easier. So much so, one begins to wonder why any other style deserves an audience.

1. Unlimited upside

This feature is very much part of their appeal to Slater.

'What excites me – what I like about focusing on growth companies – is that the upside is unlimited. If you're investing in a cyclical business, the best thing that can happen is that the company is re-rated for a short period until the cycle turns again. There's no chance of a genuine breakout. There's no chance of a very material capital gain.'

2. Unlimited holding period

It follows that, as long as the company continues to perform and the market does not get too far ahead of itself, then an investor can continue to sit tight – which is often the best strategy. As Slater observes, too much trading can hurt a portfolio's performance.

'That's particularly important if you are a tax-paying investor, because what you want is a company you can invest in and never crystallize a capital gain. You always own it. Warren Buffet has demonstrated that in the States. That's the optimal outcome.'

Slater frequently mentions the importance of running profits.

'The ideal investment for me is a company that you can buy and never have to sell, where the share price never quite catches up with the reality and the reality keeps getting better. In other words, it keeps growing very quickly, yet the rating does not go overboard, so can be held for a long time. Of course, these are exceptionally rare, and it is incredibly difficult to resist taking profits along the way. One has to try to be disciplined, asking oneself whether a

> # The ideal investment for me is a company that you can buy and never have to sell.

share remains a good investment today, and whether there are better homes for money elsewhere, and then weigh these considerations against the tax angle.'

There is an added bonus, which is a by-product of the two aforementioned benefits. If you are buying into situations where the upside is both large and potentially could last for a long period, the precise entry point is less of an issue. Which means elusive market timing matters less. Trying to catch the absolute bottom, always a bit of a guessing game, becomes a lower priority. If you can make 200 per cent, why worry about the first 10 per cent?

'If you're looking at a genuinely high quality company, the timing becomes much less significant. The price is actually less significant, in a funny sort of way. It doesn't matter if you overpay a bit. If it's a great business, it's probably worth doing. Again, Buffet has shown that remarkably clearly.'

In search of reliable growth

So how does Slater identify the best prospects that match his parameters?

'First of all, which sector are they operating in? Is it a good sector with a bit of tailwind behind it? Is it a business that is well positioned in that sector? Do they have a competitive advantage – a strong brand or a strong market position or a powerful bit of technology?'

Desktop analysis only takes him so far. The next step invariably involves in-person meetings with relevant executives, though Slater is careful to interpret the information he gathers through a more qualitative filter.

'I meet the management, mainly to get answers to specific questions. I always bear in mind that any company director worth their salt has a conflict of interest with any potential investor – they want you to buy the stock.'

The way that investment insights emerge from one-on-ones is a sensitive subject so, although he can cite several instances where he backed off a potential idea after talking to management due to their excessive enthusiasm, Slater is reluctant to name and shame.

Should the company under consideration survive this screen, there is still one more to go. While he is willing to pay up for a quality company, Slater is careful not to overpay. Even if everything else checks out, the price must be right.

'I look at all that in the context of is the price acceptable anyway? In other words, if it grows at x per cent p.a., for the next few years, which I think it might well do, do I still want to buy it?'

The importance of price/earnings growth

No one ratio can determine whether a share will make a good or bad investment, but the PEG is the one to which Slater pays the closest attention. If the PEG does not send a buy signal, he does not bother to research the business. The PEG is a means of quantifying how much you are paying for growth.

'A share's P/E is a one-dimensional measure, whereas the PEG puts price in a sensible context, at least for a growth share. Clearly, there

> Looking at cash flow is a reality check on creative accounting.

are many types of company for which the PEG would be totally misleading. Even for growth companies there can be distortions, for instance with those growing at 100 per cent for a year or two. But for most growth companies compounding earnings at, say, 15–30 per cent a year, it produces an excellent starting point. I tend to look at prospective P/Es and growth rates – after all, with any company it is the future that matters most. And REFS, which I use a lot, contain prospective numbers, too, so they are easily accessible.

'The attraction of a share with a low PEG is twofold. First, a low PEG provides a significant Margin of Safety. Second, if a company has a low P/E in relation to its growth rate, then there is room for an upwards status change in the multiple.'

Earnings growth, however, is not enough on its own. Coming a close second is cash flow. Slater wants to see that a business is capable of generating cash before he invests.

'It's still true that it's pretty easy for a company to fake profit: it's very difficult to fake cash. It's possible, but hard. Looking at cash flow is a reality check on creative accounting. It's also a check on how real is the business. When companies don't generate cash, one has to ask the question, "What are they doing?"'

Given his emphasis on growth, he is willing to recognize that there can be trade-offs.

'There are times when, if a company is in a highly expansionary phase, they won't be generating a lot of cash. They'll be ploughing money into working capital and that kind of thing.'

Even then, his tolerance for companies that are slow to turn investment into positive cash flow is strictly limited.

'That shouldn't go on for very long. Most companies that meet the kind of criteria I'm looking for will, over a two- or three-year period, generate plenty of cash. There may be one year when they don't, but on average they'll be generating cash.'

Cash flow feeds back into sustainable growth: another reason to question whether growth is achievable over the long term, unless there is evidence of cash-generation capability. Companies cannot rely on capital markets to be the funding source of last resort. Internal operations must contribute.

Slater also harbours grave concerns over whether very high growth can be sustainable for prolonged periods, except in isolated examples, and is wary of racy multiples, even when apparently supported by a spurt of exceptional growth. In early unit trust literature he wrote:

> Shares with prospective P/Es much over 20 will normally be avoided, irrespective of the growth rate, unless future progress is nearly certain. The rationale is simple. A P/E of 40 leaves no room for disappointment, even if earnings are growing very rapidly. A slight hiccup and the shares will fall sharply. A P/E of 40 also leaves little room for a re-rating – shareholders are therefore totally dependent on earnings growth to drag the shares up.

The biggest challenge for Slater, and other investors who use PEG ratios, is not the computation, which is easy, or even the interpretation, which is relatively straightforward. The tricky part comes in assessing whether growth is genuine and can be extrapolated forward with confidence.

'Is it reliable, is it sustainable? That's really the only other question. Try to find a share on a P/E of 15 that, on the face of it, is going to be growing at 30 per cent p.a. for some time. Look at the consensus forecast, because you've got to start somewhere. Then interrogate the numbers. Sometimes they're too low, sometimes they're too high. Get to understand the business. It's a question of finding evidence that growth is sustainable while, at the same time, looking for trouble.'

The PEG, when you have conviction about the underlying data, seems like manna from investment heaven. Slater is careful to caution investors about pushing its use too far and warns of extra layers of complexity in comparing one company to another.

'The PEG is just a measure. Like any measure, it's flawed if you push it. No financial ratio or measure works if it's abused. You shouldn't try and use such a measure to judge a very cyclical business, for example. The growth part of the equation is too unreliable. Fifty per cent may well be the forecast for one year, but then the following year you could be looking at 10 per cent. And with a high degree of probability that will be reversed. Look back and you'll probably find that earnings per share have tended to hit a certain level and then fall back repeatedly.'

You cannot put a square peg in a round hole. So for certain sectors, most of which will not, in any event, appeal to growth-minded investors, this analytical approach is not the way to go. Cyclical businesses follow a different set of rules. Investors must recognize this and should be smart enough to follow a different set of valuation measures.

'Every sector is cyclical up to a point, but some are much more cyclical than others. Worse than that, in certain sectors there is very little companies can do to buck the cycle. You would never use PEG to value a house builder. You'd never use it to value a property company. It would be an entirely inappropriate measure for construction businesses, for chemical businesses, for anything that's cyclical or anything that should be valued on an NAV basis.'

In a nutshell, 'The PEG is a growth measure. It can only be applied to companies which are growing'.

For businesses that have gone ex-growth, it is best to go back to basics and utilize other measures, as the PEG will not give the right answer in those circumstances.

More than just one ratio

The emphasis on PEG is justified, given its importance, but investors should not rely on this – or, indeed, any other single ratio – as a one-stop shop. Slater is at pains to emphasize the complexity of the investment process and highlights several additional factors that play a part in his decision as to whether to buy or, indeed, sell a security. Largely he is looking for confirmation within the company, or externally from what is happening in its markets, that growth can continue.

1. Competition

Competitive assessment is a central part of his analytical repertoire, not only for what he can learn about the industry but also, more importantly, for insights into individual companies and their relative growth potential. A good place to start is with sentiment in the sector. The next level is to see whether that applies broadly or is restricted to only one or two leading companies, which may be unrepresentative of the rest.

'One's also looking at what's happening to other companies in the same sector. What is their management saying? If they are making bearish noises, that would clearly put you off.'

Second, he wants to get a sense of what direct competitors might have to say about the potential company contemplated for investment.

'The competition is a very good source of information. It's the only good source of bad news. I always ask who's good or who's bad. You want to hear the bad news, and you want to hear bad news before you invest rather than afterwards.'

Occasionally, Slater has been warned off as a result of quizzing a company about its competition. Sadly, he is too diplomatic to cite specific examples.

Third, is it a sector that is known for cut-throat price competition? Price-driven industries rarely contain many attractive investment candidates.

'Some sectors are well known for periodic price problems. Construction, up until very recently, was such a sector. Every ten years it used to commit suicide, prices got so crazy. Insurance is another example of a sector which is so competitive as to be absurd. Insurance companies constantly compete to the point where participants cannot make money. The only insurance company I've ever owned is Independent Insurance, the only one in the UK that makes an under-writing profit. All the others make money out of their investment portfolios. In other words, they are effectively investment trusts with an extremely expensive hobby.'

Slater steers clear of industries with lemming-like tendencies where profit is not the number-one priority.

2. Ownership of unique assets

A company that owns property, often intellectual, that is hard to repli-cate or has copyright or patent protection, has a better chance of delivering sustainable earnings growth. So Slater looks for those types of assets and, when he finds them, that is a big plus point.

'I've been a shareholder for quite some time in Britt Allcroft, which owns the rights to Thomas the Tank Engine, one of the strongest children's brands on earth. That's something that would be very difficult to replicate. There's a much higher degree of reliability in their business.'

Similarly, companies with significant market share are more likely to be able to control their own destiny than most. Market position can be an asset, even though you will not find the cost of building that position on the balance sheet.

3. Directors' dealings

Insider activity regularly shapes Slater's thinking. Its usefulness as a signal is enhanced because it is relatively easy for investors to monitor. Most countries require some form of disclosure. There are several services that release this information. In the UK, the Saturday edition of the *Financial Times* summarizes directors' dealings for the prior period.

Black's Leisure was one company where director buying attracted Slater's attention.

'At the beginning of 1996, five or six directors bought quite heavily, which jumped out off the page.'

As the price started to rise, directors bought more, and so did Slater. Trading by those presumed to know best what is going on is an indicator that flags an issue in either direction.

'Aggressive cluster buying by directors is very powerful as a buy signal. Heavy selling by a number of directors is a sign that maybe things aren't quite so good. On balance, directors' buying is more important than selling. There is only one reason for directors to buy a good chunk of shares – they believe they are going to make money. Selling is more complicated. There are lots of personal reasons why a director might want to raise cash.'

On its own, director dealing is not a sufficient reason to buy or sell, but it is a useful pointer and, when other evidence points to a similar conclusion, can clinch the case.

The art of selling

One key advantage to growth stocks is that, as long as they keep on growing, you do not have to sell and, in most cases, should not be in too much of a hurry to sell.

'You've got to run profits. Very often, a good company can go to a very high price – higher than you'd originally anticipated, and new developments keep making it look cheap. With a good quality company, it's important to allow time for those new developments.'

As important as it is to let profits run, Slater stresses the importance of not forgetting to sell. In early 2000 prices of technology shares were off the charts and Slater found himself profoundly sceptical about valuations across almost the entire sector. Slater slashed his technology positions. A severe correction came shortly thereafter. By then, he was already looking elsewhere for the best bargains, questioning both the sustainability and even the growth rates of most of the TMT sector.

If something goes up sharply, at least he wants to take a look and make sure the share is still a keeper. Any doubt, and out it goes, as happened to two excellent companies in early 1998. Slater wrote in his report that year of taking profits with regret – though locking down a large profit can never be too painful.

> Diagonal was sold after a 369 per cent gain when its rating became overstretched, even for such a fast growing IT operator. The Trust's position in Psion was also reduced after the company's brilliant mobile communication joint venture prompted a strong rise in the shares.

Slater recognizes that selling a stock can involve a more complex evaluation process than the original purchase decision. As a journalist, the sell side of the investment equation was often at the forefront of his mind.

'It is much easier writing a buy note than a sell note, because, with a sell note, the timing is much more difficult. If a share has done very well and the rating has caught up with the price, and it's suddenly a higher risk bet, then you might easily decide that you no longer wish to own it. But there's a world of difference between deciding that something is getting pricey and deciding to go short.

There's a world of difference between deciding that something is getting pricey and deciding to go short.

'The hardest thing is when a company has done well and the stock is also acting well, but is in a phase when it's difficult to value – when it doesn't really fit any traditional valuation criteria. This applies to a lot of technology companies. Often the best thing is to ease out – to sell a third, then another third, etc.'

There is a general discipline that should apply across a portfolio, and which is generally market related, but then there are also company-specific events that can trigger a sell decision if a change of sufficient importance takes place.

'Normally, one sells because a price goes up to the point where the Margin of Safety has been eroded, and where all the good news is in the price. Selling certainly makes sense when you have found a better home for the money elsewhere. With a truly great company, however, one is always more tolerant of a high rating and more reluctant to sell. The other scenario when you sell is after bad news, after a profit warning or such like, when the "story" changes. Then it normally pays to sell fairly quickly. Profit warnings have a nasty habit of coming in threes.'

Slater cautions against selling – or, indeed, buying – for the sake of it. Just as investors should move on if events dictate, equally they should not be in a rush to do something without a reason.

'Investors need to be wary when reading magazines that contain investment tips to sell or buy. Journalists are under pressure to fill magazines with copy every week, whereas, as an investor, you don't have to do anything, certainly on the buy side. That's the greatest privilege of the investor, the ability to say "No – I'll wait a bit. I'll see how it goes. I'll wait a few days."'

Slater also highlights a tendency of too many investors who do detailed research before making a purchase decision and then do not devote the same intensity of analysis to deciding about the sale. There is a need for balance, with the exit strategy meriting more weight and coming closer to equilibrium in terms of the appropriate degree of deliberation.

Several specific triggers alert Slater to the need to consider getting rid of a stock that is not acting well, but one above all sets off alarm bells. That is when a company goes ex-growth. After Azlan, a computer distributor, came in with earnings only up 10 per cent at its interim report in November 1996, as against the market's expectation for 25 per cent, Slater wasted no time jettisoning the holding. His initial instinct to unload was confirmed by a deterioration in the company's cash position. That reaction turned out to be right. The share sagged for some months thereafter and then, in June 1997, Azlan was suspended due to accounting irregularities.

Growth going forward

Even in 1997, the FTSE 100 PEG was around 1.6 times and there were only four Index shares with PEGs of less than one. Pickings for low PEG lovers have been slim among large caps for a while, so the focus has, of necessity, been on smaller shares, where the range of qualifying companies has been larger.

More recently, extreme technology enthusiasm distorted the valuations of many growth companies. If the bloom is off the technology rose, what does a growth groupie do? Slater remains upbeat about prospects for his style of investing, provided investors are not wedded to a single sector. He sees plenty of opportunities elsewhere; but, whereas his preferred enterprise was one capable of generating 15–25 per cent p.a. in earnings growth, now he is considering companies that may only offer 5–15 per cent, to escape having to pay sky-high P/Es.

'You can still buy good growth companies on normal kinds of ratings. They just aren't in the technology sector. The Whitbreads of this world, a leading leisure concern, are only growing at a few per cent per annum. But they have become so de-rated over the last couple of years that they're getting to the point where they compare very well with cash and superbly well with some of these companies on crazy valuations. At the moment, exciting tends to come at too high a price. It's a novelty for me to start buying those sorts of companies, because they're not dynamic. The growth rate is unexciting, but there comes a point at which that's in the price.'

This is not the sort of argument that springs to mind when talking growth, but Slater's logic is compelling. He makes a convincing case for a safer form of growth as suitable during times when markets that, for now, at least, seem uncomfortably turbulent, also are unable to provide investors clear direction. His solution in spring 2000 was to switch to stocks where almost all the conceivable risk and all realistic operating problems were already factored into the price. These names were not his natural constituency but, when valuations of traditional growth stocks make no sense, Slater turned to non-traditional sources for more reliable, if lower, growth at a sensible price.

'Take Whitbread. The only way in which you can argue that their price is wrong is if they massively miss their earnings targets. That can happen. They are quite highly geared, and maybe consumer spending is about to collapse, or about to disappoint. You could argue they still might be expensive. But, on balance, a lot of companies like Boots, the pharmacy retailer, are cheap.'

Later the same year, Slater found himself in truly foreign territory buying house builders whose growth was being upgraded and where PEG rates were declining. Many in the sector suddenly lit up his screen. So Barratt, Bellway and Wimpey all attracted attention. The good yields meant these shares were almost proxies for cash, but there was also potential upside, which cash can never offer. Slater is flexible enough to consider companies he had ignored in prior periods, but his flexibility does not extend to mucking around with his analytical approach. He will own what fits the discipline rather than stretch parameters to renew investment in old friends.

Safety first

The other strategy to consider is cash. There are times when a low profile is necessary. If you are a growth investor but growth is so much in vogue that investors push valuations to silly multiples, it pays to sit on the sidelines. There is nothing wrong with holding cash in that environment. At least, in the middle part of 2000, that was the right place for Slater and those of his ilk.

'I was very unsettled by the intensity of the enthusiasm behind technology. Having been investing in these sorts of companies for a long time, long before they were fashionable anyway, it was alarming to me just how blind and indiscriminate buying was. It was panic buying at any price. And 30 or 40 new technology funds were set up. They raised money very easily, which is never a good sign. Everyone and his wife was investing in these things, and you couldn't go anywhere without people telling you which shares you ought to be buying. It was indiscriminate and crazy.

> # Cash is a very good investment because you don't have to be too clever with it.

'Cash is a very good investment because you don't have to be too clever with it. I think the technology sector is overvalued, and I think that's going to change. My biggest holding today by a mile is cash. I think that is probably still the best investment.'

When all else fails, investors can sit on the sidelines and wait for better opportunities to arrive. Which is exactly where Slater was when NASDAQ, TechMARK, Neuer Markt and all the other new economy indices were falling off a cliff for most of 2000.

'Terry Smith of Collins Stewart quoted this in one of his books. He said that, at the racetrack, your only privilege is the ability to say "no". You have no obligation to bet. It's like Warren Buffet's baseball analogy for buying shares. He says, "Just keep waiting. Don't swing. Wait until you've got a real sitter and then clobber it."'

And cash can be comforting indeed in times of extreme turbulence. For those who wish to stay in the game, there is an alternative, even when markets are in a downdraft.

A time to short

Where valuations become extreme, Slater feels investors should be more willing to go short; although, in the UK, while gradually getting easier, shorting remains difficult for individuals. Slater's approach to selling short is straightforward. When asked what might cause him to short a stock, he identifies two drivers.

'One is serious overpricing, and the other is a near-term trigger.'

Overpricing is easier to identify. The second determinant is clearly critical because, with shorting, you can be right in the long run about overvaluation, but wiped out in the short term if you get the timing wrong. So what makes a good short? Slater identified Knutsford, a UK listed shell with a high-profile board, as an irresistible opportunity to go short in early 2000.

'All they had was 2.5p in cash, or £5 million. They were looking to do a major deal. £5 million wasn't going to be enough to pay the legal bill on a big bid. The shares peaked close to £2.50 compared with that 2.5p of assets. Including warrants, the company had a market cap of £1.5 billion against only £5 million of cash. To my mind, that was a lot of hot air to plug, no matter how good the deal.'

A compelling case, but however convincing the analysis, caution is critical over on the short side. Issues of appropriate valuation aside, when there is huge market enthusiasm for something, it means nervous moments before the inevitable arrives. In the case of Knutsford, Slater felt, sooner or later, the price would come crashing down to earth.

'It was hard to see what would make the dam break. But it clearly would. It was only going to be a matter of time. The moment they announced a deal, the shares were bound to fall. Even so, psychologically, it was hard staying short of a share like that.'

Slater stuck to his guns and, as it turned out, only four weeks after this observation reality reasserted itself and the stock took a dive to 20p. A few months later, the price was down around 6p, a decline of 97 per cent.

But events rarely arrive on schedule. More frequently the exposed short seller is left hanging, wondering why the price continues to defy gravity. Slater accepts that, on its own, overvaluation is not enough. For each time he mentions overvaluation, he stresses the need for a trigger twice. Some triggers are more obvious than others.

'You hope, if you're going short, there is bad news which the market hasn't yet fully priced in. And you hope that news comes out quickly. You might know about that bad news through people in the same industry, because companies in the same sector have reported recently.'

A good short, then, is one where overvaluation is quantifiable, but other things are also present within the company or in its markets that suggest that the price could come under pressure – soon.

'One short I rather like at the moment is Logica, because it held up pretty well in the initial technology fall, so it's still on well over a hundred times earnings. It's only growing at 30 per cent p.a. if they make the numbers, which, to be fair, they always have done so far. It's done very well over the past. A great record. But there's nothing exponential in their business. There's no rocket that can turbocharge their earnings. It's a pretty normal, straightforward business. A lot of it is fairly old skills. Yet it's on a PEG of over five.

'The accounting is quite aggressive, in my view, because they book revenue when the contract is signed. There's not much provisioning, as far as I can see. All those things make me think it's overpriced. The trigger could well be when options mature. So I think that's a company where the shares will probably halve over the next year, maybe two years.'

Since this particular conversation (which took place in April 2000), Logica's share price had come off by around 25 per cent as of February 2001.

'Probably my best short recently has been Durlacher. At the peak, in February or March, it had a market cap of £2.1 billion, yet I could not see how it was worth more than a few hundred million at most. The gap was supposedly explained by its investment portfolio, but they only invested £25 million at cost. The market is beginning to consider the possibility that it might have been a bit overpriced.'

Valuations can go to the extreme in both directions, down as well as up, which is worth remembering when selling short. Durlacher's market capitalization, as of December 2000, was barely above £100 million, off nearly 95 per cent. So how does someone in the UK short if so inclined?

'You can go short through most brokers, selling on a long settlement date. A lot more firms nowadays are also offering Contracts for Difference, which remove some of the timing pressures.'

You can see ads for these financial instruments every day in the *Financial Times* or find them in specialized publications such as *The Investors Chronicle*. In the US, of course, shorting is routine. Trading on both sides of the spread is likely to get more accessible in many major markets over time, and become routine for active investors.

Technology and more technology

Slater remains convinced that, though valuations were far too high in the short term, technology will continue to be of prime importance to investors in the longer term. In December 1999 he raised a new fund – Internet Indirect – devoted to investing in private technology companies. Far from being dismayed by the recent reverse in valuations, he is delighted.

'Our cash buys much more than when we raised it. I've spent the last few months saying "no" several times a day. I became the Gromyko of the investment world. Mr *Niet*, wasn't he? And I am delighted I did, because most "yeses" would have been very expensive.'

As to where and when he will put that cash to work, Slater has yet to make more than a small number of investments. He has, however, given thought to which areas he prefers and has ring-fenced those he is likely to avoid.

'Our bias is in favour of enabling technology, must-have content, infrastructure plays. Areas where you can, at the very least, see where operating profits are going to come from. Areas where you can charge for a product or a service which, in the consumer space, is very difficult. Companies such as Redbus Interhouse, one of Europe's leading providers of neutral collocation services, or QSA, which makes software for food manufacturers and food retailers, enabling them to trace the origins of each ingredient and increasing the ease of compliance in the food chain. B2B contains more of these commercial propositions. Our December prospectus made clear that we would be biased against B2C propositions.

'The companies we're looking to back are businesses that will have a competitive advantage of some kind that will mean they can actually charge money for something, which means that they have a more straightforward progression towards operating profit.'

The key phrase is 'charge money for'. It's no good coming up with some whiz-bang new concept if Joe Public won't pay to use it. Slater is not one to allow himself to get sentimental or stock struck; especially when evaluating new technology, which can be so beguiling.

'It's about business, and business is about making money.'

Since our initial discussion, there have been a number of developments at Internet Indirect. The company announced its interim results in September 2000, revealing that it had invested only £1 million in three companies out of a total of £76 million of available funds. The company stated:

The shakeout in public technology markets since March has had a sobering effect on valuations. It is now possible to have a sensible dialogue with companies in relation to price. However, the board believes that prices being asked by owners of private companies are, in many cases, still too high, and that a lateral approach and a rigorous focus on valuation will continue to benefit shareholders.

This announcement was followed by a series of deals worth about £4.5 million and then, in October 2000, a friendly merger with New Media Spark, another quoted technology investment company. Since Spark's shares had come down a long way, the deal can be viewed as a move by Internet Indirect to accelerate its investment programme by buying into Spark's portfolio at a low figure while getting access to its Pan-European deal flow and management team. The enlarged company will have assets of about £230 million, including £90-plus million in cash, and will be the best resourced technology investment company quoted in London.

Slater, who is joining the board of the enlarged group, says:

'This is, to a large extent, a winner-takes-all sector. We believe that we have created the likely winner. Now that technology valuations are so much lower, there are beginning to be real bargains around amongst private companies, which should prove very profitable over the next few years.'

Yet there is a sense that, for all the current uncertainty and fluctuations that make it hard to hold to a particular course, Slater is only tweaking his fundamental approach and placing more emphasis on capital preservation until market conditions allow him to reactivate his core strategy. Which sounds eminently sensible, since this strategy took his unit trust from under £1 million to approximately £200 million in five years, and propelled him into the top ranks of all UK investment professionals at an age when most are barely starting their career. If an approach is not broken, why fix it?

Slater has repositioned Slater Investments to focus on high net worth individuals, pension funds and 'special projects', after he decided, with Johnson Fry, that they should take the unit trust in-house, and after the merger of Internet Indirect with New Media Spark. Although he does not rule out managing retail investment funds in the future, his focus will be on the burgeoning high net worth market for the time being.

Growth in good companies acquired at the right price is likely to continue to reward Slater and his shareholders for many years to come. Growth provides that essential tailwind that can reward good analysis twice over. It is worth repeating, then, the stated investment policy: 'We are looking for growth which can be acquired cheaply with sustainable earnings'. That will remain Slater's primary investment focus. His first decade in the investment industry has shown it is a focus that can work, both in good and less good market conditions.

12

Catherine Tan

Avoiding losers

Top performing unit trust in Singapore in 1995, her first year of managing a portfolio, with an increase of 39 per cent

Won Best Performing Regional Fund in 1996 when managing the Shenton Asia Pacific Fund

Voted one of Asia's top ten fund managers by *Asia Money* in 1997

Ran Best Islamic Fund in 1999 with an 88 per cent return compared to benchmark returns of 59 per cent

One of the first to buy Softbank (and to sell), making 22 times her money in 14 months

It is something of a surprise that Catherine Tan has emerged as one of the bright stars in new firmament of market-savvy Asian investors, since she is so soft-spoken and understated you can be in danger of missing the insights she rattles off with devastating effect. Equally, it is a surprise she ever entered the investment world at all, since she was destined to become a lawyer and her father had a very dim view of financial markets.

'My dad was always very averse to stocks. He had too many friends who I think had scammed the public, or knew too many people who were a friend of people who scammed. I remember growing up with stories of how people pushed up the price of a stock because of some piece of land the company owned, but he was saying, "I can tell you that land's not worth half as much". He was convinced that many of these companies were pyramid schemes to inflate asset values.'

Even her introduction to the profession was intended only to be temporary – a job for a gap year before commencing articles as a solicitor. Except that Tan so enjoyed her work at DBS Asset Management that she was quickly hooked. Also, she discovered, almost by accident, that she had a great talent for stock picking, which is more useful for fund management than any other line of work.

So she left the law behind and moved into finance. Not that her training was a waste. In fact, Tan attributes some of her success in stock picking to her legal education.

'A legal background encourages objectivity. One concept behind the law is that "justice is blind". The statue outside the Old Bailey Law Courts in London is blindfolded. Objectivity is very important in investing. Also, the law teaches you how to search. Research is a key skill in fund management.'

So the switch was, perhaps, eminently suitable for someone who is a self-professed information junkie.

All successful careers usually include a lucky break somewhere along the line. In Tan's case, that came early, when, only five months after she started, several of the more senior people in the department resigned. She was given responsibility for managing the Philippines part of the portfolio; not such a mad move as it might sound, since Tan had already demonstrated, in her first assignment, a remarkable knack for finding winners.

'We had an investment game with a central dealing system. You had to choose a portfolio. It was a competition between new associates. At the end of three months, the management committee audited the result. There was a prize for coming top.'

Tan won, outperforming the Philippines Composite Index during her trial period by over 50 per cent. She soon had the chance to prove that this result was no fluke and her talent not confined to the theoretical. The first stock she recommended for purchase was the Bank of the Philippine Islands, which promptly shot up 80 per cent in three months. No wonder she can still remember that call.

'JP Morgan owned a big part of them. Their business seemed conservative. Their loan book was superior and their client list more impressive because they concentrated on the top 50 corporates, yet their valuations were much cheaper than those of other banks such as Metrobank or Philippines Commercial Bank on both price to book and on P/E, the basic investing 101s.'

Tan's views on her region have added weight because, even though only 30, she has an extremely broad experience of all South-East Asia from India to Japan, and has, during the past seven years, been responsible for investments in almost every country in the region. Having grown up in Malaysia, she worked in both Singapore and Hong Kong and spent time in most of the territories she covers. Her first field trip was to Sri Lanka, where her natural instincts took over as she made her first macro call on a country; and she was right to advise against buying in 1995 even though the rest of the investment community was besotted by Chandrika Kumarantunga's promise of a peace dividend.

'I remember coming back from a Euromoney conference and thinking, "The peace agreement is not going to work. It's not going to hold. That isn't what I heard when speaking to waiters and waitresses, taxi drivers and shop assistants. I'm recommending we stay out." And, of course, very soon after, peace fell apart.'

Looking back on that decision, Tan highlights an aspect of her approach that has been one of the cornerstones of her success.

> **In investing, it's what you avoid that's as important as what you actually do.**

'In investing, it's what you avoid that's as important as what you actually do.'

Avoiding losers

Tan makes a point which is worth repeating – more than once. There have been periods when it was possible to do very well indeed investing in Asia, both in specific stocks and also simply by riding the right tiger at the right time, but you have to know when to get off.

'Sometimes you buy because you think this is a liquid market. In a liquid market, there are times when even turkeys fly higher. You're not buying because you fundamentally believe you are riding a great value story. We've seen that with Thailand, for example. In January 1997 Thailand went all the way to 1,200, but it was purely technical and a liquidity-driven rally.'

None of which cut much ice with Tan, who saw straight through a market that was riding for a fall.

'I was running an Asian fund yet was zero weight Thailand going into the great crash. After looking at bank balance sheets and seeing the proportion of property loans, I could not fathom why property in Thailand should be so valuable. The same sort of residence cost three times as much in Bangkok as in Kuala Lumpur, but every piece of farmland was being converted into condominiums. I wondered how demand was ever going to catch up with supply.

'Offices were the same story. They were much more expensive than elsewhere. With so much new building, I thought there was danger of a glut. Yet, for the banks to make money, there would have to be further property price rises. And much of this over-investment was financed with foreign money. Foreign direct investment and exports were slowing, putting pressure on the Central Bank's balance sheet, which made me wonder about the baht. The whole situation seemed like a time bomb waiting to go off.'

If there is one thing Tan dislikes more than anything else, it is losing money. In fact, she went well over a year before she suffered a single loss. Even after living through a stock market crash, she has emerged with a low body count. Her emphasis, when first evaluating a potential new position, is very much on convincing herself that she will not lose money, and trying to identify what could go wrong.

Tan recalls several recurring warning signs where she has preserved her investors' capital by not following the crowd, and provides examples of specific companies where she stood aside after a detailed investigation. Smart investors should follow Tan's example and stay away from situations where she opts not to invest, which include:

1. A fundamentally flawed business model

Hikari Tsushin, a Japanese company where cellular phone retailing was the primary business activity, attracted a lot of speculative interest in late 1999 and early 2000. Tan was intrigued enough to take a look.

'I loved the story when I was first told it. I went to see management and came away very disconcerted. I thought their business model was flawed. And then the stock rocketed. I went and saw management again and still came away very uncomfortable with their business model.'

She did not buy because she could not reconcile the actual results, especially the movements in the cash position, with what one would have expected to see if the business model had performed as advertised. It turns out there was a subtext, which Tan winkled out of the management.

'It was supposed to be a franchise system, so its cash flow was supposed to be very positive. Everyone was projecting earnings growth based on growth in franchise sales. When you spoke to management you realized that the company was financing all these franchises. In an upturn, that's OK. But, in a downturn, you still have to finance losers, and, if I was a franchisee, I'd have no real incentive to make it work.'

But when a stock is hot, if the first story does not hold, you can always come up with another. Management created Hikari Capital and cobbled together a clutch of venture interests.

'When valuations reached absurd levels on its main franchise business, people started talking about its internet investments.'

Tan remained unconvinced. Some may succeed, but all were early stage, and speculative, and of uncertain value.

'Their internet investment is very small. They did not get in early, usually investing just before an IPO, and they had no strategy for, and had no real background in, internet investing. It's a bit late if you have nothing real to add to it.'

Shareholders at Lloyd George where Tan works should count their blessings that she chose not to follow the herd. The price of Hikari Tsushin, which hit the giddy heights of ¥241,000 in February 2000, languishes below ¥2,000, down 99 per cent, and could collapse entirely. Brokers who were recommending the shares at ¥200,000 are now crying 'caution'. These days, discussions are about when to cover short positions.

2. Bull-market stocks

Tan is acutely aware of the danger to capital when valuations detach from fundamentals. She has been consistently sceptical when it comes to sentiment which can too easily push multiples to obscene heights.

'I have avoided a lot of stocks that expect you to buy on a wing and a prayer in the hope that everything turns out perfectly. Internet stocks, in the first quarter of 2000, went up so fast it made no sense. In 1997, Asian stocks had gone to such high multiplies I really wondered why they deserved valuation premiums over their global peers. It did not seem that could last.'

Not that she is averse to taking advantage of market conditions to make a bit of money for her clients.

'You can play the market cap to exit game for a little while. Tom.com at IPO was a good stag, and I must admit we stagged.'

The critical distinction is not to get confused over why you bought a share.

'We got out of Tom.com in the first four days of trading. There was no basis for the market's valuation.'

Tan is somewhat sceptical about the merits of the whole sector in terms of its suitability for long-term investors.

'Everyone suspended all disbelief, so accounting did not matter, cash flow did not matter, earnings did not matter. All that people were betting on was a technology. It's a great concept, it's a great idea.'

This sort of speculation cuts no ice with Tan.

'I've always been, "OK, wonderful technology, wonderful concept, but what does it leave me as a shareholder? When am I going to reap any benefit?"'

Unless she gets the right answer, Tan does not invest.

3. Constant negative cash flow

If there is one characteristic almost guaranteed to turn Tan off, it is a company that cannot convert growth in sales into positive cash flow in some sort of reasonable time period. This is why, although she sees all sorts of benefits stemming to society from new technology, she is deeply suspicious about the suitability of many of these businesses as stock market investments. She uses one of the best-known internet names in the world to draw an important distinction that investors often forget.

'People fail to distinguish between the product and the company. You can have a great product and it can be a lousy investment. Amazon is a great brand, but is it a good company, if you've got to keep funding the end consumers? I love Amazon as a consumer, but it does not mean that I want to be a shareholder. It seems to me their model was to take money from shareholders to subsidize consumers. In that case, I want to be a consumer and not a shareholder.'

If you are tempted to try and make a quick buck merely on momentum, and the temptation can be overwhelming at times, Tan has this to say:

'You must remember why you are in the stock. Leave a little for Miss Manners. Know how to leave the party before they remove the punchbowl. Momentum can stop very quickly. Always, always ask yourself who the next buyer will be. You don't want to be the last idiot holding the stock.'

4. Well-connected promoters

Tan acknowledges that certain people with the right connections have been able to do very well for themselves, but she is more sceptical about whether that translates to good returns for investors. Perhaps there was a phase in the past when this was a profitable rule of thumb, but buying a share merely because there are powerful people involved does not work in 2001.

'Traditionally this has mattered in Asia. But what the crisis has shown is that if all you are buying are good connections to governments, be prepared to lose a lot of money. Reading the political tea leaves can be tricky. During 1997/8, Malaysian brokers were promoting stocks such as Magnum Bhd on the basis that they were connected with Anwar Ibrahim, who had supposedly gained the upper hand from Dr Mahathir Mohammed. That prediction proved premature. While the stock enjoyed an initial run, the moment Anwar's troubles began it took a tumble, back 50 per cent below its level at the start of 1996.'

For Tan, people are important not because of who they are, but because of what they do and, in particular, what they do for shareholders. So low marks for heavyweight directors and, in its place, a heavy emphasis on financial performance.

> **People are important not because of who they are, but because of what they do.**

'At the end of the day, it's your cash flow that matters.'

Caveat emptor

Investing in Asian equities has not been for the fainthearted but, with so much potential, and since the region has experienced periods of exceptional returns, international investors cannot afford to stay away. The bull case is easier to articulate, so a review of pitfalls that investors need to avoid is more useful. Tan has seen both the good and bad of the market. Some potential problems that can catch out unwary investors new to Asia include:

1. Inadequate disclosure

Few Asian companies provide the depth of disclosure found in the US 10K. That may be an unrealistic standard for now, but a combination of culture, past practice and lighter regulatory requirements does leave greater discretion to companies as to how much – and how – to tell investors about the business.

Tan comments that 'just because a company has a set of accounts which are audited does not mean they are accurate.'

Many of the abuses of the past are going or gone and, by and large, public company reports are better and more complete in 2001 than they have ever been. Nonetheless, lack of transparency can still catch investors by surprise. For example, inter-company relationships such as loans are not always fully documented. A classic case was Kentucky Fried Chicken (KFC) Malaysia.

'The Malaysian operation was the most profitable in the world. Chicken is the one thing all the races in Malaysia can eat. And it is a great company which is well run.'

Great product, great positioning, even great profits, but unbeknownst to shareholders or, indeed, apparently to KFC's auditor, since no mention of this crucial information appeared in the audited statements, the main shareholder had used KFC's buildings as collateral for personal loans. He then ran into difficulty and the banks tried to enforce the security.

Some recent developments appear to be more of a step back than a step forward. Tan has concerns about the GEM market in Hong Kong, where companies do not need a profit record or even a full set of accounts to get a listing.

'You have companies that have only been in operation for three months.'

Companies such as Tom.com and TechVentures debuted on GEM with sexy sounding plans but no real record, leaving a lot of execution risk in the price and more hope value than real value. Since flotation, their prices have fallen a long way from where they once were, as initial enthusiasm collided with reality. Tan believes investors are unwise to be 'buying something about which you know so little'.

2. Ambiguous accounting

Variation in accounting conventions continues to pose a challenge. Investors may need to adjust elements of both the balance sheet and income statement before cross-country comparison can be meaningful. While some adjustments are minor, others can cause considerable confusion and, almost always, the restated numbers look less attractive. Tan cites specific examples. The airline industry is notorious for using a wide range of depreciation schedules. Singapore Airlines depreciates its aeroplanes more aggressively. They use seven years, while others use as much as 15. Some Japanese car companies did not account properly for pension liabilities. They seemed superficially cheap because their balance sheet appeared stronger.

Toyota and Honda have now adopted GAAP to make their accounts more comparable and easier to decipher for international investors. The others are following suit, with some situations influenced by foreign investment such as Renault buying into Nissan. They, too, had different depreciation schedules compared to manufacturers elsewhere in the world, and cross-country benchmarking could only be truly comparable after considerable restatement.

'Headline numbers can be very deceptive. They are not apples to apples.'

For every potential distortion smoothed, Tan spots a new grey area; neither are new economy companies immune from accounting ambiguities.

'Internet sales, revenues and viewership numbers can be problematic. Not every company calculates sales the same way.'

When markets start to rely on other measures, that can create a whole new set of issues.

'Page views as a valuation metric is really meaningless.'

Inconsistencies make it difficult to place reliance on the publicly available accounts of some Asian companies. Other parts of the world are not immune from similar problems, but getting underneath accounting conventions can be more of a challenge in countries undergoing transition. Sometimes Tan finds she cannot stick as strictly to the reported numbers as she would like. In summary, if in doubt, watch out.

'If something looks too divergent, it probably is.'

3. Weak corporate governance

While, in many respects, there has been progress in this area that is so critical for investors, in part due to the 1997 crisis, Tan acknowledges that there is still much to be done. There is even danger of standards slipping. Tan has concerns about some companies recently listed on GEM, NASDAQ Japan and Mothers Japan. This issue tends to get glossed over when markets perform well. When companies have problems, that is when corporate governance assumes greater importance, and truly separates the sheep from the goats.

4. Companies run for the benefit of someone else

This, too, is not a uniquely Asian issue – far from it – but there are many examples of listed companies that treat shareholders as second-class citizens on a good day. Management may not set out to short-change outside or minority shareholders, but the way the company is run or structured could lead to that result. As long as such conditions continue, it is not sensible for an investor to own the share, and it is unlikely that the price will outperform, so the opportunity cost of staying away is low.

Tan is sensitive to several structural and/or financial characteristics that can be identified from the outside and should be seen as a potential future flash point, such as large amounts of inter-company loans. The presence of a controlling shareholder who owns other businesses that could lead to a conflict of interest should concern investors.

Berjaya Sports Toto is a very well run gaming operation in Malaysia, and generates gobs of cash, but a large proportion of its cash flow seems to be siphoned off into loans to other companies. Many of these loans are to companies that have connections to Vincent Tan, its main shareholder.

'The company itself is a great cash cow, but what they do with the cash itself is another matter.'

Cultures that place a high importance on family are more likely to contain companies where there is potential divergence between the interests of management and those of outside shareholders. Investors need to consider carefully whether the goal of enhancing the share price has a high priority, or could clash with other objectives which might be more important where a family either owes a majority of shares or somehow controls a company.

'In Asia a lot of families think of the company as their personal piggy bank.'

Behaviour which is perfectly legal can be destructive to shareholder value. Decisions taken for reasons other than investment returns, or people, often relatives, put into senior positions not because of their ability but because of connections, can undermine shareholder value. These events are still too common an occurrence. Tan and, indeed, any potential investor, needs to get a handle on whether there is a risk of a good business proposition coming unstuck due to extraneous variables.

> **Nothing beats the qualitative judgement about the people you are investing in and whether you can trust them.**

'This is why we try to visit companies. Nothing beats the qualitative judgement about the people you are investing in and whether you can trust them.'

5. Fraud

America had the salad-oil scandal of the 1960s, and every country contains examples of companies that cooked the books. Black holes continue to emerge in the accounts of companies, in spite of the best efforts of accountants and regulators. Versailles went belly up in Britain in 1999. Canada was embarrassed by Bre X in 1998. Asia has its share and, in markets where the dynamics are different and personalities play a more important role, there is greater scope than, say, in Sweden for these sorts of things to go wrong.

'Aokam Perdana was one of the highest flying shares in 1993. It went from a penny stock to a ridiculous valuation. They supposedly had timber concessions in east Malaysia, until someone actually went to see the concessions and found that there were no trees.'

The price has been basically one way ever since – down. There is little an investor who is not on the spot can do to protect themselves, other than by being sensitive to the risk.

Sit this one out

Another facet of Tan's investment persona where her caution shows up to good effect is in internal asset allocation. The correct composition for a portfolio is always on her mind. She devotes considerable time to taking the temperature of the economic environment. While most managers focus on comparing one holding against another, Tan tends to spend more time higher up the decision tree. She starts from the perspective of capital preservation as an overriding objective.

'My game plan is protecting the net asset value. One of the early things that I was taught at DBS was that there was a great stock called CASH. If you don't think that something's going to outperform that, you could always go to cash.'

This is not a point of view to which Tan pays lip service. In autumn 2000 she had a number of concerns about market conditions.

'I believed the summer was a technical bounce and that the technology correction was not yet over. Also, I had worries about what the oil shock might do. This led me to keep 45 per cent cash for my regional fund, because it seemed likely I would be able to buy shares lower later.'

Which, of course, she was.

Liquidity, liquidity, liquidity

Tan's caution comes to the fore in other ways. Investors who are successful over the longer term have some sort of model of how the market works, which provides a framework for portfolio structure. In Tan's case, her decisions are coloured by her view about money flows.

'At the end of the day, it's always liquidity. The marketplace is all about buyers and sellers. It's all about demand and supply. This is where economics comes in. What are the fuels for demand and what fuels supply? Monetary conditions are paramount. Are we entering a phase when money supply will be looser or tighter? Is there more demand for money or more supply? In a period of loose money, stocks fly. August 1998 illustrate this best. Globally, things were bleak in the aftermath of Russia. Hedge funds like LTCM were in trouble. There was real reason for pessimism, but stocks rallied. Why? Because the Fed cut rates and increased global money supply.'

> At the end of the day, stock markets crash because of liquidity.

Take Hong Kong in 1999 and on into early 2000, where the few new-economy stocks in the market seemed destined to go on going up on a daily basis. Tan did participate, owning stocks that normally would not appear in her portfolio, but only because she could see the rush of liquidity in the market and that sector.

'We were in internet stocks very early. We were early buyers of Pacific Cyberworks. What was clear in the back of my mind was that whenever you have high valuations in anything, it's because it's liquidity backed.'

But she kept one eye on the door monitoring the money flow.

'At the end of the day, stock markets crash because of liquidity.'

And the other eye was on the key influence on liquidity – interest rates.

'Interest rates are always key. I don't believe that interest rates don't matter. Every one of the past crashes has happened because of an interest rate hike. Every one of the rallies has been caused by interest rates being abnormally low. Abnormally low interest rates led to the 1993 rally in Asia. It's always interest rates more than earnings.'

And she is sanguine about the impact of intervention, recognizing that the intentions of monetary authorities alone, though an important indicator, may not be sufficient.

'Sometimes central banks cannot do very much. You have robust export growth, like Korea in 1999. Whatever you are trying to do with the currency isn't going to make a difference. But when they began aggressively loosening after the Russian débâcle, that set the stage for a global rally.'

Liquidity is also a big factor in Tan's sell decisions. If she senses tightening, she looks to lighten across the board and even exits holdings altogether. When she began to get nervous about NASDAQ, she dumped almost all her Softbank within a few per cent of the top.

'I couldn't see who was going to be the next buyer. When the last disbelievers jump on the bandwagon, that is an interesting signal. Too many people already had this as their top holding.'

Arguably Tan can go a tad over the top in extolling liquidity above every other consideration, as in her thesis about the Taiwanese market.

'In 1996 what was a signal and what was noise? If you had ignored all the tension and bought, you would have made a lot of money. In 1998, liquidity and the interest rate environment were favourable. I sometimes wonder if politics matters at all? The China crisis has shown that, if you're buying, look at liquidity and that's all.'

Even if things look very bad, the best time to buy is when there is blood on the streets. Tan is totally agnostic on the topic.

'We can sit here all day and talk politics until we're blue in the face but, at the end of the day, I'll never know and nor will you. If China and Taiwan went to war, it would not be contained. The US would be involved and it would be World War III. I can't spend the rest of my life waiting for World War III.'

Results show her interpretation to have been accurate, so it would be niggardly to argue around the margin when the main thrust of her proposition is valid. Investors should always consider liquidity carefully when setting the stance of their portfolio as well as in individual stock selection, and worry more about what the central bank is doing than what the Prime Minister is saying.

Buy, sell or hold

Minimizing losses can only be one facet of performance, and Tan did not achieve a top ranking by sitting on her hands. Her approach is broadly based, involving both a search for themes that could suggest positive price action and interesting ideas about stocks such as new products that might change their rating. And, of course, the issue of stock-specific valuation is paramount prior to any buy. Tan looks at several measures, none of which, on their own, carry the day, but she does have a hierarchy, so they are presented here in descending order of importance:

- Price to Cash Flow
- Enterprise Value to Earnings Before Interest, Taxes, Depreciation and Amortization
- Market Capitalization to Net Cash
- Price Earnings to Growth.

Two aspects of her approach mark Tan out from the crowd. First, she does not favour one style at the expense of another. She uses value ratios, growth ratios and, of course, seeks a Margin of Safety such as a positive net cash position. Second, her use of numerical tools is not static, and it is her assessment of liquidity that raises or lowers the relative importance she places on these quantitative measures. While the ranking illustrates her inclination in a steady-state environment, markets rarely linger in equilibrium for long.

'It's important to catch the market cycle right. When it's a liquid market, you're looking for growth. Values underperform. But when you're going into a downturn, for example back in 1997, you really wanted to be in companies that had a lot of cash, and that had profits and positive cash flows. They withstand a liquidity squeeze better. When liquidity's abundant, cash is a commodity, so it doesn't matter and, if you've got a lot of money, it's actually a disadvantage.'

What emerges from a balanced analytical approach is a balanced portfolio.

'Fifty per cent would be stocks that you liked, no matter what, that you are riding for the long term. It's companies that you think are a great business, great management who know what they want and, in ten years, I can still sleep with the stock and know that it's going to make me money. And then you've got the other 50 per cent which you juggle to play themes.'

There is more to Tan's decision than just numerical analysis. Like most top professionals, she likes to see companies and meet the management and prefers to do that on their home turf, since she learns a lot from a visit to their premises. Indeed, the company's office can be a factor in her thinking.

'I've tended to avoid any companies where there's too much marble in the building. If the office has designer leather chairs and too much art on the walls, I've thought, "They are doing this with shareholders' money. Either they have too much cash and insufficient business opportunities to invest, in which case profits will slow, or it's mismanagement. In either case, the minority shareholder will lose, so I stay away."'

The most important input naturally comes from her assessment of the qualities of management. Here Tan has a strong bias as to what she wants.

'You're looking for people not just with a vision, but people who can execute that vision. That's the problem with a lot of companies. You've seen it clearly with the inter-

> # You're looking for people not just with a vision, but people who can execute that vision.

net. Anyone who supposedly has a concept – has a vision – has been given a lot of money to play with. I don't think enough attention is given to people who can actually execute.'

Easier said than done, but then this is what Tan does for a living every day, and she has a way of interrogating the executive team that usually allows her to decide whether they are likely to deliver or not.

'I approach a company very much as a management consultant and say, "These are the problems that I think your company would face if this is what you want to do. What's your response to that? What would you do?" And it's interesting to see if they've thought about it. Some people are naturally optimistic. They just look at everything on the brighter side. Then you wonder if they could cope if things turn around. One of the questions we ask companies who are still loss-making is this: "What will happen if you cannot raise the next round of financing?" You would be surprised at how many of them meet the question with a blank stare.'

And Tan has found a simple solution to piercing the corporate veil so that she gets a better idea of what is really going on.

'I have found it very useful to see different people within the same company. Companies often have someone who is the face to investors. If you see that person only, it could provide a misleading view. It's good to see different layers of management again and to put different questions to them.'

In part, this is what caused her to come to the conclusion not to buy Hikari Tsushin when so many investment managers were loading up with the stock. The other thing that put her off was the impression management made when she did meet the team.

'I had visited the company three or four times and every time could not find that I could trust the people.'

Shortly after this conversation, President Shigeta resigned, a most unusual occurrence in Japan, and a testimony to Tan's ability to judge character.

A different process caused her to arrive at a similar decision in the case of Berjaya Sports Toto. Tan was extremely impressed by management.

'The guy who runs the operations is great. He runs a tight ship.'

She was poised to take a big position, but when she talked to Vincent Tan, the main shareholder, she realized that his agenda might not be consistent with maximizing value in Berjaya Sports Toto itself, due to other interests elsewhere. She has not missed much.

Trust is something that Tan stresses on several occasions. If you can trust management, that makes a big difference as to how an investor can view the business. Equally, without trust, the assessment should be more severe. Singapore Airlines and Dialog Malaysia are two companies with management that she trusts. This enabled her to buy those stocks during the market carnage of 1998 in the belief that these companies would emerge with stronger businesses. Both businesses justified her trust, delivering doubles within 12 months.

Islamic investing

Tan has a surprising area of specialization. She is the manager of Alfanaar Islamic Fund. Tan began her involvement in the area at DBS where she ran the Mendaki Growth Fund and now has six years of experience in this field.

Islamic investing has to abide by a set of rules that sets it somewhat apart from the mainstream. The first difference is in fund structure. In addition to an investment committee, Tan reports to a Sharia panel every quarter which has to confirm that the portfolio has complied with a defined set of rules. To secure its seal of approval, all securities must overcome a number of hurdles. Up front there is the well-known prohibition against interest, effectively eliminating debt instruments. Equities must meet certain tests to avoid falling foul of the interest issue:

- debt to market capitalization should be below 30 per cent;
- cash cannot be more than 50 per cent of market capitalization;
- interest income must be less than 15 per cent of sales;
- receivables cannot climb above 50 per cent of sales, because some receivables are deemed to be interest bearing.

It should be noted that Sharia panels can differ over the precise percentages in applying these tests.

Investment in certain areas is off-limits: alcohol and tobacco, naturally, and all financial institutions and gambling, but also less obvious industries are excluded, such as TV and photographic holdings, because their activities violate the prohibition on graven images. The ban applies even where a tiny percentage of a company's business is considered contaminated. So Tan cannot purchase Swire, the Hong Kong conglomerate, even though brewery profits amount to under 1 per cent of the group total.

These requirements can complicate life and, under certain circumstances, cause excessive churn which may be sub-optimal. During the 1997/8 crisis, balance-sheet ratios relative to market capitalization become a problem because so many shares sunk to such low prices. Receivables also rose during the crisis, as customers slowed payment, causing that ratio to be broken by some holdings. In spite of these limitations, Tan has managed to extract superior performance. In her first full year running Alfanaar at Lloyd George, she increased the NAV by 89 per cent. In 2000, a notoriously tricky year, she was up 10 per cent, when the relevant markets were down by 19 per cent. So these handicaps could hardly be said to hold her back.

She strives to achieve a high degree of commonality with positions in unrestricted accounts. Normally portfolios manage about a 70 per cent overlap. The biggest bugbear is banking, a major sector in Asia which has a large weighting in most indices. Areas where she was overweight, as of June 2000, included metals and retail. Tan chose companies such as Hindalco, the Indian aluminium process, and Giordano, Asia's answer to US fashion retailer The Gap, as core holdings.

2001 investment odyssey

Tan expects to expand her horizons over the next three years. One new activity is the Lloyd George Asian Internet Fund, which seems counterintuitive in the light of her scepticism over the sector. Tan thinks the timing is excellent for the new fund, post the 2000 meltdown.

'The easy money has been made. A lot of people have been burned and are throwing out the baby with the bath water. It's a great time. It's exactly like the computer industry in the 1980s. You're going to go from 600 companies to five and you will make a lot of money in the survivors.

We are looking for real companies with real technologies that are generating free-operating cash flow.

'Now the survivors are more obvious. We are looking for real companies with real technologies that are generating free-operating cash flow, or are very close to it. Their competitors have fallen out of the game. You have more trust in the execution of those still in. Since competitors with concepts only are already starting to fail, we can be more selective.'

And she makes one more interesting point about a possible in-built advantage for this regional-sector vehicle.

'In Asia, it's a little bit easier than in the US, because a lot of these companies which are supposedly internet and technology plays have got no real expertise, so you see those that will not work more clearly.'

Tan likes some of the big multinationals that are already leaders, not the obvious names you would link to the internet today, but those she believes can grow their involvement and become profitable more quickly than many start-ups. Sony is great at commercialization, a key skill to achieve success in a new technology environment.

'If you think about Sony, they did not invent the transistor radio, but they were the first to commercialize it. Sony also makes money by buying technology copyrights and exploiting them more effectively. They know how to make money from technology.'

Sony has a huge technology platform which Tan believes investors have been slow to appreciate.

'Everyone was excited about AOL having 17 million customers, but Sony's PlayStation has 70 million users. The potential network effect is mind boggling, and we know that they are going to capitalize on it because the new PlayStation PS2 has internet capabilities.'

This commercial approach fits with her focus on technology as a tool first and foremost. What excites her is not a capability now, but how to translate a technology into a commercial enterprise. Pure plays may, therefore, be of less interest than 'old-economy' companies that understand how to apply new technology to their businesses. In this category Tan highlights ICIC, a bank in India that has a strong technology orientation.

'Seventeen per cent of its customers are already on the internet. They set up a virtual network for their clients to link up with their suppliers. They do not charge for access but, once companies start using it, they have to use ICIC for managing their cash, and they charge fees for that. So they lock in their customers.'

Tan will continue to temper her enthusiasm even for the best businesses when they sit on unsustainable valuations or handicap themselves with an excessive cost structure, raising doubts about the rate of future earnings growth. She believes Infosys is one of the best companies in India and has owned the share in the past, but took profits when its valuation appeared to get ahead of events.

'It's still a great company, but valuations got too high. To justify their multiple, they decided to buy computer services companies that could increase their margins but, before that could happen, they increased their cost base substantially with acquisitions in the US. The whole reason their margins were so much higher was due to low labour costs in India, and also low marketing costs. Expanding in the US increased their labour cost. Then the reason for their premium over US company valuations had gone, so there was no longer any reason for me to hold the stock. They need to transform because of increasing Indian competition, but this period of transition is likely to be quite painful.'

In May 2000 Lloyd George Management decided to launch its Asia Internet Fund. The aim is to invest in listed companies that will benefit from the internet phenomenon. The context for creating a portfolio with this focus is compelling. Tan cites several factors that should provide a tailwind for the new fund.

'The internet in Asia is a service industry, but there is a huge techno-savvy population. Web users are expected to grow at 40 per cent p.a. for the next five years, faster than in Europe or the USA. Some estimates say China alone will have 100 million users by 2005. Also, internet commerce is growing over 100 per cent each year in South-East Asia. Services such as online advertising are set to explode. There are lots of opportunities for the early birds; and we see more room for disintermediation than in the relatively mature US market.'

Across Asia, in every category of the new economy, there is compelling evidence that growth will exceed other regions by a factor of two or three times: maybe more. Tan points to Gartner, a leading US research firm, whose studies on B2C transaction value provide supporting evidence for her views. Singapore is a model of how things might evolve elsewhere in the region.

'The government looked ahead and launched the Electronic Commerce Hotbed Programme in August 1996. This gave Singapore a head start by putting in place a leading-edge legal and technological infrastructure. Now you have 91 per cent of the top one thousand companies using the internet. Already, in 1999, 4 per cent of industry is e-commerce-enabled with $1.4 billion of B2B revenue. And the consumer is also ahead. Fifty-nine per cent of households own a PC.

Thirty-two per cent of the population uses the internet and 16 per cent buy online.'

A taste of things to come? The data suggests the best is just ahead (*see* Fig. 12.1). If so, Tan will be well positioned with winners. Not just in pure technology plays with sustainable business models for leadership, but also with companies that have core earnings from a strong base business where the internet upside is in for free. That could mean Li & Fung, the Hong Kong trading company; or Creative Technology out of Singapore which, from its origins as a PC sound-card manufacturer, has expanded into other activities, including a website called hiFi.com and an internet incubator.

Another point made by Tan was that, on the whole, valuations in this area – whether measured by revenues, or activity such as page views, or based on subscribers – tend to be lower in Asia than in the US. Valuations are very volatile, so relativity can turn but, in the summer of 2000, an ISP like Pacific Internet was at a discount to the US sector mean and traded at less than two-thirds the multiples of America Online, while Star Media was valued at less than the US mean for portal companies.

With all the euphoria and excitement, trust Tan to keep her feet firmly on the ground. She intends to seize the opportunity, but her closing comment on the subject shows she maintains her aversion to losing money at all times.

Figure 12.1 | Potential growth in Asian internet users

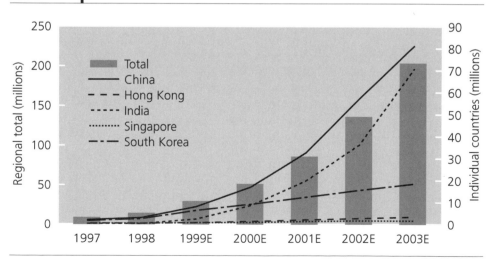

Source: Lloyd George Management

'Ninety-eight per cent of all internet stocks are over-valued. Two per cent are undervalued.'

The other area in Asia that Tan sees as a sweet spot for the future is Japan. She has just taken on a new

Ninety-eight per cent of all internet stocks are overvalued. Two per cent are undervalued.

mandate in this market, where she had been investing on and off while at DBS, and with more focus since starting at Lloyd George in 1998. Tan believes it is time for investors to revisit Japan, hence the launch of the Lloyd George Sumitomo Life Japan Fund in June 2000. There is a touch of the contrarian in Tan's rationale.

'There has been too much negativity for too long. At the end of 1998, everyone was underweight Japan and overweight the US.'

But her confidence, in large part, stems from her belief that liquidity will return to markets.

'What gets me excited is that the re-capitalization of the banks has started. Until the banks could be re-capitalized, this was a dead economy. For me a very decisive step was in October 1998, when they set up the Financial Revitalization Committee. I thought this was very interesting, because they began to put a system in place to increase lending and end bankruptcies. The Credit Insurance Association is extending guarantees for small businesses. There has been a time of tight money. That change could bring an end to the credit crunch. Since February 1999, Japan has been awash with liquidity.'

If you accept that the environment for liquidity is improving, which sectors should you target?

'Leasing companies usually move first in a liquidity rally. Orix is one of the largest, and has begun to clean up its balance sheet by writing off bad loans and making provisions for doubtful loans.'

Liquidity is a big plus, but there is a second favourable trend that increases her confidence: greater emphasis by Japanese corporations on shareholder value.

'I was a very early believer in the restructuring story. And then I bumped into someone who was working for Stern Stewart in October 1998. They are the ones who started the Economic Value Added Analysis [EVA]. Stern Stewart told me they are opening an office in Tokyo due to client demand. This meeting was pure

From mid-1999, restructuring has been an investing buzzword in Japan.

serendipity, but I thought, "Here are Japanese corporates inviting Stern Stewart in, yet the rest of the world is still saying Japan will never restructure". From mid-1999, restructuring has been an investing buzz-word in Japan. You see it at Nissan Motors, where they have shut five domestic plants, halved the number of supplier firms, intend to halve the number of platforms by 2003, and have stated goals to cut costs by 20 per cent and reduce net automotive debt by ¥700 billion.'

All of which, if achieved, should do wonders for return on capital employed. More emphasis by Japanese executives on managing their business for profit and improving returns must be a plus, sooner or later, for how the market values their companies.

Stock prices are likely to be assisted by reversal in a trend that has taken household equity holdings in Japan as a percentage of dispos-able income down from nearly 60 per cent in 1990 to around 25 per cent in 2001. While in the US during the same period the percentage rose from close to 40 per cent up to over 100 per cent. Tan expects to see net inflow into Japanese investment trusts following a decade of outflows, and increasingly back to equities, especially since, over the next two years, more than 106 trillion yen of postal accounts will mature. Both government and the consumer could be positive forces for liquidity in 2002.

Several other trends may help. M&A activity is on the increase. The year 1999 was a banner year, with 137 deals valued at over ¥6 trillion; more than the total value of the previous five years combined. Such statistics lend weight to the argument that, if Japanese companies do not take steps to control their own destiny, outsiders are now more willing to move in. Tan sums up:

'I see the start of a new virtuous cycle in Japan. Restructuring can and is happening, and is becoming pervasive. We see it at Nissan, we see it at Nikko Securities, and we see it at Itochu. Our bottom-up analysis confirms the macro story.'

In Japan, Tan is likely to be more eclectic in her choices, while cling-ing all the time to a process that weeds out the weaker brethren. She likes Bell System 24, the market leader in telemarketing, and Saizeriya, a chain of low-priced Italian restaurants.

In addition to those two main thrusts, which is where she will be spending more time, Tan highlights several themes likely to be pivotal in Asia.

1. Logistics

'Asia is still export oriented. You want to pick companies that can cope with competition. With the world becoming more global, Asia has to find a way to maintain its export competitiveness *vis-à-vis* other emerging economies in Latin America and Eastern Europe.'

Export economies generate massive demand for logistics services. Even e-commerce cannot escape the need for physical delivery. Indeed, the internet is likely to accelerate growth in delivery requirements. Sembcorp Logistics of Singapore springs to mind.

'They can take over the whole function for you. Everything is computerized and traceable.'

Another area is freight handling, where one obvious beneficiary is the airline industry.

'If you look at airline companies, cargo numbers have gone up tremendously.'

And, of course, warehouse companies such as Yamato in Japan. One knock-on effect is worthy of comment. All this activity creates yet another source of demand for power, adding to the argument in favour of utility stocks in Asia.

2. Consolidation

Tan expects to see more global consolidators starting within Asia, and some of the more successful using their strong Asian position to acquire businesses beyond the region. The automotive industry and its suppliers will be one area of continuing consolidation. Also, she expects to see more mergers among airlines that, from time to time, trade at discounts to assets, making acquisition a cheap way to expand.

In certain industries where economy of scale is vital, Tan wants to own well-run consolidators. She cites Star Cruises of Malaysia as one such company, which looks set to rival Carnival, the worldwide leader.

'They are expanding into the global market while cruises here in Asia are still growing. At one point, they were even talking about buying Carnival. They are owned by Genting, the casino company, which has great cash flow. Ships can be like travelling casinos.'

Who knows? Star might even buy the old colonial master, P&O Princess, the UK-listed cruise line company that used to provide passage around the peninsular when Malaysia was a colony.

Software provides a second example. Indian companies are likely to play an increasing role outside their home territory. Infosys has already began to integrate forward by buying professional services firms in the US to complement its core programming competence.

3. Education

The growing middle class all round the region, including China and India, will drive demand for better and more education. The internet is an ideal mechanism for long-distance learning, which can be efficient and cheaper and deliver real benefits. Why not get your degree online? Among companies that are pioneers in a sector posed to explode is Informatics in Singapore, which runs computer training schools, and is expanding into the rest of Asia. Aptech and NIIT in India run computer training schools and are likely to prosper on the back of this longer-term trend.

4. Communications

As in most regions of the world, expect massive growth in this sector. The emphasis is likely to be on mobile, especially in the two largest markets, China and India. Japan is well on its way.

'Non-PC access to the internet will be a world phenomenon. Arguably, Asians are already ahead of the rest of the world in mobile usage. NTT DoComo (Japan)'s I-mode was the fastest technology adoption ever, with 5.6 million subscribers in just one year. Asia should have a larger cellular subscriber base than America by 2001.'

Growth is likely to be very rapid. While telcos are out of favour in the US and Europe in early 2001, Asia should be more robust. Tan is, however, cautious about where investors should place their bets, preferring component makers such as Matsushita Electric Industrial as likely near-term beneficiaries over carriers like NTT.

These, and other trends, will feature in Tan's thinking as she accumulates a growing raft of responsibility at Lloyd George Asset Management. Certain common traits will carry over, whether she is running an Islamic portfolio or picking Asian internet stocks. She will strive to avoid investments that suffer from any suspicion of taint in respect of their structure, whether that be financial or corporate, or even the character of management or influential shareholders. And she will steer clear of businesses that try to substitute promises for performance. By avoiding losers, Tan is free to concentrate on making money from the positive developments she has identified in Asia without laggards dragging down a record that has so far excelled – and seems set to keep her in the front ranks of Asian money managers for many more years.

13

Francis Tjia

Rolling back the frontiers in Asian fixed income

Set up first regional fixed income fund for South-East Asia

Set up first investment firm devoted exclusively to Asian debt

Delivered 20 per cent plus p.a. returns in US$ terms with his first fund

Won the *South China Morning Post* Fund Manager of the Year Award in 1999

Created Asiabondportal.com, the first cyberbond exchange for Asian fixed income instruments

Francis Tjia was able to enter the financial industry with ease, due to an unusual reason.

'I came to Hong Kong in 1990. At that time, Indonesia was just starting to take off. They had liberalized their financial markets, and, by virtue of having an Indonesian background, it was very easy to get a job in finance. Nobody knew anything about Indonesia. Nobody spoke Indonesian. So job offers came quickly. I started as assistant fund manager at Thornton Management.'

It was Peter Everington – now of Regent and profiled in *Investing with the Grand Masters* – who was the first to spot Tjia's potential. Actually, his precise words were: 'Great! Indonesian? You've got a job!'

If his introduction to the profession was a breeze, ever since, Tjia has been active in areas that were demanding on a dull day, constantly overcoming challenges that have destroyed many careers. One notable achievement is that he has survived: survived the meltdown in Indonesian equity markets, survived the ripple effects from the Tequila crisis in 1994, survived the massacre in Asian debt instruments; survived and emerged stronger as one of the true innovators among investment professionals in Asia. In short, in a tough market, Tjia is the sort of person you want on your team, as he has learnt how to dodge just about every curve ball the market can throw at investors.

The fixed income frontier

New frontiers are very much what Tjia is all about. He set out as he meant to continue. At Thornton he was put in charge of the New Tiger Selections Indonesia Fund, one of the first equity vehicles focused on that country. No surprise, then, that he attracted the attention of one of the leading Indonesian conglomerates, Lippo Group, which he joined in mid-1991 to set up their new Jakarta based operation. Lippo decided, early in the 1990s, that financial services were a good thing and that they should have their own fund management group. Which was not, as it turned out, terrific timing, because Indonesia, in late 1991, went through a period of severe economic contraction with a tight money policy. Inevitably, in that environment equity markets did not perform well.

But what was a disappointment for Lippo contained a silver lining for Tjia. Equities were the wrong asset class, but, with sky-high interest rates, fixed income instruments had more to offer. So the team at Lippo Investment Management launched a second fund to tap that market. Tjia found himself an instant fixed income expert, and, more to the point, embarking on a new career as a pioneer in Asian debt.

'It was, to our knowledge, the first Asian fixed income fund outside of Japan and, perhaps, South Korea. We weren't familiar with any other money market or bond funds, certainly in South-East Asia. For the region, they didn't really exist. While we were at Lippo we started thinking "Why is nobody doing this for Malaysia, or the Philippines, or Thailand?"'

If Indonesian equities were a basket case, the same economic policies created a close to no-lose proposition for investors in short-dated fixed income instruments, especially for international investors. Tjia and his partner, Emil Nguy, were presented with a classic arbitrage and were among the first to exploit the gap. They created a fund that returned over 20 per cent annually, in US$ terms, with negligible volatility: almost every institution's investment dream. To see how this was possible, it is necessary to recap briefly on conditions in 1992.

'Indonesia had been running a creeping depreciation policy for its currency. At the time the rupiah was fairly robust. When you have interest rates of 35–40 per cent and currency depreciation of 4–5 per cent, that can be very rewarding. The rates were in rupiah, but you could capture most of the spread in dollars because the curve started to extend out for dollar/rupiah swaps, so you could hedge your exposure. Swap rates on the rupiah were around 7 per cent.'

That meant a nice return could be locked up in hard currency, as long as you were willing to accept the credit. And their timing was opportune in more ways than one.

'Indonesia was also starting to try to develop a local fixed income market, so more and more instruments became available. The market went from just central bank and government bills to commercial paper as well and, eventually, expanded to offer longer dated bonds.'

Which gave Tjia experience in a range of differing categories of bond and made him rather a rarity in Asia: a regional fixed income expert.

A house built on fixed income

The next logical step – especially if you are of entrepreneurial bent, which Tjia demonstrably is – is to go off on your own. Since you need to do something different, and everybody else was emphasizing equity, the logical foundation for a new firm was the area that was more or less wide open.

'Fixed income markets virtually everywhere in developed countries are much bigger than equity markets, but nobody was doing fixed income investments in Asia.'

A good marriage, since that was where he had a record that stood up to examination and could offer something apart from the normal fare. In June 1993, Tjia and Nguy incorporated Income Partners Asset Management. They have been developing the Asian debt business ever since.

Fixed income investment in Asia requires some deviation from the accepted approach to North American and European markets, which are well established and mature. Tjia initially divided his universe into three categories:

- money market instruments (debt instruments with a maturity under one year), such as:
  - Asian government treasury bills
  - Central Bank bills
  - bills of exchange
  - other money market instruments dated less than one year;
- straight bonds (of longer duration):
  - government
  - state enterprise
  - corporate bonds;
- convertible bonds.

A brief overview of where the action is in Asian fixed income as of the back end of 2000 helps set the context for the rest of this chapter.

'Today, for international investors, effectively you are talking about a US-dollar market, which means debt instruments of more than one year, issued by Asian entities: sovereign entities, or semi-sovereign, such as state banks, or private corporate. They would be grouped under the euro bond market, but with Asian credit risk.

'There are other markets. Clearly the most important is the Japanese yen domestic market, which is huge and growing. Then there are markets in other domestic currencies, the biggest of which is Korea. Malaysia, for a while, was big. Hong Kong and Singapore are not big *per se*, but are financial centres, where most banks are located.

'Each domestic market has its own specific instruments. In Hong Kong you would be talking about the equivalent of treasury bills in the US (called Exchange Fund Notes or Bonds) you have HK$ fixed rate corporate bonds issued by Hong Kong-based companies, but also by some supranationals such as the World Bank or the Asian Development Bank; bank paper such as certificates of deposit; and other bank-issued debt such as Floating Rate Notes. You have equivalent similar types of instruments elsewhere, such as Cagamas bonds in Malaysia, and Monetary Stabilization bonds in South Korea.'

Effectively, the current position can be summarized in a simple matrix (Fig. 13.1) within which all pure debt instruments fall.

For an Asian fixed income fund, a regional investment structure seemed most appropriate in 1993, because individual markets, on the whole, were neither deep nor broad enough to support dedicated investment in these asset classes on either the demand or the supply side. Tjia had been there before with a strictly single-country focus and understood the limitations.

'With a regional fund structure you can tell investors, "Listen, if we feel that Indonesia or Thailand is not the way to go, we'll put your money in the Philippines or Malaysia, thus making decisions on a regional risk/reward basis, rather than within one country". The dynamics of the market, the maturity of the market, the instruments available are comparable, or can be adjusted by setting specific asset allocations. Secondly, we felt country diversification was important.'

Nowadays the delineation is much more issue-specific rather than country-driven, though the regional or industry sector distinction still survives as a risk overlay to issuer analysis. Currency and duration are the main macro drivers.

Convertible bonds, as a hybrid, require a separate explanation as a category with unique characteristics where the emphasis and audience shifted during the previous decade.

'In the early 1990s some companies in Hong Kong, Taiwan and Korea started to issue convertible bonds. But these were really quasi-equity instruments targeted at equity fund managers as equity with a twist. Typically, convertible bonds had very low coupons in the 1–2 per

Figure 13.1 | Framework for Asian debt market

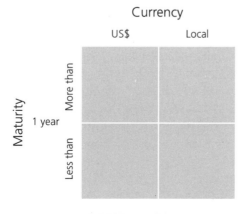

Convertible bonds are more income-oriented with an equity kicker as additional compensation for bond investors.

cent range. They came at a premium of 15 per cent or so. If you held for five years, at the minimum you got your money back, as long as the company didn't go bankrupt. Today that's changed. Convertible bonds are more income-oriented with an equity kicker as additional compensation for bond investors.'

Income Partners was set up to exploit an institutional void. Investors were intrigued both by the availability of new products and by returns which, in US$ terms, exceeded 15 per cent p.a. over the first few years, with very low volatility. So assets under management rose to US$1 billion in only four years. All good things come to an end. Conditions that were, at the outset, benign, began to suffer from a surfeit of new entrants. Tjia was early, but others soon followed as big global banks spotted the opening.

'One of the first who started to bring commercial paper to market was Citibank and, once that proved relatively successful, others, including HSBC, jumped on the bandwagon.'

The proliferation of paper contained the seeds of its own destruction.

'This corporate commercial paper market became humungous in Indonesia, with everybody borrowing short-term rather than looking carefully at their maturity profile.'

New participants comprised companies like Dharmala, a conglomerate with its origins in local commodities such as palm oil and sugar, whose bonds were 50 per cent in rupiah. At least one-quarter of all companies listed on the Jakarta Stock Exchange had a commercial paper programme, while more than 10 per cent of companies listed on the Bangkok Stock Exchange issued bills of exchange.

Obviously no-one invested in Asia escaped the crash of 1997 unscathed, and Income Partners were no exception. But they came back strongly in 1999 with a 37 per cent return for their flagship fund and achieved a positive result in 2000, another very difficult year. Throughout the life of the firm, which encompasses one of the most turbulent periods in the history of Asian financial markets, Tjia has achieved strong performance relative to the asset class. The keys to his success include:

1. Intense credit checking

Forget about S&P, Moody's or Fitch IBCA. None of the normal crutches were available in 1993. Tjia was opening up the Wild East. Orthodox credit assessment was not an option. There was every bit as much art as science in the early days.

'Financial statements are relatively opaque in countries such as Thailand or Indonesia. You needed to be on the ground, and have a good feel for how companies were doing. You were relying on a lot of anecdotes.'

Take the Dharmala commercial paper. Tjia's evaluation had to go way beyond analysis of a balance sheet and cash flow, because the information risk was high. The process was more akin to that of an equity investor than traditional quant-driven bond assessment.

> # Tjia's evaluation was more akin to that of an equity investor than traditional quant-driven bond assessment.

'We tended to meet with management, which I suppose is not that unusual, and had to take a view on the reputation of the people, which was ultimately what you made financial decisions on. Then you would talk to bankers. You knew who had been a customer of well-regarded banks for a number of years and who hadn't. Banks would tend to have better information. Companies had a longer-term relationship with banks. Bank managers would occasionally feed you information that would ordinarily be fairly difficult to get.'

The structure of markets in the region provided an additional avenue of investigation.

'In most markets, you tend to have a few business groups who are either competitors or potential partners. When you are in Indonesia talking to one of the big chicken-feed producers, there are only two others. Either they are competing head-on, or they are in a joint venture. And all you need to know is one guy in the industry and you get a lot of information about the other two companies. Second-hand evidence is valuable and can be relatively accurate, depending on your source, which is, of course, a judgement call.'

Tjia and his colleagues had to be doing something right, because, in the first five years of the business, they did not suffer a single default in the portfolio.

2. Avoiding default

As long as a bond does not default, you are still in the game. True, it can slump below par, a long way below in bad times, but, provided the company continues to pay and has the wherewithal to redeem on the due date, returns can turn out all right on the night. Which has been the most important ingredient behind Income Partners' ability to survive when other houses failed, and to make money in the most difficult of markets by catching the rebound early.

'Owning paper that hasn't defaulted, if you have the patience, if you have the stomach, where we're pretty certain that these companies will survive – then you'll get your return.'

Tjia only experienced default during 1998, and then the rate was less than 4 per cent of assets under management, while defaults were avoided altogether in 1999. In 2000 the portfolios were once more devoid of defaults, even in a deteriorating credit climate.

3. Focusing on total return

Total return is a function of not just the coupon paid on the bond but also the net capital gain or loss. In more mature markets, income is usually the predominant partner. This is not necessarily true in less developed bond markets. Over the years, Tjia has made money from increases in value, from arbitrage and from income distribution. What is hard to pin down is a consistent pattern favouring one form of return over any other.

'Every year is different. In 1994, Mexico had the Tequila crisis, which had an effect in Asia as well. Because of the flight to quality by US investors, aggravated by rising interest rates during the previous 12 months, Asian bond prices came off sharply and were oversold. Then the environment changed in the US. You started to see declining rates in the second quarter of 1994. Those Asian bonds that had been sold down during the Tequila Crisis did very well. That effect was strongest in 1995. In 1996 and 1997, the return was more from interest income and the 'cash and carry' where we would look for high-yielding domestic currency bonds and swap the instrument into US dollars – effectively currency/ interest rate arbitrage positions.'

Currency can have an influence, too, with swings sometimes larger than either the change in capital value in local currency or the income or indeed both combined. Movements in currency across Asia have more often been a minus. Tjia took an agnostic view, emphasizing capital preservation as a priority and seeking currency neutrality.

'We never set out to make money on currencies. Currencies in the early to mid-1990s were stable. Even if you took local risk and hedged it out, you'd still have a net positive return that would exceed what you would get on US dollar instruments for the same credit risk. This occurred with increasing regularity as forward currency swap premiums decreased with more investors coming into the region.'

Working on behalf of an international client base, Tjia hedged back to the US$ whenever he could, which, as it turned out, was the most sensible anchor currency. He gave up potential gains, but avoided the worst losses when the crunch came. That neutrality still prevails, even though there have been periods when relaxing hedges could have increased returns. Betting on currencies is a gamble that holds no appeal to Tjia.

The emerging market for Asian fixed income

This asset class covers all South-East Asia, excluding Japan. The evolution of the space in which Tjia operates is not well known, so merits a potted history, starting in the mid-1980s.

'If a company required funding, it basically went to a bank. That was really the only option available. Japan had a corporate debt market and Korea started, in the very early 1980s, to develop a domestic market. But, for the rest of Asia, there was no source of borrowing, aside from banks. In the mid-1980s, as economies started to deregulate and open up to foreign investment, outside influences brought industrial deregulation and also financial deregulation.

'It wasn't until 1989/90 that equity markets were starting to take off. After that, people began to look at what could be done on the fixed income side. In Malaysia and the Philippines you had a government debt market. The Central Bank was issuing short-term notes. They used these for their own funding and general liquidity purposes, and also as monetary policy tools to influence the money supply. These countries got off the ground first because they had more experience, there would be a yield curve, and there was some semblance of a risk-free rate for pricing other debt instruments. Banks at least had a basis for how to value securities and the authorities knew how to regulate them.'

A little patchy and with no cohesion or co-operation between countries. A somewhat different path was followed elsewhere.

'Second out of the starting block were Thailand and Indonesia. By constitution, both were running a balanced budget, so the government didn't borrow domestically. No domestic debt market means no yield curve. People don't know where to price. There was a small money market in Indonesia for Central Bank bills, but that was it. You were starting at ground zero.

'In Indonesia the impetus was the tight money policy around April 1991, when interest rates tripled from 15 per cent to nearly 50 per cent. Banks stopped lending. Companies were bleeding. They couldn't find funding, so had to get creative. Citibank came up with a commercial paper programme for their better local customers.'

The next step was away from the local orientation and towards a currency and structure that would attract more international interest.

'Around 1993 you started seeing Asian companies coming out with dollar-denominated debt in the euro market. Asian risk, but in dollars. You'd get two, three, even five year paper, floating or fixed rate.'

Stimulating greater interest was that once a larger numbers of issuers entered the market, the critical mass that was lacking when Tjia set up his shop began to take shape.

'In 1994 it was tough to come up with more than 40 names for the fund. Today our database shows about 850 different Asian bonds that we could potentially invest in.'

The natural evolution was given a boost as institutions new to the region, primarily US investment banks, saw this relatively immature product category as a way to open up a new customer base.

'Things were starting to take off in 1993. Lehman Brothers was active in what they called dragon bonds – basically euro bonds from Asian issuers. Peregrine started its fixed income business in 1994 when a team from Lehman defected. Then you saw the main investment banks becoming involved: Merrill Lynch, Bear Stearns and JP Morgan, among others, began to get much more active.'

By this time the space was more clearly mapped, so Tjia no longer had to explain what he was doing and could concentrate on why it was a good idea.

A trillion-dollar pot full of inefficiencies

The first goal for Income Partners was to craft a portfolio that would deliver superior returns without taking on an unacceptable level of risk. Benchmarks are less than reliable for this asset category – indeed, there were none back in 1994 – but no informed observer disputes that Tjia's performance was top-notch. The first decision was portfolio composition and, in particular, their emphasis on corporate debt over other fixed income options. Corporates tended to make up over 80 per cent of issuer names.

'The risk reward was attractive. Your yield pickup on corporate compared to sovereign paper would be hundreds of basis points. Indonesian Central Bank one-year paper in 1995 earned 12–14 per cent in rupiah. Corporate would pay 19, 20 per cent. And, up until 1996, the credit risk you were taking on what was available was pretty good. These were relatively decent companies which did not suffer from the easy money disease that afflicted later issuers.'

Efficient markets tend to drive down returns over time. The Asian debt arena was to prove no exception. Indeed, it was precisely because a few early entrants such as Income Partners were delivering exceptional fixed income returns that the balance swung too far the other way. Alarm bells began to sound for Tjia.

> # Efficient markets tend to drive down returns over time. The Asian debt arena was to prove no exception.

'We felt that, in 1996, the market started to change. There was too much money, too many investment bankers chasing too few good companies, so the overall credit quality started to come down as each banker chased a new deal. It was a period of easy money for most corporates. There was a lot of liquidity in the region and people were willing to roll-over debt, even for companies that were relatively weak financially. Increasing credit risk became the norm.

'The breadth of the market expanded way beyond the type of companies that we would be happy lending to. The first warning signs were dodgy names starting to raise money, where you were saying, "Either we're missing something, or the other guys are overlooking fundamental risks". There were companies we knew that had always had trouble finding funding, even from the traditional commercial banking source and, suddenly, some investment bank was doing a $100-million medium-term note programme for them at rates comparable to well-established companies.

'Yields kept coming down while risks were rising. Companies that, from our perspective, were borderline, where you'd maybe lend at 20 or 25 per cent in rupiah or baht, we saw that, nine months later, these same companies were borrowing at 15 per cent. And then companies you never would have touched, regardless of yield, were able to borrow at 17 per cent. That's when it became clear there was too much liquidity, and too little discrimination.'

To such an extent that Income Partners pulled almost all of their money out of short-term corporate debt by mid-1997. Sufficient signals of accumulating problems persuaded Tjia to sit on the sidelines.

'Especially popular were companies that were supposedly government risk. That is to say, majority government owned. In Indonesia, the government and Central Bank both clearly stated that investors should not assume there was an implicit government guarantee. Yet port services provider PT Dok, and third-rate plantation companies whose management consisted of retired civil servants such as PT Perkebunan IV, had no trouble obtaining funding.'

The supply and demand imbalance swung the other way, with inevitable consequences. The risk/reward ratio was ignored in the rush to clean up on spreads.

'This story was replicated all over the place in Indonesia. Thailand was slightly different. Finance companies would borrow everything short term, and then lend on at much longer terms. They made three-, four-, five-year loans for property and construction projects, and they'd borrow using 90- or 180-day paper. Third-rate finance companies that had only got a licence three months before were raising $100 million.'

South Korea was a separate story, but a classic illustration of how credit contagion could creep in the back door. Tjia observed from afar, and was not tempted to join the superficial yield bonanza.

'Korea liberalized finance company law in 1995 and 1996 and issued, I believe, more than 15 new licences. A big conglomerate would set up a finance company with no track record, go to the international markets and borrow $300 million with a guarantee but, because brand new, they would not get a favourable rate. Let's say LIBOR (London Interbank Overnight Rate) plus 200 basis points. Then these finance companies had to find borrowers.

'If you looked around Asia, the only places you could find people willing to pay more were in Indonesia, Thailand and the Philippines. So you had Korean finance companies going to Thailand to another finance company that had a dodgy book and saying, "You need money. You can't get it from Chase. I can lend to you, but it is going to cost LIBOR plus 400". So you not only had a domestic house of cards, because finance companies are lending recklessly with a mismatch of assets and liabilities, you also had a cross-border house of cards, because Koreans were lending recklessly in Thailand.

'A shopping complex with a condominium tower and office tower attached is several years in construction. As the crisis hit, finance companies needed to refinance their liabilities. It started to get more and more expensive, and more and more difficult. They ran out of cash to make their own interest payments, but couldn't go to their borrowers to get money back, because these guys were in three-year projects and weren't making interest payments. It was those kinds of situations that caused the whole house of cards to collapse.'

The question no-one seemed interested in asking, as they snapped up spreads that were chunky only compared to much higher-quality credits elsewhere, was, 'How will we get paid back?' As far as Tjia was concerned, that was the first question he wanted to ask.

> # The question no-one seemed interested in asking was, 'How will we get paid back?'

'Virtually all of the finance companies closed – over 36 in Thailand had this problem: weak balance sheets, poor financial management, and no recognizable cash flow. It was assumed that these companies would be able to roll over debt when they became due.'

Not a good assumption for all seasons. Especially when many borrowers were unsuitable for the sorts of commitments they were taking on – a weakness compounded by financing structures that were inherently unsuitable.

'You'd see companies starting to build a factory which would be a two- or three-year programme and they would fund it with 90-day paper which, of course, is ludicrous, because, if somebody is not willing to roll over your paper after 90 days, the funding for your factory stops and everybody is dead, which is exactly what happened.'

Risk piled upon risk. Tjia was having none of it, but the temptation became too strong for even some of the better names in the region, who succumbed to cheap and plentiful credit pushed at them by intermediaries whose sole interest was the up-front fee. Into this frenzy fell companies such as Anwar Sierad, an Indonesian chicken-feed producer, cement companies in Thailand like Siam City Cement, and a number of construction companies that suddenly decided they could be property developers. Tjia was sorry to see decent businesses caught up in a credit spree only to become casualties of the excesses of the era.

'In some cases companies were well run. I have a lot of respect for management, but it started to become so easy to get money through short-term paper that, rather than going to a bank to try to secure a loan with a longer payback period that would suit the capital expenditure programme, but that would be more expensive, and plan a factory with matched funding, they took the shortcut.'

Perhaps this imbalance should have come as no surprise for a market still feeling its way towards proper definition. After all, the UK had its secondary banking crisis in the early 1970s and there were shades, too, of the US Savings and Loans crisis of the late 1980s. When the crisis hit, Tjia could not escape entirely, but high-profile Peregrine went bust, while Income Partners lived to invest another year. Anticipating the deluge, Tjia had moved part of their portfolio to cash and also reallocated where they remained invested. The goal of reallocation was to seek more safety and less volatility.

'We went to more sovereign risk and eschewed new borrowers. We went to longer-dated debt instruments, often in dollars. Most companies able to issue longer-term dollar debt were much better quality. They underwent a higher degree of scrutiny by the international investment community, especially in the US and Europe, where significant portions of these issues were placed. These investors were more careful and more sophisticated.'

And another consequence of this shift in strategy was that Income Partners sold nearly all its local currency paper and owned almost exclusively dollar-denominated paper, so did not have to cope with cascading exchange rates.

Adolescence is awful

The fixed income market in Asia received a severe jolt in July 1997 when the Thai baht broke.

'It was a banking crisis where you had a combination of three factors: lax supervision, which intertwined with corruption in many cases; secondly, imprudent practices in general; and, thirdly, imbalances in the way money was allocated and borrowed. Typically, the borrower, whether it was a property project or a new factory, had used a successful but relatively short track record to persuade lenders that the same formula would work on a much larger scale. As the crisis struck, it wasn't only an inability to roll over short-dated paper. Longer-dated loans and bonds started to default because cash flow from existing smaller scale operations was insufficient to finance larger, uncompleted projects.'

The collapse of these categories of Asian debt is well documented. Most 'go-go' issues from 1996/7 were worthless. Tjia has an interesting perspective on the nature of this problem which still persists today, since, fortunately, he is able to take a more detached view of life.

'You can still find some of this debt traded today at a couple of cents on the dollar. If you were to apply a proper, commercial law approach, it's probably worth more, but you need a reliable legal system to make claims and collect on your claims. That doesn't really exist yet in these countries.'

Lack of such structure meant it was much more difficult to contain the extent of the knock-on effect and also effectively made it impossible for companies to rise from the ashes. With no framework for restructuring to reassure new investors, few were willing to risk fresh capital and there was little possibility for secondary trading to provide a safety valve. At this juncture, more or less the whole region was tarred with the same brush.

'Everybody was allergic to anything Asian. They just didn't want to touch it.'

Adulthood at last?

As is often the case when panic consumes an asset class, the nadir of 1998 was precisely the point at which investors should have stepped in. Twenty per cent US$ yields, which were available at the depth of the crisis, disappeared in short order, with deeply discounted bonds from solvent issuers mostly back close to 90 cents two years later. The swing has been largely sentiment more than substance but, either way, the shape of the market has changed to take into account investor concerns. The response has seen a more conservative and more comparable debt market emerge, with inevitably much greater correlation to US fixed income instruments. That still left openings for out-performance, and Tjia found five for Income Partners.

1. Anticipate re-rating

'If you buy at 50–60 cents on the dollar and people change their mind and see that the credit is actually not as bad as they thought, bonds rally, and you can get very good returns.'

This was one of those once-in-a-decade type opportunities. Tjia read the environment correctly, loading up on large tranches of the better credits that had been beaten down along with the dross. Names such as the Korean company, Pohang Iron and Steel, or Philippine Long Distance Telephone and Petronas Malaysia were never in dire straits, but were treated, albeit briefly, as distressed.

'By 1999, people felt that, from a credit perspective, you could already say that if a company were going to fail, it would have, or the signs would be so abundantly clear that you could steer clear. For companies that were going to survive, their bonds looked very cheap.'

Tjia took full advantage, acting ahead of the market's reaction.

2. Shift relative risk

Migrating along the credit curve as circumstances dictate can be a way to enhance performance, especially on a risk-adjusted basis. Tjia responded to the new climate by moving up, since he was not being paid adequately to accept higher risk.

> # Why buy corporate debt at 40 cents on the dollar if you can buy sovereign at 50 cents?

'Why buy corporate debt at 40 cents on the dollar if you can buy sovereign at 50 cents? Sovereigns bought at 50 were able to generate returns in excess of 50 per cent, including interest. Given what was possible from semi-sovereign credits, aiming for an extra few percentage points return by taking pure corporate risk against a backdrop of the 1998 economic crisis did not make sense.'

One name that caught his attention was Tenaga Nasional, the national power grid in Malaysia.

'Tenaga Nasional is majority owned by the government, so effectively sovereign risk, since it is a crucial utility within the country. Tenaga was trading at 50 cents in early 1998. At the same time a Malaysian corporate, Rasshid Hussain, a financial services conglomerate, for example, which had not defaulted, was trading around 40–45 cents. Whilst we felt relatively comfortable with that corporate, for a few points difference I would much rather buy sovereign risk.'

3. Change countries

The lucky ones were those who came late to the party and so avoided the worst of the hangover. In Tjia's region, China emerged more or less unscathed from the 1998 contagion.

'China just started tapping the international debt market in 1996, so were laggards. They weren't really affected by the crisis. They looked to be getting through it OK, although they had their own internal problems.'

A new tranche of Chinese companies got issues away during 1997 and even in 1998. Tjia bought a bit, but most were sold fairly soon, as many early issuers did not use the proceeds wisely.

'Towards the end of 1999 you started to have problems in China. The central bank put stricter lending policies in place. Supervision and central government direction started to dry up lending. Additionally, the government embarked on a huge state enterprise reform, closing scores of old and decaying industrial factories and liquidating loss-making state enterprises. The result was a significant contraction in domestic demand, resulting in financial pressure on many Chinese companies that had borrowed overseas. There have been high profile bankruptcies.'

New countries can offer options for improving the credit profile of a portfolio, but only if they avoid the same path that clogged up the credit market in Thailand. What matters most to Tjia is not to lose sight of the sovereign-risk element in the equation.

'The relative cheapness of a bond in Indonesia needs to be higher than the relative cheapness of a bond in Korea. Inherently, Indonesia does have higher risk than Korea. That plays a part but, ultimately, it is really company-specific information that we are looking at now, rather than a more top-down approach.'

4. Focus on a few favoured sectors

However bad conditions become, there are always bright spots. There was carnage across the corporate debt market in Asia, and even sovereign issues were under pressure, but Tjia was able to pick a few spots of relative safety which have been rewarding. Sound credits had to overcome economic and currency issues. The ideal candidates were companies with a high percentage of sales exported and invoiced in US dollars.

'What type of company would be able to continue and survive in this environment? We stuck with the Asia Pulp and Paper Company, where all its revenue's pretty much in dollars, because its commodity is priced in dollars. Petronas Malaysia, another US-dollar earner, had the same sort of characteristics and was well placed to bounce back.'

Many companies operating in the agricultural field exhibited these attributes.

'Typically, agriculture-based companies have most of their costs in local currencies. Fisheries, some canning industries and food processors were relatively attractive. From a profit perspective, they were doing better with each drop in the domestic exchange rate because they booked profits in the weaker currency.'

5. Rotate into restructuring stories

Restructuring takes the fixed income investor most of the way over to an equity mentality. Even though legal and regulatory uncertainties made this an immense challenge, a few companies were willing to work with creditors and, in some instances, something could be salvaged. The key was to identify companies where both sides believed there was a business worth saving.

'If liquidation value is higher than where the bond is trading and you can assess how likely it is that you would get that value, you can make money. We bought Astra International, the automotive market leader in Indonesia which derives 70 per cent of its bottom line from car and motorcycle manufacture and distribution, at 22 cents on the dollar. Today it's trading at 60. They had quality management and a huge franchise. Astra was worth something. It was just a question of how many cents on the dollar.

'The restructuring plan proposed by the Astra's management came up with a NAV on the bond of about 65 cents. We felt that, even if you discounted their projected cash flows, you were still looking at 35 or 40 cents on the dollar, so buying in the low 20s was worth the risk, especially since risk was primarily measured in the time it would take to see the restructuring completed and accepted by creditors.'

There is a steady flow of these sorts of opportunities, which continued in 2000 and into 2001.

'We bought Guangdong Enterprises in the low 20 cents range. It is now trading in the mid 40s. Guangdong Enterprises pulled in Goldman Sachs. Obviously Goldman is sitting at the other end of the table. But what you do get is a lot of information and, when you are doing credit analysis, it is always good to have more information. The intrinsic value of the bond was not more than 10–15 cents on the dollar, but the provincial government proposed to inject a huge waterworks project to help bond holders. This company supplies a lot of the drinking water to Hong Kong, and also to southern Guangdong. So then it was a matter of coming up with a valuation for the water company. If it goes through, the bonds are probably worth something like 55 cents.'

The lessons of the past are still working through the system painfully, and painfully slowly, but many elements of a platform are more solid, as of 2001, which would suggest a more prosperous future for investors in Asian fixed income. Tjia's perspective on this realignment deserves note.

'We had the key ingredients in place in 1995, 1996, but then too much money started to come in. So we have to go back to where we were then. You need both the buy and the sell side to make it all work, and see organic growth.'

Maturity by 2005?

Before forecasting a rosy new world, it is important to recognize that real obstacles still remain. Tjia is under no illusion about the task ahead.

'You have everything from information risk to no pricing transparency in the instruments themselves, to few corporates that are credit worthy, and, last but not least, there is finite domestic investor base.'

That said, there are encouraging signs of problems being addressed. Tjia and his partners are at the forefront, offering relevant and innovative solutions that could revive the appeal of the asset class both to issuers and investors.

1. New products

One hurdle was credit and the ability of investors, particularly overseas institutions, to evaluate, especially at a distance, the true creditworthiness of individual issuers. Solution: Collateralized Bond Obligations (CBOs).

'They follow the US mortgage-backed bond structure. We take a pool of Asian bonds and put them into a Special Purpose Vehicle [SPV] and, rather than raise pure equity to buy these bonds, the SPV would issue bonds itself.'

Income Partners structured the first four such vehicles in 1997. Their positive reception was indicative of a growing sophistication and awareness of how more mature fixed income markets slice and dice to fulfill investors' objectives.

'Let's say a $100 million pool of Asian bonds would yield 15 per cent. You'd earn $15 million in interest. The SPV would raise $70 million by issuing five-year bonds at 8 per cent. So we have cash in at $15 million a year, and cash out at $6 million. The other $30 million would be equity. Those investors receive the balance, so $9 million, which, on $30 million, yields 30 per cent.'

Tjia has not cracked the alchemist's quest for converting base metal into gold, but he did use structuring to enhance his shareholders' returns significantly, in return for taking on a greater degree of principal risk – which has been an excellent exchange thus far.

'Now, why would somebody be willing to accept 8 per cent? We'd go to a rating agency and say, "Here is our pool. It's got diversity; this is its credit risk, cash flow and collateralization." Then we got a rating. Our bonds are rated either AA or AAA or A by Moody's. Of course, if anything went wrong, it's the equity that would take all the initial hit. On $100 million, if $10 million went to zero, the bond holders would still get their money back.'

The new instruments, which typically contain around 35 bonds, have nifty names such as Asian Recovery CBO and Balanced Asian Credit Corporation. The plus point is that the pooling and subsequent rating allows institutions such as US pension funds or insurance companies to purchase Asian debt instruments that they would not, or even – in certain cases – could not buy as an individual exposure. While liquidity in these instruments is actually lower, because they are locked up inside the pool, the overall market benefits through broader exposure and greater availability of

> **CBOs potentially combine better risk management for fixed income investors with superior total return.**

primary capital. With pent-up demand, especially in infrastructure, CBOs seem one answer, as they potentially combine better risk management for fixed income investors with superior total return.

'A pension fund has trouble investing in anything rated lower than single A by bond agencies. They have a very small component of portfolios that will go to triple or double B. Same with insurance companies. They face much higher risk ratings in measuring their capital when they go down the credit curve. Taiwan is investment grade, as are China, Hong Kong and Singapore; Korea just went up to triple B, as did Malaysia. But those are sovereign ratings and, by definition, corporate ratings are lower. There are almost no corporates in Asia rated at investment grade.'

But parcelled together inside one of Tjia's SPVs and, lo and behold, the merchandise is fit for all comers, while Income Partners' investors gain access to a higher-yielding asset class.

2. Stronger issuers

CBOs may be the only way for most corporates to go, given rating constraints.

'If you're a corporate and get double B, there's only a few specialist funds that can buy your bond. And, to make it worse, both issuers and investors in Asia are coming off a very poor few years. Even with a triple B, people are more cautious.'

That may change. The first few Asian corporates to regain investment-grade status are already in the market. Tjia cites MTRC, a semi-sovereign credit which is the national railway operator in Hong Kong, and Hutchison Whampoa, the Hong Kong conglomerate which owns Orange, as two names that are Asian bond blue chips. Tjia sees his home base, Hong Kong, as the only clear-cut example, so far, of a country where economic conditions are ripe for nurturing corporate issuers, but Taiwan could come round, as there are suitable candidates if the political backdrop permits.

3. Greater liquidity and transparency

One problem has been the lack of a strong secondary market, a situation that may, in the short term, be made worse by the trend to lock up tradeable paper in CBOs. Difficulty in dealing and the size of spread deter potential entrants. That is assuming you can get a price at all, which has not always been the case. Information on credit, too, remains in short supply. Making a decision to buy or sell is that much more difficult, especially if you are not a top-tier account at one of the big firms.

'A smaller financial institution, regional pension fund or regional bank does not throw a lot of money at the market every year. It's too expensive for an investment bank or bond dealer to service such a small institutional client every day with prices, research and news, when all they do is buy a million dollars of bonds once a month.

'If you ask, people tell you that it is difficult to get consistent sales coverage and research updates. And the quality of Asian fixed income research varies greatly. Some analysts are excellent on Korean issuers, while others are strong in Chinese toll roads. Investors spend a lot of time aggregating research from a number of sources. Plus every time they want to trade, they are on the phone for an hour getting prices from a number of houses.'

Enter Tjia with asiabondportal.com, which went live in January 2000. The electronic trading service was launched in October 2000 – the first multi-dealer electronic platform for Asian debt trading. Pull up www.asiabondportal.com for a full picture.

'asiabondportal.com is a financial services B2B platform intended for leading securities dealers and institutional investors. The primary services are electronic trading of bonds and electronic distribution of investment research for OTC-traded Asian debt. We aggregate research from a number of buy-side and sell-side institutions, with online trading for a wide range of investments from Samurai credits to Singapore dollar bonds. asiabondportal is positioned between fixed income institutional investors and leading securities dealers, who are the industry market makers.'

The roster of backers is distinguished: Daiwa SBCM, Deutsche Bank, JP Morgan, ABN-AMRO, UBS Warburg and the Government of Singapore Investment Corporation. Tjia explains the rationale behind his new venture.

'We feel there is a huge pool of qualified, *bona fide* investors in Asian debt that don't get serviced and, as a result, don't have information, don't know what prices should be, and don't get research. The internet is a perfect medium for distributing all of that. We started with everything we know ourselves. We put all our 850 Asian bonds on the database. We add about 70 company credit reports that we update, and we put notes of our daily morning investment meeting online. The next step was allow people to trade, because nobody reads about Asian debt for fun.'

Tjia explains how this will work in practice.

'You still need banks to execute. JP Morgan, Deutsche and other dealers will make prices. A small pension fund in Taiwan, as long as it's credit worthy, can click on a bond and send an enquiry saying, "I want to buy Korea Telecom 08 – what's your price?" Banks will reply online, and the investor then can transact, or can try to negotiate for a better price online.'

User-friendly, intuitive and easy to use. Tjia emphasizes one key advantage.

'Today, if you want to buy a bond, you'll have to make five different phone calls or go to five different sites. We've seen a lot of single-dealer websites. Ours is the first in Asia where you've got a multiple-dealer base.'

To get a sense of what is on offer from Tjia and his team, log on and take a look. The introductory tour is worth the time. The extract from 5 January 2001 in Fig. 13.2 illustrates the scope of the service.

The community is still in its infancy but, as of its one-year anniversary, was attracting more than 150,000 hits per day, more than 35,000 daily page views, and had several hundred active participants.

If all asiabondportal does is generate more information, that will be a plus for the market, if not for Tjia and his investors. Even if it is only a partial success, there can be little doubt that others will follow with variations on the model, but all intending to generate more openness and more liquidity, which has to be positive.

Figure 13.2 | Opening page for asiabondportal.com

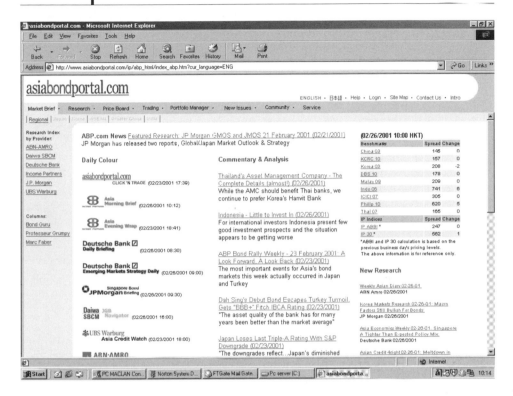

And, if it does meet Tjia's objectives, the service should stimulate more issuers, since debt can be distributed at lower cost. A logical extension is to allow smaller issues which could interest tier-two institutional buyers. All of which has yet to play out. It is still early days, but initial indications are promising.

4. New buyers

Tjia identified another barrier as the small number of purchasers for this type of paper, which is one of those classic chicken-and-egg circles.

'The investor base is pretty limited. Pension funds and insurance companies are the natural buyers, because they have long-term liabilities which they need to fund with long-term assets. In our region, you have few well-established provident plans. If you don't have a buyer, you don't have issuers.

If you don't have a buyer, you don't have issuers.

'There is a civil servant pension fund here in Hong Kong. Indonesia and Thailand have them, and Singapore has a huge one, but we need a much bigger base. It's nothing like what you have in Japan and the US. Same with life insurance. These are big investors, and the life industry is just getting off the ground in most of Asia. Outside Japan and Korea you don't have it.'

That, too, may be changing.

'In Hong Kong they launched a Mandatory Provident Fund on 1 December 2000. MPF requires people to put 5 per cent of their salary, up to a certain maximum, into a compulsory pension fund scheme which is purely private, and the employer matches the 5 per cent. It can be invested outside Hong Kong, but we believe a lot of that money will stay within Asia. With a city of 6 million to 7 million relatively wealthy people, funds available for investment from saving soon add up: that should be very good for the market.'

The impact in the immediate future is likely to be nominal, but there are positive precedents for the medium term.

'Australia introduced superannuation around 1990, which had a profound effect on the domestic debt market. In the 1980s, it was moribund. Today, you see a fairly large debt capital market.'

There are also few private pension plans. That industry, too, is just getting off the ground, with only a few specialized local offerings.

'It takes two to tango. You need a buyer and an issuer. Both need to have the same demands at the right time.'

asiabondportal is likely to play a part. The current service enlarges the circle of institutions able to invest efficiently, and it is the intention to accommodate individual investors at a later date.

The future for Asian fixed income

Looking across the region, Tjia predicts a varied pattern of development. International issues are where the action is. Domestic markets are likely to remain subdued for a while, due to continuing concern over currencies, though with signs of life in India and Korea. The big exception to all of this is, of course, Japan.

'Japan will be very interesting, because they don't really have a corporate high-yield market, but I think all the ingredients are in place.'

These ingredients are:

'A well-established liquid corporate credit market – rating agencies and companies that have found it more difficult to borrow from banks, simply because the banks are in such poor shape. So you have to find other ways to borrow. The bond market obviously is one way.'

Tjia has a vision for how he believes this will unfold.

'You have such low interest rates in Japan. Insurance companies have negative cash flows. They need higher yield. And the only way to find that is by taking slightly more risk and looking at lower credit qualities. You will start seeing smaller companies get a rating. The industry's becoming more sophisticated, and information is becoming more readily available.'

> # The industry's becoming more sophisticated, and information is becoming more readily available.

When announcing that Income Partners Asset Management had won their Best House of the Year Award for 1999, the Financial Intelligence Agency, an Asian-based publisher and provider of financial services, stressed not just success at making money in the sector and ability to outperform peers, but also the very fact that Income Partners had survived when so many had fallen by the wayside, and added plaudits for the innovative way in which the firm bounced back. Few people experience as much turmoil in a lifetime as Tjia has lived through in his first decade as an investment professional. His ability to overcome adversity and maintain a position as one of the industry pioneers throughout suggests he will be around for a long time and should continue to provide superior returns to clients in an asset class – Asian fixed income – that is likely to be a lot larger and more important ten years from now.

14

Investing for the future

The biggest problem investors face today is change. The pace of change shows no sign of letting up. If anything, the reverse. Consider the profile of the top 100 British companies a century ago. Railway stocks accounted for almost half the market's capitalization. Oils, pharmaceuticals, telecoms and media companies, which now weigh in with over 50 per cent combined, back then made up less than 4 per cent. This cycle of destruction and reconstruction continues to accelerate, unleashing a new round of challenges for investors to master.

Technology represented about 15 per cent of the US economy in 2000. According to Wardlink Information Technology Systems, it is forecast to breach 50 per cent within a decade. Among ideas coming reasonably soon to commercialization near you are:

- smart dust – computers so tiny (say about one-tenth the diameter of human hair) that they could go anywhere;
- smart sensors – which will travel in our blood stream or, more mundanely, sit inside a refrigerator and warn when food is stale;
- virbots – visible but virtual people who are capable of a multidimensional human interaction reacting to non-verbal cues as well as words;
- moletronics – electronic fibres so finely woven they can approach the architecture of human brain cells;
- customized medicine – with designer drugs modified to match the patient's unique genetic profile; and
- nano technology – the next generation of artificial intelligence, where computers are capable of creating their own brain cells without human intervention.

The precise when, by whom and how are not yet known. In whatever form they arrive, one can safely conclude that radical developments on a scale sufficient to redefine industry economics are not necessarily good news for today's technology giants. These, and other breakthroughs that have yet to see the light of day, will destabilize established companies, but they will also bring new opportunities for wealth creation.

Active portfolio management is essential in such an environment. The era of buying blue chips and leaving well alone is well and truly over. Investing has always been a dynamic process: never more so than now. The only constant is change. Investors who do not adapt will get left behind. Only those who stay at the leading edge, all the time adjusting for their personal-risk profile, can expect to power ahead.

If this sounds too daunting, do not despair. The success of 12 young professionals profiled in the preceding chapters provides pathways through the minefield; and their knowledge of markets allows us to identify potential clusters of companies where capital correctly allocated should prosper.

Peering into the future

Taking a top-down view, the first question was, 'Where are the most promising parts of the market?' There was a range of answers, as one would expect, but also a degree of consistency, which is encouraging or, for contrarians, may suggest investors should avoid these areas altogether. Sectors that seem set to deliver above-average growth ranked, in descending order by frequency of mention within our sample of young superstars, are:

- internet infrastructure providers
- outsourcing
- asset gathering/fund management
- education
- manufacturers of fibre-optic components
- providers of broadband access
- logistics
- semiconductor equipment manufacturers
- creators of media content.

Obviously there is some overlap in selection – logistics could be seen as a subset of outsourcing, for example – but generally the ranking reflects areas of the economy that are likely to continue to prosper. Strangely, there were no fans of biotechnology, but perhaps that is because it is such a specialist sector. Biotech aside, superior growth prospects are a good reason for investors to take a hard look at these sectors. The selection of individual investments is something else entirely.

By their very nature forward looking, such observations are generic and, in using particular companies as illustrative, no-one – least of all this author, nor the *Financial Times*, nor the people profiled in this book, nor the firms for which they work – should be seen as making any specific recommendation. That said, and, alas, disclaimers are mandatory in today's litigious climate, readers may want to consider the implications of those themes on existing holdings and prioritize those areas of activity if growth is a portfolio priority.

So, with all the usual caveats attached, the company that came in for most mentions as an investment that could do well in 2001 and beyond was Bank Julius Baer, a Swiss financial services institution which emphasizes asset management, and primarily caters to high net worth individuals.

Again, in descending order of frequency, based only on the number of times they received a favourable mention and only including companies that received positive endorsement from at least two contributors, the remainder of the favoured few were:

Company	Country	Business
STM Microelectronics	France	Semiconductor equipment
Commerce One	US	B2B platforms
ASM Lithography	The Netherlands	Semiconductor equipment
Giordano	Hong Kong	Casual-wear retailer
Trend Micro	Japan	Anti-virus software
Li & Fung	Hong Kong	Procurement and supply chain management
Infosys	India	Software support
HCA	US	Healthcare

Not surprisingly, these names mostly reflect the growth sectors highlighted above. They tend to be innovators and leaders in their competitive arena. Whether their share price does well or not, as of January 2001, these are companies which should do well in their industry.

Do not rush out and buy a stock simply because it is mentioned in this book. Superior operating performance and positioning does not always lead to superior share price performance, especially in an environment where rapid obsolescence is the norm, business models are in a constant state of flux, and market valuations fluctuate like yo-yos. Barbel Lenz was a big fan of Sonera at 20 euros in late 1999, but a seller at 80 some eight months later. Fast forward eight more months to March 2001 and she is considering whether to re-enter with the stock now back well below 20 euros. Sonera is a serious company, not some fly-by-night dot com. Take the nine names mentioned: two – Li & Fung and Infosys – though highly regarded and expected to outperform long-term, were also considered fully priced as of mid-2000. Even for the best quality names, price is important, as is picking the right time to buy and, indeed, to sell.

Roger Guy can flip from buying to selling and back within a similar timeframe. One-third of his portfolio is effectively on six-month probation at all times. Catherine Tan, too divides her holdings into two categories: keepers and trades. Dan Chung has been in and out of core names such as Amazon, America Online and Exodus. Sam Lau bought and sold one of his all-time favourites, Li & Fung, within the same year. Even people who prefer to invest

Flexibility is the only sensible response to volatile markets and stocks with generous trading ranges.

for the long term have to accept that extreme price movements can render a buy-and-hold strategy irrelevant. Slater went so far as to short companies he liked because valuations got so out of line. Flexibility is the only sensible response to volatile markets and stocks with generous trading ranges. Or, as Nadig points out, perhaps all investors are now citizens of Day Trader Nation.

One other observation jumps off the page. Even though US managers make up the largest constituency in *Investing with Young Guns*, the list is almost all non-US, raising the question of whether large cap stock-market stars for this decade may come from elsewhere, in part as the rest of the world plays catch up and, in part because the US may lose leadership in key technologies such as next-generation semiconductors and wireless. And it is interesting to note that both Morris, who was 85 per cent concentrated in the US, and Garrett-Cox, who, until 2000 was exclusively invested in North America, have recently launched new funds that are global in scope where they expect to have a significant percentage of the portfolio in non-US holdings.

Readers should not make too much of this. The US will continue to incubate a disproportionate percentage of the world's most dynamic growth companies for the foreseeable future. More transferable are insights that can be distilled from identifying the factors that have enabled talented individuals to outperform in current market conditions. These, in turn, have to blend with views on forces likely to affect markets. The end product is a series of guidelines intended to help investment performance, especially in equities, and a collection of insights, both timely and relevant and, more important, that could give readers of *Investing with Young Guns* an edge over other investors. There are 12 in total.

Let's start with a general proposition that cannot be reduced to a catchphrase. Superior returns come from seeing something that most of the market has missed, and going long or short against prevailing opinion. This is not simple. Taking a contrarian stance is no guarantee of beating the index. Consensus can be correct – often is. But you will not get rich following the herd. While academic orthodoxy would have everyone in tracker funds, outperformance logically can only be achieved where investors challenge conventional wisdom; and investments that outperform arise when the consensus turns out to be wrong. Or, as the OpenFund manifesto puts it, 'The key to successful investing is original insight'.

Most of our young professionals have a slightly different take on how to unearth these truffles among stocks. Cooperman likes to catch a change in an industry that alters the economics, and thus the profitability, of companies within that industry. A shift in pricing environment is often the most profound and easiest to interpolate: better margins, therefore profits ahead of expectations. Kennedy looks at the relative progress of similar businesses in different countries to get a head start. Internationally minded investors should be able to see cross-border trends coming even when they are not yet obvious to a domestic analyst. Nadig prefers to find themes that are not properly appreciated, since companies that harness exceptional growth dynamics should exceed expectations. Morris is more concerned with company-specific events, such as a new product line, which will have an impact beyond what is anticipated.

In Lenz you have an extreme example, as she has access to an organization whose entire existence depends upon identifying discrepancies between market expectations and reality. Grassroots' research tells her what is really happening, as opposed to what the market thinks. Chung is on a similar track when he creates multi-layer financial models, hoping to throw up discrepancies from the accepted range of predicted profits: the same goal in each case, though the methodology varies. Garrett-Cox takes the position that it is through meeting management face to face that the investor can learn something unique, even if what is said in private does not differ from what is in the public domain. How something is said can influence interpretation. Even the SEC has yet to come up with a way to regulate eye contact.

Tan has a series of war stories that confirm the value of in-person conversations, mostly of bad decisions avoided. Lau spends more time in meetings than in any other activity. The attitude of management to the market can have a material impact on share performance, quite apart from the financial results, enhancing or undermining how the price responds. All of these are variations on the theme that the market, at any given point in time, may be far from perfect and presents opportunities to profit both on the long or short side.

No-one can be everywhere but, by picking a few spots, Main Street can outperform Wall Street. Garrett-Cox and Guy represent the majority of our twelve pros in finding little use for analysts who regurgitate the official company line, or gravitate to the middle of a narrow range of projections. Information of that ilk will already be priced in. Investors need a point of difference. Differentiation usually requires specialization – maybe in an industry, perhaps even on a couple of companies – allowing the investor to attain advance warning of change, both good or bad, and reposition accordingly ahead of the crowd. Slater points to director buying and selling as one sign that the market has missed something.

With these generic observations as a backdrop, I have extracted a series of shared views from our young guns which should help all investors improve portfolio performance.

1. Elevate growth above everything

If there is one common theme that overwhelms all others, it is that investors should go for growth. Just about every top performer in the next generation is a growth junkie to a lesser or greater degree. The only real debate would seem to be between those who emphasize growth at a reasonable price and those who are willing to pay over the odds for the *crème de la crème* of companies. Garrett-Cox, Slater and Tan tend to fall into the former camp, as does Lau, though what is reasonable growth in a Chinese context might show up in the fast lane elsewhere. Chung, Lenz and Nadig, on balance, favour the second position.

There is no Berlin Wall between their positions. All agree that the priority is to find companies where sustainable growth is achievable. Even our lone value representative, Wayne Cooperman, accepts the argument that cheap growth is a variant of value. He is more than happy to own a decent business on an undemanding rating at a discount to his estimate of its future growth.

We need to be clear that going for growth has nothing to do with momentum investing. Momentum is about price action in a stock. The focus of our top young professionals is on growth, by which most mean in cash-flow earnings. All concentrate, first and foremost, on finding a business with top quartile prospects. Most make the point that sustainability of growth requires a capable management team, so that adds an additional hurdle that prospective investments must pass. The valuation test usually comes third, though Slater still sees merit in using quantitative screens up front, and then turning to the other two tests to sift out suitable stocks.

This conversion to the supremacy of growth comes after a period when growth has been almost all that counts. Taking the long view, by which I meant the last century, classic value stocks outperformed growth stocks. The growth versus value debate will run and run, and also runs into the problem of data definition. Regardless of what has happened in the past, our next generation of investment superstars is convinced growth will triumph for the foreseeable future. In their opinion, that is where the largest gains are likely to be made. Given what is going on, it is hard to argue against their convergence on the superiority of growth.

> ## Our next generation of investment superstars is convinced growth will triumph for the foreseeable future.

What is critical is to distinguish between businesses which can deliver sustainable growth with positive cash flow as opposed to the majority of new-economy companies which, as in all prior technology revolutions, from railroads to mainframes, will lack staying power.

2. Let winners run

Or, better yet, add to a position that is up, as Dan Chung does at Fred Alger Management. How many times during interviews did I hear the refrain: 'If only I hadn't sold', or some such similar variation on that all too common theme. Almost every person had an 'if only' story, like Cooperman on Oracle: 'Unfortunately I sold it many years ago after making a large amount of money, but leaving even more on the table ...'

This problem seems particularly acute among technology stocks. How hard is it to hold on, once a share has doubled, especially if the rise was rapid? And how much harder if the price has quadrupled? There is always the fear that a star may morph into a supernova. As many do. And investors are constantly reminded to leave something on the table for the next buyer, a dogma that has been around since Rothschild made it famous in the early nineteenth century.

Caveat vendor. If there is one common failing to emerge from this research, it is that readers must forget, for a moment, how well these investors have done. Every one could have done even better by hanging on to their best-performing holdings a little longer. Fine to top slice. By all means take partial profits. Slater suggests easing out a third at a time when you start to feel uncomfortable. But only by continuing to own companies that continue to deliver and find favour in the market can you realize those elusive ten baggers. The strength of mind to let winners run is the single most marked difference between outperforming professionals and the rest. Look at how Kennedy continued to recommend Infosys for five years from 1994, or Lau, who stayed put in Li & Fung while it went up ten times in four years. As Garrett-Cox observes, 'Generally we have a strategy of running with our winners. I very much believe that the trend is your friend.'

The flip-side is to be ruthless in eliminating losses. That holds true irrespective of what the price was at the time of investment. Guy is most decisive in this department. Indeed this is one of his Golden Rules: 'The price paid is irrelevant: do not be afraid to close at a loss'. Garrett-Cox also emphasizes the need to take action once decisions are made. Slater, too, argues for selling losers, especially on bad news, since problems tend to travel in packs. Once the growth trend is broken, get out fast. Cooperman and Lenz both give examples of stocks they sold at a loss where they were happy to have got out so lightly – and where the loss would have been much worse had they hung on.

3. We are all venture capitalists now

Investors who want to make serious money have to be willing to make earlier-stage investments. Many investments that produced the greatest returns were made before it was clear that the company concerned would be successful, or even survive. The jury is still out on whether many new economy stocks will ever turn a meaningful profit. The environment in 2001 is more discriminating, and speculators who were sucked into the specu-

> **Investors who want to make serious money have to be willing to make earlier-stage investments.**

lative 'dot com' frenzy of late 1999 and early 2000 have the sour taste of large losses in their mouths. Even so, most early-stage investors, including some of those in high-profile flops, had a chance to bank fantastic profits.

An investment approach that requires earlier-stage commitment implies a higher risk profile, but diversification comes to the rescue. Venture capitalists expect to back investments that go belly up, counting on a handful of big winners to compensate for a sackful of losers.

As Nadig points out, investors seeking superior returns must be willing to invest in innovative companies without well-established earnings records. Of course investors should demand a clear path to profitability, but they cannot expect certainty into the bargain. Even Slater, who has been more cautious than most in committing cash to this strategy, still endorses the principle.

Regardless of suitability, public markets – especially in the US, UK, Europe, and increasingly in Asia – are opening up to relatively untested businesses. Indeed, that is where most of the largest percentage gains have been made. On NASDAQ, AIM in the UK, Neuer Markt in Germany, or GEM in Hong Kong, companies are coming public earlier. Listing rules have been modified to facilitate these types of offerings. Many investments available in 2001 would have been off-limits to individual investors until recently, open only to institutions and insiders.

Not everyone is a fan. Tan is sceptical about the durability of many companies she saw coming to market in 2000. That said, she is still willing to participate and turn a quick profit to enhance total return. The majority of our young guns have backed immature companies and ridden their success. Chung achieved dramatic returns by being early into America Online. Lenz and Guy made exceptional profits by being among the first institutional investors to own Nokia at a time when mobile-phone handsets made up a minority of the total enterprise. Kennedy was recommending Infosys of India years before the software innovator attracted a following. Fidelity did extremely well out of owning it in several portfolios. Lau made his mark because he was willing to buy Chinese companies when they first became available, even if some were not properly prepared for life as listed entities. His investors enjoyed an outstanding period because he was one of the few to see value there and take the plunge. Closet venture capital comes in a variety of shapes, but shares a common feature. Exceptional upside potential compensates for the downside risk.

It is getting easier all the time to follow this advice. An increasing number of listed companies are, in effect, a collection of early-stage investments that may or may not offer incubator type services as a fig leaf of value-added. Nadig refers to one of the smallest, Harris & Harris Group, in which he made money. The best known is CMGI, but there are 20 or so in the US, and around the same number on various UK exchanges. In London, New Media Spark, where Slater is a director, is probably the leader. Asia has also embraced this business model. Softbank of Japan is the name almost everyone knows from that region.

Maybe more relevant, individuals can now get in on the VC act directly through the web. Sites such as vcapital.com are arguably self-selecting, since you need $200,000 to participate, but universityangels.com has a more realistic $50,000 threshold, and offroadcapital.com starts from a modest $25,000 minimum.

In the UK, VCTs (Venture Capital Trusts) are the poor investors entry point, with some accepting subscriptions of as little as £1,000, and, for many, there may be tax benefits to boot. Returns are not always spectacular, but the industry is in its infancy. Singer & Friedlander deserves its good reputation. Foresight has done well so far. The Allenbridge report is an objective guide to the best and worst VCTs. Every serious UK investor should get their hands on a copy.

Venture-type situations are likely to get more accessible everywhere. Leading firms have begun to jump on the bandwagon. In October 2000 Credit Suisse Asset Management unveiled its global Post Venture Capital Fund, which is effectively a follow-on fund that goes where reputable venture capitalists have already dared to tread.

More investors can now participate and, based on the experience of these 12 talented young investment professionals, more should; with one crucial qualification: spread risk. Never hazard too much on one story, however beguiling. Sage advice, especially in respect of new-economy companies. No-one can know, with any degree of certainty, whether some new competitor may not emerge out of the woodwork to undermine the business proposition, or whether a new technology may suddenly overhaul and render obsolete today's promising new venture. This is Risk Capital with a capital R. Plan on allocating whatever sum you risk across ten plus situations or stick to pooled schemes.

Even Morris, who restricts himself to more mature new-economy companies, has a limit of 3 per cent in any one position. Most top-performing portfolios that emphasize technology prefer lower concentration in their holdings than was the norm for successful investors of past periods. *Investing with Young Guns* gives a green light to include venture capital category investments, but also an amber light that warns investors to limit their total exposure and to own enough individual positions to spread the risk.

4. Embrace disruptive companies

During a period of intense and unusual instability, investors need to seek out companies that are change agents. These are the businesses that will create the greatest shareholder value in the shortest time, leading to the highest possible compound rates of return. Sure there will be casualties: another reason to have multiple holdings. Disruptive companies may end up emulating Samson and destroy themselves along with everyone else. Amazon has changed the retail world though the jury is still out on whether its shareholders will be rewarded. Irrespective of the impact on an individual company the arrival of new technologies almost always signal the end of an era, and such a signal is usually bad news for incumbent businesses better known as blue chips.

Identifying disruptive innovators is a common strand that runs through the themes that underpin MetaMarkets.com. Nadig constantly cites these companies as potential longs and also assesses their impact as a signpost to potential shorts. The force of disruption is no one way bet. Viisage may yet succeed in bringing fundamental change to the way the corporate world protects premises, making obsolete all existing security systems – or it could collapse under the strain of trying to drive such a far reaching transition.

While not the precise word he employs, disruption is what Kennedy has in mind when he talks about companies such as Trend Micro that take business models cross-border. Tjia has himself created a disruptive force at asiabondportal, and it is through the use of techniques that have changed and continue to change the Asian bond market that he has been able to extract top-tier returns.

Change of this kind is not just about new entrants. Established organizations are capable of reinventing themselves. Those that can should prove investment gems, since the degree of disruption can be more profound when emanating from a larger company with greater resources. Nadig has found a few familiar names with suitable culture and characteristics, such as Home Depot and Domino's Pizza. He urges investors to 'learn to identify those rare companies with the unusual ability to nurture innovation within the context of existing franchises'. They combine some margin of safety with the potential for higher rates of return. It is, however, vital to differentiate between reluctant revolutionaries and true converts.

Disruption can assume many shapes, some less obvious than others. Hoechst was considered disruptive in Germany, when the chemical giant became a pioneer in shareholder value. Lenz found that form of disruption can also generate superior stock performance. Tan believes Nissan could be capable of exerting leadership on a similar scale in Japan. At the same time, and in the same country, relative newcomer Trend Micro is destabilizing an industry through both its attitude to shareholder value and its approach to delivery of its services to clients. Getting on board corporate innovators early in their transformation often leads to superior capital appreciation.

5. Don't underestimate the soft stuff

If traditional quantitative tools are not always able to provide accurate answers, there are elements of the analytical suite that still have relevance. The character of the people in charge and the way they operate can provide investors with indications of how likely it is they are backing a winner or a company that will disappoint.

Garrett-Cox is a leading exponent of the importance of blending art with science. Her checklist of management 'no-nos' is worthy of serious consideration. The much-repeated mantra about the depth of corporate carpets as an inverse predictor of future profit has proven accurate too frequently for the result to be random.

It is not just a question of character. The attitude of top management to shareholders and public markets is also one aspect several of our young guns take seriously. Morris makes a point of investigating previous employers when key managers change at his holdings. In emerging markets, this is even more of an issue. Lau makes sure always to find out the background and prior record of management before he invests. In China, sympathetic executives are an essential ingredient to sound stock-market performance.

Do not underestimate the value of good corporate governance. Tan cites several examples of its importance and impact on share prices. This may seem self-evident, but what is largely taken for granted in the US and UK does not necessarily apply elsewhere. Investors can continue to find ways to profit from this development in maturing markets. Lenz did well out of following the theme in Germany as recently as the second half of the 1990s. You still

> **Do not underestimate the value of good corporate governance.**

see examples. The recent attempt at reinvention of Degussa, the company whose history was linked to the Third Reich's gas chambers by a former director of Hoechst, Utz Felcht, could be a watershed. Felcht is on record as saying, 'What Thatcher did in Britain is much the same that we still need to do in Germany'.

Kennedy and Tan both are benefiting today in Japan, which is undergoing something of a sea change in attitudes to shareholder value. Kennedy highlights companies such as MEW and Sony, which are pointing the way forward. All our Asian experts, to a greater or lesser degree, agree. Other things being equal, the market will assign more value to a company that adheres to good corporate governance and respects outside shareholders than to a similar company that lacks transparency and places a low priority on those obligations.

Best of all is to catch a company at a relatively early stage in transition from a history of poor practice. This holds true for bonds as well as equities, as Tjia's experience shows when buying, at a deep discount, companies where management was sound. The market may well re-rate such a company, on top of giving credit for any operating improvements. Multiple re-rating and profit growth can compound to a heady cocktail. The opportunity to achieve outperformance from finding companies that have only just started to accept the importance of corporate governance is still very much alive, even in major markets such as Japan, in varying degrees across most of South-East Asia, and in whole regions such as Eastern Europe. Kennedy believes that, if Samsung follows through on its conversion and completes the course to total disclosure, its share price could also complete the journey from historic discount to a comparable global rating.

Corporate governance can also work as a contra-indicator. Management that rides roughshod over shareholders' legitimate rights should be avoided. This is true, even in countries where governance is generally good, as investors in Maxwell should still remember.

6. Seek out the competition

Information has long been recognized as a key variable in determining relative investment performance. For individuals, access to basic data has been getting progressively easier and cheaper. For retail investors and professionals alike, the search for proprietary information has been getting harder, but the quest is as critical as it has ever been, and wider dissemination of standard documents only underlines the need to go beyond the company for a full evaluation of its business.

Our young guns are already ahead of the crowd. They all recognize the critical importance of understanding the competitive context. Chung would always cover the competition in almost the same degree of depth while creating the type of detailed financial forecasts discussed in his chapter. Benchmarking is an essential reality check on achievable margins that drive future profits and cash flow.

For Slater, the emphasis was on whether growth is sustainable; and, while some of the answers can come from assessing the business model of a single participant, part of the answer lies in making sure the overall sector can support growth. What the management of other players in the sector is saying can be a valuable guide. He makes sure to monitor all relevant pronouncements from competitive companies before concluding he has found a growth story. Garrett-Cox believes that quizzing management about their competition is often extremely informative. Executives tend to be a bit more relaxed when talking about another business.

Where information is in short supply or the reliability of information is uncertain, competitors can become a critical source in building up a clearer picture of a company. Tjia points out that, since disclosure is incomplete in some countries, there is no substitute for primary research. Which also goes to show that this approach is every bit as relevant for corporate bonds as it is for equities.

It is not realistic for individuals to expect much access to management, but data mining can get you a long way towards building a picture of what is going on in a sector. Professionals who can expect opportunities to ask pointed questions ignore this source at their peril. The main message to get across is that investors need to cross-check the company's view of its prospects, as articulated in its public pronouncements or elsewhere, with what others in the sector are saying – both about the environment and about the company. And, as Slater observes, and Cooperman also made a similar remark, this kind of intelligence can be even more helpful when considering a short sale than when thinking about a long position.

7. New metrics: new valuations

Don't rush out to discard Enterprise Value to Earnings Before Interest Taxes and Depreciation and Amortization (EV/EBITDA); and, by all means, hang on to cash flow analysis and Price-to-Earnings Growth. These, and other measures, are still critical to determining intrinsic value. The period when clicks and page views replaced financial based measures came and went.

Their passage still leaves a market containing many billion-dollar companies with prospects but lacking in profits and with negative

> The period when clicks and page views replaced financial based measures came and went.

current cash flow. Some will fail, but other valuations arguably underestimate the transformation that can follow fundamental realignment of an industry. The current watershed finds investors in something of a no-man's land. Traditional techniques from the 1980s cannot cope on their own. Many of the new measures that markets rushed to employ in the late 1990s have already been shown up as a busted flush.

Apart from the observation made by most of our young guns – that investors need multiple measures to pick investments – their own experience confirms that a blend works best; a blend that still leans heavily on financial ratios, including snapshot analysis of current performance, but which places greater emphasis on estimates of future earnings expectations. So Price Earnings to Growth replaces Price/Earnings. Discounted Cash Flow ranks alongside today's EV/EBITDA or Price/Cash Flow. Almost all the 12 managers profiled here prefer forward-looking measurements. And, while clicks may not mean much, metrics like subscriber growth – both absolute and relative – can be invaluable in modelling future revenue and earnings growth.

Investors may also want to employ specific analytical tools, designed to box businesses of tomorrow with measures that mean something today. Morris has devised what he calls a Practical P/E Ratio (*see* page 215). This concept helped him hang on to winners and stay away from losers. Chung addresses exactly this problem (pages 21–3), in a section that repays careful consideration. Another measure that has adherents is growth flow, popularized by technology guru Michael Murphy. Price to Growth Flow was created to allow for fairer comparison between leading-edge companies, which could be enhancing shareholder value through research and development. Most R&D shows up as an expense, so penalizes the earnings of a business investing for the future. To adjust, you add back R&D cost to pre-tax Earnings Per Share (EPS). Then price is divided by the restated EPS. As with traditional P/E, other things being equal, the lower the ratio, the cheaper the stock.

A shift in the way a traditional tool is put to work can be as profound as the development of an entirely new analytical measure. Margin of Safety has long been a concept that investors of all stripes have utilized, but the value community has perfected its usage and developed workable definitions. Its genesis was the net current asset test devised by Benjamin Graham. The net value per share derived from the balance sheet should exceed a company's stock price. One school of value thought expanded the components in this computation to include the market value of tangible assets, investments and real estate held for sale. The definition was further extended in the 1990s by some practitioners to include the value of readily marketable intangible assets, such as music rights and media content, brands, or even the firm's franchise, if capable of quantification.

A shift in the way a traditional tool is put to work can be as profound as the development of an entirely new analytical measure.

Now comes Cooperman with a further refinement. His rationale rests on the proposition that it is possible for value investors to find a new Margin of Safety in cash flow rather than, as in the past, relying exclusively on assets. He still uses assets. Indeed, he is keen on the idea of two ways out to demonstrate a really robust Margin of Safety. But, in times when asset values can fluctuate as alarmingly as everything else, he is wary of placing too much reliance on assets alone. Reliable proceeds are rarely there when you need them. Predictable cash flow may offer more of a Margin of Safety as, provided cash flow continues, management will have a range of options as to how to enhance the share price, including going private.

Fans of growth argue that growth, *per se*, can fill the role of providing a Margin of Safety for investors. For me, such a claim goes too far. It is when growth falls short that you need something else to rely on. Cooperman's focus on cash flow is more realistic. Cash flow often remains positive even if reported profit turns negative and net cash flow may increase when top-line growth falters. Sustainable cash flow especially on an ex-growth basis suggests a route to a new Margin of Safety but only to complement, and not to replace, the more traditional balance-sheet based approach.

Other tools have evolved that extend previous techniques with an overlay of 'new' thinking. Goepel McDermid, a Canadian broker, has developed a 'market value slide rule' derived from three key factors – size of potential market, expected market share and time to market, which sits rather well alongside discounted cash-flow analysis. Measurement of performance has to become much more forward-focused. Past margin is only relevant as a departure point. What matters is Commerzbank's growth Estimate in Margins (GEM). You see something resembling GEM as one among many inputs if you delve into the small print of Chung's model in Fig. 2.1 on page 32–3.

Chung makes the point that, 'Often, companies with the highest market cap to sales or operating income are those that are moving the fastest to claim new markets'. Provided the new market is worth owning and the valuation aberration temporary, sticking strictly to traditional measures might produce the wrong result. Market share usually deserves a premium rating, and leadership deserves to be even more highly rated during the race to stake out the most profitable position in lucrative new markets.

Nadig employs consumer loyalty tests to capture corporate tribalism as a measure of earnings sustainability. Individuals will find some 'new' analysis hard to emulate, but you, too, can stand at the cash register and observe reactions to new retail concepts. Chung also emphasizes the value of personal experience of a product or service. The mother-in-law test may have become more sophisticated, but still has its place.

All these tools assist in an assessment of the likelihood that a business in expansion mode has a path to profitability that makes sense in the context of its market; also in answering the question whether rapid growth in revenues really should translate to positive EBITDA numbers; and within what sort of time frame investors might realistically expect profitability. New measures are necessary, because disruptive companies and early-stage innovators both require a more complete and complex evaluation. That is the bad news. The worse news is that everyone will have to learn how to combine time-tested benchmarks with new metrics; or give up on those areas of the market offering the greatest growth and containing the stars of tomorrow. Analysts and individual investors alike will labour under the same imperative to adjust.

8. New economy, new M&A

Traditionally, businesses have been bought for their assets, cash flow and earnings. Nothing wrong with that, you might say. Nor is there. Investors, however, who want to position themselves in front of the M&A wave of the future, so as to enjoy the uplift that usually accrues to shareholders in the acquired company, may want to consider new criteria.

The business cycle will continue to ebb and flow, and the search for scale economics and market share should drive further consolidation in mature industries. But the number of such deals is bound to decline. There comes a point at which industry structure nears a competitive equilibrium or bumps up against regulatory limits on market share. How many more takeovers can possibly occur in the beer or cement or paper sector, all of which are already reduced to a handful of global players? The January 2001 decision by the EU Commission requiring Interbrew to divest its recent acquisition of Bass suggests some sectors are up against the limits now.

So the search for areas of intensive corporate activity is likely to lead to new pastures. This quest was a recurring topic. All investors keep at least one eye on M&A action. While some industries mentioned are old chestnuts where fragmentation persists, particularly in the field of financial services, it is the need to maintain growth momentum among the technology sector that is seen as a new driving force for deal flow. Our young guns have less conviction as

> **It is the need to maintain growth momentum among the technology sector that is seen as a new driving force for deal flow.**

to premiums which will be paid, or whether stock will progressively replace cash as the currency of corporate takeovers. Their view is that there may be more mergers than acquisitions, which would make the game less worthwhile. But investors should not underestimate the ability of investment bankers to persuade their corporate clients to overpay and over-leverage.

New-economy companies have barely begun to exploit the possibilities of M&A as a tool to accelerate or extend growth. A few notable exceptions have already begun to employ acquisition as a key plank in their strategic thinking. As always, it pays to play follow-the-leaders. In years gone by, investors tried to second-guess active acquirers such as Hanson or BTR/Invensys or Tyco. Now upside comes from figuring out Cisco's next move, or spotting what is missing from the repertoire of services offered by American Online or EBay. Cisco understands that the next generation of products is rarely home grown and a quantum change almost always occurs outside the mainstream. There is no debate over build or buy. It is buy or lose leadership. This shift in objective requires investors to pay more attention to capabilities and technology, rather than valuing hard assets, when thinking about whether a company might make a suitable acquisition target. It also means we have arrived at the age of people power.

Many acquisitions in the decade ahead, and arguably in decades ahead, will be driven as much by the need to buy specific skill sets where demand exceeds supply as by anything else. Such an approach can be seen as accelerated recruiting, with investment banks replacing head hunters – or perhaps recruitment firms may drive these deals leaving financial intermediaries out in the cold. Either way, investors should prosper by spotting particular pools of high-value talent. Specialist programmers, biochemists, optical engineers, chip designers and other leading-edge artists can be expected to be among the targets in greatest demand. Perhaps talent scouts, too, will become more valuable.

Content will also continue to be key; but not just ownership of the asset or the right to exploit an event. The evolution of MP3, the reincarnation of Napster, and the rapid spread of Real Networks and other similar enterprises will challenge traditional concepts of content exploitation and increase the value of organizations able to generate a continuous flow of original material. Companies such as Othnet.com, which seem to have solutions to the problems of online revenue generation and royalty preservation, should be in demand.

Morris has benefited from Cisco's expansion programme. Other areas likely to see increased corporate activity are:

- biotechnology
- broadband access
- content management
- media
- optical component manufacturing
- outsourcing.

The geographical location of M&A activity is also likely to shift. This is not to say that time has been called in those most active of markets, the UK and the US, but that greater growth lies elsewhere. Lenz points to increases in continental Europe, where closer ties at every level, including the euro, are likely to lead to a second round of consolidation as national competitors either expand or disappear. Technology catch-up will also require more sectoral M&A if Europe is to have any hope of closing the gap on the US.

Kennedy observes that the role of corporate activity is achieving greater acceptability in Japan. Tan has telling statistics that confirm that this development is more than merely anecdotal. M&A will be much in evidence across all South-East Asia. There were a number of high-profile deals in Singapore in 2000. Japan, though, is the big prize, where enormous value waits to be unlocked. The process seems finally to have started, with boutiques leading the way, but management, even at large companies, also appears ready to accept the legitimacy of external corporate activity, and in certain circumstances a hostile takeover can happen.

9. We are all citizens of Day Trader Nation

This is one of Nadig's refrains, but he is not alone in emphasizing the need for investors to be more active and less passive. Taken too literally, hyperactive turnover is bad. Day trading requires a specific mentality – specifically a trader's mentality. Few people have the staying power or emotional fortitude to cope with a lifestyle glued to a screen, fighting for every tick. Empirical evidence from the US shows that, over time, most day traders lose money. The serialization, in *The Sunday Times*, of John Urbanek who sold his house to try this lifestyle and, so far, is well under water confirms the danger.

Equally, to achieve an optimal rate of return, it is almost certainly the case that investors need to be more proactive and willing to turn over their portfolios more frequently than has been either desirable or ideal in the past. The logic is clear.

First, barriers to trading have come down dramatically almost everywhere. Costs have fallen from around 5 per cent 20 years ago to less than 0.5 per cent today, with some brokers even offering zero commission to secure order flow. One of the best reasons not to trade has always been that frequent transactions enriched the broker rather than the client. The ease of execution and nominal transaction costs remove that restraint, though the Treasury's perverse obsession with 0.5 per cent stamp duty is a serious drawback to placing UK equities on a level playing field.

Second, the world is changing so much faster that it is simply not safe to sit still. Buy and hold worked in an era when a large number of companies could roll out results year after year with steady sales and profit growth, and were able to achieve this over long periods. In this day and age, that does not work. How are the mighty fallen? Take Xerox and Procter & Gamble in the US, or Marks & Spencer and

> The world is changing so much faster that it is simply not safe to sit still.

Rentokil in the UK. You could hardly ask for safer or better blue chips, yet the prices of these large cap stocks have fallen by unthinkable percentages over the last couple of years; not quite dot-com style, but destroying a lot of savings in the process. Investors had thought of these long-time leaders as safe and secure. Not any more.

It has always been true that sentimental attachment is not on in the stock market. Never more so than now. Investors must be ruthless in pruning and must remain open to new ideas. High turnover should no longer be seen as a sign of weakness or inconsistency, but of vigilance and decisiveness.

It is not just Nadig who expressed this opinion, though he is at one end of this particular spectrum. Guy is of like mind. Lenz totally overhauled her portfolio in 1998, and her winners in 2000 were an entirely different set of companies from those that lifted her results in 1999. Kennedy saw a high degree of turnover as necessary in Japan in the first half of 2000. Tan has also seen many holdings come and go within the year. While he is not personally comfortable with too much trading, Lau recognizes its role in the context of investing in China.

A willingness to accept turnover translates into the ability to buy and sell the same security times over, which appears as a common trait among our young guns. Cooperman traded Prime Hospitality with great success, Garrett-Cox managed more than one round trip at Micron, and Lenz has been in and out of SAP more than once. Tjia sold debt holdings when credit conditions deteriorated in 1997/8, only to buy back some of the same positions less than 12 months later, but at much lower prices. Investors used to hold bonds to maturity. Asia Income Partners achieved exceptional returns, in part by trading. What is good for equity investors can be just as good for bond investors. Complacency is a crime for professionals and a luxury that investors can no longer afford.

10. There's something about the air in Palo Alto

One other attribute deserves comment. The great investors of yesteryear were largely generalists, well rounded men – and they were only men – whose education often came largely from the school of life. Academic achievement was not a useful indicator of investment performance. Many had not 'wasted' time to go to university. Experience was what mattered. The market was their teacher.

Today's top professionals come from a different mould. Most have gone on to earn postgraduate qualifications on top of a good degree at one of the world's best universities. Perhaps that reflects a new form of gate-keeping in the profession. Those without MBAs need not apply. There is some truth to that; along with a lower tolerance today for learning on the job. I also think it is a reflection of a shift at most large asset management houses to more holistic analysis. Add on the growing complexity of listed companies, especially leading-edge technology stocks, and the need for a more structured skill set is obvious.

So rather less of who you know and more of what you know, though maybe a new set of networks has arisen. The educational establishment that tops the table in *Investing with Young Guns* is my own *alma mater*. Chung, Cooperman and Morris all went to Stanford. Let me be clear. I had no idea where these guys had been when they made the cut. Could that common background be a statistical fluke, or something more meaningful?

Obviously the area around Stanford is buzzing with entrepreneurial energy. This has been true from the early 1970s. Ever since the phrase 'Silicon Valley' was coined, the peninsular has been famous as a centre of early stage excellence and a magnet to ambitious entrepreneurs. Sand Hill Road, that crucible of the venture capital industry, is barely a mile away. New economy start-ups abound in the area. The culture is consistent, on and off campus. Everyone knows someone who successfully started their own company. Students are exposed to many pioneering enterprises that have been among the top performing investments during the past two decades. These companies actively recruit at Stanford and go to great lengths to make sure students are aware of their activities. A Stanford education, in the broadest sense of the word, is ideal for understanding stock market stars especially the most recent advance guard of wealth creators.

Apply that education in an investment environment and it is possible that Stanford *alumnae* are better placed to appreciate the virtues of this technology transformation than other graduates. The old boy or girl network is also a plus when so many in the venture community and so many top executives at the most successful enterprises hail from Stanford. Intel, Oracle, Sun and Yahoo, among others, are chock-full of Stanford grads. Access is that bit easier. Information flow, that critical currency for investors, is that bit more fluid. *Alumnae* reunions take on more significance.

There are other pockets of similar activity and culture elsewhere. Austin is another centre, though on a smaller scale. Boston still leads in biotech. Cambridge stands out in the UK. Adjacent incubators and research parks have germinated some of the most impressive débutants on the UK Stock Exchange, including ARM Holdings and Autonomy. Finland has managed to create clusters of entrepreneurial excellence around Nokia. Scandinavian institutions embraced wireless and spawned several innovative companies in that sector. Singapore looks likely to stimulate more entrepreneurs in Asia. Emerging markets have cloned their own equivalents, such as Bangalore in India.

Since education has been identified as one of the most exciting investment themes of the decade, expect more of the same. Investors should seek out centres of excellence, as early-stage success stories are likely to fare better when they have roots in communities with the capability to provide a complete support system.

Which brings me back to a couple of old cherries. Just as the best fund managers of the past seemed to select many of the same stocks, often by sharing ideas and even monitoring each other's holdings, interestingly, today's top young professionals, too, seem to gravitate to a select few companies which recur even in their relatively short investment history.

11. Buy Nokia

You tend to find some of the same shares in the portfolios of top performing managers. Every so often, a stock and a story comes along that is so important that owning this one name can make an enormous difference. There are no rules of thumb for picking blockbusters. If only! What investors can do is examine portfolios of top managers, most of which are publicly available. Identify those shares that appear frequently. They should be holdings of sufficient size to reflect conviction. That shortlist is a great place to start.

For the top UK managers of the 1980s, Shell Transport and Trading was such a share. For the global young guns of 2001, the one company that they nearly all owned, if it fell within their remit, was Nokia, the Finnish mobile phone manufacturer. Nokia drove arguably the most important consumer development of the 1990s.

Buying the exact shares that have been thoroughly vetted by multiple experts, each with an outstanding track record in stock picking, but a somewhat different analytical approach, is like getting a free ride on the best investment due diligence money can buy. Candidates can be found among selected names cited earlier in this chapter, such as ST Microelectronics, ASM Lithography or Infosys but, in all likelihood, the next Nokia will be a name no-one has yet noticed. And even a company the calibre of Nokia cannot be bought and held with impunity. Shell Transport and Trading could be owned comfortably for ten-plus years. Nokia achieved uninterrupted heroics for five-plus years. The next blockbuster may only be able to maintain pole position for a couple of years.

12. No one right answer

I would like to wrap up with the closing observation from my last book, *Investing with the Grand Masters*. Researching this next generation of superstar investors confirms that an important characteristic of global markets has stayed the same: there is no one right approach to superior investment performance. That proposition has always been true in the past, remains true today, and it is a safe bet that the conclusion will be exactly the same when I come to write the next edition five years from now.

> # There is no one right approach to superior investment performance.

Horses for courses. No single style suits all – at least, not for any length of time. Growth investors, momentum investors, value investors, East European regional experts, telco sector specialists: all have their year in the sun. The secret of successful investing is to find out which way works for you as an investor, stick with what you know, build in as many parameters for flexibility as can be consistent with your chosen strategy, make sure you allow for your ability to tolerate risk, and then apply those guidelines in *Investing with Young Guns* that match your personal profile.

Let me add a word of warning: never convert your personal comfort zone into a cocoon. The successful investor has to be ready to respond to change and must be capable of adapting. Shorting should be carefully considered, but requires a totally different temperament and does not suit all investors. Still, it is noticeable that most of our young guns, even those not running hedge funds, are increasing their results more and more through judicious use of shorts. Active investors need to spend more time exploring the potential of shorting within the context of a diversified investment strategy.

If that does not appeal, or even if it does but the market makes you nervous, there is always CASH, as Tan points out. Capital preservation is essential to long-term performance, especially in markets that are unpredictable and volatile. Slater reminds us that investors can always choose to sit on the sidelines until the right opportunity arrives.

In today's increasingly complex investment world, there are only three viable options for individuals. If you have the ability and the confidence, and are able to enjoy yourself, then commit to becoming an active investor, but recognize the time commitment involved. The key to superior performance lies in understanding an industry or a small group of companies in sufficient depth to identify gaps between market perception and reality – which takes a lot of time and a degree of expertise. Listen to our young guns and you hear, over and over again, that determination to discover misunderstandings in the market that create mispricing is the single best way – and possibly the sole realistic route – by which an individual and, indeed, a professional, too, can outperform.

If such a scenario seems daunting, then a passive approach may be a better fit. Investors who prefer to retain a degree of control over their own portfolios, but are reluctant to make the full commitment required by an active approach, should consider adopting a higher-risk profile than has been recommended historically. Be prepared to forage for companies that are at an early stage of development and offer immense upside, but also, inevitably, greater downside. Such a shift carries with it the need for a more diversified portfolio. Consider a greater allocation to earlier-stage investments, perhaps through third parties, and also to investing more in growth markets such as China – again, for most investors, that means through a fund rather than directly.

The third, and arguably most sensible solution, is to ride on the coat-tails of those who know how to cope with difficult conditions and spend every waking hour working out how to improve returns for their shareholders. And, of course, what every investor needs to know is not who are yesterday's heroes, but who will be the stars of tomorrow. *Investing with Young Guns* has profiled 12 exceptionally talented individuals, each of whom has already, even early in their career, been able to demonstrate unusual investment acumen. All are capable of continuing to outperform their peers and are able to deliver superior returns. Their stories are worth a close look, always recognizing that, just as with top stocks, so fund managers, too, can come to the front only to stumble.

That caveat apart, looking forward at the next generation and placing at least a portion of every investment portfolio in the hands of younger professionals makes sense, since, on the whole, they are better attuned to current market circumstances, more flexible in outlook and have the survival skill set to match the climate of 2001. Even more relevant, they should be able to flourish in whatever conditions prevail in 2006, and may only reach their investment prime around 2011.

The insights from the next generation of investment gurus summarized in this final chapter ought to make a difference, if systematically applied – however erratic and inconsistent the behaviour of financial markets. Investors who read *Investing with Young Guns* should find something to help with their own performance and, having reached the final page, should emerge better equipped to face the investment challenges that lie ahead. Making money in the first decade of the twenty-first century is likely to be harder than it was during the closing decade of the last century, and may require a more eclectic approach. I hope I have given readers of this book an advantage by sharing the ideas of 12 young professionals whose remarkable successes contain valuable lessons for every investor.

Index